TIMELESS VOICE
of
RESURRECTED MIND

Bible Talks of The New Testament
by Master Teacher

ENDEAVOR ACADEMY
Certum Est Quia Impossibile Est

Published By:
Endeavor Academy
501 East Adams Street
Wisconsin Dells, WI 53965, U. S. A.
Tel: +1 (608) 254-4431 Fax: +1 (608) 253-2892
www.themasterteacher.tv
Email: publishing@endeavoracademy.com

Contents

Let us today open God's channels to Him,
and let His Will extend through us to Him.
Thus is creation endlessly increased.
His Voice will speak of this to us,
as well as of the joys of Heaven
which His laws keep limitless forever.
We will repeat today's idea until we have listened
and understood there are no laws but God's.

CHAPTER 1

The Inevitable Altruism Of Enlightened Mind

It is amazing. You come together to try to figure out, as a Christian, what Jesus meant. It is an amazing idea. You are going to look at it and say, "What did He mean by that?" First, He meant that you can contact God directly and that is what we will do here for a moment.

He said that there is a God who creates Heaven and earth, everything that is and ever will be. It is a God that doesn't decide what cultures or what practices or what apparent affiliations of civilizations are involved. Very simply, in the universe there is a whole God. He teaches us to contact God directly. He says, as humans you have a Creator. This is very basic to this teaching. He is a singular Creator. Because you have a singular Creator, you are all created in the totality of that association of mind.

This was an entirely new idea. This was even a new idea to the Judaic tradition which had maintained that their god was somehow superior to other gods. The idea that all gods would be equal would be fundamentally not acceptable to civilization very simply because everybody would have the same advantage over everyone else. Nobody was really disadvantaged by their own god – they wouldn't have a god that disadvantaged them, it doesn't make any sense. Any god that they had would be one that was going to present them with superiority over their apparent associations with each other. Do you see how very fundamental this is? The idea that there would be one God for the whole universe, including a God for all the animals – although some were more sacred than others and everything that goes with that – is rejected by the fundamental concepts of the human mind. Do you see?

The human mind absolutely rejects it in a very fundamental sense because it is a discrimination of the associations of cause and effect. It sets up within its own mind parameters of ability based on all sorts of things – what a great variety – all subjected to the whims of environmental association. Quite literally, man is taught by the nature god that he is at the mercy of the nature god. So his prayers are to that god. Man is a god-inventing animal. He is aware that he is at the mercy of his environment. An animal does not question that he is at the mercy of his environment very simply because he is his environment. He doesn't suffer from an illusion that somehow he can control nature. Do you understand? The animal is a whole part of that nature.

The son of man has no place to lay his head. (Matthew 8:20)

Is this a Christian church? I am teaching the teachings of who you call Jesus Christ of Nazareth. How many have heard of him? Oh, He's your savior! The words that I am offering you, the basic, absolutely fundamental philosophy — you like the term *psychology*, so we will use it — are exactly and only the teachings of Jesus of Nazareth. Here we have a dilemma: we have the invention of a god, which must be feared very simply because lightning strikes the good guys and the bad guys. Do you understand? So the prayer is, to be relieved from or exercise control over your apparent environment. "God help me build a better house." "God help me get a bigger dog to protect me." "God protect me from the bigger dog." "God protect me from what is outside of me." This is the basic teaching of all religions and is the teaching of the human condition today. Can you see that? All of the teachings today are exactly what they have been as long as there has been a man on earth.

When he separates his cause and effect, he ends up attempting to control the effects. Obviously there is no fundamental admission of the teachings of Jesus Christ. Number one, which is rejected, is God does not discriminate. Therefore, if he will not admit to the causation of the environment, he must suffer from the effects of something that is apparently not caused by him. The entire teaching of the Sermon on the Mount is that the universe, or God, is thought and that God is a thought contained in your mind and that it has absolutely nothing to do with what appears to be the effects outside of you. It has nothing to do with it at all! Jesus will say, "Can you control anything? Can you do anything? Are you going to change one hair of what you are?"

Which of you by taking thought can add one cubit unto his stature?
(Matthew 6:27)

He says, no you can't! What is He saying? Change yourself! The entire teaching of Christianity is *change yourself*. There is a fundamental admission that is very prevalent in this teaching that you are the cause of it. How directly does Jesus say that in Sermon on the Mount? He says it directly and He says it repeatedly.

If it is fundamentally true that there is one single, whole, eternally-creating God, of which you must be a whole part, it must then fundamentally be true that God did not create the world – presuming that there is perfect, eternal Happiness. Here is where you sort out. Jesus calls this the great sorting out of your individual, uncompromising determination to accept unqualifyingly the inevitable altruism of any enlightened mind.

Did you hear that? I'll try it again. To an association of a disciple of Jesus who has undergone a transformation of his mind which will be very much a part of the Sermon on the Mount, the idea of altruism – the idea that there is a single, whole God of which he is a whole part – is very easy for him. So his rejection of it, and the necessity to defend himself from his apparent environment, disappears. To him, to an enlightened mind, it seems perfectly reasonable that God creates everything perfectly. To a perceptual mind, it seems perfectly unreasonable. You think it is reasonable to perceptual mind, but it is not, very obviously because his judgment in regard to perfection belies the certainty of the perfection of a whole God. Did you hear that? I am preaching here. I want you to see what Jesus says. His entire teaching is the necessity, using the power of God with your own mind, to undergo a transformation wherein you can see that you are perfect as God created you. Yet if I take the sentence – if I pick up Matthew, and I read *therefore* in Matthew 5:48 – and there is a lot before that – but let's start with *therefore: Therefore, be ye perfect, even as your Father which is in Heaven is perfect.*

You immediately say, "What do you mean by that?" I mean be perfect as your Father in Heaven is perfect! "But what you *mean*..." I mean be perfect as your Father in Heaven is perfect!!

The rejection of altruism is fundamental to the conceptual mind. He cannot accept it without becoming all true! The whole teaching of the New Testament:

Judge not, that ye be not judged. (Matthew 7:1)

I can read them if you would like me to. You can pick it up and read it just as well as I can. That is so basic.

So, here we are faced with altruism. "Let's not be naive. Let's not be naive and think that Jesus actually meant that." Why not? I know perfectly well that this is hell. I know perfectly well that I am suffering here. Everything here gets old and sick and dies. Don't tell me that's not true. I can see it is true. I also know perfectly well that somewhere in my mind there is a whole, eternal, creating, loving God. It seems very reasonable to me that one or the other is not true. Yes or no? What Jesus says is that you have the power to make the decision. He says flat out that you have the power to make the decision of whether you would rather be on earth or in Heaven. You say, "He doesn't say that." The hell He doesn't! I'll stand up before any Christian association that ever was and teach fundamentally the total inability and unacceptance of the basic teaching of Jesus. Of course it is true!

And I don't blame them. How could you accept uncompromisingly that you are perfect as God created you when you have admitted to His creation and find yourself in this abominable association? There is no solution to it except what? You have to change your mind! That is the teaching. *Know ye not that ye must be born again?* (John 3:7)

Know you not *you* must undergo an individual change in your own mind, not someone else's mind, *your mind* – not in the adulterer's mind, in *your* adultery; not in the stealer, in *your* stealing. Do you understand me? If the causation of this world comes from God, and you are a total product of God, either you are not carrying the true message of God in your own perfection, or God is whatever this world is. But one or the other is not true!

Heavenly Father, we thank you that all of your ideas are a part of us, and your idea of us, which is our perfection, is true because you say so – no matter what we say. Therefore, we are determined not to express what we believe we are, but allow us to be what we are through you. Amen.

You act as though that is hard to do. "Well, that is very difficult for me." Of course it is very difficult for you to do. It is too altruistic for you. Those of you who are laughing at this message are obviously not going to hate me and revile me and kill me. Jesus says this message is absolutely not acceptable to you because it has no qualifications in regard to what you determine that your existence is. It simply tells you that you are perfect and whole and in Heaven. Now you are going to hate me and revile me. It doesn't seem as though you do, but watch, I am going to test you on this. There can be no compromise between totality and separation, between what you call good and evil. If there is such a thing as good, it is all good and there is no evil. If there is any evil, there is nothing good. If there is such a thing as all power, weak power is totally meaningless. If there is such a thing as eternal life, time is totally meaningless. See how you are rejecting it? Somewhere in your mind you are saying, "He doesn't mean that," to everything that I am saying. I mean that! I mean it! Until you get to the point of a fundamental acceptance of the message of Jesus Christ of Nazareth, there is no way possible you can hear it.

That doesn't mean that you are going to believe it. It doesn't mean that you are necessarily going to accept it. But it does mean that you are going to have to finally admit what it says. Your acceptance of the fundamental nature of salvation by the terms that are set forth by Jesus of Nazareth to you are beginning to become acceptable to this world. And I am talking to *you*, individually, and I am saying *individually* in its entirety so you won't get it mixed up somehow with altruistic statements of sharing with your so-called brother the idea of freedom from this world. It is beginning to be acceptable to you that if God is, in His entirety; this isn't. This will be the entire teachings of Jesus. That is what He says.

Not only does He say that, but He says that when you change your mind, the world will change. He says all power is given unto you in Heaven and on earth. He says you are using the power of God's mind to determine the outcome you want in regard to what you believe is a part of this association.

Once you get the hang of Jesus' teaching, it becomes more and more enjoyable to you for one single and very simple reason: *It is true!* "Yeah, but..." No, no yeah buts – It's true!! Therefore be perfect as your Father in Heaven is perfect. It is true. "I can never know that." Why would you have to know it? You already are it! What is it that you are trying to prove by changing the world out there? If you are the cause of this, you accept Jesus Christ as your savior, risen. He has set the terms for your salvation based on His own illumination. You have absolutely nothing to say about it at all except to determine your own illumination and your realization that there is no world. That's what is coming about in you.

Are we in a fundamental understanding of this? This is called altruism. The entire unacceptability of the *Course in Miracles* in a very fundamental sense is that it is absolutely and totally altruistic. Its entire psychology or philosophy is that if this world is, God isn't. Its entire method of bringing about a change in your mind gets you to look reasonably at the idea that if life is eternal, death is impossible. If life is eternal, there is no such thing as death. There's no such thing as death? Why? Life is eternal! What's wrong with that? Now I am talking to you from my illuminate mind. That seems completely reasonable to me. What will be the result of that? I got the result of that! The result of it was instantaneous when I changed my mind about my relationship with myself in regard to what I am. This is Sermon on the Mount. It had nothing at all to do with the world! It has nothing to do with deciding I am going to change the effects of what is out there.

The *Course in Miracles* teaches that it is much too late for that. You will just end up changing the effects of your old association with yourself. What is that? Nothing! The entire fundamental teaching then, very simply, is that this world is nothing. Zero. At least when you pick up the *Course in Miracles*, hopefully you will see that it says this world is over and gone a long time ago, but it is being retained in your mind as a justification for a cause-and-effect relationship through the previous projections of your mind that were determined to justify an eye-for-an-eye – to justify a temple, to justify a priesthood, to justify the laws of man. I herewith deny the laws of man and declare the law of God which is my perfection. Now you better crucify me quick. You better get me because I am a revolutionary. I am telling you there is no world. I am telling you that you should not adhere to your establishment. You don't like this at all. Suddenly you are very suspicious of me. Do you understand me?

Yet it should be readily available to you that any compromise in this teaching will simply throw you into what? A denial of God! The teaching must be that you, individually, are in an active denial of God. This nonsense about neutrality is absurd. There is no such thing as a neutral thought. Every thought that you are empowered with – this is Sermon on the Mount – will give you the attention you want in the conflict of your own mind. What an idea! So if I change my mind the world will change? "I tried it and it didn't work." I guess what God says is not true, and you are right. You don't like that kind of teaching. You

CHAPTER 1: The Inevitable Altruism of Enlightened Mind

don't like it because you are accustomed to determining the outcome in your own mind. I am giving you the fact of the matter. All of your outcomes are totally meaningless and mean nothing whatsoever. You won't like that because you have a need to die.

Reviewing the problem for you who want to hear this: *Most of you have no intention of hearing this.* Isn't that amazing? You have no intention of hearing it. Your intentions are not to hear this. If you had any intention whatsoever of admitting God is perfect and you are divine, you would hear it. You believe that you must determine the outcome of your own mind, and quite literally invent God in your own mind. You have a very serious authority problem. You believe that you can conceptualize an association of eternity. Yet conceptualizations are nothing but a justification for your apparent body. *I am not a body, I am free, I am still as God created me.*

Why don't you deny that? Why don't you deny that you are perfect as God created you and you inhabit a body that is going to rot and get old and sick and die because that is the condition of this place. I am telling you, and you have rejected it, that you are the cause of this condition. This is Jesus. Should I read that to you? I have said it for 2000 years. I'm not going to read it again. You say to me, "Well, where does it say that?" Where does it say what? What is it that you are battling in your own mind in your determination to what? To reject the altruism of the teaching. Is your mind split? Of course. But it is impossible to split your mind and have any truth in it whatsoever. The moment that you split your mind you become totally untrue. Can you really be separate from God? No! Well then what are you doing here? "Oh, you are threatening me." Yes! I am threatening you! Evidently you are an advocate of death. What else are you doing here?

Does the devil depend on you? Is there a devil? You bet. What does he depend on? You! What would happen to the devil if you change your mind? He won't be there. Obviously you are advocating pain and loneliness and death and using the power of your mind to get the result of your own mind. God is going to be true whether you advocate Him or not. He couldn't care less about you. He cares nothing at all about your sickness, loneliness, pain and death. Can you hear that? If God sees you as perfect, why would He be concerned about your denial of Him? He doesn't know of your denial of Him.

Who knows about it? The devil. The devil is very active in your mind to determine an outcome that you want to be true. You like that.

Now you say, "Ah-ha, now I got him to admit there is a devil." But there is only a devil through your advocacy of him. The step made this morning by a pastor that I heard on television was that the devil is an objective association and the opposite of God. To me, that is totally senseless. I thought we agreed that there was only one divine, perfect, living God. You mean that God allows an evil force to exist? Shame on you! Then He's not all good. If He can't do anything about it, He's not all-powerful and He's not God. Now I can decide whether I would rather adhere to the devil or to God.

You have me in an objective association. The hell with you. I can understand perfectly well my fundamental causation of this, and that I am going to get the result of my own mind because it is true. What I can't accept is that I am uncompromisingly responsible for it because I am determined that in the condition in which I find myself, somebody has to share it with me in order for me to tolerate it at all. The simple fact of the matter is that all of my relationships that I have with my family, my friends and the things that I love are based on death.

Did you hear that? All of us agree that we come here together to share pain and loneliness and to die. Everything that we do in the fundamental nature of our culture and in association with each other guarantees our temporal pain and death. Is that so? Into this impossible situation, I come as a whole mind to tell you, individually, that that is not true. I am now what? Threatening you with your relationships. Now you must hate and revile me because I am offering you your perfection and denying you the necessity for you to sacrifice and die – or do anything. I'm teaching Jesus of Nazareth.

I deny that you must do anything to be perfect. And, as a matter of fact, I tell you, that in all of your doings of your relationship, you are simply denying and attacking God. Do you like the uncompromising teachings of Jesus? Planning for the future is an attack on God. That is the teaching of Jesus Christ. "Oh, no it's not." Yes! Yes it is! The question is not that. The question is: *therefore be ye perfect even as your Father in Heaven is perfect*. Greater things will you do in your own mind because I am telling you this with my mind. Your acceptance of the necessity for your own saviorship to save the world is the entire teaching of Jesus. Why aren't you standing up and saying, "I am the savior of the world"? If you, in fact, intend to follow Jesus Christ, He says to you very emphatically that, "What I am doing, you will do and greater."

He that believeth on me, the works that I do shall he do also; and greater works than these shall he do. (John 14:10)

He is saying that He is demonstrating to you the manner by which you can come from your sick, false self to the entirety through what? The transformation of your mind. Is that what is happening here? That Sermon on the Mount is something else! What am I performing? Sermon on the Mount! That's quite an ordeal isn't it? You are going to have to change your mind about everything that you thought you were. Fortunately, God is on your side. Fortunately, God does not take sides. Fortunately, the answer to your problem, taught by Jesus of Nazareth, is Forgive Your Brother! Of course. I don't find in Leviticus a lot of references to the necessity to forgive my enemy. It is not there! Jesus says you must forgive your brother:

Love the Lord thy God with all thy heart, with all thy soul, and with all thy mind. This is the first and great commandment.

And this is the new one:

Love thy neighbor as thyself. (Matthew 22:37-39)

Your neighbor *is* yourself! Who did you think he was? Somebody else? One thing for sure – this is Sermon on the Mount – he isn't going to be any more or less than what you have decided you want him to be. Until you change your mind about him, there is no chance for you because he is you. That is the teaching. And that is what this says.

Is this like it was 2000 years ago? It is exactly the same. You are accepting it, and the world is about to attack you. The question is not that. The question is whose side are you going to be on this time? I am telling you this is going on all the time. The decision to listen to this is being made by you in your own mind all the time.

Here is the entirety of the solution: you came here determined to die, and I am going to prevent you from doing it. You say, "No, you're not." And I say, yes I am. You say, "No, I am going to get cancer and die." And I am saying, no you are not. You may believe that you will succeed in dying, but you will never succeed in my mind because my mind is in direct association with God. So is yours. Why do you then believe that I am different than you? Why do you believe that I must have accomplished something within my own associations, like you are doing right now.

Somehow I have done something – I have looked at scripture, I have determined in my relationship with man what God is. What an absurdity that is. Yet how determined you are to justify the associations of yourself from where? Outside of yourself rather than admitting the necessity for the fundamental connection of you. This is all Sermon on the Mount. It says don't try to prove anything out there. You come into your own closet and you talk to God, and God will give you the answers. The answers are not out there. The answers have nothing at all to do with the world. Do you have anything to do with this world? No! How come? There isn't any world. This is the whole teaching of Jesus of Nazareth. I came to tell you that you never left Heaven. In the next sentence Jesus says that we all came from Heaven together, and we are all going home. But we never could have really been separate from God. It is not possible.

This is a place of separation, isn't it? What is it separate from? The whole. Doesn't the whole miss you when you are separate? You miss yourself apparently. Most of you wouldn't know the Christ if He came up and bit you. The whole teaching is that the Christ is standing right next to you and you are trying to determine with all of your so-called purity of mind who the Christ is. Well, the Christ is sitting next to you in the pew. Where do you think He is? If everyone is perfect within your own sight, He must be. This is the teaching of Jesus.

Most of you get to the stage where you go into your closet and you find a little purity. Somehow you know the Christ is somewhere but you can't admit that He is in you, and therefore you can't admit that He is in your brother. The entire teaching is that the salvation of the world depends on you. "Doesn't it depend on Jesus Christ?" If it depended on Him, you would be gone already. You wouldn't be here. How would you be here? He is resurrected! If He's not here, and He is your savior, what are you doing here? He is resurrected! You are the denial of that. "Oh, Jesus is resurrected and I have to get old and sick and die." That is absurd. That doesn't make any sense. It is senseless. See how uncompromising this is? What you are doing is totally meaningless. It has no meaning whatsoever. You are perfect as God created you. What a threat! Talk about a threat! Talk about a revolutionary. Talk about a guy who absolutely denies the establishment all together.

Most of you in this new continuum have come through the determination of your own new self that there is no world. The entire teaching of Jesus Christ risen is that there is no world, that you cannot be separate from Eternal Life, and that the solution must be in your mind.

For those of you who are leaving, who are going to recognize this, there is a real high association of contemplation going on in this church. Do you understand contact with God? Most of you do. Contact with God is nothing but the release of your own protective devices to keep yourself from contacting God. God didn't go anywhere. He is here. He is a whole part of you, yet your constricture of yourself in your identity of yourself or your prayer for continued death will justify the need to die in your mind. The simple prayer:

Father, into thy hands I commend my spirit (Luke 23:46)

is all that you would ever have to do. You might want to ask for a little help. My teachings are of a conscious contact with Universal Mind through your individual transformation, which are the entire teachings of Jesus.

You wouldn't be able to get the associations of this world to become altruistic in their determination to change their mind. It seems to have worked pretty well here. You haven't jumped up and said, "No, I am going to go out and die some more." You haven't jumped up and said, "What about my aunt who is dying? What about the children that I love?" – the children that you have condemned to death along with you. So far you haven't jumped up – most of you will, because most of you are hell-bent on justifying your associations with yourself. I am telling you that you are wrong. It would have nothing to do with me. It could if you want it to, because I am speaking from my own certainty. But I am telling you flat out that your condition with yourself is absolutely wrong. It is not true that you are a body and can get old and die. That is not true. You are a liar. And you always have been a liar. You cannot be separate from God. Will you defend yourself from me? That is what you are doing. You are in a condition of defense from your own Christhood, from your own totality of what you are. You are being attacked by your own thought association. This is Sermon on the Mount. I am just repeating it for you so that you can see it.

There is one thing we know for sure in this teaching, and that is that we are teaching only power of mind. We have absolutely no concern about what occurs out in the world. Our concern is only that you are mindful and that you think and that you can change your own mind. And in that change will you realize that you are whole and perfect. There is no other manner in which that can come about. Most of you have accepted that on some basis; I am telling you there is absolutely no basis for your acceptance of it whatsoever. It is either totally true

17

or it is totally false. Now you are going to deny me again. Why do you deny me? You are the denial. All conceptual judgment is a denial and an attack on God. Can you hear that? Was that okay with you?

So you're not going to attack anymore? But to do that, you would have to forgive your brother. To do that, you would have to lay down your arms. To do that, you would have to walk the extra mile. To do that, you would have to turn the other cheek. It is impossible for you to do that because you are already being threatened by the associations out there. You believe somewhere that I am demanding that you forgive the junk that is going on in the world. I am not demanding that at all. I am telling you that you are the cause of it! I am not asking you to forgive sin. Are you kidding? If sin is real, it is not forgivable. How would it be forgivable if somebody is hurting you? How can you come to know it? Don't defend yourself. Immediately you will have the freedom of your own whole mind without the necessity to defend yourself, because that power is given unto you.

What you will notice mostly, and books are starting to be written about *A Course In Miracles*, the fundamental problem remains: There is no world. "What about... what about... what about..." No, no, no. You cannot be separate from God. Obviously you are proving that I am wrong about this. And you will probably prove it for a very long time. Certainly nobody in the universe can stop you from proving to yourself that you can suffer sickness and loneliness and pain.

The fundamental necessity of your admission of causation is what the Sermon on the Mount is. It says that you are the cause of this. As you think, you will get the result. What goes around comes around. There is no such thing as an idle thought. Everything is contained within your own association of yourself. That is the entire teaching. What a threat! I am threatening you with salvation! The whole teaching of Sermon on the Mount is that you don't know what anything is anyway. You can't control it. There is not one single thing that you can control. Nothing. You can't even observe it. Every time you see it, it is always gone.

How have you evolved in your new associations with your new mind? You no longer, most of you in your Christ Minds, justify your old associations of cause and effect with your own previous mind. You don't need, in the experience of the miracle which is going on all around you, to justify it by a relationship of yourself. Can you understand that?

Do you know what happened this morning by my house? I looked out into the field and there, growing out of the field, was a miracle. It was a flock of robins. And they weren't there just a minute before that. Suddenly I was harvesting out of my field 24 robins – I tried to count them. I usually get 12 pairs. This is an indication of an early spring. First I saw one, and I said, "Oh, there's a robin." A minute ago that robin wasn't there. Was that a miracle? Tell me it was a miracle. I don't have to know what that robin is. "Oh, that's a harbinger of spring." That's all well and good. Then I looked, and there was another one. And then suddenly they were all over the place. It's good to see them, I'll tell you that! Most have wintered down South. They don't fool around here. The energy of a robin is different than other birds. He's pretty regal, you know. He has a certain independence about him that you can really feel. It's really nice to have them back. Was that a miracle? I am telling you about it, but if I can get you to look at my certainty of mind, that is the entire teaching of Jesus, that all around you are miracles going on that you are rejecting because of your old associations. Those miracles are actually happening to you, and you are rejecting them.

What do we have, real basically, here? We have for you to evolve in yourself an uncompromising determination to seek an alternative to the world. You don't have to prove it to the world. How could you possibly prove it to the world? They are already a part of your rejection of it. Your necessity is to prove it to yourself, if need be, by constantly seeking the alternative, which is God, which is available to you through the rejection of this world.

Does that mean, as Jesus says, that I have to hate my mother and father and come to God? (Luke 14:26) It means that, but you have no intention of understanding that. I can read you that sentence, but you have already rejected it. Somewhere I would believe that you might want to progress, as my mind progressed, to where I knew I was sick and tired of the injustices of this world – I was just plain tired of being told that all of my brothers would be killed and that I would get old and I would die. I could also see that everywhere I looked in every human establishment, this was exactly the result that I was going to get. No matter where I looked at the establishments of man, I saw that the result was going to be the same – more sickness, pain and death. So it was necessary for me somewhere to follow the directions of Jesus Christ risen, who said, "Why don't you deny death? There is no death." *Whosoever believeth in me shall never die.* (John 11:26)

It has nothing to do with getting old and dying. If you believe this message, you will never die. There isn't any such thing as death. So the salvation of the world does depend on you.

I'll show you now how rapidly you will reject the teachings of Jesus. If you show me a congregation of 1000 Christians, I would stand up and read this, and you could watch how they attack Sermon on the Mount. Should I do that? What good is it going to do? If they don't want to hear it, they won't hear it. If you are determined to justify pain and death, you love it. I am threatening you with the things that you love. I am threatening you with an alternative – you are going to lose all the things that you love, all of your need to protect, your cancer. I wouldn't want to be sick and be in a body and die. Do you? Well, don't! You have the power to change your mind so that will not be that way.

Be ye therefore perfect, even as your Father which is in Heaven is perfect.

Take heed that ye do not your alms before men, to be seen of them: otherwise ye have no reward of your Father which is in Heaven.

It doesn't say you will get some reward; it says you will get none. If you take any credit for your associations here, you will get no reward in Heaven. "Oh, well, I am rewarded for what I do." No you're not. All you have done is say that you can exist and die separate from God. I couldn't even read the first sentence of Matthew 6, and you reject it.

Take heed that ye do not your alms before men, to be seen of them, and take credit in your own ego, *otherwise ye have no reward of your Father which is in Heaven. Therefore when thou doest thine alms, do not sound a trumpet before thee, as the hypocrites do in the synagogues and in the streets, that they may have glory of men. Verily I say unto you, They have their reward.* (Matthew 6)

Those of you who can hear that can leave with me. If you can't hear that, you are never going to get out of this. They are getting exactly the reward that they want from the associations of themselves. They cannot get more or less than that because that is the demand that they made. This is going to say, "Don't lay up stores at all." This is going to say, "Give everything away and come home." If you would have done that, you wouldn't be here. Why are you here except that you have refused to give everything away and come home to God. Now you defend yourself by saying, "Well, no one here does that." That's why they are here! Why would you want to share sickness and pain and death with them? Never mind that you are the cause of it. I am telling you that you are the cause of it.

But when thou doest alms (when you give), *let not thy left hand know what thy right hand doeth: That thine alms be in secret: and thy Father which seeth in secret himself shall reward thee openly.* (Matthew 6:3-4)

What this says is the more you change your mind about yourself, the happier you are going to be through God. It has nothing to do with the reflections of your own projections that justify your conceptual need to give at all. Until you give entirely, you are not giving at all, because God only gives. If your salvation is your entire dependence on yourself, why are you asserting the necessity for your existence at all? Why don't you simply be perfect as God created you? These are amazing associations! So go into your closet and pray to God, and the answer will come from God.

Don't use vain repetition because God is hearing you all the time anyway. This is the same idea as the question: should you perform a healing more than once? If you look at somebody and you say, "You are perfect as God created you," he is, despite your subsequent denial of it. The dependency is on the transformation of your mind. That is what I am offering you.

Then comes the Lord's prayer: *And lead us not into temptation, but deliver us from evil; for thine is the kingdom, and the power, and the glory, for ever. Amen.* (Matthew 6:13) You say, "But that wasn't added on until the fourth century." Which part? *For thine is the kingdom, and the power, and the glory.* That wasn't in the original. It was added on 400 years later. So what? God is still the kingdom and the glory. It is an extraordinary thing. Whatever you do, justify your objective associations so you can deny yourself access to the entirety of knowledge that is available to you.

But thou, when thou fastest, anoint thine head, and wash thy face: That thou appear not unto men to fast, but unto thy Father which is in secret: and thy Father, which seeth in secret, shall reward thee openly. (Matthew 6: 17-18) The justification for good deeds is a futile attempt to remain separate from God. All I ever told you was to give everything away and come on home. Any suffering that you do will be the possession of your own self in association with your own self.

Lay not up for yourselves treasures upon earth, where moth and rust doth corrupt, and where thieves break through and steal; But lay up for yourselves treasures in Heaven, where neither moth nor rust doth corrupt, and where thieves do not break through nor steal: For where your treasure is, there will your heart be also. (Matthew 6:19-21)

I am afraid that I am going to have to tell you that what isn't love is murder. Since the whole basis of this talk is that there is no compromise, I am going to have to tell you that this world is an attack on reality. It is an absurd attack because obviously the whole mind of God knows nothing about it. Up until this point, you have believed that this so-called existence in time is what life is. This is not Life! How come? Life is eternal. What am I doing here? Shall I answer that for you? You are not here. This is the whole teaching. There is no reality here. This is the Third Patriarch of Zen. There is no reality here. You are not here. "Yes I am." No you are not. What you think is you is not created by God and is not real. One thing for sure, what you lay up you are going to treasure and use up and die.

If I lay up a lot of stores and then I die, then other people get to use my stores? I got a thing in the mail to buy funeral insurance. I was thinking about it. I have no objection to doing that. I would want to be sure that it was used properly. How would I know whether they followed my instructions? Somewhere I must feel that I am going to know how they follow my instructions. What a place to be! Jesus says that if you don't buy burial insurance, you can't die. That was one of the old favorite expressions: "I'm too poor to die. I can't afford my own funeral. I'll get even – when I die they are going to have to bury me." Isn't it fun not to be able to die? Nothing is more fearful – illuminate minds, followers of Jesus – nothing is more fearful to the human conception than the idea that he can't die. Nothing. He is depending on it. Look at humans. I see how dependent you are on dying because of that condition you have. You think the relief will come from dying. It won't work. Now I am really threatening you. Do you know why? You are going to have to suffer forever. Of course! Death takes many forms, including the body. Is this death? Is this dead here? Is this what being dead is? That's what Jesus says: *Let the dead bury their dead.* (Matthew 8:22)

Nobody alive would bury a dead body. That is absurd. Why would you bury your own mother? Shame on you. If that's not a denial of God, what is it? Are you going to pretend that God, in His infinite mercy... That's crap! Why would you possibly justify a God that caused you pain and loneliness. Don't tell me He's acceptable to you. What's actually happened is you split your mind. Do you want to know what else? Nothing is happening! You can't decide at any moment whether you love Him or hate Him, because you do both love Him and hate

Him, and if He is responsible for the death of your son, you have every right to hate Him. Yet somehow He has to be justified in your mind. What have you done? You have cancelled yourself out. Nothing is happening. Nothing!

What is this thing you call death anyway? What if you do drop your body? Actually nothing is really happening, except just for a moment you freed yourself. And you will see eternal life and… plunko! You're right back into the same junk that you were in before. And you're doing the same thing, over and over and over again. So the entirety of this solution is being offered you now in your own mind. I'm going to read one more sentence here.

For where your treasure is, there will your heart be also. There is a very strange sentence in here. It says: *The light of the body is the eye: if therefore thine eye be single, thy whole body shall be full of light.* (Matthew 6:21-22) What does He mean by that? Boy, that's getting pretty mysterious. That's pretty mystical. He tells you that you can enlighten your own body. He says that through your mind, you can have an experience of singularity of thought that will actually resurrect your body. He says that you are having dark thoughts. This is exactly what this says. He says that your mind can exercise control over its associations and justify this world as thoughts of your own mind. Is that what that says?

But if thine eye be evil, thy whole body shall be full of darkness. If therefore the light that is in thee be darkness, how great is that darkness. If you accumulate light forms in your association, the power of the light will be manifest in the darkness. That's what you do with your body. You manifest yourself in your body association and justify your temporal existence using the power of God. One thing for sure: *No man can serve two masters: for either he will hate the one, and love the other; or else he will hold to the one, and despise the other. Ye cannot serve God and mammon.* (Matthew 6:23-24) Notice that the word is not neutral. Notice that the word is "despise." Therefore you will hate and despise me as savior of the world. Did you hear me? I am offering you entire freedom and you continue to judge me in relationship. As soon as you judge, you hate me and despise me. "Well, no I don't. I'm just examining you." Under what terms? You are examining me under the terms which you have established to justify your own hatred and death in your own mind.

So the entire lesson for today is what? Altruism. You cannot compromise time with eternity. Eternity, which is what Life is, is not waiting for time to be what it is. You are not deciding that Life is eternal. You are simply deciding whether *you* want to be eternal or continue to operate on the ridiculous premise of your own aging and death.

So that we understand this, I will pick up the Workbook of *A Course in Miracles*. *A Course in Miracles*, for those of you who don't know, is a direct message from Jesus Christ, out of time, entered into this continuum, offering you a new mind training association where you can come to know this. Let's just do a lesson. I'm going to show you how rapidly you will reject it.

It's going to say, "I will that there be light because the power of my mind is to will for light." All right? The next one is, "There is no will but God's, and therefore I'm using God's will." The next, Lesson 75, is, "The light has come," and that I'm entitled to vision and will now experience it. Everybody nods their head until they get to Lesson 76 which everybody is going to deny because there is absolutely no sympathy whatsoever in Lesson 76 for the laws of man. It is just not there. What I'm curious about is, if somebody reads this who pretends to be a follower of Jesus, what does he do? He will just say, "It's not so." Or "I don't believe that." This says:

I am under no laws but God's. We have observed before how many senseless things have seemed to you to be salvation. And they are all senseless. And this world is senseless. *Each has imprisoned you with laws that are just as senseless as itself.* Listen: You are not bound by the laws of your mind. *Yet to understand that this is so, you must first realize salvation lies not there.* There is no salvation here. *While you would seek for it in things that have no meaning* – things that have no meaning, these *things* have no meaning – *you bind yourself to laws that make absolutely no sense. Thus do you seem to prove salvation is where it is not.*

Today you should be glad you cannot prove it. How do you try to prove it? You die. Heretofore your human condition was hell-bent on justifying your own associations with yourself by proving that you were right. Are you good at that? Sure! No one is better at it than you are. Who could possibly be better at denying God, your eternal Creator, than the human condition? Why else is there a human condition? You are an expert at it, and that is what prevents you from seeing the altruism of the *Course*.

How simple is salvation. All it says is that there is no world, that this never happened, and you are not separated from God. Yet when I tell you that, you just stare at me and you analyze in your own mind how that could be true. Just as obviously the analyzation of *A Course In Miracles* is an attack on it because it says that the analyzation of Jesus' teaching is an attack. For goodness sake! I'm getting letters every day, attacking me. Do you know that? Because I'm teaching uncompromising Jesus. They have got to attack me. Stand by. Do you think that you are going to be allowed to perform miracles? Do you think that you are going to be allowed to raise the dead? There are so many Pharisees around here, they are going to tell you that you are healing evilly. That's the next step. The next step is a lot of miracles are happening. He's going to tell you, "You're healing evilly because you are not healing through Jesus Christ." What kind of nonsense is that? Jesus doesn't want your praise. He wants your acceptance. He wants you to admit that you will do these things.

For if you could, you would forever seek salvation where it is not, and never find it. The idea for today tells you once again how simple is salvation. Look for it where it waits for you, and there it will be found. Look nowhere else, for it is nowhere else.

Think of the freedom in the recognition that you are not bound by all of the strange and twisted laws you have set up to save you. This is Sermon on the Mount, incidentally, if you would like to know. Well, I just thought you might have seen where this is rejected. *You really think that you would starve unless you have stacks of green paper strips and piles of metal discs. You really think a small round pellet or some fluid pushed into your veins through a sharpened needle will ward off disease and death. You really think you are alone unless another body is with you.*

What is it that thinks that? *It is insanity that thinks these things.* How will you reduce this? You will "Christian Science" it. You will say, "He just told me not to push fluid in my veins." That's what you just did. I saw you do it. "He just told me that I'm not supposed to..." I didn't you tell you anything of the kind. I tell you *it is insanity* that thinks that. I am telling you that you are not true. *You call them laws, and put them under different names in a long catalogue of rituals that have no use and serve no purpose.* **No use and serve no purpose!** You say, "He doesn't mean that. He couldn't possibly mean that there is no purpose here at all. He couldn't possibly mean that this world is over and gone." I just thought you might like to look at it. You have no intention of hearing me. You would rather die. But the simple fact of the matter is that I am speaking to you from not-here. I am not here and neither are you, and that's what you are going to come to know. There is no world!

You think you must obey the "laws" of medicine, of economics and of health. Of course! "This couldn't be Jesus of Nazareth speaking." Then who is it? This is exactly what He said 2000 years ago. It is identical to what He said, and everybody that heard Him is not here. In a particular sense the only one that didn't hear Him is you. In a particular sense the only one I am speaking to is you, since you would be the part of me that hasn't heard this. This is Jesus of Nazareth. The only part of me that couldn't have heard this is you. Notice that I don't divide up the various parts of who you think you are to study your relationships with each other. The whole teaching of the uncompromising miracle working of your mind is that one miracle is no more difficult to do than the other. I positively guarantee you that I can heal your cold as well as raise you from the dead. Why? None of it is real! If I see *any* of you as real, I have denied my Creator. Believe me or believe what I say.

Protect the body and you will be saved. These are not laws... "Oh, these are the laws of man." The hell they are! They're nuts. They are madness. *These are not laws, but madness.* You can't be separate from God. You're nuts. You are insane. Anything that doesn't know what it is, is insane. You have come to a place where nobody knows who they are, where they are going, or what they are. Imagine a man not knowing who he is. Human beings confined to space/time have no idea who they are, where they came from or what they're doing. The beginning of salvation is the admission that you don't know what anything is, because you *don't* know what anything is. Yet not knowing who you are is nuts. One thing we know for sure: if there is a reality, everything knows what it is. Do you understand me? Consciousness is the domain of the nothingness of the ego. Everything here knows perfectly well what it is.

The body is endangered by the mind that hurts itself. The body suffers just in order that the mind will fail to see it is the victim of itself. Could you hear that? This is why nobody wants to be healed. If they're going to be healed, they won't have any reason to be here at all. What is the greatest threat to you? Being healed. See it? I know most of you do. The tenacity, the determination to believe that the body can act outside of the mind is a sure sign that you believe the world can act outside of your mind. You now are at the mercy of this world. Shame on you! Shame on you for believing that somebody out there can set the stage for what you are supposed to be – can dictate terms of the littleness of your body, can tell you what you are. Shame on you! You are under no laws but God's! And until you stand up and say that, there is no hope for you. If you stand up and say that egotistically you will get the result of your ego. You are not going to escape the consequences of your own mind.

The body's suffering is a mask the mind holds up to hide what really suffers. It would not understand it is its own enemy — (the mind); *that it attacks itself and wants to die. It is from this your "laws" would save the body. It is for this you think that you are a body.* Did you hear that? This is all happening in your own mind. There is absolutely nothing outside of you. You are attacking yourself. You inherently defend yourself in your own association from your own thoughts. No more. *It is for this you think you are a body.*

There are no laws except the laws of God. Is that so? *There are no laws except the laws of God.* What are they? That you are perfect and whole and in Heaven. That's the law. How do I get there? *Love the Lord thy God with thy heart and thy mind and thy soul and thy neighbor as thyself.* I have given you everything I have to offer. Those of you who know my mind, know that my mind will not be here in a moment. Those of you who know my mind as you know your own will understand that I have offered whole-mindedness to the limited association, that I am declaring to you, individually, not to your projections, but to you individually that the salvation of the world depends on *you.* Is this the teachings of Jesus of Nazareth? Solely and simply. He didn't come to save the world; He came to save you. I have come to save you. What do I care about the world? It's not real.

There are no laws except the laws of God. This needs repeating over and over and over and over and over and over and over and over and over, *until you realize it applies to everything that you have made in opposition to God's Will.* Because this world is in opposition to God's will. "How altruistic of you! Let's examine what you just said." What do you want to examine? Time, sickness, pain and death is in opposition to eternal life. Why is that difficult? "Why is it I don't know that?" You do. You just don't want it to be true because you are going to lose your cancer. And if you can't get cancer, how are you going to stay here?

If Aunt Tilly can't die and leave you everything, how are you going to be here? What a terrible ambivalence. You want her to die and you don't want her to die. What is that called? Guilt! Boy, are you guilty! You are guilty of your own thought associations with yourself. "Well, I'm not as guilty about some things as others." What kind of nonsense is that? You are guilty of being you. You are guilty of existing in your association. If you are going to be guilty, be guilty of being perfect. Then you don't have to measure it. At least you can say, "Hell, I guess I'm perfect." That's called a little willingness. Jesus says somewhere you are a little willing to let it be true. It is going to be true despite your willingness. Wow!

Your magic has no meaning. Ready? Here's a sentence for you if you want it. *What it is meant to save does not exist.* I don't hear *Course in Miracles* teachers teaching what it says. What you are attempting to save is totally meaningless and doesn't exist. The ego does not exist and it is nothing. Why do you study your relationship with yourself and your ego? You already are non-existent.

The laws of God can never be replaced. We will devote today to rejoicing that this is so. I don't want to read you this because then you will really get me. *We will begin our practice periods today with a short review of the different kinds of "laws" we have believed we must obey.* You can ask God this if you want to. You've got to obey the *"laws" of nutrition, of immunization, of medication, and of the body's protection in innumerable ways...you believe in the "laws" of friendship-* (Let's die together.) *of "good" relationships and reciprocity. Perhaps you even think there are laws which set forth what is God's and what is yours.* Most religions are based on this. What an absurd idea! So everybody either believes in themselves, or themselves and God, but not in God alone. It's an amazing idea. Wow! *Many "religions" have been based on this. They would not save but damn in Heaven's name.* This is the basis of all established Christianity today – that somehow you have to suffer pain and death in order to be with God. I hated it. I couldn't understand the idea that you would have to suffer pain and death in order to justify your return to God. It doesn't make any sense. It is totally senseless.

Yet they are no more strange than other "laws" you hold must be obeyed in order to make you safe. Safe from what? From nothing? What are you protecting? Nothing. *There are no laws but God's. Dismiss all foolish, magical beliefs today, and hold your mind in silent readiness to hear the Voice that speaks the truth to you. You will be listening to One Who says there is no loss under the laws of God.* You can't lose. You can't lose the things you love.

I hate this place. I hate to have you tell me that my mother is dead. In my life as a human I saw people grow old and die. That's why I hate the world. Can you hear me? Did you hear what I just said? I hate the idea that you would have to justify the pain and death that I experienced. You do that. I don't do that. I offer you a solution to your declaration, "There is no death." That's called a renunciation. The basic teaching of this is: There is no death and we renounce it right now. We will not operate on the premise that we are a body, locked forever in space/time. We are going to declare our freedom to be as God created us. You are going to use the power of your mind to deny death. I assure you that you cannot die. If you are determined to die, death is an idea and the purpose of your own body will be to get old and get crippled and die. Shame on you! I hated it. Right? You too? I didn't want to be a body and get old and die. I didn't want to crouch down here. I wanted to be free. I wanted my mind free to be as God created me. I am perfect and whole as God created me. Now, if that requires through Jesus Christ the denial of this world, I intend to deny it. You don't. You believe that you are actually locked in your own mind and that you are at the mercy of this world. Obviously somewhere you must be applying the power of your own mind to justify this world. You would have to be. Otherwise, what are you doing here? If all power is given unto you in Heaven and on earth, you are doing everything you can to keep from hearing it. My goodness!

Payment is neither given nor received. Exchange cannot be made; there are no substitutes; and nothing is replaced by something else. God's laws forever give and never take. Who heard that? What is the best way to get out of here? Give everything away. We are barely existing here. We have given everything away and the world's going, "Ha ha ha ha, we've got you now." Little do they know. Listen.

Hear Him Who tells you this, and realize how foolish are the "laws" you thought upheld the world you thought you saw. Isn't that a lovely sentence? *Then listen further. He will tell you more.* He will tell you *about the love your Father has for you. About the endless joy He offers you. About His yearning for His only Son, created as His channel for creation; denied to Him by his belief in hell.* So there is no Heaven without you. And there is no Hell without you. Now you can make a choice. What I bind on earth will be bound in Heaven. (Matthew 16:19) I thought that Jesus said that 2000 years ago. Well, He did. Well, why don't you do it, then? Do you believe that that is true, that your mind is a decision-maker in regard to this? An incredible idea!

Your Father will tell you *about His yearning for His only Son, created as His channel for creation; denied to Him by his belief in hell.* Oh, I love this. I really love it. I knew that I yearned for something. And I knew that when I yearned, everything must be yearning because I could not see beyond my own yearning. This is the human condition. I knew that somewhere in my mind there was an alternative to what I was being directed to associate with here. That's called the Christ. I knew that the Christ was in me somewhere, but I couldn't find Him because He was only available to me under terms of God, not my own terms. As long as I kept setting the terms, I couldn't see the Christ. As soon as I laid down my burden and said, "God, I can't. Help me," I began to emerge as a wholeness of my association with God rather than my association in the limitation. Is that clear? This is the entire teaching of: You are the Christ, and as that Christ emerges in you, it will emerge in your projected association very simply because you are sharing Jesus Christ. You are sharing the single wholeness of your mind, that there is only one Self and that Self is you.

You offered me your saviorship and I accepted. Why are you so afraid of that? Obviously my salvation depends on you, at least as long as you think so. I want you to emerge in your own Christhood. Jesus says, "What good does it do me to save the world and be gone if you are still here in the junk of your own mind?" *Know ye not ye must be born again?* Followed by some of the most beautiful sentences that have ever been written anywhere.

Let us today open God's channels to Him, and let His Will extend through us to Him. Don't tell me that's written by a human being. There is no human being that could write that. That says that our will is the Will of God and our channel is His channel and that we are singular in that association. *Thus is creation endlessly increased.* Do you see that? If you are God creating, it extends forever. There is nowhere it begins and nowhere where it ends in your own mind. *His Voice will speak of this to us, as well as the joys of Heaven which His laws keep limitless forever. We will repeat today's idea* over and over and over again *until we have listened and understood that there are no laws but God's. Then we will tell ourselves, as a dedication with which the practice period concludes: I am under no laws but God's.*

You are under no laws but God's? Really? What are you doing here? "I'm not going to stay here." Oh, I see. There really is a Universal Mind. There really is an experience that I can have. I don't have to operate on the premise of this world. I have been dreaming. I have been hallucinating. I have been locked in my own mind. *We will repeat this dedication as often as possible*, at least 240 times.

You don't have to go out there and do it in the world. You don't go to a guy who tells you to pick up a shovel and say, "Screw you! I'm under no laws but God's." That is not what I am telling you to do. I know this is difficult for some of you still, but I'm telling you, when you change your mind, the world will change out there and the situations that you previously found yourself in will change.

I'm going to finish this up with part of the problem that you have. I don't generally do Chapter 17. But when this is presented to the world, many associations for the first time are going to begin to suffer the conflict in their apparent environment about the change in their own mind. Listen to me all human beings: As your mind changes and matures, the direction of your purpose changes. And this will be viewed as conflictual. The reason I am going to allow you that conflict if you want it is because I'm leaving here. Listen. Understand me. There appears to be a compromise, a dichotomy – that in the change of your mind you will obviously be threatened by the condition that you were previously in. This is absolutely inevitable. You think you will be more peaceful? It is exactly the opposite. Once you decide you want to fulfill that role, you will suffer the previous conflicts of your own determination of mind.

The solution is very obvious if you'll let it be: *You are the cause of it.* Once more. I'm only going to do this once more for those of you who want to teach this. If you are the entirety of the causation, the conflict of the reassociation will not last very long. It cannot, simply because you will admit that you are the cause of it. You will step back from it and stop trying to defend your new-found freedom. In your non-defense of that freedom will be the extension of the freedom from your own mind. Could you hear that?

I'll tell you my illumination. I am illuminate. I had the most devastating experience that any human being, including you, could ever have. I am pressed up, my body is raised up, the Voice says I'm whole. The next morning I walked out into the living room and in the process of conversation, I said, "Well, of course, the world's not real." I actually said that. I said, "Well, this world's not real." And everybody at the table turned and looked at me. You still turn and look at me. I am telling you the fact of my illumination, that this world is not real. This is the entire teaching.

Everyone must come to know there is no world. Coming to know that is the transformation of your mind. My next sentence was: "You know that." My next sentence to all the humans is, "You know perfectly well this is not a real world." I will try it with a human being: You know perfectly well this world is not real. Otherwise, why are you establishing a reality? You must know of an alternative, yet you continue to operate on the premise that this world is real. This world is not real. I discovered that through my illumination. In my discovery of that was your salvation, because previous to that I intended to stay in this nightmare and kill you and honor you and love you and die with you and do all the things a human being does to honor his position. I don't do that any longer.

Most of you in this room have never seen death. I never could justify death in my own mind. They had a little shoot-out two weeks ago, and half the people are under therapy. They have no idea of death. The idea is much too traumatic. They just want to see it on video games. That's not what this is.

Just one sentence in Chapter 17 (The Two Pictures) real quickly. First of all it talks about the picture of light and how you blocked yourself. *The ego is alert to threat, and the part of your mind into which the ego is accepted is very anxious to preserve its reason, as it sees it. It* (the human condition) *does not realize it is totally insane. And you must realize just what this means if you would be restored to sanity. The insane protect their thought systems, but they do so* how? *Insanely.* You can't protect your insanity sanely. You can think you can. To you it seems sane. It's the same as: *My meaningless thoughts are showing me a meaningless world.* (Lesson 11) If the thoughts were meaningful, the world would be meaningful.

And you must realize just what this means if you would be restored to sanity. The insane protect their thought systems, but they do so insanely. And all their defenses are as insane as what they are supposed to protect. The separation has nothing in it, -- doggone it! – no part, no "reason," and no attribute that is not insane – totally nuts! And its "protection" is part of it, as insane as the whole. The special relationship, which is its chief defense, must therefore be insane – completely nuts! The idea that you can reproduce a body in the association of your own mind and justify it through the use of a carbon-based life in this little hell-hole of nothing is totally meaningless if you are as God created you. Now, obviously your entire attribute of mind is the use of the apparent form that you find yourself in. You were born here, weren't you? And you are going to die here, aren't you?

The holy relationship is nothing but the discovery of your mutual Christ Minds. It is nothing but the admission that everyone is perfect as God created you, with the further admonition that there is only one Self. Jesus says, my Self, your Self and the Self of God. Now suddenly here you are, with all of these new bright alternatives being offered to you, which cannot be understood by the conceptual mind. Quite literally, the world cannot understand you are new. Everybody knows that. They will not understand that. Behold, I show you a mystery. In a moment you will be transformed. The world does not understand that. The requirement is that you understand it, not the world. But therein lies the conflict. The only place Jesus uses the word "phenomenal" in the entire *Course* is in what I am going to read to you now. It's not noumenal, it's phenomenal!

A holy relationship, the idea that you could join in minds with what was previously dedicated to the separation, is a phenomenal accomplishment. Why? Every single attribute of that quality, that justification with your body, was to justify sin and death. Into this impossible situation – this is the whole *Course* – comes a mind that says, "No, the world is not real." So it depends on not only you changing your mind, which is the essence of the teaching, but that it's possible for other associations that were previously in the rejection of God to change their mind. That can be a little uneven. Can you hear that? That can be a little uneven because everyone is inhabiting their own space/time. And each one has constructed in his own memory patterns various symbols or forms that he justifies in his own mind. Quite literally the manner in which I see you is different than the manner in which you see me. You see me within the perspective of your own association with yourself. I see you in my perspective, which is totally whole and Universal Mind. Or, if you are separate from each other, you see each other in perspectives that justify the special relationship through the formulation of forms, of body, in which you then exist. What an idea!

The holy relationship is the expression of the holy instant in living in this world. Literally, if I don't decide each moment, I can live in a holy instant with you because the world is over and gone already. This world lasted but a moment in our mind and it's over. I can live in that moment of return to Heaven if I choose. You can join me in that because our minds are joined, because our minds cannot be separate.

Like everything about salvation, —(I love this) *the holy instant is a practical device, witnessed to by* what? *Its results.* If you are not getting the result of the holy instant, you are still going to be pissed off in your own mind. If you are getting the result of it you are going to be very happy in the realization that you are under no laws but God's. If God is only happiness, why are you angry because you're not happy? I can't do anything about that except to tell you that your anger is a denial of the perfection of your own mind. *Like everything about salvation, the holy instant is very practical.* Because it's an offering of a totality from a totality of separation – that's how practical it is. It doesn't have to be examined. The experience cannot be examined. In fact, the examination of it is what reduces it. Then you can compare your old holy instants. And you remember back in 1972 when you found all that love. Now you are an old rotten thing and you hate it. Guys, thoughts don't get old. You can't get old.

The reason I seem maybe kind of young to you today – and I'm the oldest guy here; am I the oldest guy? No, I'm the youngest – is that I don't have old thoughts simply because I don't know what an old thought is. An old thought is nothing but a comparison with another thought. If you don't compare your thoughts, all of your thoughts will be brand new each moment. You don't have to study that; it's true. You are always examining your old thoughts and justifying them, and then you wonder why your body gets old and sick and dies. What an amazing idea! "Well, I can tell the difference in my thoughts from 40 years ago." My thoughts of 1934 are just as vivid as my thoughts of yesterday. In fact, in some cases more vivid.

The holy instant never fails. Listen. See if you can hear this. *The experience of it is always felt.* You are experiencing it at every moment, otherwise, you wouldn't be you. There is no question that at each moment you are whole – you believe that you're whole. I tried to teach that as "eternal time." The moment that you experience that, it is whole and perfect, and that moment is eternal. You like to block off little moments of eternity, where you come together at the motel. Talk about 1947! The greatest moment I ever had. You know the fun part about that? I just had it. Isn't that amazing? Actually I could hold a grievance that there was no room at the inn and I did it in the back seat. I don't hold a grievance. There is no reason why you should be guilty about your experiences. It is who you are. You are so afraid of being happy, you don't know what to do.

The experience of it is always felt. Yet without expression it is not remembered. Doggone you! If you're going to declare this, you have to stand up and declare it! You have to give it away! My experience when I turned my will and my life over to God – as many of you know, I was an addict – I discovered I was free of that addiction. The requirement for me was to give it away. There was no way that could work except by my giving it. That's all I'm teaching you, isn't it? Through this experience with God you have recovered from the disease of human-ness. You recovered from that disease through God, through turning your will over to God. And that's what you are going out into the world to teach. Can the world hear it? Based on their admission of the need to hear it, they will hear it. If they don't need to hear it, you won't hear it. You will go on with your addiction to what? Death.

Yet without expression it is not remembered. Listen: *The holy relationship* – now, what we're sharing together, here – *is a constant reminder of the experience in which the relationship became what it is.* I couldn't care less about your old associations with me. They are totally meaningless to me. All I know for sure is that at this time, in this place we are ascending to Heaven. That has to be true because in this time, in this place, we came here. If I can get you to come into that *now* with me, you can have that experience not based on your old references, which are going to condemn me to the death of our association. I have no intention of sharing that with you. This is the Workbook of *A Course in Miracles.* Here we go.

And as the unholy (unwhole) *relationship is a continuing hymn of hate in praise of its maker, so is the holy relationship a happy song of praise to the Redeemer of relationships.* It's time to cash in your holy instants. Can you hear that? Why don't you look at your holy instants as S & H Green Stamps that you put up into a warehouse of holy instants, because nothing is ever lost to you? The reason the instant was lost was because you forced it into an association of cause and effect. Now that's gone. What does that cause? A grievance. That's why you're grieving, because you think you have lost the holy instant. Amazingly enough, holy instants are accumulative and they form new spatial references called the Borderland, where you can enter with me. You are what? Redeemed. Whatever price you thought you had to pay has been paid. I am telling you I know that my Redeemer liveth. Of course! He has redeemed me from my thoughts of pain and death. Listen: *The holy relationship, a major step toward the perception of the real world, is learned.* Ready for this? Nothing is outside of you. *It is the old, unholy relationship, transformed and seen anew.* It isn't that any of the circumstances are different. It's that all of the circumstances are different because you look at them in a different way and they have a different purpose to you. By changing your mind about the purpose of this world, the purpose of you and your relationship changes. Your sole responsibility in this world is to escape it. You have no other reason except to get out of here. And on that basis, the holy relationships here have been formed. Can you hear that? That's why the world denies you. You are saying, "No, there's another alternative." I say, "I agree with you."

If you agree with me, we are going to get the hell out of here through this teaching. You cannot fail. Since you're coming from all over the place, you have no standard here. You are so deep that obviously you killed your savior. Everyone we have sent into this area, you killed before he even got started. Finally we just send in the form. We send the teachings in to a scribe and it is still immediately denied and rejected. There's no admission of its truth at all. I'm a professional, as you know. I'm not from here at all. You think I am from here? Why the hell would I be from here? I can't be. Nothing is from here. I'm a complete insertion. There was nothing religious about my awakening at all. I couldn't stand this place. So I'm teaching you service and giving and loving through my transformation. Obviously I couldn't possibly be from here; there is nothing about me that is, except what I share in our holy relationship. I can share perfectly well, but I can only share your wholeness with you. I can't share your determination to stay separate. Why? It's not sharable. When you lock yourself in your own mind, you are non-communicative. You are blind, deaf and dumb. Nothing is happening because you close down in your mind. A holy relationship is nothing but a moment of communication which continues in your determination of the entirety of your Creator in relationship with you.

*The holy relationship is a **phenomenal** teaching accomplishment.* And the reason that we are so happy is that every one of you sitting together had every intention of not doing this. Don't pretend that you had any intention of coming to God. That's nuts. Nothing would ever stop you from coming to God. You have been a seek-and-don't-finder. The idea of a spiritual path is obviously an attack on God. It would have to be. How would there be a path from nothing in separation to God? This is the whole *Course.* Listen: *The holy relationship is a* *phenomenal teaching accomplishment. In all its aspects, as it begins, as it develops and becomes accomplished, it represents the reversal of the unholy relationship. Be comforted in this; the only difficult phase is the beginning.* If you are beginning to have experiences of God, if there is one thing this world is going to do, it is going to deny you that experience. I'll do it once more for you. If there's one thing this world is going to do, it's deny your out-of-body, out-of-world experiences. It will allow you to have Christian mystical or mystical ideas as long as you continue to formulate them in your own temporal death. But as you expand in your association you will begin more and more to deny this world and assert the reality of your relationship with God.

Be comforted in this; the only difficult phase is the beginning. For here, the goal of the relationship is abruptly shifted to the exact opposite of what it was. Not a little shift. The moment that you recognize that you are whole and perfect, the world will have no meaning to you. And that's not because it's a discipline. That is simply because the world has lost its meaning. It doesn't have any meaning to you. Now have you become a threat. Now suddenly, you don't want to participate in the world. You are looking for a solution. Or, more likely, you are looking somewhere in time for someone who can share with you that experience. This is called the evolutionary process of man to remembering that he's God. You are very capable of doing that now as a species. Listen: *This is the first result of offering the relationship to the Holy Spirit, to use for His purposes.* The first result is that you will see it as exactly the opposite and it will be conflictual.

This invitation is accepted immediately, and the Holy Spirit wastes no time in introducing the practical results of asking Him to enter. It is impossible that you ask for God's help – and mean it – that it won't occur. When it does not occur it is because you don't want it. That's the fact of the matter. Now you have opened up that portal. Now you are in trouble. Unless you can close it down, it's going to grow. It may initially not get more beneficent. It may even get more conflictual. Did you hear that? Suddenly the relationship that was so dependable – where she had cancer and you see that she got chemotherapy – doesn't have any meaning to you. All of the *things* that you associate in your mind begin to lose their value. They become less and less valuable to you.

The Holy Spirit accepts it immediately...At once His goal replaces yours because He is a simultaneous corrector. If there's a field of energy of correction, which we call the Holy Spirit, a unified field, it is not at all concerned about your conflict, but only the conversion of it. Who heard that? It awaits its use. And if you dare to open up that door, it will begin immediately to convert. And this, of course, is where your fear is because you are afraid of the loss of your own special relationships. This just makes sense if you will let it. Stop studying it as concepts. This is what's happening in your own mind. Then it gets fun. You can sit here and go, "Those villains – wait a minute. I'm doing this to myself! I am the cause of this. I am not going to let that affect me." See that? See how valuable this teaching is? Then you can rant and rave all you want. You can hit yourself, kill yourself, go get therapy, do anything you want, but it's too late. The human condition is too late. It knows about an alternative.

Seek, and ye shall find; knock and it shall be opened unto you. (Matthew 7:7)

At once His goal replaces yours. Listen: *This is accomplished very, very, very rapidly.* Because the Spirit doesn't know whether you are ready to hear it or not. How the hell does God know if you're ready to hear it? You asked God, and He said, "There you are!" And you said, "Oh, shit!" Do you see that? This is called Fear of Enlightenment. You opened it up and now you can't get it closed. How many here can't close their gate? You can't close it. You went too far. Jesus says you went a step too far. Now what happens is, your past winds up behind you and when you turn around to finally get out, there's nothing back there. Now you might as well just say, "What the hell! Into Thy hands I command my spirit." You might as well take that step. I cut off your retreat. I did! I made you examine your own associations and decide you didn't want them. And the more you decided, the more you experienced. But you remember this, it is completely abstract. It is very possible for you to disappear from this world right now and go home. Many of you are aware of that.

At once His goal replaces yours, introducing the practical results of asking Him to enter, which you have done. *At once His goal replaces yours. This is accomplished very rapidly, but it makes the relationship seem disturbed, disjunctive and even quite distressing.* Even quite distressing! *Disjunctive* means you have always been meeting at the verification of death. You have been meeting at a juncture of death. If that juncture is not in our associate minds (which is death), sitting right here we are in agreement about a juncture of the termination of us. This is why we have food and life insurance policies and all of the things in our own mind. This is very disjunctive because I don't recognize what I previously agreed with you. I've lost it. It's not in my mind. It is sitting right next to that. But as yet it has not phased into your association.

The reason is quite clear. For the relationship as it is, is out of line with its own goal, and clearly unsuited to the purpose that has been accepted for it. In other words, if your purpose is to get to God, obviously it's a denial of your existence here. That's what this says. So now you have a hell of a time. "Well, which am I?" Now you can decide for yourself. "Am I confined to this body? Am I limited to being old and dying, or is this alternative that I see true? Is there really a God? Has my Christ at last caught up with me?" This is the *Course.* "Am I going to have to admit that there's an alternative that I've been walking around with all the time and until this moment have refused to accept?" Okay?

The relationship as it is, is out of line with its own goal and clearly unsuited to the purpose that has been accepted for it. In its unholy condition, your goal was all that seemed to give it meaning. Now it seems to make no sense at all. And this is frustrating as hell. You get into your own room and you've been doing everything, and you say, "What the hell is the purpose in this? I have done all of these things. I can't do this." These are moments of despair. These are dark nights of the soul for some of us, aren't they? Of course. How would they not be? You are at Gethsemane. You are in that association. I have never taken your bottoms away from you. I have told you very emphatically, you are going to have to come to that moment when you can make the choice through desperation of not being here and finding God. That is my entire teaching. How that occurs and when it occurs, I have no concern. But I can guarantee you that it can occur in an instant and you will be gone from here in another instant.

Many relationships have been broken off at this point, and the pursuit of the old goal re-established in another relationship. You are always meeting each other in holy relationships. You keep searching for solutions in other bodies when it gets too conflictual because your goals have changed with each other. Each one of you is peopling your own associations to justify the old memories of your own mind. *For once the unholy relationship has accepted the goal of holiness, it can never again be what it was.* Never! The old man has passed away, as Paul would say. That old man is gone forever. Never again will that relationship be what it was.

The temptation of the ego becomes extremely intense with this shift of goals. For the relationship has not as yet been changed sufficiently to make its former goal completely without attraction, and its structure is "threatened" by the recognition of its inappropriateness for meeting its new purpose. That's about as great a sentence as I can offer you, if you can hear that. Everybody. There is no one in this room who has not had that experience. Do you hear me? You had to begin to question, "What am I doing?" Many of you have left the world. Some of you have said, "The hell with it!" Some of you have said, "I'll be so successful, I can prove this is real." You have all used all these methods in your own mind. Now the world is getting ready to hate and despise you. Yet the decision is going to be yours because *you* are the cause of it, and that is where the solution will be.

Set firmly in the unholy relationship, there is no course except to change the relationship to fit the goal. Until this happy solution is seen and accepted as the only way out of conflict, the relationship may seem to be severely strained. "What the hell happened to you?" I don't know. I saw a Light. I want to be with God. "What are you talking about?"

It would not... not! This is why you got me. At this level, I required your acceptance of an uncompromising alternative, otherwise there was no hope for you. This is as low as I go with this. I am telling you that I am offering you this, and it would not be kind of me to condemn you to the cancer that you've got. My responsibility is to offer you that alternative. *It would not be kinder to shift the goal more slowly, for the contrast would be obscured, and your ego* (human condition) *given time to reinterpret each slow step according to its liking. Only a radical shift in purpose could induce a complete change of mind about what the whole relationship is for. As this change develops and is finally accomplished, it grows increasingly beneficent and joyous.* Why wouldn't it? It is your way out of hell! If you dedicated yourself to sharing sickness and pain, the change of your mind is real because it is real; there is a God, and you are perfect, no matter how much conflict you inflict on yourself.

But at the beginning, the situation is experienced as very precarious. A relationship, undertaken by two individuals for their unholy purposes, suddenly has holiness for its goal. Obviously it is a complete conversion. Every emotion that you have that you call love is actually hate and pain and death, without exception. Now, boy, what a phenomenal accomplishment this is. *As these two contemplate their relationship from the point of view of this new purpose, they are inevitably appalled.* Can you hear this? They suddenly look at each other and say, "What the hell were we doing? Why do we want to stay in a place where there's murder and death and pain? Why did we ever think that we could justify this? There is a whole loving God." They are appalled! This is a slaughterhouse – I'm sure you are aware of this. As your mind emerges and you look at it, you literally cannot understand why you would have participated in it. That is what causes the conflict. They are appalled. *Their perception of the relationship may even become quite disorganized. And yet, the former organization of their perception no longer serves the purpose they have agreed to meet.*

This is the time for faith. You let this goal be set for you. That was an act of faith. Do not abandon faith, now that the rewards of faith are being introduced. If you believed the Holy Spirit was there to accept the relationship, why would you now not still believe that He is there to purify what He has taken under His guidance? Have faith in your brother in what but seems to be a trying time. The goal is set. And your relationship has sanity as its purpose. For now you find yourself in an insane relationship, recognized as such in the light of its goal. Which you don't want any more! Wow!

Now the ego counsels thus; substitute for this another relationship to which your former goal was quite appropriate. You can do that forever, can't you? *You can escape from your distress only by getting rid of your brother. You need not part entirely if you choose not to do so. But you must exclude major areas of fantasy from your brother, to save your sanity.* What an incredible idea. Now you close yourself in and reject the world, and you become an agreement to die together to justify the continuation of this place. That's where you found yourself. Wow! *Hear not this now! Have faith in Him Who answered you. He heard. Has He not been very explicit in His answer? You are not now wholly insane. Can you deny that He has given you a most explicit statement? Now He asks for faith a little longer, even in bewilderment.*

You will find many opportunities to blame your brother for the "failure" of your relationship, for it will seem at times to have no purpose. A sense of aimlessness will come to haunt you, and to remind you of all the ways you once sought for satisfaction and thought you found it. Forget not now the misery you really found, and do not breathe life into your failing ego. For your relationship has not been disrupted. It has been saved. (Text, 17:5)

Wow, that's nice. Is that in this little book? It's called *A Course In Miracles*. It's in a little book called *The Holy Bible*. It says that the world is your doing and all the power of your mind to change your mind is given through God to you. It says you have been dreaming a dream of death. It says you are not really separated from God at all. It says in just a moment you are going to awaken and remember that you are in Heaven. That is a little altruistic. Now look at the chaos of this world. Look at the attempts to take the *Course in Miracles* – a major attempt now (another new book is coming out) – and analyze it in association with the conceptual mind when it is exactly the opposite of the teaching.

So you are whole and perfect as God created you! Everyone knows this. You have been locked in this little box of space and time and it is time to leave it. You have come together with a new purpose. And the world cannot recognize your purpose. But through your healing grace, you are able now to demonstrate, if you choose, the power of my mind to heal. I am a healer. I am trying to heal you and you are trying to keep from being healed. That is just the nature of it. There is nothing I can do. If you do not want to be penetrated by the love that I am offering you, you will deny your own healing. That is why your need to get sick and die is constantly being justified in your own mind.

Now I ask you this: Everything else being equal, wouldn't you rather what I'm telling you be true than what is in the world? Until then, there is no hope for you. None. You will continue to close down your own mind because everything you do justifies that old rotten carcass that you are in. That's how I heal. I heal literally by denying *you*. That's what our little book, *Miracle Healers Handbook*, says. How could I possibly heal you if I acknowledged your sickness? It doesn't make any sense. If I acknowledge that you are really sick, how would I heal you? The sickness is in my mind, not yours. That's what that little book says. Raise the dead! Some of you guys are getting real good at healing. If you have any problems, call me and I'll raise it right up. Is this healing really going on? You bet! The question is not that, the question is whether you really want to be well or not. If you are well, you will have no reason to stay here! If you can't die, what is the sense in staying here? Now you see how afraid the establishment is of what I am offering. It is totally afraid of it because I am a denial of the entire system. You can't get old and you can't get sick and you can't die.

Fortunately, we're not really threatening anything. Can reality really be threatened? By who? There is only one mind! The lesson that you guys have learned in the presence that you are experiencing is a very joyous happening. The whole teaching is that you have been living in the past and that everything you see is already over and gone, and you feel very resentful because you can't hold onto it, so you get old and die.

We are showing you a presence. This goes beyond perception. This is the teaching of Chapter 17 of the *Course*, where you are inhabiting the associations of your own mind with pain and death that you no longer want to do. The whole perspective of the physical association of the body can then change because, literally, the resurrection is occurring each moment. The resurrection of your body is occurring each moment. At no single moment is your body real at all. "Well, I'm going to keep mine real, and I'm going to close in on that association. And though there are angels all around me, I won't glance up because I might see them and they will threaten me with my own perfection." You don't have to do that, brother, you are already whole and perfect. To do that, you must face the fear of the opening up of the portal. Everyone must come to this place of fear and death, and go beyond it in the realization of your whole mind.

Verily I say unto you,
Whatsoever ye shall bind on earth
shall be bound in heaven:
and whatsoever ye shall loose on earth
shall be loosed in heaven.

CHAPTER 2

Double Or Nothing: Let It Ride

You think that I'm telling you not to prepare to teach, and that's not true. I am in constant preparation. This is one of the greatest – or better, fairly good, no good at all – talks that I have given in a long time. Well, there's a progression to humility, if I've ever seen one. Ha! Did you see what I did? Down, down, down. Now I'm free! Because my expectation of return to a manifestation of knowledge gained by my preparation is no longer necessary for me.

What I'm saying is that if you can hear this in our association, that would be the entirety of the demand, and it really wouldn't make any difference what I'm saying. Yet your need to hear what I'm saying is based on your accumulation of form associations that require you to identify yourself in a relationship of exchange.

You are in a relationship of exchange in your own mind. The entirety of this teaching, those of you who are in illumination now – and many of you are – the requirement of this teaching is, very simply, that you understand that in the process of exchange, you are retaining a portion of your own creative energy and that the Universal Source of Reality only gives. That is, there would be no requirement for exchange if there is only one association. This is the teachings of Jesus of Nazareth.

This will be the teaching of *your* mind as it proceeds to the wholeness of its realization of its Universal Mind. That's what's happening here. We're starting with a premise that there's a God, and that He creates eternally, and that you are in a conceptual association of yourself in that exchange. So my offering to you is that in the action, or process, of your mind – whether it's giving or getting – you are re-enacting an association of creative purpose. You cannot *not* be, simply because your procedure of self-identity cannot *not* be what it represents in its entirety in the exchange. Do you see that? There's no possibility that it can be anything but that.

The problem is not that. The problem is, in all of your observations of yourself, you believe in the utilization of mind separate from its Source. This is called the *Course in Miracles*. Do you understand me? So that by utilizing the process of exchange, you can mature in the apparent growth of you, based on your abundance of space/time identity, that is, what you have contained within the association.

Here's the fundamental lesson of this, if you would like to hear it. Since there is only one creating true Source of Reality, He can only have one continuing eternal extension, which is *you*. This is called the philosophy. If this is true, you can literally only give to yourself. Once more. If this is true – presuming that this is true, presuming that God only gives – *you can only give to yourself*. And that sounds very simple to say, but it's quite another thing when all around you is an exchange going on or a process of the retention of yourself.

Without digressing into things like "Everything here is a projection of your own mind" (which it is), and all the other things that go with this teaching, I'll advance you very rapidly because your mind is ready to hear it, to the certainty that you can come to know that – through the *action* of your mind – not in the observation of the exchange. Once more. You can come to know that through the *act* of giving rather than the recognition of *what* you have given. Class? Do you see that? This is forgiveness. Of course! That's what it is. Through the *act* of giving, you can come to know that you are as God created you, very simply because God is the act of giving. Is that so? So the joy that you're experiencing is actually in the act of giving – of giving yourself.

The entire nature of the teachings of a whole mind – and I'll demonstrate with myself – would be an expression of... (should I take a chance on this?) *"double or nothing!"* Can you get that? Double or Nothing! Quite literally, if you're only giving to yourself, every time you give to yourself, you've got twice as much as you had before. Could you get that?

You don't mind that, but the idea that it's an entire double is what disturbs you. I'm sure a lot of you will take the chance on double or nothing, but the idea that you give yourself for a moment in its entirety – and it doubles – is very difficult for you. Why? Until you give yourself at that moment, it can't double. It has nothing to do with your idea of what you're giving, but in the act it square-roots – doubles. Just as the doubling of the energy of the association of the form accumulates to light energy as you double it. Is that so?

So all I really teach you as a philosophy is "double or nothing." What's the psychology? Class? Who can do this with me? What's the psychology? This is from a movie. "Let It Ride!" Got it? That's the whole philosophy of Jesus Christ. *Double Or Nothing; Let It Ride!* It's the same idea as "What the hell have I got to lose?" I have nothing to lose. I don't know if it's going to work, but certainly I enjoy the act of the bet. Certainly there was a great deal of joy in the freedom I felt. This isn't a Gamblers Anonymous meeting. Ha ha! No. You understand I'm speaking of the mind here, not the physical act. There's a certain thrill of going to the races, you know. I'm very much aware of that.

It's taking a chance on love. Do you see that? It would be impossible for you to be with me in this church, offering you the lesson unless somewhere you had rather an adventurous spirit. Can you hear that? I'm asking you to give everything away. You have no idea what you're giving to; you have no idea where you're going. You're liable to hear this yet. Wherever two or more are gathered is where you hear it, not in the definition of it.

Yes, it's an adventure. But see, you don't have to define it. You can't define totality, anyway. The secret is that each time you take one step, it's total. All of this is going on all the time, anyway. You say, "Well, it represents the total." Fibber. It *is* the total. If the Christ is risen, if He actually has demonstrated the re-formation of His body, He is always present with you in that exchange, representing the explosion, or what you call ultimate devil, which is nothing but coming from the black hole up into reality, that's going on with you all the time. The whole New Testament says this. And it shows you the ways in which that can be accomplished in your mind.

It starts with some very fundamental premises, getting to the Bible lessons now. It starts with some very fundamental premises that the power by which this can be and was accomplished is where? In *your* mind! There's no question that the entire teachings of Jesus of Nazareth are that all power is given unto you in Heaven and earth, and the power to perform this act of creative energy is contained in *you*.

Our lesson for today will direct your attention to two things: One, all power is given unto you in Heaven and earth. Secondly, your creative energies of association of your mind cannot be more or less than what you are. Do you see that? As you identify yourself, you will identify your brother. The interlude in between is called the Holy Spirit or the Christ, which was a requirement through the resurrected Jesus Christ, that you recognize the totality of you in His organizational association of His resurrected body. Who heard that?

I'll give you an example. Stand up. Here. If I'm standing here in a body and I'm practicing giving to you (and I'm not exactly good at it, so I'm oscillating in my determination to re-associate the energy of the factoring of the reflection of my own mind – all human beings do this – you're doing the same), standing between us is the entire conversion of the act of giving. The whole lesson of the New Testament is Jesus saying, "Lo, I'm here with you till the end of the world because I am your resurrected factor." Did you get that? I am That, standing here. He's standing right here now. I don't know whether you can see Him with your body eyes, but why would you have to? Certainly, you've evolved a capacity of looking through the reflections that used to hinder you, and recognize that your brother must be the Christ, if there is one. If there is a Christ, your brother must be Him because there is only one Son of God. We have an agreement somewhere that God only has one extending eternal energy, and that's what *you* are.

Obviously, if you divide it up and exchange it, you will reap what you sow. Notice there's no denial that you're going to get back what you give away. The question is not that. The question is, why do you hold onto anything if your true creative source comes from God? Yes or no? Christians?

I bet I could give this talk in a church. So far I could give this talk to anyone. I mean, anybody that's open. I'm not sure the minister would approve of my gambling mode. You've got to gamble on salvation, or you can't get it. There's no possibility you can get it because your definitions of it are what are keeping you from it. Gambling on salvation is the same as faith, having faith in God, betting everything that you have.

So the power of my mind, the power to do that, will be indicated (we're into a Bible reference) in Matthew and John and the Text of *A Course in*

Miracles and the Workbook and anything else – the Smucker's peanut butter jar. As your mind begins to open up to this process of "I don't know what anything is," you're always being told new associations within your own mind. The whole basis of this teaching is to vacate your exchange procedures. The verification for this occurs, and you've heard this before, but it has a particular context this morning, Matthew 18:18: *Verily, truly I say unto you, whatsoever ye shall bind on earth shall be bound in Heaven: and whatsoever ye shall loose on earth shall be loosed in Heaven.* That is actually the only thing that you have to know. Why the hell else would you have to know anything except your incredible denial that your own mind could actually bind Heaven? But since there is only you, since you represent Heaven, since yours is the Kingdom of Heaven, obviously, if you bind yourself through your refusal to give (to bind means to possess; to be possessed by yourself) you will literally possess Heaven. Possessing Heaven is the same as space/time. Do you see that? Possessing Heaven is the same idea as the fall. If you bind it in your mind, if you retain it, you will base your reality on the retention rather than on the giving. You cannot *not* because you can only give to yourself. If you limit yourself, you will prevent the double or nothing that occurs.

"I'll double what I give away." That may or may not be true. But there's very little usury involved. Whoops! I got into the talents. There's very little usury involved. You're going to have to get some interest, or you wouldn't exchange at all. So your getting some interest must be denying your brother the access to the profit that you received in the exchange. Tell me you heard that. This is how I got to be the manager of a very large company. This is the whole basis of exchange. You must render together in association that benefits both of the concerns.

That's not the problem. The problem is, you're sharing in the limitation rather than in the entirety. Do you see that? So the solution to that problem in its entirety is always standing next to you. It cannot *not* because you're searching for the solution. The search for the solution of organization of your mind in exchange is what salvation is. Because if you search for the wholeness of you contained within yourself in an attempt to justify yourself, it must be based on the Christ, or the totality of you that is inherent in you. It cannot *not* be. Does it say that here?

And whatsoever ye shall loose on earth shall be loosed in Heaven. Again I say unto you that if two of you shall agree on earth as touching anything that they shall ask, it shall be done for them of my

49

Father, which is in Heaven. (Matthew 18:18-19) That's one of the most extraordinary statements. Nobody understands that. If our minds touch for just one second in the giving, we have performed the action of love in entirety. That's what that says. For goodness sakes!

Hold it. Hold it now. Was that too much energy? Did you see that? What is that called? A Holy Instant! I had an instant of communication that the Father immediately came into. You see it was in the action, not in the reciprocity. Love is only giving. It isn't in the recognizing that you have love. It was in the admission of the totality of you using God's mind in order to unconditionally love your neighbor, who is *you.*

Most of you that are coming into Light simply recognize that the universe is what you are. God is your entirety of creation, and you'll be damned if you're going to admit to the continuing exchanges of the gift that Jesus Christ resurrected has offered you in the entirety of His Self. Whose Self is His Self? Your Self! There is only one Self. If you can only give to your Self, why do you prevent yourself from having everything by not giving everything away?

I want to be sure that we've got this clear. The very fundamental lesson involved in this is: *All power is given unto you in Heaven and earth.* This book is going to reflect the idea that whatever happens in the universe, *you* are the cause of it and it's happening within your own mind. That has to be the truth of it.

Now, that does not mean you will not see the evil and sickness and the pain. But it does mean that you admit you're getting back what you give away. Sermon on the Mount. You can't get away from that idea. And I know you like to con around with it because you believe you can gain by exchange, but you can't. How could you if you are only giving to yourself? That's the forgotten quotient that always occurs in the thoughts of demonstration of it.

For where two or three are gathered together in my name, there am I in the midst of them. (Matthew 18:20) It's very interesting that He uses His name. And the interesting part about that is, your heritage – which is God – is the name of God just as it's the name of your brother. We gather together in the totality of our apparent separate names with the knowledge that the heritage of God has named us.

Once more. We don't try to be someone else. What's the sense in being someone else if he's only going to be a projection of your own mind, determined to justify the limitation of what you are? Quite literally. Everybody say their name. That's the Christ. That's what this says.

Now, the acknowledgment of Jesus will have a great deal of value to you if you'll let it, since He is representing your name in the entirety of your Christhood. I know you think, "Well, I'd rather have a different name." But having a different name is not going to change what you are if you will remember that God's name is what your inheritance is.

Inheritance is the fundamental idea that in time you accumulate salvation. And there isn't anything wrong with that idea if you remember that your inheritance is that God is always giving you all that you are. If God is always giving you all that you are, your inheritance must be the entirety of Universal Mind. So we have that. What you bind on earth you will bind in Heaven. I am with you, offering you Heaven because I have *unbound* myself on earth. This is called the resurrection. Is it going on all the time? Is it going on at this moment? Yes. Is Jesus saying to you right now, "I am resurrected?" He says, "Don't bind anything. I have unbound you in our minds together. I have unbound you of my previous definition of you. I have unbound you. I have freed you from the devil. I freed you from the name that the earth had given you. I freed you from the advocacy of the devil – of death. I have freed you to see that you are perfect and whole as God created you."

Don't get me excited here! It's pretty hard for me to teach this without demonstrating it. Do you know why? I'm teaching you have to demonstrate it to know that you are it. Do you see? Let it ride! Double or nothing – let it ride!

Do you understand how you're so happy here? How could you possibly prove that to the world? They haven't been willing to relinquish themselves. The only thing they could properly relinquish is the Christ. They can't relinquish fear. They already are fear. But they can't know that it's the Christ until they relinquish it. If they keep it, it's going to be fear. If they give it away, it's going to be Love. Isn't it?

I want to be sure you've got the talents story right. (Matthew 25:14-30) The Talents is one of the great parables of all time. To one guy the master gives five talents, and the other guy he gives two, and the other guy he gives one. So the guy with five goes out and doubles his money. He's got ten. He says, "You're going to be with me in Heaven." This is real simple. This is part of this teaching. It's just the next page. The guy that's got two, he says, "Oh, I got two." What does he do? He doubles his money. The guy that's only got one is fearful of sharing it, so he buries the talent in his backyard. And he says to God, "I know that you reap what you don't sow. Therefore I saved this for you so I could give it to you." He casts him into hell.

Obviously, Jesus, or your mind, reaps what it doesn't sow. Is that true? If you're doubling it all the time, you're always reaping what you don't sow. Can you get that? Do you hear that? Somewhere they say that to Jesus. "How are you able to do that?" Jesus says, "I give everything away. My reaping and my sowing are simultaneous." Actually, they are. If you give everything away, your reaping and sowing, your harvesting, would be the same time as your seeding. That's called the birth and maturity of the Christ. It could not *not* be so. Do you see that?

Wow! So what you bind on earth will be bound in Heaven. I better not do the sheep and the goats. (Matthew 25:31-46) Does anybody understand the sheep and the goats? The goat is the male, and the sheep is the female. And the sheep are willing, and the goats, of course, are stubborn and resist. You have your right hand and your left hand and... Oh, never mind.

That comes right after the talents. *When the Son of man shall come in his glory, and all the holy angels with him, then shall he sit upon the throne of glory.* And then the sheep and goats. *Then shall the King say unto them on his right hand, Come, ye blessed of my Father, inherit the kingdom prepared for you from the foundation of the world.* (Matthew 25:31, 34)

I'm going to make you listen to this because there's a lot of emphatic-ness in what Jesus says here now. He wants you to hear the entirety of the necessity of your service to your brother. I know that you believe you benefit from service. And you do. You benefit from service to the extent that you think you can alleviate your brother's pain through sharing his pain. And to that extent, you share the retention of some of you with the totality that you're willing to exchange. That way, you can measure the degree of your giving.

Yet, if the Kingdom of God is only in the giving, if you have retained anything, you have literally not given to the king, who is you. That is, all Heaven and earth depends on you as a creator. There is a Kingdom that you must rule. The only way you can possibly know that is by giving yourself away. Whatever you give to will be the establishment of the Kingdom in the act of giving. In the *act* of giving must be the entirety of Universal Mind.

This is somewhere in the ministry of Jesus. And here's what He's faced with: *Come, ye blessed of my Father, inherit the kingdom prepared for you from the foundation of the world.* Uh-oh. This is God speaking. This is the entirety. This is the entirety of the expression. You might as well hear this. I know this is reduced a lot, but it shouldn't be. *For I was an hungered, and you gave me meat. I was an hungered* is "I have a need that you fulfilled in the mind."

Here we go. These are the six necessities for the totality of you. These are the things that you will perform within your act of entirety to your brother. I'll do them without reading them to you if you want me to. Hunger and thirst, clothe and house... Got it? External and internal. Clothe and house; hunger and thirst. I better read it to you because it's real nice stuff. He's so determined that you see it that He does it in its opposite regard to show you that any retention of anything in this lack of finally performing this act will bind you at that moment to the restrictions contained within your own body form. And that's the truth of the matter. Here they are. *I hungered and you gave me meat: I was thirsty, and you gave me drink: I was a stranger, and you took me in.* That's coming into my house. *I was naked, and you clothed me.* Are you ready for the last two? *I was sick, and you visited me: I was in prison, and you came unto me.* (Matthew 25:35-36)

That's it! I healed you and I forgave you. You see, the final two are the actions that are performed in your own mind. Who did you give that to? The King! God! You! You gave it to yourself. You forgave yourself. You healed yourself. You fed yourself. You clothed yourself. You sheltered yourself. Who do you think you're doing this to? But you can't know that until you give to those that you have denied in your own mind because in the denial of them is the denial of yourself.

Well, that's what that says. It goes to great lengths to say that. *Then shall the righteous answer him, saying, Lord* (and these are the righteous guys), *when saw we thee an hungered, and fed thee? or thirsty, and gave thee drink? When saw we thee the stranger, and took thee in? or naked, and clothed thee? Or when saw we thee sick, or in prison, and came unto thee? And the King shall answer and say unto them, Verily I say unto you, inasmuch as you have done it unto one of the least of these my brothers, you have done it unto me.* (Matthew 25:37-40)

I know that's what all the Christians say, and that's nonsense. By *least* they mean "doing for no reason." Could you hear that? "You do it to the least of *me*." It doesn't concern you. You just see his plight. You don't care who he is. What the hell do you care who he is? *But what you do to the least of me*, that is, for no reason except the compassion you feel in the necessity to give and serve, you can't know the Kingdom of God. That's literally true. Is that so? Wow!

Then shall he say also unto them on the left hand, and he is going to curse and condemn them to *everlasting fire, prepared for the devil and his angels.* (Matthew 25:41) Is this everlasting fire? Where are you right now? You're in the everlasting fire, you dummies! Where do you think you are if you're not in hell? It isn't that there is one. Look at this place! Come on! Is it everlasting? Of course. It lasts as long as there's time. Of course it's everlasting. Eternity has nothing to do with lasting at all.

So he goes through the repetition of saying *I was hungered and you gave me no meat. I was thirsty and you gave me no drink. I was a stranger and you took me not in. I was naked and you clothed me not. I was sick and you let me rot in prison.* And all the other things. *Then shall they also answer him, saying, Lord, when saw we thee an hungered, or athirst, or a stranger, or naked, or sick, or in prison, and did not minister unto thee? Then shall he answer them, saying, Verily I say unto you, in as much as you did it not to one of the least of these, you did it not to me.* (Matthew 25:42-45)

What he wants you to see there, very simply, is that every act of a denial is a condemnation of yourself. I'm sorry. *What isn't love is murder.* You are either for Him in this or you are against Him. That's the truth of it. That's why he does that twice in that association.

Okay? So give everything away. Come unto me, ye who are heavy laden, and I will give you the rest of you simply laying down your burden of the necessity of the exchange contained within you. Are you comfortable with that?

See if you can do this with me. I want to show you how a resurrected mind works. Would you like to see how your mind is working now? I want to show you how your mind is working now. What you bind in Heaven will be bound on earth. When you unbind your associations here and ascend to Heaven, it will be because you unbound your brother. But it was impossible that you did not unbind your brother by the admission of the unbinding. I'm going to do that once more for you. You ought to be able to hear this with me now. At the moment of unbinding, we shared the totality of our singular Self. I literally depend on you for my salvation. Can you hear this? I don't know if you can hear this or not. There is only one Self.

Listen. I have no concern about what you think you are in your associations. Obviously, you cannot be anything but a projection of my mind. You say to me, "Well, why do I have to participate in the act of your undoing?" And I'm saying, you don't, but I include you in because you are a part of my mind. If you are a part of my mind, you cannot *not* be included in. If I remain in any association following the resurrection, I will feel the obligation of service to you.

Once more. I'm talking for myself. I'm an illuminate. I'm telling you, I feel the obligation that I owe you this. Can you get this? I have freed myself. You are freed with me because of *you*. If you are freed because of your Self, I am freed because of you. How else am I going to get free if you have bound me in your mind? Not only is that true, but after I am unbound, I will appear with you and say virtually the same thing that I said: What you bind in Heaven you will bind on earth, except I'm going to change it just a little bit. Are you ready? I'm resurrected. I am no longer bound.

And the same day at evening, being the first day of the week, when the doors were shut... Uh-oh. Here the disciples were assembled for fear that they were all after them. And suddenly, boom! Peace be with you. Do you hear that? It's the same as saying, "Don't be afraid." *Peace be unto you.* All of a sudden, He's here. (John 20:19) And they look at Him and say, "Holy mackerel! I thought you were dead." He says, "No, I'm resurrected. I'm here to tell you that you can't die. You have nothing to worry about. I'm going to show you how you can bring this about now." And it's subtly different than "what you bind in Heaven" because it's the direct admonition from the awakened mind. In that sense it's not instructional except in the veracity of the new mind He has become with the certainty that you must carry His message in order to know who He is. There's no other manner that that can be accomplished.

Here's what he says. *Peace be unto you. And when he had so said, he shewed unto them his hands and his side. Then were the disciples glad, when they saw the Lord.* Did He show them His wounds or did He show them that He was healed? Since they saw Him get pierced with a spear.

"Anyway, what do you want me to do to prove that I'm resurrected? Bleed some more for you?" *Peace be unto you: as my Father hath sent me, even so send I you.* If you can recognize the resurrection of Jesus – use me, my resurrection – it is impossible that you will not resurrect because I am resurrected. It is also impossible that you will not participate through the example I have set in the experience that you can have by the Light I am offering you in your resurrecting mind.

That is, you become willing to participate in it simply because you have viewed the resurrection within your own mind.

But look out. *And when he had said this, he breathed on them, and said unto them, Receive ye the Holy Ghost.* (John 20:20-22) This is the practice that we now undertake. This is *A Course in Miracles.* As we resurrect, we breathe, we offer the light of our breath, of the Spirit, to our associations that they may share in the resurrection. That's what's happening right here and now. You are becoming fine demonstrations, literally, of your own resurrecting body.

"Oh, that's very occult and mysterious." Nonsense! Only because you would like to get a reflection of your own mind that keeps you from seeing that He is resurrected and you are resurrecting with Him. Or that I'm resurrecting. Or that your brother is resurrecting.

So the process of unbinding is changed just subtly and it says, *Whose soever sins ye remit, they are remitted unto them; and whose soever sins ye retain, they are retained.* (John 20:23) That's a literal example of everything we're teaching. Everybody got that? It's subtly different because it's the *remission* of the sin.

I'll see if I can teach you this. I have a debt to you because of my resurrection. I am remitting – I'm giving – to you what I owe you. I'm remitting to you what I owe you for the love that you gave me. Will you accept it? I need your acceptance. You've got my marker! You are the one that gave me enough dough to bet in the first place. Did you hear that? "Lend me ten bucks. I'm going to the race." Is that true? Did you get it? Literally, I owe you. You were the one that got me started.

What you are going to discover as you progress in this, you're going to start getting phone calls from people who actually helped you along the way, even though they didn't get it themselves. Look at this. Here's a good example. Actually, he's further along than she is. That's not true because I say it's true. It's true because it's true. Because he holds it in his closet doesn't mean he doesn't know. You can have a fully matured Christ in your own closet. Can you see that? He's bursting out finally because he's going to stand next to a resurrected body. That becomes irresistible to him. He can't resist the Light of God resurrecting.

Any limitations you impose on him are simply ones you have imposed on yourself. Do you get that? In Luke 17 He says that you're going to be working in the field, and one of you will spring into Heaven, and the other is still going to be here. And you, righteous one, will be here and he'll spring into Heaven. And you'll say, "How the hell did he get to go to Heaven?" His going to Heaven had nothing to do with you at all because your definition of him was what kept him from being in Heaven. *He cometh as a thief in the night.*

What did he learn? Expectation. Give through expectation without reward. And the joy that most of you have now is a preparation. When I used to teach this originally, I would get all excited. "I'm going to go and teach!" And I would go to church and nobody would come. It had nothing to do with it. I still had to be what I am in the teaching of it. I could not *not* be. Actually my salvation was in the teaching of it, in the preparation for it. It's embarrassing when you've got the wrong day. You get all dressed and you get there, and there's nobody there. The church is empty, and it's Saturday instead of Sunday. That's called the original mistake. Can you hear this? It's a slight deviation in time. It's the difference between Saturday and Sunday. Can you hear that? It's the difference between resurrection being on the first day rather than the last day. Can you get it? Is that true? Did I get it?

Whosoever sins ye remit, they are remitted unto them. And whosoever sins ye retain, they are retained. And then it describes how He holds out his Hand and shows them all those things. He is resurrected. And they are very glad to hear it.

I'm going to bring this down to what you think is earth for a minute. The idea of multiplicity, or the possibility of a direct contact with God is what salvation is. And in a very real, real, real, real way, it doesn't have anything to do with the entity that performs the act. Can you get this? In other words, Jesus Christ is not a definition of Jesus. He is a resurrected association.

Let's go to the *Teacher's Manual* just for a minute. There's a question that arises in the *Manual*. It's a very real question which would be asked by you. And I'm presuming that you understand that Christ is risen and all that. You have an inquiry. You say, "Can God be reached directly?" In other words, you say, "Is it actually possible for me in that Holy Instant to experience God?" Notice I said "experience." Is the answer to that yes?

It is possible? Christians? People in this earth? Is it possible for you to experience God directly?

Will the experience of God be the same for everyone?

Participant: No.

The first thing that comes to your mind is wrong. How the hell would it be different? Come on. This is the whole problem. Your thinking salvation is different for everybody is why you're here – because the manifestation of it immediately becomes different. But it has nothing at all to do with the experience itself. You got it? Oh, yes. That's why *you* are the only living Son of God. You can give vision to your brother, but it comes through your experience.

The idea of multiple saviorship is, first of all, almost impossible to describe because it hasn't occurred in this association. Secondly, it must involve the power of your mind to work magic and be evil. I'm not going to get into that because that's in here. If you want to get into the idea that you're going to take that contact with God and use it for evil purposes, go ahead because that's what you're doing right now. I'm going to stay out of that. This will say there's a great deal of value in that, too. *Are "Psychic" Powers Desirable?* Oh, sure. There's a great deal of value in whatever you think that is, because it's a contact you are making within your own mind. You can't be any more evil than you already are. Don't be finding somebody else guilty of black magic. Nothing is blacker than you are in your determination to deny this message. It's impossible there be. At least there's a worshipping element involved in that of the passion of the determination to establish its reality. Can you hear me? I have absolutely no concern about your so-called judgmental perceptual associations – only the energy of your mind of coming to know that you are whole and creative as God created you.

Can God Be Reached Directly?

Was I able to share with Shirley Christ that experience? Why? I didn't try to figure out who was doing that or what was happening like you are. I simply shared in her resurrection. Do you see that? What you have to remember in multitudinous resurrections is that everybody finally is participating in it, and that it's only a matter of time. You cannot *not* be participating each moment. Somebody goes to Heaven and comes back and is offering you another solution to your problem and/or you are offering him another solution. Do you see this? This is called "The Great Reversal." Everyone you meet, you're either justifying each other – he's trying to instruct you on something – or you're trying to instruct him. Always between you is the certainty of the entirety of you, if you will stand still for a moment and let it be. That's actually what's happened in this place, isn't it?

God indeed can be reached directly, for there is no distance between Him and His Son. He's everywhere. *His awareness is in everyone's memory, and His Word is written on everyone's heart.* Got that? His word is Love on your heart; His awareness is your recognition in your mind. That's called your mind and your heart. *Yet this awareness and this memory can arise across the threshold of recognition only when all barriers to truth have been removed. In how many is this the case? Here, then, is the role of God's teachers. They, too, have not attained the necessary understanding as yet, but they have joined with others. This is what sets them apart from the world.* Until that, no progress is possible. Until you can share in the admission that you want to have this accomplished between you, you couldn't possibly succeed in it because you'll begin to work the *Course* which says I can't succeed by identifying you. In our freedom of the release of our identification from each other is where the Christ is, not in the exchange that brings about a body.

The reason that's important is this. *This is what sets them apart from the world. And it is this that enables others to leave the world with them. Alone they are nothing. But in their joining is the Power of God.* In the *act* of joining you leave the world. It's impossible for you to meet anyone in time and not resurrect him or him resurrect you. I don't know what the hell you think is going on here, but I'll tell you, it's nothing. But once the resurrection has occurred, you have a model that is always present with you if neither one of you will judge the other guy. That's just true. I'm not talking about it Socratically. I'm telling you, that's how your mind operates in the new Light that it's coming into. That's a nice thing to know.

But in their joining is the power of God. It goes to plurality here. This is real difficult. I'll read it. What it says is, there are those who have reached God directly and have gone. They are all around you – unless they just left altogether, or they stopped back to see how the hell you're doing. Obviously, you are an aggregation that came into the world together and left together. You cannot *not* be. We came here together; we're leaving here together. We are that aggregation, the twelve tribes of Israel. We are performing that act.

There are those who have reached God directly, retaining no trace of worldly limits and remembering their own Identity perfectly. Is that possible? I'm giving you a pretty good description of what has happened to *you*. Do you want to share this with me? I'm giving you a good description of you sitting in this pew. You have begun to recognize who you are! Nothing can stop you from recognizing who you are. At that moment you are literally in Heaven because you never left. Class? You are literally in Heaven!

Now, if you remain in an operational procedure, you will come from Heaven each moment, and offer the conversion to the association. If he accepts it, he will literally join you in Heaven. He cannot *not*! Obviously, I'm taking a batch up here. But there's nothing I can do if you insist on identifying your brother as other than the savior. The only way you can know he's the savior is by not identifying him at all. If you identify him at all, you will identify him falsely. For goodness sake!

Listen: *There are those who have reached God directly, retaining no trace of worldly limits and remembering their own Identity perfectly. These might be called the Teachers of teachers because, although they are no longer visible, their image can yet be called upon.* Quite literally! You can call on anybody and you will get exactly the help you need at the specific time. Could you hear that? I promise you that because *that whole veil is open.* There's a specialist in your problem. You like to call them angels. I don't care what you call them. They are available for you from someone who is transformed – and I'm saying "someone" in its broadest sense. What difference does it make who it is if he's the solution to your problem? Your need to know who he is, is preventing him from being the solution.

Can you hear this? I'm going to try this with you. Your identification of the savior is what continues to crucify him. Any anonymous association that springs into Heaven is gone. You think that they write about him in the history books? Do you really think that they wrote about me when I resurrected and came back here? No. They may begin to write about us now. Can you hear this? But when the operation was done on me, it was done by anonymous associations who literally operated on my head. They said, "Can we do that? Can we do it?" Obviously, these are associations that are perfectly aware of the entirety that surrounds this world. That's a fact of the matter. Have you got that? Do they have names? Nah. In fact, one of them seemed to be more an apprentice than a technician. That's why I have a little problem in actually visualizing a lot of Light. I convert thought factors. That's called the "Whoops!" factor. Right in the middle of it, one of them went, "Whoops!"

Do you believe when something divine is happening to you that it's divine? Not necessarily. It's only divine as it is in that association. "Whoops!"

All they told me to do is "Let It Ride". They opened up a channel for me. It came about because of my service, not my doctrine. I had had an inclination or a realization of surrender, and I was out doing high service, and I reached a certain point in my service in response. That's what this says. It didn't have anything to do with the doctrine at all. I discovered that my salvation came from giving it away – or my sobriety or whatever the hell you call it. And the more I did that, the happier I got in a function that gave me some sort of gratification, called love and forgiveness. You have a mind that teaches only action because Jesus Christ teaches only action. He doesn't teach anything but the action of service, forgiving, or giving to your brother, or loving. Does He? No! So that's what's occurring in this action.

And they will appear when and where it is helpful for them to do so. I love the "when" and "where." When *and* where. Because if they occur visually, it would be both when and where. That's an amazing idea. The only problem you have with that is you may believe that they're phantom figures. And they're not! They can be the guy walking down the street with you. He suddenly hands you a note. The telephone rings. Come on! He is there to solve your problem at that moment. It has nothing at all to do with what you think he is. Do you see that? Is he available to you? Yes, because you really asked for the answer instead of deciding what the answer is. Literally, at that moment you said, "Shit, I don't know what to do." Boom! Come on. That's the whole practice. This is the whole *Workbook*. Never know what to do.

And it may come from strange places. Why wouldn't it? You have alienated yourself and called it strange when actually it's perfectly normal in your own mind. The weirdos out there are nothing but *you*. They are nothing but you.

Listen to this. *To those to whom such appearances would be frightening, they give their ideas.* This is really wide open. Why don't you take a look at this. The other guy gets to sort it out because he's afraid of the direct approach. Listen to me. If you're not afraid of my direct approach, you will resurrect instantly because I'm offering you the entirety of the solution. If you're not, if you're afraid of me, I'll pretend to instruct you. I'm going to give you an idea. I'm going to give you an idea about this and I would like to have you examine it. I know perfectly well, your examination of it is nonsense. Why would you examine it? You could only be examining it in your own mind, anyway. But you're scared to death of this message of love that I'm giving you, and you want to have a respite from it so you can examine yourself and decide whether you would rather die than hear it. And heretofore you've always decided to die rather than hear it.

There's a natural progression from what I am offering you to the certainty of the instantaneousness of salvation and how you delay it in time in order to re-image associations of your own mind. In one of the most dramatic passages that will occur in the *Course* is the use of multiplicity to describe singularity. It's the section called *For They Have Come*. Quite literally, any aggregation of perfection can represent itself in the entirety of the aggregation to any aggregation that gathers, using the sufficiency of the entirety to define it.

Five talents, two talents, one talent – don't bury it. Because the moment that the one talent would have been given away, the guy would probably get to Heaven quicker because he only had one thing. Can you hear that? Nothing doubles faster than the square root of one. Why? It has to go back and repeat the one if it doubles at five. Did you hear that? That means you didn't lay it all from the first race. In "Let It Ride!" he lays it from the very first race. Everybody got that? If you haven't seen the movie, there's a great moral principle involved in it: Give it away to have it. By the end of the race, everybody wants him to win. Before then, he's a flake and nobody wants him to win. They see his willingness, his alacrity and determination to let it ride based completely on guessing. He doesn't handicap it at all. He gets advice from everybody.

Finally, his final salvation – where does the advice come from? The horse! See the movie, please. Can you hear that? The fix is even in with the horse! In the end he doesn't know who to bet on and says, "I'm having a very good day." He's having a very good day. He's sitting out by the stable. It's the last race. He looks around and the horse winks at him. Notice he had to get prepared for the idea that the horse would wink at him. Through his giving he saw that the fix was in. And he actually looks at the horse after he goes like that, and he goes, "Ha, ha, ha!" And he goes down and he sings to the horse.

So when I say to you, "The fix is in. Bet everything you've got," *I mean it*. It may take a minute for that to accumulate because there's probably seven or eight races, including fillies and mares and three furlongs and all sorts of good stuff at the track. I used to think the horn before races was Gabriel's horn. I thoroughly enjoyed going to the races, and going back down in the barn and looking at the horses myself.

To those to whom such appearances would be frightening, they give their ideas... Who is this? All humans. The entire aggregation of your own thoughts is always available to you. Isn't that nice? That's what you're doing right now.

Nor is there anyone of whom they are unaware. It's impossible. Notice it says, "they." There's no one that *they* are not aware of because *they* are your aggregation in the borderland or out into Heaven. You may meet them in the borderland, but they will always be coming from out of time to help you. Who are they? They! They! All of your projections converted. All of the things that you put out there, converted *en masse.* Got it? All right. Good for you.

Listen: *Nor is there anyone of whom they are unaware. All needs are known to them, and all mistakes are recognized and overlooked by them.* What that really says is (and it's time for you to hear it), I'm not concerned about the manner in which you come to know this. I overlook it entirely because there is no world. This is the offering that I always gave to you. I did not preclude your finding God in the struggle of your own mind. I didn't preclude that from you. I just told you you're struggling with yourself and that any single admission of that would get you out of here.

There are very sacred saints who have worked their little butts off for forty years to find the Christ – and have succeeded in it. But it's almost inevitable that they will measure seeing the Christ by their procedure. Have you got that? Who didn't hear that? It will seem as though it's a form of sacrifice. It isn't that they didn't catch glimpses of it. They could have whipped themselves, gone and served the orphans; they could have literally done anything to catch that glimpse. You call them saints. You worship them. You raise statues to them. Mother Theresa had glimpses of God. But inevitably she continued to serve in her own mind the evilness of the world. That's true because it's true. Now, you can identify with her if you choose. Or you can identify with the resurrected Jesus, who is not in body except in the body of your reassociation with yourself. Thank God!

Does it say that here? Oh, yes. It does. *The time will come when this is understood.* Has the time come that you understand that? If all of this is nothing but your mind, everyone can offer you the totality of where you are in space/time. If they don't offer it to you, don't worry about it. It simply means that you have asked for something that you've progressed past. Always simply let it go and don't struggle within your own determination to justify the method by which you are coming to know God because it doesn't make any sense. The entire establishment of this world is an attempt to establish within the form a way that you can come to God.

The time will come when this is understood. And meanwhile... in the meantime, "in between time, ain't we got fun! Anyway, dear, we'll stay as we are." All around you are these high scriptural notations. And all around you are demonstrations of those who did and remain poor. But they are only demonstrations of your poorness, because in the giving they sprang into Heaven. That's what I just read you a minute ago. You can't know that because you want to be poor, or you were the cause of their poorness.

And meanwhile, they give all their gifts to the teachers of God who look to them for help, asking all things in their Name and in no other. It doesn't make any difference who you ask. Ask for everything always all the time and you can't fail. Don't play the odds. Let it ride!

"Can I play in a game where there's no possibility of losing?"

Not for very long. Why? The croupier will be fixed. Can you hear this? If you can't lose, if you're going to win on every number, they either won't let you play or the game will be over. They need the handicap of possibility. In *Rainman*, they won't even let the computer (Dustin Hoffman) play – "take your money and go away; you're not a human being." He's counting seven decks. It's virtually impossible. He knew every card that was being played out of seven decks – that had been played or could be played – and they wouldn't let him play anymore. That's why I don't stay here. I have the fun of not being able to lose because I share it with your discovery of not losing. I know you can't lose. I keep telling you you can't lose. If you think you can, you must venture what you have to know that you can't. Until you venture it, you can't know that you can't lose. Yes or no? You can't lose love, you dummy. If you give love away, you'll have it. I'm liable to release a little love here. Easy now. Hold it a minute. I have to bring this around for you, because it will come around as *A Course In Miracles*.

Sometimes a teacher of God may have a brief experience of direct union with God. This is exactly what you're working on. *In this world, it is almost impossible that this endure.* Because if it endures you wouldn't be in this world. Do you see that? So you end up just getting old. It's not that. *It can, perhaps, be won after much devotion and dedication, and then be maintained for much of the time on earth. But this is so rare that it cannot be considered a realistic goal. If it happens, so be it. If it doesn't happen, so be it as well.* Stop trying to measure Sister Teresa. I don't care what Sister Teresa did for you. I'm concerned about you in your own mind. You make a saint in order to deny the resurrection of Jesus. If He's resurrected, why do you need sainthood? *All worldly states must be illusory. If God were reached directly in sustained awareness, the body would not be long maintained.* Guys, I don't know if you want to hear this. That's exactly what's happening to you. You are in a sustained awareness of God, verified by the forms of your previously rejected association.

Listen to this. Here's why He loves you guys so much: *Those who have laid the body down merely to extend their helpfulness to those remaining behind are few indeed.* Can you hear this? Somebody who lays his body down and springs out of here is gone forever. There isn't any such place as this. There are very few associations that we have been able to recruit who are able to come back into this association at all, once they lay their body down. They need your help as a body (I don't know if I can teach that) in order to convert. I used to try to teach this. To that extent, you assume a role and I help you. At the point you assume the role, you really don't know the answer. But you do know that the answer is there. That's what the conversion from body to resurrection is. This is a little apologetic because it says you have to be in this in order to come to know it. That's why I say to you that you've got a pretty good part; but once you hear it, you can get out using that part. Don't try to change it because the aggregation of the entirety of a solution is already evident.

Don't try to change who you are. Whatever you do, don't try to emulate something else outside of you. I want you to be you. I don't want you to look at her and figure out how she's doing. It can only be you I want because you are the savior of the world. There is nothing but *you.* He doesn't think he's ever going to get it. That's all right; let him stay here. Whatever help he can give me I appreciate. I finally may look at him, and like the Holy Spirit, shrug my shoulders. He says, "I don't know why you would want to stay here and justify the pain and death of this place." But there's no one in the Universe that can stop you from doing it because there isn't anyone else but you.

They need helpers who are still in bondage and still asleep, so that by their awakening can God's Voice be heard. I really love this! *Do not despair, then, because of limitations.* You are an imperfect perfectionist. Don't despair. My whole teaching is, "Don't worry about it!" You define it and you are hell-bent on finding it in your own association.

It's always only the continuing act and nothing is ever completed here because there's nothing here to be completed! Do you understand?

It is your function to escape from them, but not to be without them. If you would be heard by those who suffer, you must speak their language. If you would be a savior, you must understand what needs to be escaped. You have to escape this world. *Salvation is not theoretical.* Salvation is literally the act of you coming from time to eternity. *Behold the problem, ask for the answer, and then accept it when it comes. Nor will its coming be long delayed. All the help you can accept will be provided.* You decided to accept it all, and it's been provided for you. *And not one need you have will not be met. Let us not, then, be too concerned with goals for which you are not ready.* When you are ready for the goal, it would be available to you. If the goal is not ready, it just simply means you don't want it or you're afraid of it. *God takes you where you are and welcomes you. What more could you desire, when this is all you need?*

Is that all right? The question that is now being asked, after *"Is Direct Contact Possible?"* is *"How Many Teachers Of God Are Needed To Save The World?"* One. You act as though this is big news. The fact of the matter, if that's true, is, why are you here at all? Except that you are going to help your brother. Let's go to the fundamental teaching here. This is a community of Singular Mind, or the admission that in the Universe there is only One Self. If that Self is in separation, it will be in separation and aggregate with the separations of its own mind. As it comes to the union of who it really is with itself, it will organize a union of realization of God and aggregate for that single purpose at which time that purpose would and did take place.

How Many Teachers Of God Are Needed To Save The World? Here's the answer: One. *One wholly perfect teacher, whose learning is complete, suffices.* He's not too much and he's not too little. He's just enough. He's a sufficient number. All he can be is sufficient. Sufficiency does not compare too much and too little, because it can finally only be just enough anyway. *This one, sanctified and redeemed, becomes the Self Who is the Son of God.* Boy, that's lovely – sanctified and redeemed. *He who was always wholly spirit now no longer sees himself as a body, or even as in a body. Therefore he is limitless. And being limitless, his thoughts are joined with God's forever and ever. His perception of himself is based upon God's Judgment, not his own. Thus does he share God's Will, and bring His thoughts to still deluded minds. He is forever one, because he is as God created him. He has accepted Christ, and he is saved.*

I have a great deal of trust in you that this is what has happened to you because I promise you and guarantee you that until it happens to you, no salvation or escape from this world will ever be possible. Class? Got that?

Thus does the son of man become the Son of God. It is not really a change; it is a change of mind. Nothing external alters, but everything internal now reflects only the Love of God. God can no longer be feared... I'm in a presumption that you have accepted the Atonement for yourself and are determined, if you are here, to justify the reassociations of your own mind – singularly in your own mind, not outside of you.

This is a description of you: *Everything internal now reflects only the Love of God. God can no longer be feared, for the mind sees no cause for punishment.* Where before you thought you must have had to do something, you see no cause and so you are not afraid of God. Is it really that simple? Is that all right with you? Did that happen to you? The world is not real to you. And you are joining with others who know the world is not real because they are simply of like mind, which is your mind or the Mind of God. Got it? Wow!

God's teachers appear to be many, for that is what the world needs. Because there is so much broken up here. *Yet being joined in one purpose, and one they share with God, how could they be separate from each other? What does it matter if they then appear in many forms? Their minds are one; their joining is complete. And God works through them now as one, for that is what they are.* You mean *they* are one? You mean your mind is joined with the single Mind of the Universe? *I am one Self, complete and healed and whole, shining in the reflection of His Love.* Isn't that nice?

Why is the illusion of many necessary? Only because reality is not understandable to the deluded. The moment you understand it, everyone around you must understand it. You don't think that they do if you remain to help the deluded, but you have the certainty of yourself which was all the requirement was for a savior. I never asked you to be anything but to be certain of who you are. If there is one thing in the Universe you can be certain of, it's who you are. *Only very few can hear God's Voice at all, and even they cannot communicate His message directly through the Spirit Which gave them.* It's too thick. *They need a medium through which communication becomes possible to those who do not realize that they are spirit. A body they can see. A voice they understand and listen to, without the fear that truth would encounter in them.* See, I'm pretty good at that! All I did was threaten you with your ultimate fear – which was nothing but fear of God, which doesn't make any sense to you. *Do not forget that truth can come only where it is welcomed without fear. So do God's teachers need a body, for their unity could not be recognized directly.* How could it be? If it was, they would be gone!

Yet what makes God's teachers is their recognition of the proper purpose of the body. Which is to transfigurate. *As they advance in their profession...* Profession – I love it – they're getting paid for doing this! Each time I take one of you home, I get paid for doing it! I am indebted to you. I told you that before. I am indebted to you, and you are going to have to accept my forgiveness whether you like it or not. I'm going to pay you or I can't get out of here. You say to me, "Well, you don't owe me anything." Oh yes I do. Yes I do. The idea that I don't owe you anything is not true. I am determined that my salvation comes from you, and you can't possibly change my mind. My salvation comes from the conversion each moment of this world. And I have no intention of justifying anything within my own association. That's what my freedom to be the Christ is! What does that depend on? Complete dependence on you is the same as complete dependence on God.

They – your Christ and the memory of God thereof – once more, your *Christhood* (your heritage with God) and the *memory* you share thereof with each other at this moment at the end of time, you are sharing the aggregation of the moment of your separation. And you are Home and free as God created you.

Now, if you need to let the dead bury the dead, it's very important that you get this. I can't be concerned. I see people sitting around here. I don't know what the hell they're doing. I have no idea. They don't need me. They're not even open to the possibility of me. Quite simply, they've solved their problem. Their problem is to be here and get old and sick and die. That's the answer to their problem. I have no concern about them because they are literally dead. Dead. I'm only concerned in activating the dead to Life. This is all that the resurrection is. You believe that there's a partial death and a partial life. That's not so. Do you hear me? Prior to Jesus' appearing behind closed doors, He says, "Don't touch me yet. I'm in resurrection. I'm going to my Father." And that's in there.

As they advance in their profession, they become more and more certain that the body's function is but to let God's Voice speak through it to human ears. And these ears will carry to the mind of the hearer messages that are not of this world, and the mind will understand because of their Source. From this understanding will come the recognition, in this new teacher of God, of what the body's purpose really is; the only one there really is for it. The only use of your body is to remember who you are and get out of here. I don't need you to tell me, "Well, I've got to exist." That's all just pure nonsense. I'm talking about the power of your own mind, individually, to awaken from your own dream of death.

This lesson is enough to let the thought of unity come in, and what is one is recognized as one. By one single thought. Doggone it! What's recognized by one is recognized by one single thought. If you can recognize one single thought with me, you're gone from this world. One single thought. One single teacher. Because there is only one problem. Any one single thought of salvation is all that would ever be required of you. And it's too late for you to turn back because you've had that thought. The gratitude that some of you are feeling is because *now* in you is the thought of God. And once you see that, you look around the world and you say, "I don't want this." That's a fact.

The teachers of God appear to share the illusion of separation, but because of what they use the body for, they do not believe in the illusion despite appearances. That's the most difficult thing I have to show you, simply because you believe in your own appearances. And if you have constructed me as a part of your appearance, you will believe that that is true. I'm offering you the solution contained within yourself, that we share that single Selfness with God. Isn't that nice!

Here's the truth of the matter: *The central lesson was always this; that what you use the body for it will become to you.* This is the whole Sermon on the Mount. Whatever that body is for, it's really not there at all except in aggregation of your determination to use it to justify your own association. It's always over and gone, anyway. You're always resurrecting all the time, anyway. *Use it for sin or for attack, which is the same as sin, and you will see it as sinful. Because it is sinful, it is weak,* and because it is weak, it's going to suffer and die. *Use it to bring the Word of God to those who have it not, and the body becomes holy.* Literally. The merger of your body with an illusionary body is what holiness is. I wouldn't dare read you that. The actual climax of this is in the Text. The merger of the Christ that's standing next to you is the most holy place that there is. It's as holy as Heaven because it is a mutual recognition of the totality of your causation as God created you. What an idea!

See if you can get this: *Because it is holy it cannot be sick, nor can it die. When its usefulness is done it is laid by, and that is all. The mind makes this decision, as it makes all decisions that are responsible for the body's condition.* My condition is one of continuing revelation and reconstruction of my body. It makes absolutely no difference how you see me here, because here is not here. There isn't any such place as this. Many of you are now in that realization. Quit examining it. Remember that it's going on all the time. Your examination of it will only slow you down as you prepare to leave here. Do you see that? You don't have to do that. I can't speak of that, but I can tell you that's the experience that you're having.

Because it is holy, it cannot be sick, nor can it die because it's not really here because it's not anywhere. *Yet the teacher of God does not make this decision alone. To do that would be to give the body another purpose from the one that keeps it holy.* Because he would give himself his own purpose, and he wouldn't be here at all. If he's here at all, he's given himself his own purpose and will be locked in that association. It's a direct comparison of the ego with the Holy Spirit, or the wholeness of you.

God's Voice will tell him when he has fulfilled his role, just as It tells him what his function is. He does not suffer either in going or remaining. Sickness is now impossible to him. Really what we're saying is that you're standing well among the sick. You are not going to be sick in your fight to leave here, and you are not going to be sick in your coming back. You are always going to know that your kingdom is in Heaven. The security that you're feeling in your own mind now is the self-same Self that is in Heaven because anything that's not in Heaven is not real. Now, when you attempt to describe it, you are atoning for the illusion. But if you can remember that it's only going on in your mind, it will begin to be shared by other minds who recognize in themselves their own Christ. Got that? That's the whole teaching. You got it!

It does not suffer either in going or in remaining. Sickness is now impossible to him. Oneness and sickness cannot coexist. God's teachers choose to look on dreams awhile. It is a conscious choice. For they have learned that all choices are made consciously, with full awareness of their consequences. It isn't that I'm not aware of the consequences of coming into hell; it's simply that I convert the consequences because my mind *is* the consequences. And by accepting that responsibility for my own mind, I can convert it. You bind it in here; you bind it in hell. There is no hell without you. There is no Heaven without you. Got it?

If you made a conscious decision, you would not stay in this slaughterhouse. Come on! Are you nuts? Nobody's that nuts. I'm offering you a decision that you must have already made because I made it and it was made at the time of the schism. You have nothing to say about it. You can say, "I have the time to decide it," but that's totally meaningless. The one problem you have is you believe you have time to decide it. I'm in the *Text.* You believe I'm really offering you time in order to choose. I'm not really offering you any time at all. You can only choose one thing, and you did; and you're gone.

It is a conscious choice. For they have learned that all choices are made consciously, with full awareness of their consequences. The dream says otherwise, but who would put his faith in dreams once they are recognized for what they are? Listen, class: *Awareness of dreaming is the real function of God's teachers.* Can you hear me? I might as well tell you. The awareness that this is a dream and not real is your only function. If you are aware that you are hallucinating, you won't hallucinate. Awareness of the hallucination is the separation of your Self from the dream.

Listen: *Awareness of dreaming is the real function of God's teachers. They watch the dream figures come and go, shift and change, suffer and die. Yet they are not deceived by what they see.* How many are in that condition right now? You better raise your hand! You are in that condition whether you like it or not. If I'm in that condition, you cannot *not* be. The only requirement is that you believe me. And if you believe me, you will be in that condition because you are.

I'm doing the same thing over and over. You know perfectly well this is an illusion. That's how you got this far. That's what sorted you out from other human beings. This is a dream.

"Somebody else is dreaming me. I'm trapped in here."

No, you're not. You're the cause of the dream. You can dream right out of here. You're east of Eden. Where does it say you woke up? You are dreaming. You went out east of Eden and you're in a dream. Don't worry about it.

They watch the dream figures come and go, shift and change, suffer and die. Yet they are not deceived by what they see. They recognize that to behold a dream figure as sick and separate is no more real than to regard it as healthy and beautiful. What a step!

So I don't pay any attention to what you tell me at all, and that is your salvation because you're going to be perfect whether you like it or not. And I intend to show you that perfection despite your protestations. But until you guys aggregated, they had nothing to compare themselves with in their own aggregation. You offer that guy sitting right there a good comparison if he wants it. If he doesn't, he'll just stay aggregated with the dead ones. But the dead ones are a product of his mind just as the live ones are. If he sees them as whole and perfect, he will have seen himself that way. If he doesn't, he'll just stay here and die with the rest of them, which are no more real than he is because this is not what Life is.

Unity alone is not a thing of dreams. And it is this God's teachers acknowledge as behind the dream, beyond all seeming and yet surely theirs. The act of unity is what truth and love is here – not the comparison of the separation. It's all around you. Particularly in the evidence of the conversions of your individual minds are guys who have helped other associations and can now help you – or through helping you, they can help other associations because in your non-defense of yourself was offered the entirety of the solution without the specific necessity for it. This is the same as "raising the dead," is the same as healing – atonement. I am an atoner or a raiser of the dead. You can have all the phenomena you want to of being healed, and that's perfectly all right with me. Why? You're being healed all the time. You *are* perfect.

What I'm showing you is the entirety of the solution within your own mind. The acts that you are performing are an aggregation of re-associations in another continuum of time, quite literally in another continuum, where you recognize yourself as a single Self and shine the energy of Love that you manifest in the sharing with God into the chaos that's down below, or the separation of you below. Some of you shine from up there. Some of you come back down into here. But I can guarantee you at the opening that occurs now, everything has been made available to you.

Why is everything available to you now when it wasn't before? You have lost your aggregated fear. You have decided to be totally fearful in yourself, and in being fearful in yourself was the salvation.

The salvation of the world depended on *your* conversion, not the aggregation of fear that locked you in the grid of the dark form where you thought communication was possible. You are actually starting to communicate. When you look at each other and laugh and shine, that's what you're doing. That's what that is. It's just Love.

You have lucked out. Sometimes you guys get lucky. I catch you in a moment where you say, "What the hell!" You took the afternoon off; you went to the races. Suddenly you start to have *a very good day,* where you begin to play your intuition rather than the favorite. Can you hear this? This is literally true. You have opened yourself up to possibility. Since all things are possible, you immediately experience the love and happiness that you are. And you are very, very happy for no reason at all except the recognition of your happiness, which really had nothing to do with why you're happy. That's what salvation is.

The fact of the matter is, you're going to the window to collect. You won! You know you're a fraud. You know you lucked out. You know you had nothing to do with it. Finally you discover that God's on your side, anyway. You won't try to run your own show and decide what odds you have of being successful, because there's no way that you can fail at this. You're the guy behind the window, you're the bettor, you're the jockey, you're the horse. You're just playing your own mind. You can agree with anybody to bring this about and they will not fail you, because the agreement is only with yourself in your determination to want it to be true. If you want it to be true that you're happy in Heaven, it's impossible that it won't be true.

I understand the aggregate of you has entered this continuum. The energy of your Love is being expressed in the aggregation of the entirety of you, coming from that certainty that you are in Heaven together. And in that sense it is an aggregation. But each one of you separated expresses the whole of any association, so that no matter who you meet, if he is a part of your aggregation, he will immediately begin to recognize you. That's what everybody in this room is doing. I'm not concerned about the world.

That does not mean that the invitation is not open to anyone, because no one is really determining where you are in your own time except you. What you may have discovered when you tried to leave here was, you saw a real alternative in what was being offered you. That's a very true thing. But as you've learned now, it really doesn't have anything to do with the world at all. It has to do with all of us being gone and coming back for a moment.

This is the resurrection of Jesus. I am resurrected. It is impossible that you are not resurrected in me, and we are gathered up here to come back and perform this association. This is probably the greatest thing ever written in the English language. Maybe you can hear it with me. It's going to begin on the page that says time and space are one and deals with *the immediacy of salvation*. It's impossible that all of this is not going on right now. Sentences like *Future loss is not your fear. Present joining is your dread. The plans you make for safety are all laid in the future, where you can't plan. Salvation is immediate. Unless you so perceive it, you will be afraid of it, believing the risk of loss is too great... The working out of correction takes no time at all... Be not content with future happiness.* Lay it all on the line now. Put it on the line. Bet everything you have on this moment. The freedom that you will feel in doing that is nothing but a dependence on God. It is nothing but the freedom of your dependence on your Self. And that's what you're experiencing here now.

For you have cause for freedom now. What profits freedom in a prisoner's form? Why should deliverance be disguised as death? Delay is senseless, and the "reasoning" that would maintain effects of present cause must be delayed until a future time, is merely a denial of the fact that consequence and cause must come as one. Because they are. *Look not to time, but to the little space between you still, to be delivered from. And do not let it be disguised as time, and so preserved because its form is changed and what it is cannot be recognized.* Don't look at your brother and tell him you're going to die with him. Look at him and tell him you're going to resurrect with him and you will take your place as a future-past-timer, one who recognizes that this is over and gone.

I'm going to read *For They Have Come*. (Give me a little soft music.) I would really like to have you see this with me. The "They" that it's speaking of here is *you*. It's going to be a dream, but it's a dream where you have saved yourself in your aggregate association. It's as though you now see that you were lost in time, but there's an aggregation, there's a search party that has found you. And it begins to pick up other people who know the answer to this. And finally there's a sufficient aggregation where you come into your own mind to let that be true. That's the "They," and that's the *"You."*

Think but how holy you must be from whom the Voice for God calls lovingly unto your brother, that you may awake in him the Voice that answers to your call! They're the same. How holy are you who call to him and how holy is he in the recognition of your shared holiness. I'm going to read it without comment. You can read it on your own. Ha ha – that will be the day!

Listen. *Think but how holy you must be from whom the Voice for God calls lovingly unto your brother, that you may awake in him the Voice that answers to your call! And think how holy he must be when in him sleeps your own salvation, with his freedom joined!* You are shining on his Christ. He can awaken very rapidly to that because you are representing his Christ to him.

However much you wish he be condemned, God is in him. And never will you know He is in you as well while you attack His chosen home, and battle with His host. Regard him gently. Look with loving eyes on him who carries Christ within him, that you may behold his glory and rejoice that Heaven is not separate from you. Is it too much to ask a little trust for him who carries Christ to you, that you may be forgiven all your sins, and left without a single one you cherish still? I want to give you this, Shirley the Christ. If I looked at Shirley as a human being, I saw her as a human being. If I look at her as the Christ, she immediately matures and becomes my salvation. Then I recognize her as we share that saviorship together. Listen: *Forget not that a shadow held between your brother and yourself obscures the face of Christ and memory of God.*

So that you can hear this, from now on, whenever it says, "Them," it will refer to your face and your memory of God in the other faces. There's nowhere that the "Them," (*They Have Come*) is tracked except there. It is tracked in the image of the entirety of *you* in the reflection of the Light of God as the face of Christ and the memory of God, who is your brother, and the memories that you share with the separate associations – each one of you whole, but only in the totality of you.

Forget not that a shadow held between your brother and yourself obscures the face of Christ and memory of God. And would you trade Them for an ancient hate? The ground whereon you stand is holy ground because of Them Who, standing there with you, have blessed it with Their innocence and peace. This is nothing but the agreement of any two guys, as you have done now, to come and do this for the world. You have no conflict in your own mind about what you are in this association. Wow!

The ground whereon you stand is holy ground because of Them Who, standing there with you, have blessed it with Their innocence and peace. All of the memories of their holy minds now contain the certainty that their source is Heaven and God.

The blood of hatred fades to let the grass grow green again, and let the flowers be all white and sparkling in the summer sun. What was a place of death has now become a living temple in a world of light. Because of Them. It is Their Presence which has lifted holiness again to take its ancient place upon an ancient throne. Because of Them have miracles sprung up as grass and flowers on the barren ground that hate had scorched and rendered desolate. What hate has wrought have They undone. And now you stand on ground so holy Heaven leans to join with it, and make it like itself. The shadow of an ancient hate has gone, and all the blight and withering have passed forever from the land where They have come. Not *when* They have come. From the land *where* you have come to redeem the lost ones. *You* have come. Where you have come to redeem *yourself* in the aggregation of this lost tribe. Lost in space somewhere.

What is a hundred or a thousand years to Them, or tens of thousands? When They come, time's purpose is fulfilled. What never was passes to nothingness when They have come. What hatred claimed is given up to love, and freedom lights up every living thing and lifts it into Heaven, where the lights grow ever brighter as each one comes home. The incomplete is made complete again, and Heaven's joy has been increased because what is its own has been restored to it. The bloodied earth is cleansed, and the insane have shed their garments of insanity to join Them on the ground whereon you stand.

I think it covers just about everything. This is one of the most beautiful things you will ever read. This was turned in as a graduation exercise. This paper was picked out. Can you hear this? I mean, there's a lot of mixed metaphors in this passage. This little passage has every metaphor mix that there is. It goes from insanity to the grass to the sun. It's lovely. And it's so good and it's so innocent and it's so beautiful that it was chosen to represent your new innocence. Whoever is responsible for this, thank you. Wow!

Heaven is grateful for this gift of what has been withheld so long. For They have come to gather in Their Own. What has been locked is opened; what was held apart from light is given up, that light may shine on it and leave no space nor distance lingering between the light of Heaven and the world.

The holiest of all the spots on earth is where an ancient hatred has become a present love. A new Field of Dreams, of forgiveness of a present condition that can come about with no regard to space/time at all. You invite them to come so that you can forgive them, and they will come, and that's what they are now. The invitation to be forgiven has been offered you and you have accepted. And in the acceptance of that forgiveness are you forgiven. *And They come quickly to the living temple, where a home for Them has been set up. There is no place in Heaven holier.*

And all the lights in Heaven brighter grow in gratitude for what has been restored. Whoa, I better back up. *There is no place in Heaven holier.* That moment, that spot here, is just as holy as Heaven because it is. It's a spot of Heaven where the pain was. Boom! Pain, death – Heaven! Out! See, it never could have not been a little piece of Heaven that got lost. But if the Heaven broke away, it could not be anything but Heaven. If you still identify it in space/time, it becomes hell rather than Heaven. So your responsibility, as Jesus says, is not to escape the world in the sense that you can die, but to convert where you are. And that's what is happening to you. Wow!

And They have come to dwell within the temple offered Them, to be Their resting place as well as yours. What hatred has released to love becomes the brightest light in Heaven's radiance. And all the lights in Heaven brighter grow, in gratitude for what has been restored. I love it! Any definition of Heaven would be brighter than Heaven, not dimmer, because it's an aggregation of God creating. God creates from pure Light to the Light of Heaven. Your aggregation from evil goes beyond Heaven to God. Can you hear this? With no association at all, you just come together with all the power of the Universe in that moment of realization, which is actually what sustains the creation of God's Mind.

The idea of multiplicity, the idea that you are using that energy, is literally the only way you could express creation here. The secret for you is to remember there's no opposition to this. If you can share that with me, you'll have no problem at all. Nothing is denying you this, including yourself.

Around you angels hover lovingly, to keep away all darkened thoughts of sin, and keep the light where it has entered in. Your footprints lighten up the world, for where you walk forgiveness gladly goes with you. There's a nice talk on your footprints lighting up particular places where the association can be distracted from the route that he was taking. He comes to a certain spot where you have met him in a future association. He sees the Light of your footprints and they give him a new direction, another direction from the one that he was in. Can you hear that? I'm always turning you around. Turn around! Stand still for a minute and you will see the Light, or the path of these footprints that are leading you to Heaven. They are there. And they're there right now, at this place, at this time. Don't be going off somewhere else. If you do, it will be because you've judged the manner in which you want to proceed on this rather than let the Light be shown to you from the you of *They* who is gone. They wait at intersections for you to answer all your problems.

It's absolutely true that you've come in twos and threes from out of time to help somebody: "Hey, let's go down to Section 4. There's a guy there who may be able to hear it." Hope always springs enough at this level that you can hear it because once you do, you begin to aggregate all of your memories of the separation. That's how simple this is.

No one on earth but offers thanks to one who has restored his home, and sheltered him from bitter winter and the freezing cold. And shall the Lord of Heaven and His Son give less in gratitude for so much more? Of course not! You've square-rooted your gratitude. You can't give any more than God. Each time you came, it was doubled. Each time you converted it, it doubled. Each time you gave it away, for that moment when you didn't hold onto it, you doubled your own salvation. You literally doubled your own life. It's a pyramid. As long as it doesn't collapse, you never have to collect. It's like chain letters. "Send this letter on and eventually you'll collect this." You never do. You spring into Heaven. All it requires is that you give everything away in order to know that.

Now is the temple of the living God rebuilt as host again to Him by Whom it was created. Where He dwells, His Son dwells with Him, never separate. And They give thanks that They are welcome made at last. Where stood a cross stands now the risen Christ, and ancient scars are healed within His sight. An ancient miracle has come to bless and to replace an ancient enmity that came to kill. In gentle gratitude do God the Father and the Son return to what is Theirs, and will forever be. Now is the Holy Spirit's purpose done. For They have come! For They have come at last!

Those of you who are sharing that writing with me have come to see how obvious it is that the rejection of this simple message is the insanity of this world. Do you understand what I said? You, human? (If there's any human in here.) Any human that can't see what this says and what is written here is simply locked in his own necessity of death and there's no hope for him. The magnitude of the message that I just read you would be impossible to overestimate because it's the entire solution that you are being offered in your own mind. Now, at this time, in this place.

The *Workbook* lesson that goes with this is Lesson 191. *I Am The Holy Son of God Himself. Here is your declaration of release from bondage of the world. And here as well is all the world released.* Read it!

Dear Heavenly Father... Perhaps some soft Christian music... This sojourn that I have had the privilege of sharing with you in the establishment of this church has given to you and to this aggregation in time a great deal of joy. This morning is the sixth anniversary of our church in this building. What you call six years ago, much to the concern of the neighborhood, including our denial by the Ministerial Association and the beautiful response that allowed us to enter in here, is an occurrence that measured, in whatever this time is, six years. Actually, about 2600 years has passed. If this became a holy spot, there isn't anyone in this area who has not had the experience of his holiness because there is only this area. This apparently may have resulted in the Academy, in the Cheese Factory, the message going out. But those are nothing but holy spots of aggregations of *They*, which is *you*. This is an agreement that I made with you. I'm paying you back for my resurrection. Can you hear this? I'm staying here for a moment to remind you that you were responsible for me getting out of here. You are sharing that I escaped the world.

Now, I understand that most of you aren't going to be here in about another second. You carry it to the point of the Second Coming, obviously. But remember, all of this has already occurred, anyway. You are the cause of this. You are taking all the sacred moments of your Christianity, when you resurrected instead of crucifying the Christ. And you are letting them each moment be applied to this holy place. And that's what's happening. Of course – because it's *you*, albeit it's a later time association where you continue to resurrect.

So Happy Anniversary, New Christian Church of Full Endeavor! We're not "New-Agers." We're "Old-Agers." We accept the fundamental teachings of Jesus: "I must be born again. I must be resurrected. I must forgive. The salvation depends on me. Christ represents me. I am true because He is true. I believe Him, so I can't die." All we've done is taken what's right there and shown, in the light of the new you in your love for God and each other, the recognition that God is Love.

You're looking good. Not only do you look good, but you're planning – you plot among yourselves. When the solution is really obvious to you, you begin to plot among yourselves. You're not sure what you're doing, but you're not concerned about it because your kingdom is not of this world, anyway. This is what I just read you. You can screw it up but you can't sin. You're just dedicated to this, and all of your energy goes to it, instead of fear that you might fail – or fear that somebody might look at you and say, "What is that? How dare you tell me I'm perfect? How dare you say there is no sin? How dare you tell me that God creates perfectly eternally? How dare you tell me there's no world and I never left Heaven?"

Yeah, I dare to tell you that. I dare to tell you that because of the energy of my laying it on the line. And the energy of my daring to put it all on the line is what salvation is. You have learned to let it lie. Let it go. Let it ride. Let Love ride and it will ride you right out of here. Thank you! I have a tremendous amount of temporal energy, which I've always had. You have to remember this, aggregates of They, when you begin to aggregate, you provide a spatial reference that will justify the Light.

Remember: I'm not from here. Nobody is from here. So if you'll let me not be here for a moment, we will have a place that's not from here, which is your temple of God, which is really what you're doing. The problem that I have is that if I'm carrying that Light around, you activate it by the centering of your own associations here. Can you hear that? You actually begin to activate it. I have no real resistance to it at all – except the resistance that you might enter into fear in this association. If you've gone past that, your fear is simply converted to the place where salvation occurs. Where did salvation occur? Right here! That's literally true. You come here; that's it! But you don't struggle with your determination to remain. You let it be so because it's true.

There's a tremendous amount of Love and change going on. The factor that has grown in you, individually, is the certainty of your Self because there is only your Self. See how easy it is? Thank you, God! Thank you for that association. That's a gratitude for the recognition of your Selves compared to the old you that's gone.

We were in the middle of a prayer: *Heavenly Father, thank You that we are able now to remember together not only our revelation with You, but the congenialness of a place where Your Light, through our revelation, could shine on this world of loneliness and death, and in that be converted to the glory of a new Jerusalem, wherein God is with us and we are a part of His whole Love. We thank You for the provisions of community of the Guide You gave us to even be here. We came to know that nothing happened by accident. That we were in a field of possibility which, if we didn't guide ourselves, would lead us immediately to where You have come now. This world is going to be over and is over, and we have come together in this aggregation, and these final moments will be very joyous and happy, not because of the moments of joy and happiness but because there is nothing but You in happiness. We won't try to explain it to the world, but we will offer it to the world as a new vision of what we are in our mind. Amen!*

May the Lord bless you and keep you, may the Lord make His face to shine upon you. This is both the beginning and the end. Happy Anniversary! The moment you walked in here six years ago, this is what was going on. This is actually what was going on! There's no such thing as a past. This is going on right now! Where you stand now is Holy Ground. Holy Mackerel! It doesn't matter how you got here; you're here! If you're not judging it, you can feel the joy of letting God be God.

Verily I say unto you,
Whatsoever ye shall bind on earth
shall be bound in heaven:
and whatsoever ye shall loose on earth
shall be loosed in heaven.

CHAPTER 3

Finding The Present

We are teaching to the certainty of our singular atonement together with God. We offer love. We are going to introduce the teachings of Jesus from the Bible from 2000 years of expressions, at least in the script of conceptual association of what He says. And suddenly you say "Oh, I hear what Jesus of Nazareth said 2000 years ago." How is it that you now, here in this time are suddenly able to hear what He says?

It's going to amaze you, I positively guarantee that most of you are now amazed by the fact that as you listen to the New Testament, you are hearing what it says. You must understand this. Jesus in the New Testament is not saying anything that has not been said for 2000 years. You are standing up and reading the Sermon on the Mount. You are declaring the teachings of Jesus of Nazareth! Now there's no question of what He says. Why? Because it says that He says it. And you're hearing it.

What is going to astonish you in the particular event in which you find yourself in your time association is that literally the contemporary association denies what He says. I don't know how else I can offer this to you. If Jesus Christ appeared suddenly at this moment and declared to you "I am giving you the Kingdom of Heaven; if you bind on earth, you will bind in Heaven, if you release, you will be free," He is obviously declaring to you that you have the power of God. You immediately deny it.

Here's a lesson that you must learn if you are going to progress past this. There is nothing about the association of the establishment of the religion of Christianity that has anything whatsoever to do with the teachings of Jesus Christ except an attempt to verify the inevitability of your perfection in the limitation of your conceptual association. That is the fact of the matter. Do you understand me?

Now you are saying to me "well, all of a sudden I like the idea that the solution to my problem of pain and death, the sufferings that I'm undergoing, that my solution is not of this world at all." Quite literally, all that Jesus of Nazareth ever said is: You can't solve your own problem! Let go. Let God solve your problem, and He'll solve it. You say to me, "what is this world doing here?" The world has not acknowledged the saviorship of Jesus Christ. Why do you question it in the relationship with your determination to justify your old associations if Jesus tells you directly – do not justify your own associations.

I don't understand why you stand up in front of me on television and offer me an eye-for-an-eye solution to the problems of the conflict of my own mind, if, in fact, the whole requirement is to release them and let God be God in the perfection He has constructed me: *Therefore be ye perfect even as your Father which is in Heaven is perfect.* (Matthew 5:48) It doesn't say anything else.

I don't know whether you want to believe that the message *Therefore be ye perfect even as your Father which is in Heaven is perfect* is rejected, but I assure you that if you look at it, it is being rejected here. Yes or no? So don't be surprised when you pick up the *Course in Miracles*, which is nothing but a vivid elucidation of exactly what Jesus teaches, that it is rejected. What will surprise you is that if I actually open this *Course in Miracles*, you will see that in 20 years no one has really made an admission of what it says. All Jesus ever said to you is: Don't bring your own memories of yourself in conflict with yourself to this altar of truth that I am offering you. If you do, you will not be able to resurrect, you will not be able to be born again because you will be locked in Isaac and David. You will be locked in the continuum of your own association with your own mind. What surprises most of us now is the refusal of the world to acknowledge what the *Course in Miracles* says. Most of you in your new light are saying, "why isn't it okay that this is heard?"

I'll read you the impossible one: *To perceive truly is to be aware of all reality through the awareness of your own.* This is Christ's teaching.

But for this no illusions can rise to meet your sight, for reality leaves no room for any error. This means that you perceive a brother only as you see him now. His past has no reality in the present. (T13:6) Jesus declares to you that each moment of every day you are deciding what – against God and for the associations you have in your own mind. The fact of the matter is the world, as it is constructed, doesn't want to hear what Jesus is teaching. Is that so?

Reasonably, if I sit here and teach, for example: *Therefore be ye perfect even as your Father which is in Heaven is perfect* – God has created you perfectly as His living Son – I am offering you the solution of your problem through the transformation of your own mind. But I must tell you that as you are constructed in your own identity, you are not as God created you.

This is the whole teaching of Jesus. You must come to know, this is Sermon on the Mount, that there is no world. And the method by which you must come to know that will be a rejection of this world. Now we are about to part company. That is the simple fact of the matter. Those of you who are having your *born again* experiences will continue to look around in the world and attempt to correlate the data of those who have come to this place to deny the teaching. You will do it because it is the nature of you to justify yourself where you find yourself in your own space/time reference.

The entire teaching of Jesus of Nazareth is that yours is the Kingdom of Heaven, that Heaven is within you, and that the salvation of the world depends on you being born again. I'm not saying anything that has not been said for 2000 years. The very fact of the matter is that until this moment, you have been unwilling – and that would include, then, unable – since you are unwilling to accept the fundamental teaching, you are unable to accept it. Since you are unwilling to admit that you are perfect as God created you and that the Kingdom of God is in you and that the salvation of the world depends on you and that what you bind in your own mind here you will bind in Heaven and that God is lonesome without you and that the whole universe is waiting for you to wake up and acknowledge it, you will simply stay bound in your own dream of death.

Now the solution that you have finally admitted is the necessity for you, personally, and individually, to undergo the experience of your own enlightenment. That is precisely and exactly and only what any savior would offer you. If you stand here with a very rapidly evolving whole mind, what you call brightness, in the expression of your new determination of yourself being born – not based on the old reference of you – that will not be understood or admitted to by the associations. You cannot not do it.

This is Chapter 13 and 14. Beginning at Chapter 14, Jesus says to you: *Why aren't you happy to hear that all the pain and death and everything that you thought was occurring here, the loss of the things you love, is not true?* (T14:2) Come on, why aren't you happy to hear that? Obviously, in your new enlightenment you look at a human being and say: Why aren't you happy to know that God is perfect? Why aren't you thrilled with the idea that you never left Heaven? Why aren't you excited over the prospect that this world was over a long time ago? I don't understand why aren't you happy to learn that there is no world? Why aren't you happy when I say you're going to do even greater things than I did? Because you brought this world with you and when you leave the world will be gone. And you sit there scrunched in your own mind. Why? Because space/time is the nature of your denial of what I'm teaching. You can't see beyond it.

Your conceptual identity is what the design of the denial of eternity is. The truth of the matter is the teachings of Jesus are rejected because He says you are totally meaningless. Now reject me. See how simple that is? He says everything you do is totally meaningless. All the pain you are suffering is for no purpose whatsoever. This is Sermon on the Mount. Now you're really going to get me. What an astonishing idea!

As you look with open eyes upon your world, it must occur to you that you have withdrawn into insanity. You see what is not there, and you hear what makes no sound. (T13:5:6) This is the exact teaching of Jesus. So we are teaching you, then, as you come into here, that the necessity is for the experience of you being born again. The requirement, if this is so, is that when you come together to proclaim the Kingdom of God, that you acknowledge that your own worldly goods have no value to you, that all of the things that you have heretofore defended have no meaning to you, and that you will not hold them within the bondage of your own mind.

Now the relevance to this continuum of time of the teachings of Jesus is not evident. Those of you who intend to leave the world, this is the whole teaching: Come and leave the world with me. *He that believeth in me, though he were dead, yet shall he live...and shall never die.* (John 11:25-6) I have no understanding of why that is not taught from the pulpits of this world. Hopefully, you don't either. Because when I listen to what's being taught from the pulpit, it says that God sent His Son to be torn apart and crucified and killed in order to justify and atone for your sins. Guys, my mind will not accept any manner by which the teachings of Jesus could have been reduced to a denial of Jesus! But the fact of the matter is: What isn't love is murder. The fact of the matter is that if you are conceptualized to identify with pain and death, you will what? Love pain and death! I know you don't want to hear that. You love to lose the things that you love because by losing them you can justify your need to possess your own love. That's the fact of the matter. Do you hear me? Of course. You love it! Winning and losing are a part of your association with yourself. Actually, what I am denying you is the necessity for you to verify your existent association whatsoever. That's why you won't listen to me, because you are a verification of the separation contained within your own human purposes. Is that so? You don't have to hear me. Why would you want to hear me? What I am teaching you is not relevant to the problem that you are trying to solve.

You asked when you were ten years old, or maybe five, "what's the meaning of this?" You were very aware that you are conscious. You said, "what is this, mama? What is the meaning of this? What are we doing?" And she says, "you've got to give purpose to your existence." The meaning of life is to give purpose to where you find yourself in your own association. You must then what? Give purpose to existence and separation, to pain and death, because what? That's what the meaning of life is! Why? Meaning and purpose are the same. Do you see that? You can't have a meaning in something without it having a purpose. It's not possible. But somewhere within your own nightmare, you have said "if the meaning of life is this existent association, I can't understand it. What does it mean that I must exist and die?" Your whole meaning is based on you losing the things that you love. If you accept that as a contingency for your existence, that's exactly what you'll get. And the meaning of your life, I'm talking to you human being, the meaning of this is to exist in this little world based on a universe that is over and gone by the acknowledgment, and you get old and sick and die. That's insane. Jesus says to you in the Sermon on the Mount that's not so. You are perfect as your Father created you.

Now, here's the crucial test. The question is not whether the world, in your objective association, is ready to hear it. Why? When the world is ready to hear it, it is accepted and resurrects. I'll do it once more:

The moment that Jesus appeared on earth, He formulated a continuum of time that denied the necessity to continue to participate in the separation. At that moment the world was over. That's the fact of the matter. Jesus saved the world. Why you would stand up and say, "Jesus saved the world, therefore I must struggle" when Jesus told you to stop struggling in order to know you're the savior—which is the antithesis of the teaching—I have no idea. Except that remember this: what you bind on earth you will bind in Heaven because your mind is the determiner of the outcome that you want. *As you sow, so shall you reap.*

Obviously you deny it. Obviously you are not willing to admit that you are responsible for your own thoughts in your own association; were you to do so, you could not stand them for a moment. Wow! Obviously what Jesus said is: You are the cause of this. You are the cause of the universe. If your mind binds it, holds it, causes it pain and sickness, it will be you that is causing it to who? It cannot *not* be so. If you will free the Son of God to be born again, he will be born in the light of your new mind because you are both the denier and the freer, which is the Holy Spirit, in the certainty that you are perfect as God created you. It's very important for you because as you go out to teach this conceptually you will not understand why the world doesn't immediately admit that what Jesus says: Give everything away; I'm not from here, neither are you; there is no world, it's over and gone; we made a little mistake and it's not true; you must awaken from your own nightmare or dream of death and return home. Now, if I can get you to admit that salvation depends on you – *know ye not that ye must be born again?* You must have the experience within your own body association and the solution to your problem will be very simple.

So the simple reason that the conceptual mind does not hear when you present him with this is that he doesn't want to. This world does not want to hear that you're perfect as God created you. It is a place where people come to deny Him. So why are you searching? Why do you look where it isn't? It's not here. You are searching where it is not.

All Jesus really tells you is that there is no solution to your problem. How you can form that in *Course in Miracles* groups that study each other's separate solutions to problems is entirely beyond me. So why would you wonder about that for 2000 years; you have a church that literally depends on the companionship of death to justify the teachings of Jesus, which makes absolutely no sense. He tells you literally in the Bible, He's very succinct in telling you that every personal relationship you form in death will deny you the Kingdom of God. (Luke 14:26)

That's what you don't want to hear. You don't want to know that your personal relationships justify your own kingdom of death rather than letting God be God. Do you get that? Let's be perfectly clear that the whole teaching of Jesus in ranting against this world in all of your special relationships is only that you have designed them – your offspring – to die along with you. And your father has taught you to be old and die with him. And you will teach unto the seventh generation of vipers – this is a tough talk – your determination to murder God and attack reality. Obviously that teaching is rejected because when it's accepted this world is gone.

As you awaken from your dream, you are discovering in the cause and effect or consequential relationships, or what are termed the continuum of time, that no one here is hearing you. They are in a structure of cause and effect relationship where they will for a moment stand still. This is what I am going to read from Chapter 13 so that you can see the very simple teaching that you must be born again.

This means that you must perceive a brother only as you see him now. This is the entire teaching of Jesus. *His past associations have no meaning to you, they have no reality in the present, so you cannot see them. Your past reactions to him are also not there, and if it is to them that you react, you see but an image of him that you made and cherish instead of him. In your questioning of illusions, ask yourself if it is really sane to perceive what was as now.* In your question of illusions, is it really sane to say "I'm studying a light that's seven minutes old?" What the hell good is that going to do you? Is it really sane to say, "I'm studying some light that is a thousand million years old. And if I can study it far enough back, I can determine in my old reference what I am." That's insane.

There is no association between quantum physics or quantum reality and objective association; none whatsoever. If every association or particle of your mind is entirely whole and creating eternally, the idea of sequential time is absurd. The idea of time is valuable to you very simply because time is an invention of your mind. But that being said, for you to sequence it is absurd. All you are possibly going to be able to say about you when you came into this church is that you are over and gone. Jesus Christ resurrected teaches you only that that is true. You are over and gone. At this moment, if you'll stop crucifying the Christ, you will resurrect. That's in here. It says: Each moment in time, each hour, each second that you are here, you are either crucifying Him, killing Him in the denial of His message or you are resurrecting along with Him. That's His entire teaching, that's what He says. That's exactly what He says, that this moment, this is a denial of the teaching that you are perfect as God created you. It's always going to based on what? The references of your old mind in time! Release the past and let it go for it is gone and all of this happy new bright reality will be available to you.

Here's what Jesus says: *You,* all humans, *consider it "natural" to use your past experience as the reference point from which to judge the present. Yet this is unnatural because it is delusional.* All you could possibly say about it is that it's over. Yeah, but if that's true, the simple solution would be to turn your will over to God. The simple solution would be to simply admit "Father I can't solve the problem." I don't have to sell you that, brother, that's just a statement of fact. "I'd rather do it myself" is exactly what your problem is. "I can solve the problem in my own association." Based on what? "All of my old memories." Were you able to solve it in the past? "No. But I'm going to keep trying to solve it; I'm going to die trying because my reality is based on dying trying to solve the problem. The meaning of my life is to exist and die trying to justify the meaning of life." As though meaning of life requires justification. Why isn't God simply what He is? Perfect and eternal forever.

When you have learned to look on everyone (being born again each moment) *with no reference at all to the past, either his or yours as you perceived it, you will be able to learn from what you see now*...right now at this moment. Most of you in this church, sitting in these pews, have come into a new association of yourself in regard to what you are in your existent association in universal mind. When you look at an association who is trapped in his own mind, you literally will not be able to understand him because he is only a containment of his own mind. Each human is inhabiting his own association, which is totally uncommunicative. Your new communicative devices, which are the enlightenment of the energy of your own mind, are offering him an entire solution to his problem with nothing to do with the reference that he had in his own conceptual mind.

Quite literally, the teachings of Jesus have nothing at all to do with the dilemma of the cause-and-effect of the earth. Nothing! You are offered a solution that is not of this world. Do you understand? Heretofore your dependency has been on yourself. You've discovered that your dependency on yourself simply doesn't work. Now, obviously, the requirement is your enlightenment. Just as obviously, if you are determined to sit there in your own mind and justify the association, what could I possibly do about it? Not only will you justify your own association, you will justify me in the reference of the projection of your own mind as to what I am in our relationships together.

You're a liar. I'm teaching Jesus. You are a liar. There is no truth in you whatsoever. The cause of you is gone. That's why you are not allowed to teach this. As soon as you begin to teach it, you begin to teach the unreality of the world. But if the world is not real, neither is the human in his egotistical associations with himself. Yes or no? So, what you're really saying as we leave here – obviously you're in a different continuum of time. You've shortened time to the extent that you are resurrecting all the time instead of killing God like you used to do.

What can I do about that? I can only offer you the resurrection, the perfection, of your own mind. Why don't you have the experience? You're afraid. The fear of God is the most ridiculous, incredible jest that could ever happen to this world. Yet, if the purpose of this world is to justify the meaning, then the meaning of this world from God must be for you to suffer sickness and death, and send your son to be torn up in order to justify you. It's exactly the opposite of the teaching. What's mostly rejected is the simple teaching of Jesus that if you don't get this now you are condemned to eternal hell forever. That's exactly what He's teaching. He says that you are condemned to eternal damnation. "Well, I guess I condemned myself." I have no idea.

I'm telling you that you are responsible for what you see. Things are happening because of you and I have offered you the most fearful alternative you could ever experience. What is it? The loss of your self identity. Give up the world and come home with me is exactly what you are being offered. Do you know what your defense is? "How come no one here has done it? If what you say is right, Jesus, how come none of the priests or anybody that's here, how come established Christianity hasn't acknowledged what you've said?" Because established Christianity is the denial of the teachings of Jesus.

I'm doing that *Time Magazine* article we wrote, "Jesus Means Exactly What He Says." There's not one single teaching that Jesus offers you that is accepted totally by the establishment. If it were, there would be no establishment. The absurdity of going back to the Old Testament to justify Jesus is so senseless that you in your own mind really will want to say to the association "why are you doing that?" He's doing it because he has to deny the teachings of Jesus. How they do it with the *Course in Miracles* is amazing. The whole Course, coming from out of time, is nothing but the certainty of your own eternal mind.

Here's the crucial element of the teaching of Jesus. This is the *Course in Miracles* as it will be presented to the world, using me or using you. Jesus of Nazareth is your personal savior within your own mind. What He is offering you has absolutely nothing at all to do with the world as you conceive it. He has overcome the world and is offering you the solution to the revelation of His own mind. All He says is, "What I have done you will do and have done along with me. It has nothing to do with the world at all, except the denial of it." This is the teaching.

Are human beings in their associations going to hear this? No. You say to me, "Well, a human being can come to this." No it can't. There is no possibility that a conceptual mind will hear this. None. Zero. How could there be? Life is eternal. It is forever. Objective reality is not true. You are determined somehow that what I am offering you can be formulated in your own mind association. It can't be. I'm teaching be born again! The experiences that you are having in your own mind in your resurrection are nothing but indications you have become single-eyed so that your body can be enlightened.

I don't see any way, if you're going to present this, that you shouldn't just begin to teach personal transformation. At least let the denial be in the associations of their individual mind. Then there is some hope for them. Otherwise there is no hope. Do you see that? The association that is in denial in his own conceptual mind is nothing. *If I have not love, I am nothing.* (I Cor 13:2) It does not say I am something without love. It says I am nothing. That Corinthians talk is in print, in a booklet called *Love*, you ought to read that. The love of God is everything you are. Anything else that you do will be what? Nothing. It's not you having nothing. It's you being nothing. Except for God's love, you are nothing. You say: "How can I be God's love?" You already are. Admit it. Jesus will say in the Course, *My meaningless thoughts are showing me a meaningless world. Come on back to Heaven with me, I'm offering you the keys to the kingdom because your mind is the denial of God.* I can't think of anything simpler than that. Go ahead, examine it in your own mind. And you'll reach the conclusions of the justification for your own entrapment in time.

Each one of us has peopled his own world with what he is determined he wants to be the result. And we share the results of our own mind, which are already gone. If we share the results, we can't come into the present condition. What are the results of our own mind? Loneliness, pain and death. What a peculiar place to find yourself where the existent association depends on justification for loneliness, pain and death. Listen. This is an insane world. Most of you in this room recognized early the insanity of the world simply because when you asked "what is the meaning of life?" you were told to exist and get old and die. That is the purpose of this world. So you got involved with the purpose and you said, "but what's the meaning, what's the real meaning of this?" For you to die.

The meaning of life is for you to die, for you to suffer pain and death and then there will be an alternative. And you said, "why isn't the alternative available to me now? Why can't I come to know now the true meaning of life?" You can! But only by the denial of your existent association. This is the whole teaching. You can't see two worlds. That sure sounds like you can't serve God and mammon. (Matthew 6:24) You'll love one and hate the other. Loving the existence of death is the denial and hatred of eternal life. In the admission of the perfect love of God will be the denial of this world. So the whole necessity for you, as Jesus would say, is to hate the world. You say, "no, it doesn't say you've got to hate." The fact of the matter is you've got to hate everything about it; you've got to hate the murderer, the justification for the world, all of it.

It becomes very simple for you because as you progress in your own mind, you don't want to be of this world. Can you hear me? You don't want to be here. You have found a total alternative, but you see that the alternative has nothing to do with this world at all. Nothing. If the alternative has something to do with this world, you'll still be condemned to your own conceptual association. The teachings of Jesus or any risen mind have nothing to do with the world at all. It literally tells you that your kingdom is not of this world.

So stop looking in established Christianity for Jesus' teachings. They're not there. It's only been 2000 years – do you know how long that is? Do you know how long this continuum intends to go on? Another 8000 years based on the slow flodging of the denial of what you were offering. You go on national television and authenticate this with the certainty of your own mind, they'll all dial off to something else. They don't need to know what you are offering them. You got that? Their needs are to continue to justify their existence because that's the purpose they have given life. Shame on you! What you're really saying to me is "I can't stand this place anymore. There has to be an alternative not of this world." Come and find it with me. Jesus says, *"I will give you the keys to the kingdom."* Isn't that nice? See how simple it is? He means this is literally true. He means exactly what He says. *There is no death.*

The solution has become so evident to so many of you now that any perceptual discernment of it is causing you to undergo enlightening experiences. That's the whole purpose. You like to study other associations and wonder what experience they're having. All you're really doing is justifying them in their own search. You say, "how did you get to be born again? How were you able to know that? How did you figure this out?" This is the establishment. Who is it you are asking? You are asking associations of your own mind. Do you understand? They are justifications for you asking the question. You ask the one thing in the universe that doesn't know what it is. Any human being you ask is the one thing in the universe that doesn't know. You ask, "what the hell are we doing here?" Yet the question justifies a response from him in your own mind. He must justify you because you're a projection of his mind. You must justify him because you are a projection of his mind. So you live in your own projections and continue to ask the question "what am I?" to the one thing that doesn't know. And it's he who gives you the response. And you hear exactly what you want to hear within your own mind, not any more than that. Why? You can't hear more than you intend to hear. And heretofore you have intended to justify your own associations for existence. Now you have said "the hell with this, I intend to go home to God." What have you done? You have given the entirety of the purpose in your illusory association to find a solution that is not of this world. Do you understand?

Love the Lord thy God with all thy heart and all thy soul, and all thy strength, and with all thy mind, and thy neighbor as thyself. (Luke 10:27) That's exactly what the teaching is. There's another way to look at this. I'm not from here. I can take the power of my mind and direct it to a solution that is not of this world. I can literally remember what? Now! In my remembering of the old association, I will remember the moment of the schism. Now I can't remember the moment of the schism, but I can experience the fear and horror of it if I'm willing to. That's the way: through the death of the necessity for my existence I will be born again. I am having a continuing fearful reassociation with God. But since any reassociation with God is happiness, my fear has become joy.

I'll read Chapter 14, just a couple of pages. Quite literally heretofore you have not been a happy learner. You are not happy to learn that everything you have done here is totally meaningless, and you have no purpose here whatsoever. Now when I tell that to you, instead of going, "what the hell are you talking about, what do you mean there is no meaning to me? What do you mean the things I love aren't valuable? What do you mean I don't have to die?" That's what I mean. You're not entirely happy about that. Most of you in this association are very happy to learn that you are perfect as God created you. You say, "well, I'm not very happy to hear that." Why not? "I need to justify myself in my own mind." Yet there is nothing outside of you. If I justify myself, I will be condemned to that association.

Do you know what you are laughing at? You're not from here. All of your efforts are entirely futile. Give up. Go home to God. You're perfect. And you love it. Some of you still say, "what in the hell does he mean by that?" Your bottom is the same as your salvation. In the moment of horror when you stand in Gethsemane for just a moment and say, "God why did you do this?" is also when you are saved. I've led you directly into fear and you love it. It's an amazing thing. And this is exactly why the establishment denies Jesus Christ. Jesus Christ is offering them the most fearful message they could ever hear – that God did not create this piece of shit! Nothing is more fearful to them than that God didn't have anything to do with them.

Quite literally, Jesus says that the conceptions of your own mind are meaningless. They lead you nowhere. They are over and gone. And you're so happy to hear that. I don't know, maybe at some point they'd say "that's what He means! He means what He says." Now does that require an enlightenment occurrence in your own mind? Yes. You don't have to identify it, but you have to have had the experience very simply because you are hearing differently. Let those that can hear, hear. Let those that want to hear, hear. If you want this, there is nothing in the universe that can stop you from hearing it. If you want the Kingdom of God, if you want to remember you are perfect as God created you, nothing can stop you because you are perfect as God created you. The only thing that could possibly stop you are your own misconceptions about yourself that are over and gone and not there. How excited you've become over this message! What an amazing turn of events. And how individual that is in your own mind! It doesn't have anything to do with the world at all. Release the world and let it go for it is gone. You've gone a step beyond that now, a step that has brought you to the borderland of your mind.

I'm not sure whether you are ready to go on national television, on the Oprah Show, and Oprah says "who are you?" and you say "I'm the savior of the world. No one can save it but me, and I intend to do so." She's liable to be like Helen Schucman who told Jesus "you're a paranoid schizophrenic that has delusions of grandeur..." What does Jesus say to Helen? And on Oprah you say, "I don't know about that, but God gave me all power in Heaven and on earth." Of course the teachings of Jesus are nuts to the world. Do you see that? Just as this world has become totally meaningless to you. If you're not the savior of the world, who in hell is? Jesus? Well, He's resurrected, so I don't have to worry about it. All I have to do then is acknowledge Him and I'll be Home because He must be a part of my mind. Now I'm going to have to listen to what He says. And the world denies what Jesus of Nazareth says.

This is the only track that Jesus wants as we leave this place. Those of you leaving with me, the only real track He wants is to introduce to the denial of God the possibility of reality through transformation of the conceptual mind. Let that be introduced as a science and an art; that the science of the transformation of your mind be introduced to the world, and that it would have nothing to do with the old conceptual associations at all, that knowledge can be gained through enlightenment – and, in fact, knowledge can only be gained through enlightenment. Do you understand? So that your sole purpose in the world is to escape it. The only reason you could possibly be here is to get the hell out of here. You cannot be here for any other reason than to find a way out.

Somewhere it must occur to the objective mind – there's no sign it is, they talk about billions of worlds and aliens and all that objective nonsense. Their minds are so contained that the idea of a beautiful quantum realization in the relationship with God is not a part of this association. That's a fact of the matter. Don't let that concern you. You should not be concerned about that. Your requirement is to awaken from your own nightmare; you'll have none of it. This world is an illusion of your mind. Now, when you awaken from it, will you escape and be gone? Yes. Where are you going to go? I didn't come to save the world, I came to condemn it and tell you it's not true. I can do it any way you want me to do it. My message is for you personally. Not only personally, but completely personally since you believe there are personal thoughts, you must sort them out in your own mind – not that they're not true, but I assure you that the power of your incredible mind directed to an escape from the world, is going to happen very rapidly, particularly at the level I'm offering it to you because I am offering you this out of this world. I am not in this world at all. Neither are you. I'm not even from here.

The joy of you coming together to worship God with the certainty that the only requirement was the relinquishment of the authority of your own mind, and the admission that God has created you perfectly is a joyous occasion. You could not have gathered together except for any purpose and to acknowledge that you are perfect as God created you. Any other purpose is totally meaningless. Any other purpose you gather except to admit the necessity for your personal experience, being born again, is totally meaningless. We have come together in your new aggregation of love for God and each other – *Love the Lord thy God...* and each other – *thy neighbor as thyself*. Do not expect the world to admit or understand this. They will murder you. I might as well tell you this. The conceptual mind which has no reality is the denial of what you are offering. So that is our message for today.

So now we will begin our church service as soon as possible, we're starting a half hour early. Many of us will be visiting Minnesota at noon today. You say, "how dare you accommodate watching the Packer game by setting your service time?" What's wrong with that? It's amazing how the mind is going to judge you in association with what it considers to be sacred. Everything is sacred. Any single thing that you admitted to in its entirety would spring you into Heaven. Does that include the Packers losing? Well, no! You are experiencing the intense competition of your own mind in the joy of the new association with yourself. You say, "what you're teaching me is that it doesn't matter whether I win or lose." The hell I am. I am teaching you that your need to win can be transcended in your need to win and represent God in the wholeness of your own mind. It's the action of your own mind, not what's going on here. Is this competitive? What do you think Jesus is? If Jesus of Nazareth is not in competition with this world, what is He? He is forgiving God in His perfection and you are maintaining the world. That's a competitive association. You think you can win. So we participate in the illusion of your winning. Obviously you can't win.

The volume of our literature is increasing. Jesus really wants this, guys. This has pretty much been settled. The more you can get out of this now, the better, because we'll be leaving here. But you need to keep this flowing out into the world now. It's going to be more and more difficult for you to assemble without undergoing the totality of the experience. You're saying finally that the aggregation simply transforms and turns to Light and is gone. It's important to remember there is no world. You're at the borderland between time and eternity. This is just a little place that you came to. But I assure you, I positively guarantee you that this is over. You're here for a moment, it will be over in a moment. That is our whole teaching for today. You've gathered together at the end of the world. The time of resurrection is at hand.

CHAPTER 4

A Lesson In Forgiveness

This is a Sunday school class where we teach you that you are an establishment of a deifying association of yourself in an image comparison of a god of fear rather than a God of Love.

How would you not need a god of fear if you are fearful? My condition (as Moses) is an apparent self-identity based on a relationship that has no order, since, in a particular sense, it's a teaching that I must survive – that I must survive individually in my own associations with myself. My life, then, is based on my survival. Is this true humans, human beings?

My life is based on my survival. But it appears to be that my survival has a longevity of identification that is different from other animals, in the sense that I seem to be living in an association that demands my attention to a propagation that guarantees my continuation in protection of what I appear to possess in my identity of self.

This is for those Christians who want to hear the teachings of Jesus. Would you like to hear what Jesus teaches? Have you ever heard it? It would be extremely unlikely that you, in your condition of fear, could have heard the simple teachings of Jesus of Nazareth, who is nothing but an offering of a God of Love in a totality – singular – rather than a god of fear. That's why you're here. You could not *not* possibly be here had you not, at this moment, a structure of your relationship with yourself and this world that is what fear is. Is that so? Space/ time association *is* fear. You *are* fearful, aren't you?

How would you present to the world your newly-discovered certainty that there is an eternal life of Love that lasts forever, based on the power of your individual self-recognition of the wholeness of you? It would be impossible to present it to you. How could I possibly do it for you if your doctrine of containment or structure is based on a god powerful enough to destroy your enemies – which justifies your continuing fear? The condition right now in this world is precisely and exactly the condition of when Jesus was here 2000 years ago. It's precisely and exactly that.

I'm coming as an illuminate mind, whatever you think that is, offering you the peace of God with no relevance whatever to your god of fear. And just as obviously, my cultural associations with you in the fabric of our memory of historic identities are based on a god of fear, because in this world all gods are gods of fear. Listen to me. Not because some culture has formulated that as so, but because the nature of separation from a single reality is what fear is.

The newly-evolved ability for you to understand the emotional context of what I'm offering you is an extraordinary thing because it's impossible for me to involve you in this without involving you in the totality of your relationship with love and fear. The single requirement that I would offer you if you wish to progress in the nature of the totality of unconditional Love is that you understand that literally in this training device you are always either fearful or loving. The whole nature of Sermon on the Mount (Matthew 5-7), if you would like to hear it, is very simply that God is Love, not fear. And any justification for you to fear your brother or to attack him or to defend him or to judge him or to organize in your own mind alternatives that justify your existent fear association will be the opposite of the teachings of me, or Jesus of Nazareth, or anyone who is going to teach unconditional Love. It will come down to the fact, if that is so, that *any condition* is fearful.

Now we're making a little progress, after what appears to be 2000 years. Jesus stood up in Sermon on the Mount and said very simply, any condition of association of your own mind will be what fear is and will be a denial of the eternal Love of God.

What is your association in your own mind, based on the relevance of what I am telling you, in regard to your apparent objective condition within this world? I have absolutely no idea, but I can guarantee you this: If there is a single, whole, loving, total Eternal Reality, this ain't it!

But how the hell am I going to stand up in this world and say, "This is not created by God?" It is created by your god, because your god is one of fear and protection, as predicted by the circumstances of the burning bush. Do we need a burning bush? Without a burning bush there would be no religion. The protection of the devices of civilization in separation are a fundamental requirement of conceptual association. They cannot *not* exist because they are a sharing of the element of fear, based on a power of god that will overcome its enemies. Is this true? It's the whole Old Testament. All it says is that Yahweh is going to protect you.

Not only is that true, but it is true in the physical sense that Moses on Mt. Horeb – and we're going back some years here now – was called by God in the performance of the Ten Commandments. Of course! What a beautiful, incredible, structural idea, that man, who lived as a beast in separation, would have to come together and share, objectively, an association that guaranteed his survival. This is what the Old Testament is. Is there a question on this? That's what you do.

So your very survival is based on adherences to a code of fear that guarantees your survival as an adversary to the enemy that's outside of you. Nobody really questions this. Everybody's nodding their head and going, "Oh, yeah. Well, we got that settled."

When Jesus Christ of Nazareth 2000 years ago stood up to teach, all He would really teach you is that God is Love. He cannot *not* teach "Love your enemy" because you hate and despise and reject your enemy. This is how simple this is. Don't you see?

And I can pick up the Holy Bible and read that to you and that might or might not mean something to you. It hasn't meant anything to you in 2000 years. The idea that you should love your enemy hasn't meant anything to you in 2000 years, and it would be very unlikely that the circumstances in which you find yourself will allow you to love your enemy *since he already is your enemy.*

This is the whole problem with trying to teach *A Course in Miracles*, as you are aware, because the idea of forgiveness – the forgiveness of your enemy – is not possible if you live with a god of fear. It is impossible to forgive your enemy if he is constructed separately from you, because your fear of god would demand your attention to the fear of him, so that forgiveness becomes meaningless. Do you see that? The idea that you would have to forgive somebody who could actually wrong you would make forgiveness impossible. This is the dilemma of the rejection of the teachings of Jesus and, obviously, the *Course in Miracles.*

"I threw the *Course* away," said somebody last week, "simply because it's not relevant to my condition." That's a fact of the matter. "I threw away the teachings of Jesus Christ because the teachings of Jesus Christ are not relevant to my problem. The *Course* says to ignore my children, let them starve, and go to Heaven." That's exactly what the *Course* does *not* say. Yet that's exactly what that woman heard that the *Course* says. So do you still. You actually believe the *Course* teaches you to forgive your enemy – that you must practice forgiveness of those outside of you who are wronging you and causing you the problems in your association. It's exactly the opposite. The entire teaching of Sermon on the Mount, of all whole minds is that *you* are the cause of this.

Once more: The entire teaching of Jesus Christ of Nazareth is: As a man thinketh, he will get the result of his own mind in relationship with himself. Period.

Now we're at the crux of this teaching, which you have become ready to hear. *All power is given unto you in Heaven and in earth.* (Matthew 28:18) There is nothing that you cannot do. Giving power to God without your entire association will just give you fear of God. The idea that you would fear God is simply the idea that you would fear something outside yourself. You then require the power of that something outside of you to justify your continuing separation from singular reality.

Look at this. Do you guys see this? It says *Holy Bible.* This is a holy Bible, isn't it? Look at it. Look at all this stuff. This is the entire history of *you* since the beginning of time. Nobody really likes it. The civilized world is only about 3800 years old. This says it began about 1800 BC – you went through Exodus, coming up out of Egypt. So that period of time, pre-Christ, would be just about the period of time that you're experiencing post-Christ, if you would care to look at it. So the element that is occurring now is just about 2000 years after the beginning of this cultural association.

So all of this time there had evolved a culture, a civilization, based on a powerful god – I mean, the single most powerful god in the universe – that single most powerful god, the god of fear, that would strike fear into his enemies. Into this condition comes the reality of the teaching of unconditional Love. You can feel me because I'm loving you. All I can say to you is this: When we say *Love is letting go of fear*, we mean it literally – *and forgive*.

The lesson I intend to do today, to make you listen to, in mind-training, is going to be a lesson in forgiveness. I know it's impossible to teach a fearful thing to forgive, but it is possible to teach him to let go of his fear in faith in God. And in the release of his fear will he discover Love and in no other manner. And I know that this is what Jesus teaches you, and what I'm telling you, but it remains a fact of the matter.

This is a Bible class. Let's look at the fact of the matter of the relationship between the Old Testament and the New Testament. The word "forgive" from the Hebrew is used in the Old Testament 28 times in the entire 1800 years. Wow. Here's the shocker. The word "love" or "loving" in the entire pre-Jesus, 2000 years of all of the documents, is rarely used. The word "love" does not occur in the Old Testament, except in a relationship with fear – "Love the Lord thy God" through fear. That's an amazing idea! How can that possibly be so?

There is inherent fear in establishment of emotion that cannot be recognized objectively. Could you hear that? There's an inherent fear of Love because Love, to an establishment, would be: "Every man for himself." Do you know that Jesus of Nazareth, or my whole mind teaches you: "Every man for himself through the Love of God"? Do you understand why you reject quantum healing, why you reject the moment when complete randomness, or Love, would overcome you in the recognition of the transformation of your own mind to be born again?

I know about the word "love" because somebody gave me a new Bible, and it's the King James version of the Bible. This is right after Elizabeth. This is James I. Somebody said, "Why don't we get together and write these scriptures of 1600 years?" This is 340 years ago, isn't it? So this is getting together to describe the association of a man of fear with a man of Love. But this Bible has a concordance in it (that's copyrighted, incidentally – this is a little dig at *Course in Miracles*, the Foundation's teaching). They couldn't copyright the King James version, so they copyrighted the concordance, which makes it very valuable. I don't know if they will object to me saying that "love" is only mentioned in their concordance five times in the Old Testament, because it was a great shock to me.

Song of Solomon is the most passionate love association ever told, but it's completely objective. It's an astonishing thing that Song of Solomon is completely objective. It's love of body. It's love of identity – not love of the totality of yourself in your relationship with God. So your passion becomes objective, which is what fear is, since objectivity is fearful. What an amazing idea!

So here's Jesus, through His own revelation discovering that God is only Love, and attempting to find, in the associations of the establishment of the Judaic tradition, the entire idea, the justification for what He was teaching. And it's there – but it's there only to the extent that it can be verified among the chosen ones.

Let's see what He found. He says, "I've got to find somewhere where I can show you this God of Love, which is with you all the time." So He looked at all the commandments in Leviticus and Deuteronomy, which were written by Moses. The five books of Moses – Genesis, Exodus, Leviticus, Numbers and Deuteronomy – were actually written by Moses. Well, Deuteronomy, perhaps he wrote after he was dead.

It is a great dilemma with my mind to direct your attention to my certainty that your culture is actually based on love, not fear. Even though you appear to fear God, you actually love Him. It's very hard to teach that since you are dependent on fear. Do you see? And this is the dilemma that you find yourself in your apparent hallucination, as Jesus would say. Your emotions are exactly the opposite of what they are.

So Jesus is looking for it. He does a direct quote. He's teaching Mind. In Sermon on the Mount, He is teaching you that your mind is all that there is: "As you think, it will come back to you. You are contained within your own relationship of yourself through an entirety of your relationship with God, if you will let it be so." The practice of that, which is the Beatitudes, is give everything away, love your enemy, and all the associations that go with Sermon on the Mount.

When He looks in the Old Testament for it, He finds it in Deuteronomy 6:5 and expresses it as the commandment that says: *Thou shalt love the Lord thy God with all thy heart, and with all thy soul, and with all thy mind.* (Matthew 22:27) *And...Thou shalt love thy neighbor as thyself.* (Matthew 22:39)

That actually isn't in Deuteronomy. It's in Leviticus 19:18. The further commandment that, "You will love your neighbor as yourself" doesn't follow in Deuteronomy. It occurs in Leviticus, two chapters back. Let's understand that Jesus very rapidly had become a scholar of the Sanhedrin and Pharisaical associations that demanded His attention.

Now let's see if He cheated here. Let's look and see. He needs to teach you to love one another through giving, through forgiving. The most unjust, traitorous thing you could ever ask any human being to do is forgive his enemy. Come on, guys. You act as though that's easy. It's not. It is impossible for you to forgive your enemy and remain on earth. It is literally impossible for you to do it. If you forgive your enemy, you will disappear from here.

He finds Deuteronomy 6:3-5: *Hear therefore, O Israel, and observe to do it; that it may be well with thee, and that ye may increase mightily, as the Lord God of thy fathers hath promised thee, in the land that floweth with milk and honey. Hear, O Israel: The Lord our God is one Lord: And thou shalt love the Lord thy God with all thine heart, and with all thy soul, and with all thy* **might***.* Might. Love the might of the fear of God. Not with your **mind**. It doesn't say, "mind." He cheated. Surprise. I got you. Did I get you? That's what it says here. "Fear God with all of your might" is what this says. "Love the Lord thy God and fear Him with your might." The next page will say very simple things like: *Thou shalt fear the Lord thy God and serve Him and shall swear by His name* through your own fear.

So Jesus took it out of context and changed "might" of fear to "mind." But the idea, the mere idea that there is a power of mind within man to heal or forgive, is what blasphemy is. And I can read this to you if you want to see it in Matthew where they say, "How dare you tell us that you have the power to heal?"

Yet notice how He changes "might" to "mind." So you love God with all of your heart, which is what love is; all of your soul, which is the Holy Spirit; and all of your mind. And in loving God with all of your mind, you become a relationship of God that creates as He does. There's nowhere in the Old Testament where that is even considered. The dependency of the Old Testament, or all establishments of this world, is always on the establishment; fear of God, which causes fear and acquiescence to an establishment, or you would have no authority on earth at all. Yet all authority of separation is what fear is. Tell me you heard that – fear of the income tax, fear of the associations of what constitutes your apparent necessity to survive with your enemies.

"How dare you say you have the power to heal?!" (John 5:18) "How dare you say, 'Go and sin no more?'" (John 5:14)

105

Are you suggesting to us that there's a power contained in *you*, Christians, as taught by Jesus – that you would take on the power of God in a direct association with God, not concerned about the laws of Moses?

"How dare you tell us you operate under the single rule of God rather than the rules of this world?"

Now you can look at what your condition is. Now perhaps you can see what, as an illuminate mind, I am offering you in your own illumination. You will have a god of fear, which is what this establishment is. "Fear God." Or you will have a God of Love that says you are eternal and loving forever, and there will be no compromise to that.

Love is mentioned in Deuteronomy where Moses says to love God no matter what He does to you. And love is in Psalms, where there's a good pastoral setting. But except for that, and I hate to tell you this, it's not mentioned much. There's a great deal of fear of the passion of Love because it would immediately become uncontrollable. Do you see that? "How dare you offer the teaching without according the might of your capacity to teach to a human purpose?"

Here's the Holy Bible, and there was a lot of struggling going on. I assure you that the formulation of this Bible had absolutely no intention – none! – of acknowledging the teachings of Jesus. Are you kidding? How would they get it published? Answer me. You couldn't possibly. Come on. We're under the authority. Who's going to let you publish this? James. You're not going to be able to publish it. He set up the commission through Elizabeth in order for you to do this. You better give thanks to him. You can include God in, but you better not subtract the authority of man to be involved in this or that's blasphemy. Don't you dare tell me that what Jesus teaches does not require King James.

They wouldn't think of doing it. Do you know why? They know that they do depend on him, and they want to get the message out, and they know perfectly well that the message finally is one of fear, any scholar that really teaches it.

Great and manifold were the blessings, most dread Sovereign, which Almighty God, the Father of all mercies, bestowed upon us, the people of England, when first he sent Your Majesty's Royal Person to rule and reign over us. This is the prologue to the King James version of the Bible. You guys laugh at that, but I promise and guarantee you that your idolatry in your relationship with the laws of man is exactly the same. Any dependency on an idol will be a dependency on your own relationship in sickness and death rather than God. I'm not going to do Lesson 76: *I Am Under No Laws But God's*. Look at it!

Also, obviously, King James guarantees your death. You need a sovereign of this world to guarantee you your establishment in this association. And that's exactly what is offered to you here. There's a lot of arse-kissing (pardon me) that goes with this – including the approbation at the end that not only is it not going to be accepted by the papists, the guys who are trying to keep you from reading it at all. I suppose there's progress in the Reformation, isn't there? Because somewhere the teachings of Jesus are so fearful that the constrictions of the last 800 years have been to keep even what He said away from you in order that it could be interpreted by the establishment. Lutherans? Come on.

You said, "No, I want to know what Jesus says directly." You discovered to your surprise that He was teaching you that you could have a direct contact with God without an intermediate association. Why you continue to use an intermediate association remains a mystery. Obviously, you have protested against your condition and established another condition that allows you to continue to protest against the Love of God. Say Amen! Obviously, any protest that you would render would be against a mistreatment that you believe that you are receiving in the condition of your own mind.

This prologue is beautifully funny. I'll just finish it up. *The appearance of Your Majesty, as of the Sun in his strength, instantly dispelled those supposed and surmised mists and gave unto all that were well affected exceeding cause of comfort; especially when we beheld the Government established in Your Highness, and Your hopeful Seed, by an undoubted Title.* I mean, there is no question they're going to blow a lot of smoke in here. When they're all done with it, they're going to admit to the conflict that they experience in the translations and the attempts to bring it together.

In the English language, this is probably the most passionate determination of the creativeness of man inherent in his need to communicate Love that you will find. Obviously, I'm including the Old Testament and the New Testament. You have to remember, this is an attempt at communication of a singular reality based on the separation. It is impossible that those who came together were not being directed to the totality of their intentions to discover the single wholeness of themselves. The value of the *Course in Miracles* is the admission of the incredible communicative devices used by the mind of Jesus to direct your conceptual associations to the creative ability inherent in you, in your need to represent yourself in relationship with separation and the totality of God, which you must now give your whole attention to. That's called forgiveness.

Anyway, they're very much afraid that they're going to get torn down. *And now at last, by the mercy of God, and the continuance of our labours, is being brought unto such a conclusion, as that we have great hopes that the Church of England shall reap good fruit thereby; we hold it our duty to offer it to Your Majesty, not only as to our King and Sovereign, but as to the principal Mover and Author of the work: humbly craving of Your most Sacred Majesty, that since things of this quality have ever been subject to the censures of illmeaning and discontented persons, it may receive approbation and patronage from so learned and judicious a Prince as Your Highness is, whose allowance and acceptance of our labours shall more honour and encourage us, than all the calumniations and hard interpretations of other men shall dismay us. So that if, on the one side, we shall be traduced by Popish Persons at home or abroad, who therefore will malign us, because we are poor instruments to make God's holy Truth to be yet more and more known unto the people, whom they desire still to keep in ignorance and darkness* (that's a little slam at the Catholic Church); *or if, on the other side, we shall be maligned by selfconceited Brethren, who run their own ways, and give liking unto nothing, but what is framed by themselves, and hammered on their anvil; we may rest secure, supported within by the truth and innocency of a good conscience, having walked the ways of simplicity and integrity, as before the Lord; and sustained without by the powerful protection of Your Majesty's grace and favour, which will ever give countenance to honest and christian endeavours against bitter censures and uncharitable imputations.*

The Lord of Heaven and earth bless Your Majesty with many and happy days, that, as his Heavenly hand enriched Your Highness with many singular and extraordinary graces, so You may be the wonder of the world in this latter age for happiness and true felicity, to the honour of that Great God, and the good of his Church, through Jesus Christ, our Lord and only Saviour.

Okay. What we're saying to you is that the idea that Jesus offers you of *every man for himself* is the same idea that you believe that you had to overcome in order to organize civilization, because to the conceptual mind, *every man for himself* means attack, defend and kill. Is there anybody that didn't hear this? This is the entire basis of the *Course in Miracles*. I am declaring to you the power of your own mind through the power of God.

In a very literal sense the teachings of Jesus are *every man to himself* because every man is perfect as God created him. Class, do you understand what I said? That's why it's rejected. To a human being it would appear very chaotic because it would obviously be an attack and defense association separate from the other attack and defense associations. Yet the entire Sermon on the Mount is nothing but an admonition to you to give up this world and come to God, which is obviously not acceptable to you.

Listen to me. The idea of democracy – this is the nature of the civilization of man admitting to the idea of a single authority of God through individual associations. The idea that a man could actually think for himself has always been a danger to the establishment. So all establishments must perform acts of associations of self within the context of the establishment, and do. Do you understand that? So nothing could be more frightful and chaotic than what I am standing up here and offering you in your own mind.

What is the solution? *It's in your own mind.* Once more. The entire teaching of Jesus – or of me or of you when you see it – is that you are the cause of this in your own mind. That's what He says. So you could have all the chaos you want in association with yourself, but it is within *you*, the power to simply say, "No, I am under no laws but God's." That's why they are afraid of you here.

You remember this, and here's your problem (it still may be yours or someone's here): If you believe in a shared association of fear, earth, separation, *and* love, truth and wholeness, you will become a condition of fear. *You cannot serve God and mammon.* (Matthew 6:24) What isn't love is murder. You hear the principle of it, but deny it by the nature of your relationship because that's what you are.

Now I'm teaching fundamental Christianity that says you must undergo an experience of transformation or illumination or be born again to know there's a God. (John 3) And there's no other way you can do it. How come I don't have a million people gathering around me to have the experience? They are very fearful of the experience very simply because it belies the laws of man on which they base their reality. If they have no laws of man, how could they possibly survive on this earth? They couldn't! They absolutely could not.

There would be no way that you could be here except in the establishment of your own constitution of your conceptual reality based on who you think you are. And who you think you are ain't who you are.

"Yes, I am, and I can prove it."

You can't prove it by God, but you can sure as hell prove it by your establishment, which is exactly what you do. But by proving it by your establishment, you prove that you can be a body, get old, sick and die. Yes or no? What's your problem? If you want to get old, sick and die, go ahead. All I've given you is the power to change your mind. The teachings that I'm offering you from Jesus are – if you change your mind, the world will change. When you forgive your brother you will be forgiven.

Does Jesus dare to teach that there is a single God who doesn't show favor to some human beings? You don't realize what I'm offering you. There would be no culture. There would be no civilization if there's only one God and He only loves. Your enemies would have the same power that you have. You go, "Uh-huh," but it's true. Anything outside you could attack you and kill you, based on the power that you have given it in order to be powerless. Yet you are not powerless since your power comes from God and not from yourself. If your power comes from yourself, you are indeed powerless. What a strange idea, that I would try to stand up and teach this to you!

What Jesus really says, and what I'm teaching you, is that reality is the action of an association of a totality of beingness that we call Love. It does not involve establishment or formulation of the containment of the creative power of God, which would be what the human mind is. In no regard would Jesus, or would any awakened mind or would what you have come to discover, give you any possibility of self-conceptual association at all. *It's not there.*

The practice of loving your brother in order to love yourself is simply because you hate your brother and therefore hate yourself. And if you hate yourself, you must also hate what God has created. And if you hate what God has created, you will hate God.

Well, come on. You nod, "yes" at me because I'm very reasonable in my mind. Yet it cannot *not* be that the alternative is in *you* and that's where your fear arises because your fear is of a complete dependence on a single reality rather than on yourself in your own establishment. Yes or no? Certainly! What's hard about that? Nothing, once you begin to see it. Why? You have begun to practice non-defense. You have literally (this is the entire teaching) begun to say, "No, there's an alternative not contained within my own conceptual self." Is that true? Yes. Is that the teachings of the New Testament? Absolutely! God is a God of Love and eternal happiness, not a god of fear and death.

There is no world apart from what you wish, and herein lies your ultimate release. Change but your mind. (Lesson 132) Isn't that amazing!

The secret of salvation is this, says Jesus: *That you are doing this unto yourself. No matter what the form of attack, this still is true. Whoever takes the role of enemy and attacker, still is this the truth. Whatever seems to be the cause of any pain and suffering you feel, this is still true.* (Chapter 27) Sorry about that. So what do you want from me, sufferers? All you've really done is decide not to suffer. But in your decision not to suffer has to be the rejection of this world, and there's no other way that you can do it since the world is a construction of your own mind. How the hell are you going to know there's a God if you don't reject your own constrictions? They are what are binding you to this association with yourself.

Real choice is no illusion. But the world has none to offer. All its roads but lead to disappointment, nothingness and death. There is no choice in its alternatives. Seek not to escape from problems here. The world was made that problems could not be escaped...Yet there is no living thing that does not share the universal Will that it be whole, and that you do not leave its call unheard. Without your answer it is left to die, as it is saved from death when you have heard its calling as the ancient call to life, and understood that it is but your own. (Chapter 31)

I don't know why you wouldn't begin to like the idea that this is true. I know this is going to require (sad as it seems) a rejection of death. Listen: This cannot *not* require your rejection of death. This world has no meaning if you can't die. Yes or no, dead one – one who is determined to stay within his own association and suffer the consequences.

The concept of yourself you now hold would guarantee that you are going to stay in hell forever. Jesus Christ's Sermon on the Mount: Give everything away and come on home.

"He doesn't mean that."

What does He mean if He doesn't mean love your enemy? What does He mean if He doesn't mean if you lust in your mind it's the same as if you lust out there? What do you think He means if He's not telling you that your mind is the structure of this world? That's the whole teaching.

I'm not concerned about what you do with it in your own conceptual association, but only that somewhere you admit fundamentally that you are the cause of it. Then at least you have the alternative of deciding you don't like what you caused. If you decide you don't like what you caused, you may even be able to make a decision that God did not cause this. If you can make that decision, salvation will be very simple for you. But the admission that God did not cause this would be the admission that God is the God of unconditional love rather than the god of fear – and that's where your problem lies.

Did you hear what I said: God is love!

"Oh, what am I going to do?"

Love!!

"That's easy for you to say."

It's easy for me to say because I don't know what you think you are, and I don't know why you would think forgiveness would be required, but any illuminate mind knows perfectly well that this world is not real. If you don't know that yet, you are going to struggle with this world as a part of your fear adverse to the whole mind that knows perfectly well you're perfect as God created you. All I really want you to see is that one or the other is not true.

You have two emotions: One is love and the other is fear, and right now you are fearful. I'll do it once more for you because you like to study the idea of love. Studying the idea of love – establishment – is what fear is. Have you got it? What an idea!

A concept of the self is made by you. It bears no likeness to yourself at all. It is an idol, made to take the place of your reality as Son of God. The concept of the self the world would teach is not the thing that it appears to be. For it is made to serve two purposes, but one of which the mind can recognize. The first presents the face of innocence, the aspect acted on. It is this face that smiles and charms and even seems to love. It searches for companions and it looks, at times with pity, on the suffering, and sometimes offers solace. It believes that it is good within an evil world. (Chapter 31)

The concept that you have of yourself is totally meaningless. It means nothing. Now you see why I am rejected. I am looking at you and telling you that you are locked within your own conceptual self association and that it has nothing whatsoever to do with love. At best, you spy love, and justify your fear in association with eternal reality. Now fear becomes your eternal reality from which you cannot escape. Can you escape from it? No. Is there a way out of it? No. What's the way out of it? *It's not true!* It's not real! The only possible way out is forgiveness; that sin is not real. If sin is not real, why are you concerned?

"Oh, Lord, forgive me, I am a sinner."

You're forgiven.

That's not acceptable to you. Your definition of yourself requires that you be a sinner. It's impossible to forgive someone who believes he's a sinner. Impossible. His whole relationship with himself is based on being able to sin and be guilty of death and murder.

A concept of the self is meaningless, for no one here can see what it is for, and therefore cannot picture what it is. Yet is all learning that the world directs begun and ended with the single aim of teaching you this concept of yourself, that you will choose to follow this world's laws, and never seek to go beyond its roads nor realize the way you see yourself. Now you need some help. And this is the help you are getting from this.

You will make many concepts of the self as learning goes along. Each one will show the changes in your own relationships, as your perception of yourself is changed.

The reason you are in this room with me is to get you to be in a continual change in your conceptual association and nothing else. You were given change by God to guarantee you an alternative not of this association. You are fearful of change and when I offer it to you, you cling to the establishment of your own mind and justify this little place of nothing in relationship with the reality of what you are. Have you got that? Holy mackerel!

What does the world have to do with this? Nothing! Who does it have to do with? *You!* And me, if you want it to. Or the guy sitting next to you. All you would have to do is look at him and say, "I love you as God loves you; let's go home." You act as though that's difficult. Do you know something? It is! It's scary. Do you think you can get away with that?

(He sits between two parishioners and softly says to one: "I love you.") I might invade your privacy. Do you see what you're afraid of? My motivations – because they are yours. We protect each other from Love.

If we were sitting in the theater together and I didn't know you, and I offered you my popcorn, which is really an offering of sharing, you would be very frightened of my motivation. Why? All motivations are frightening. All motivations of this world are what fear is. You are very suspicious of the purpose of the other guy because you are suspicious of your own purpose. It's not yet vicious, but it may likely become vicious very soon (as he reaches for her knee, she slaps his hand).

The two emotions you are capable of in fear are suspiciousness and viciousness. There are no others. The whole nature of fear is being suspicious of the other guy. You're suspicious of yourself. You don't know who you are or what you are doing here; how do you expect him to? But you believe since he is outside of you that he can help you solve the problem. (He kisses his hand; offers it to her, and she kisses it.) You depend on suffering pain in order to offer ourselves relief! That's what we do, isn't it? We teach fear and we teach pain. We teach the little kid, "Don't get burned." And we call it love. What a place to be! "Is it love?" You bet. Why isn't it eternal? Why doesn't it last forever? I'm not taking it away from you. I'm telling you to love as God loves. Love totally in the certainty that there is one universal love. Love doesn't change; love doesn't turn down. You can't get old and you can't die. Why would you love death? Why would you love to suffer pain and sickness and loneliness? Obviously that's why you are here, because you love it! You don't hate it – you hate parts of it. There are other parts you are going to love in order to justify the necessity to suffer in order to be eternal. My whole teaching, teachings of any whole mind, are literally (this is Jesus on the Mount) *this is not what life is. This world is not what life is!* You are going to have to let the dead bury the dead. (Matthew 8:22)

I want to be sure you've got this. What do we have: What is the world? A human condition is an establishment of a god of fear. That's what a god is: a god of time and a god of space. Since you are time and space, your god will be timeful and within your spatial association. I am telling you that you may construct that as life, but that is not what life is. I am telling you directly, in your own mind, that life is eternal and so are you.

Now the manner in which I could teach that could vary to almost anything, including you are dreaming a dream of death; you think you are separate but you're really not – but all I will finally really tell you through this resurrected mind is that your kingdom is not of this world. You came from Heaven, you've come down here and you are going home. If you don't object to words like "Heaven" and "here," you can make very rapid progress with this because the here and now is what you are. If you construct it in time, you will be the here and now that is in time. If you release the necessity of the defense of your fear of God, you will love instantly because God is love.

The God of love does not require your love in order to be what He is. The God of fear and hate requires your fear and hate or your advocacy in order to be a perpetrator of the defense of yourself through the fear of him.

I'll try that one again: Fear of God, which is what the human condition is, since the condition is an invention of god, is a justification for death based on the invention of time.

If there is one thing I knew coming over here, looking at all the people – what I discovered in my own revelation (and what most of you are sharing now) is that death doesn't make any sense. Look at it with me. There is no sense in being sick; you can't die. I'll do it once more for you: You can't die. What's death going to be? Tell me what death is like. You say, "I don't know." What do you mean you don't know. How do you know you can die, then? You won't answer me. You depend on death to justify your own sickness and pain. I'm telling you there is no death.

"Well, I'm still going to be sick and painful."

Well then be sick and painful forever. See? Do you see where you reject me? You are not a body. You cannot get sick and you cannot die. Your body identification is just a justification for death. Yet when I ask you what death is, you say, "I don't know, but everything around me is dying." And you prove it by the demonstration of the body getting old and dying.

You can't die. This is an illusion. I just healed you. Healing is nothing but my determination of your own perfection, regardless of what you think. If you want to bring fear into your own associations, go ahead. Who will you find to justify you? The whole world! Of course! The guy sitting next to you is an image of your own body in your own relationship with yourself. What do you expect him to say to you?

115

You have given him careful instructions to be fearful along with you. That's what you have been taught. You teach God is a god of fear. All of these churches here – the churches of Jesus Christ teach fear of God! That's the most absurd thing I've ever heard. They teach that you have to die in order to get to Heaven. That's the most absurd thing I've ever heard. It's exactly the opposite of the teaching. Death won't work.

The difficult part of it is that your structure of conceptual self is the nature of what separation is. And everything is a reflection of you in that association.

Do you know what would have convinced me? Somewhere I always thought of myself as somehow being able to discern within myself a purpose for myself. And that might include sedating myself because I couldn't stand the pain; all the things that I would do in a need to justify my temporal association – my intellect. And I'm very much aware that your present condition, sitting in these pews, is one of justification for yourself in the arrangement that you have made.

What amazes me is the unwillingness of the so-called intellect of conceptual associations to acknowledge the magnitude of the communicative device of *A Course In Miracles*. I mean that flat out. Don't give me this shit about, "I should study the poetry of it." I know all about that. I can read you a simple lesson from the *Course in Miracles* that contains not only a passion of realization of creative reality, but is constructed so beautifully in the creative purpose of our association with the world that it is virtually impossible to ignore. Your attempts to ignore both the teachings of the *Course in Miracles* and the manner in which it teaches and directs you to teach astonishes a mind that wants to wake up.

The idea that the establishment must reject this beautiful work of art in its entirety in order not to hear what it says is amazing to me. And I'm speaking as an atheist! Listen to me: I'm not speaking to someone who has to do with all the covenants of Moses. It would be impossible if you handed me this, and said, "I want you to do a lesson," and I read, *nothing is outside of you; you are the cause of this; if you defend yourself you are going to be attacked,* that it wouldn't begin with the simple lesson of the necessity for you to forgive. *Forgive and love.* That is not in your vocabulary of entirety of association because you have the requirement of being sinful.

Now, the joy of this lesson is the manner in which you are offered the training device by which you can recognize your own Self. But you must accept the fundamental admission that there's nothing outside of you. Come on, now. You don't have to tell me this is in the *Rig Veda* or the Buddha said it. I'm well aware of that. There is nothing outside of you. In that fundamental admission is salvation, if you will continue with the admission: "If there is nothing outside of me, and I do not know who I am, what I'm doing, where I'm going or why I am here, I will therefore practice the negation of my conceptual objective association in order to discover an alternative not contained within my choices." That's called *A Course In Miracles*. That's a mind training going on in your mind – not out in the world at all. It doesn't have anything to do with the world. It has to do with *you*.

You insist you can turn to the other guy and give your attention to your mutually-shared dream of death. That's absurd. The whole teaching is that I am talking to *you*. *You* are the one that has to undergo the experience of being born again. *You* are the one that has to have the revelatory association. There is nothing outside of *you*!

Obviously this starts with the premise that this *Course* didn't come from this world. Am I able to admit that? I can admit it because that's what it says. I don't have to verify it. I could then pick this up and begin to read it, and begin to read Lesson 121: *Forgiveness Is The Key To Happiness*. And I would immediately say, "Who is the author of this?" I am talking to you as a human being. Obviously somewhere within my association with myself, I had found an alternative that had given me a peace of mind – hopefully that's where you are. I don't know what you are doing sitting here if somewhere you haven't caught a glimpse of an alternative that solved a problem for you that you couldn't solve. That's why you are sitting here with me. I am showing you that all of your problem-solving techniques are going to fail because they solve to death rather than life. But the practice of that, based on the passionate vocabulary of the action of your mind contained in the possibility that you could actually choose God is amazing.

What has irritated the Source of this *Course* more than anything is the simple refusal to admit what it says – not in the rejection of what it says. Obviously you are a rejection of the eternal Love of God. But to deny that this message from out of time teaches that there is no world; teaches you are not real; teaches all pain and death is not true; teaches you never left Heaven; declares to you that you are perfect as God created you is not even admitted. The groups that you formulate won't even admit what it teaches — of course, neither do Christians admit what Jesus teaches. It's the same thing. They simply reject it.

So the necessity for personal, individual transformation is this entire teaching. It cannot be accomplished if you hold a grievance of pain and death against your brother, because your brother is you.

Here is my final declaration on this: There is only one Self, and that Self is *you*. If you manifest yourself as pain and death, so will the guy out there. The guy out there will then suffer the consequences of your mutual denial of God. You have no reason to do that.

Is it possible for you to take these words, admit to your own humanness, and begin to include the power and discernment of your mind (remember, we said *mind* not *might* – soul, heart and mind), to reach an alternative that must be somewhere in your mind? This is an extraordinary idea. Yet it cannot *not* be somewhere since you are searching for it. This is going to require the fundamental acceptance of what you call self questioning. Big deal.

"I've got to carry on a dialogue with myself about this."

You are carrying on a dialogue. That's what you do. You're talking to yourself all the time. I'm telling you that both selves you are talking to are not true. If you shut up long enough in your own mind, you will see an alternative that is all around you. This is the whole teaching. This is what this says. But as long as you justify it in your own association, you are going to be locked in it.

Look in your own mind, just for a second. This is the mind training. Are you holding a grievance against somebody? Come on. It's a fun thing to do. Generally speaking, things are happening outside that you don't like. This is obviously the practice that you are going through in your own enlightenment. In your own realization that there is no world, this is the practice that you would have, isn't it?

Do you know what's tough to teach about this? I'm not concerned about the concepts at all but only the emotion of the concept. I'll do it once more for you: this is a very emotional undertaking because you are nothing but a bundle of emotions. The question is not that; the question is, are you emotionally fear or emotionally loving? If I can get you to see that there is no in-between (which most of you have discovered) then you can release your own fearful self concept which gives you the Love of God which is what you are. Is it that simple?

"How come I wasn't able to do it?"

Because you need some help! The last thing you want to accept help from is your own image of rejection. That's why you crucify Jesus

Christ. The image that you crucify is what your salvation is! If you judge your own savior, you will become the judgment that you have imposed on yourself! The one thing you don't intend to forgive is me. I'm telling you that you are home and perfect and loving as God created you.

And you ask me, "How do you know."

Do you know what my answer is?

"You told me."

I am evolving a great love for the mind capacity of *A Course In Miracles*. Once I got out of the way of my own revelation (and I'm teaching this from revelation) the manner in which this is presented – including that it's in English, in a message you can understand within your own dream, directed specifically to you – is extraordinary. These are from Lessons 121-126: Complexity. Intricacy. Eccentricity. Divergency. All those are in those five lessons. Isn't that amazing? "Well, I'm going to have to look them up." Look them up! Alacrity. Priority. Lots of "...y's" in there.

I want you to understand that this is an offering that you can take with you into the world. It requires practice, not out there, but in your own mind. Everyone who would finally begin to come into this teaching would begin to share with me what I am offering based on first the admission of causation and then on your determination to change your own mind so that the world can change – so that no matter what happens to you out there, it will not affect you.

"The dilemma I have now is that you are asking me to forsake and give up the world."

That's exactly the opposite of what I am doing. I am asking you to give up your own idea about yourself. When you change your mind about yourself, the world will change. If the world does not change it is simply because you are determined to hold onto your own association. You don't like that. And you don't like me telling you that. But it cannot *not* be so.

These are the lessons of the Workbook of *A Course In Miracles*. We will do Lesson 121. This is communication of the very highest order as performed by a mind in its entirety which is actually your mind offering you the solution of yourself. The mind that constructed this is actually you in a different temporal association since all time and space are only organizations of separation coming to the truth. But the verbiage of this lesson, which we would generally pass up in order that we can get to "I'm doing it to myself", is the simple message that if you are doing it to yourself, salvation will be forgiving the acts of your own mind. That may very well include forgiving the acts of your brother. But if the acts of your brother in pain and death are separate from yours, they are unforgivable. This is the Sermon on the Mount: *As I think, I will be. As I am, this world will be.* It cannot be different.

The simpleness of this teaching within your own mental and emotional makeup will afford you a solution through your admission of our need to communicate our love for God and each other rather than reject each other and suffer pain and death. It is very, very important for you to hear that my concern is obviously not of this world at all. I am telling you *there is no world.* I am telling you as a fact of the matter there is no little enclosure of nothing with a trillion, trillion stars outside of yourself. That is not true. Apparently it is true in your mind. I am telling you, *in your mind*, that it is not true. Now you can get to Lessons 130, 131 and 132 because they will tell you that you are going loose the world from all you thought it was within your own association.

I want you to feel the simplicity of this message because it can have a very major effect on you. It's a very simple admission that you Love. You don't even have to announce it to the world. I guarantee you don't have to announce it. There is no action involved in it. What would it have to do with action if all of your action is false – if everything you have identified yourself with is literally a denial of your own Self? The moment that you don't do that, all of the organizations immediately reassociate in your own mind.

The miracle does nothing! It does absolutely nothing. *You* are the do-er that's keeping you from being the miracle that you are.

"It is this I have done. It is this I will undo. I am not going to do this any more."

Who are you talking to? Yourself. Darn right you are.

"How can I figure that out?"

Stop trying to figure it out. Figuring it out is your problem. If you are perfect as God created you, why would you have to figure it out? I'm not talking to this world. This world is a place where life is figured out; where knowledge about yourself must be gained and protected and justified in the super ability to see your conceptual satiation in a rotting bag of nothing. That's what this place is. Jesus says it a little better actually.

You are very joyous about the nothingness that you were? But you are joyous because you ain't it any more. If you're not joyous about it, it is because you are still protecting it. Did you get that? So protection is what the fear of this message is. Joy is the admission of the message and the experience thereof, because it is impossible to have a message that you are not experiencing. The question is not that; the question is what message do you want to hear within your own mind? To say that the *Course in Miracles* doesn't teach this, is insanity of the highest order. I'm talking to any teacher. At the minimum you are going to have to admit that this is what this says. The avoidance of it in writing books about the *Course* is nuts. It's totally meaningless.

Lesson 121: *Forgiveness Is The Key To Happiness.* What's the key to happiness?

Audience: Forgiveness.

What? Forgiveness! Really?! "The hell with it. I don't care what it is, I'm going to forgive it."

Does that involve the indifference to the crap of this world? Does that generally mean you've tried to figure it out and can't? That's what your happiness is. As soon as you stop trying to figure it out, you begin to have happiness experiences. What did you do? Did you turn your will and your life over to God?

"Well, that was back then. What am I going to do now?"

Why don't you try it again?

Listen: *Here is the answer to your search for peace.*

Are you searching for peace? Who here isn't searching for peace and eternal happiness? What do you have to do to get it? Forgive!

"I'm never going to do that."

I know. That's why you can never find peace and happiness. Who are you complaining to?

Here is the key to meaning in a world that seems to make no sense. The key to giving meaning to what doesn't make any sense is forgiveness because the conflict is in the retention of the grievance. Grievances cannot make any sense because you don't know what you are grieving about. You can objectify it and believe that that is true, but you cannot know. Remember, now, we're on Lesson 121. There is a presumption that you have done the first 50 lessons. What I just did was review the first 12 lessons of *A Course In Miracles*. That was the requirement for you to release the grievances that you are feeling.

Here is the way to safety in apparent dangers that appear to threaten you at every turn, and bring uncertainty to all your hopes of ever finding quietness and peace. I'm very uncertain about whether I'm going to be able to find this for all of the reasons that there are because my uncertainty about myself and the protection thereof is what a denial of God is.

The association of yourself that is uncertain about who you are is nuts! It isn't that you have not tried to establish it, but only that it could not be true. *Here are all questions answered.* Where? In that forgiveness is the key to happiness. *Here, now, is the end of all uncertainty ensured at last.*

"Yeah, but then I would have to be as God created me. If I exercised forgiveness, non-judgment – if I don't judge myself and this world in association with myself – I will be empowered with the eternal Love of God's Mind?"

Here is the condition of an unforgiving mind. Everyone in this world that you meet on this street, in this grocery store, on that television set, walking around here, this is a description of him as unforgiving in his fear of God. It is literally a position of unforgiving and defense of his association with himself. That's what fear is. If I can get you to stop trying to measure other human associations within contexts of what is not going to be real no matter how you identify it, your solution can be evident to you.

Do you know the act that I just performed for you that you don't want to do? I brought your enemy and your friend together for you. This next lesson actually teaches you to be a Holy Spirit arbitrator between your own thoughts. I'll do this for you because it is a practice that you have to do in your own thoughts:

The unforgiving mind (the human condition) *is full of fear, and offers love no room to be itself.* Could you hear that? Love is going to be what it is anyway. It doesn't depend on you to be love. Love is what God is. Love is what eternity is. But if you keep closing off love in your own fear, in your own unforgiving action that you can be wrong through guilt, there's no room for love there. "Make way for love through the release of the necessity of you to defend yourself," is the entire teaching.

The unforgiving mind is full of fear, and offers love no room to be itself, no place where it can spread its wings in peace and soar above the turmoil of the world. The unforgiving mind is sad, without the hope of respite and release from pain. It suffers and abides in misery, peering about in darkness, seeing not, yet certain of the danger lurking there. The unforgiving mind is torn with doubt. I wish I had said that. Doubt tears! Doubt splits your mind into separate camps. It is literally what the schism is. The schism is the apparent tearing off, which is what doubt is. You tore yourself off from your own reality and now doubt. Now I've got parables of seamless garments and a bunch of others – it's not rending your own garments; it won't do you any good.

The unforgiving mind is torn with doubt, confused about itself and all it sees; afraid and angry, weak and blustering, afraid to go ahead, afraid to stay, afraid to waken or to go to sleep, afraid of every sound, yet more afraid of stillness; terrified of darkness, yet more terrified at the approach of light. What can the unforgiving mind perceive but its damnation? What can it behold except the proof that all its sins are real? Which one of you wrote that? That's real nice. It sounds like a condemnation of the unforgiving mind.

The unforgiving mind sees no mistakes, but only sins. The definition of a mistake in an unforgiving mind is what sin is, and must be compared with other mistakes to make them more sinful rather than less because one totally forgiven act on your brother would forgive the whole world. What do you do? Organize different forms of sin? You have misdemeanors and felonies? What a strange place to be. *It looks upon the world with sightless eyes, and shrieks as it beholds its own projections rising to attack its miserable parody of life.* Nobody reads this. It's talking about you, isn't it? *It wants to live, yet wishes it were dead. It wants forgiveness, yet it sees no hope. It wants escape, yet can conceive of none because it sees the sinful everywhere.*

The unforgiving mind is in despair, without the prospect of a future which can offer anything but more despair. That's literally true. Are all things outside of me the same? They are projections of my own mind.

"Well, if that's true, why can't I just forgive one thing?"

You can! Of course. But in order to do that, all things would have to be the same to you. It's an amazing idea. Wow!

Yet it regards its judgment of the world as irreversible, and does not see it has condemned itself to this despair. It is corrupt. And it can't see

123

apart from it. It has already judged, hasn't it. It has already determined the outcome. But in already determining the outcome, isn't it already gone? So everything that it sees will give it an outcome that is already gone. No wonder I felt the futility of this place. No matter what I did it was going to result in me getting old and dying anyway. Are you still accepting that? Look at yourself. All of your alternatives are based on being here and getting old and dying because you refuse to forgive – refuse to give up your grievance against God and this world.

It thinks it cannot change, for what it sees bears witness that its judgment is correct. It does not ask, because it thinks it knows. It does not question, certain it is right. The practice that is emerging in most of you is always asking rather than telling. If it begins with, "I don't know what anything is," everything I see in this practice I will not let be a judgment of my previous self. Do you hear what I am offering you? Do you practice the *Course in Miracles*? Do you? That's what it says. It says that everything you see is a projection back into your own mind based on the grievance that you hold in your separation from God. If you don't do that, it will immediately disappear because it is a correspondence of your own mind.

Why is that hard? Because the practice of it would be a denial of what you see. The minimum solution to your problem in mind training is to ask it what it is because you don't know. And if you don't decide previously what it's going to be, it will open all the doors around you of the continuation of the new Self that emerges. What lesson is that? Lesson 7. "I don't know what anything is. I'm going to ask it what it is."

Then what do you do, ask the church pew what it is? Does the church pew know what it is? Of course. Why wouldn't it? It's an integrated association of itself. What is it? Life! Is everything Life? Is that church pew alive? Who says so? "I do." Why? Is it going to be alive whether you say so or not? There aren't going to be different kinds of life? Everything is alive!

What's the difference between animacy and inanimacy? Who wants to know? I guess inanimacy is the idea of death, which is really absurd – the idea that things die.

Here is an interesting idea: *Forgiveness is acquired.* Because you think sin is real. Sin is not actually real. There isn't any such place as this world. You have *acquired* the idea of your conceptual sins, and in that sense, forgiveness is an acquirement – a requirement. But it is not a requirement based on your old associations, but of the release of them. The requirement then of the miracle is that you release your identity and experience the joy of your own perfection. *It is not inherent in the mind, which cannot sin. As sin is an idea you taught yourself, forgiveness must be learned by you as well, but from a Teacher other than yourself, Who represents the other Self in you.* And if you would like to have that be Jesus of Nazareth, I would be delighted that you do so, since everything that He tells you affirms that He is with you and is, in fact, the whole Self of you, offering to your false self the truth of what you really are.

So walking around with you is a Teacher who knows perfectly well who you are and is answering every question that you ask if you will allow Him to do so. *Through Him you learn how to forgive the self you think you made, and let it disappear.* Disappear! Really?! Oh, yes. *Thus you return your mind as one to Him Who is your Self, and Who can never sin* or be separate.

Each unforgiving mind presents you with an opportunity to teach your own mind how to forgive itself. How is that done? Don't judge him. Regardless of what he does, it will not be true. Stop organizing in your own mind what is not true with what is also not true. Your judgment is going to be false no matter how you judge, because there is no such thing as judgment. The only possibility of judgment would be the judgment of separation with wholeness, which would be impossible for wholeness and only possible for an instant in separation, because the instant of judgment in separation would have to include the entirety of the whole. So that while God does not judge, by including yourself in with God's Mind, you will lose the capacity and necessity to judge, which is what fear and death is.

This is an amazing idea. See if you can hear this: *Each one awaits release from hell through you, and turns to you imploringly for Heaven here and now.* And if you refuse to recognize yourself in your relationship with God – this is tough for you – and continue to justify him as you have made him while he is imploring you each moment to forgive him so that he can be forgiven, shame on you as *A Course In Miracles* student. You're going to stand up here and give him an identity based on what he thinks he is. Actually it's not what *he* thinks he is; it's what *you* think he is. Do you understand me? You justify him – and I know you love to do it, and I know you're going to do it, and I know you're going to justify his fear because that's the justification of your own – it's why you're here. By justifying his separate body association, you justify your own and condemn yourself to the Old Covenant, where we must fear God together but our God is more powerful than our fear. That's nonsense.

All I've led you back to is your requirement that you change your mind. When it doesn't work, it's simply that you would rather be who you are than what you really are. I guess that requires practice. Here's why. It requires practice because it's *all only in your own mind.* If you've decided that he is sinful because you are and attempt to repair him outside of yourself, you must fail because he's not outside of yourself. Do you hear me? You can't possibly repair the effects of your own mind. You will just get other effects that continue to sin in relationship with yourself. Got that?

It has no hope, but you become its hope. Because you are its hope! *And as its hope, do you become your own. The unforgiving mind must learn through your forgiveness that it has been saved from hell. And as you teach salvation, you will learn. Yet all your teaching and your learning will be not of you, but of the Teacher Who was given you to share.*

The unforgiving mind does not believe that giving and receiving are the same. I'm going to wrap this up now for those of you who are here. You are doing this to yourself. The emotions of your comparison of yourself with something separate from you is what fear is. Each time that you separate something within your own mind, you separate it in its entirety and become two separate pieces within your own mind, neither of which is true. This is the definition of the ego, or your conceptual self. The moment that you release that identity, you experience the wholeness of you.

I'm going to give you something from my whole mind that may be difficult for you. I hope not. One separation from God or from reality, based on a conceptual association of self, will be the same as all separations. Tell me you heard that. That is, the justification for the conceptual association of separation will not make it more real because it's different than another one. They are all going to be the same. But if that is true, and you as a human being are a concept of my own mind, if I forgive *you*, singularly and only you and no one else, I will have forgiven myself in my entirety because there is nothing outside of me. I'm only meeting myself.

Do you love yourself?

"Well, I'm working on it."

Why don't you let God love you and then you don't have to worry about it. The self that you want to love is unlovable. You couldn't possibly love him, and I don't blame you. How could you love your own guilt and the pain that you're in?

Here's the practice. *The unforgiving mind does not believe that giving and receiving are the same. Yet we will try to learn today that they are one through practicing forgiveness toward one whom you think of as an enemy, and one whom you consider as a friend.*

Notice that it doesn't ask you to practice finding an enemy and forgiving him. It doesn't say that. That's too late. What it does say in your mind-training procedure is to find somebody that you really don't care much about and somebody who you trust and love, and compare those two in your mind. Do you see this? See, both of them are separate from your mind.

Is there anyone here who hasn't had an experience of liking separate people who don't like each other? Yes or no? Yes. And you'll say to the one, "Geez, he's really a great guy." You have reorganized it sufficiently. There's nobody who hasn't had this. You say, "I can't see why you can't forgive him." You're always acting as an arbitrator. What this really says is, the true arbitrator of you in your relationship with yourself will always give you the answer if you won't judge the evil from the good and that's an action that's actually going on right now in your own mind.

Will this work? It's an extraordinary idea that it would take the practice. Obviously, it would take the practice of the release of your judgment. And obviously, you then are still going to see something that you love and something that you hate. So the action of your mind in the admission of the Will of God will relieve you of the necessity? That's an amazing idea.

I'll just finish this. *Yet we will try to learn today* (we are going to *try*) *that they are one.* They're actually the same because they're both thoughts in my own mind. They're the same because they're in my mind. I hate one of them, and I love one of them. Really?! But he's become a condition of my love. He has become a condition of my enemy. You and I love each other because we can hate him together. Once more: You and I love one another because we can hate the other guy.

I'm going to ask you to take your mind – your mind, individually – to take somebody you hate and somebody you love and practice bringing them together in your own mind rather than practice the continuing separation (Old Covenant) of the justification for your shared fear with the exclusion of someone who God loves equally with you. Do you hear that? That's what's not acceptable to you. Yet the practice must be in your own mind, because that's where the problem is. I have got you certain now that the problem is not outside yourself. You're making me very happy. Because if the problem is not outside yourself, you can admit that you have one problem, that's your judgment; and one solution, don't judge. It doesn't require any more than that.

I don't know if this would actually work. *Yet we will try to learn today that they are one through practicing forgiveness toward one whom you think of as an enemy, and one whom you consider as a friend.* Friend – enemy. *And as you learn to see them both as one, we will extend the lesson to yourself, and see that their escape includes your own.*

This is actually going on in your mind! If you look for just a moment on what you hate and what you love, and don't judge it in relationship with your own mind, it creates a holy instant of the reality of who you really are. If you continue in that aspect, you will not have to judge your own self against who you really are, but simply will become the non-judgment of the separation that you have made between yourself and yourself.

Listen. *And as you learn to see them both as one, we will extend the lesson to yourself, and see that their escape includes your own.* Where two or more are gathered, you are there in the perfection of your Self. And believe it or not, since you are the savior of the world, you can actually bring the world together through your forgiveness of yourself with God and the offering of forgiveness to your brother – as tough as that may seem to you. Why? There's nothing outside of your mind. You are in your own hallucination anyway, aren't you?

Begin the longer practice periods (this is half an hour) *by thinking of someone you do not like.* Everybody? Come on. I want to see if you can do it. Take me out of the equation. Think of somebody else. Everybody think of *who seems to irritate you, or to cause regret in you if you should meet him.*

"I don't even want to meet him. I'm so guilty, I'm going to avoid him."

It doesn't matter what it is. Have we got it all? Irritates, regrets, or *one you actively despise, or merely try to overlook.* That's such a beautiful thing. It covers virtually all of your conditions – all of your conditions of hate and dislike are pretty much covered. Aren't they?

"I'll put him out of my mind altogether." "I'm afraid to look at him." "I hate him." Actively: "I'm going to get him" – which is usually what the condition ends up as.

It does not matter what the form your anger takes. Anger. You're pissed. That's why you are defending yourself. Your condition of fear (which is what anger is) is angry at God for causing you all of these problems. Yet God didn't cause the problems; you are causing them to yourself. You have every right to be angry, but what is your anger with? *A slave to death is a willing slave.* You change your mind about yourself and you're going to be very happy. That's the teaching.

It does not matter what the form your anger takes. You probably have chosen him already. He will do.

"Well, I haven't chosen him, but I chose her."

That's called "missing the mark." That's missing the mark entirely. That's deciding to concentrate on a specific.

Now close your eyes and see him in your mind, and look at him a while. "I hate to look at this sonofabitch." Everybody try it. *Try to perceive some light in him somewhere.* This may manifest itself as: "Well, I know he's doing the best he can." See the sympathy? "I know he's really working on this. I know that when I went through this..." All of the things that are involved in your own mind will pertain to the most ugly enemy you have if you will let them. Is that so?

Let's see if I can teach this: *Try to perceive some light in him somewhere; a little gleam which you had never noticed. Try to find some little spark of brightness shining through the ugly picture that you hold of him.* I promise and guarantee you that directly behind your association of the projection of your own ugliness, literally behind the projection of *your own* ugliness in the thing you hate, is exactly the same Christ who's shining behind the thing that you love – that all of our Christs together are singular, not based on our body judgments of ourselves. That's what we call "looking through," isn't it?

Look at this picture till you see a light somewhere within it, and then try to let this light extend until it covers him, and makes the picture beautiful and good. Does this work? Will this work? I'm going to include it in with somebody that I love. But that would be an indiscriminate love of my association with God, wouldn't it?

What I'm describing to you is what most of you are doing. Can you hear this? What I'm describing to you is actually what you are doing now in your own mind. And the joy that you're feeling is nothing but your release of your need to defend yourself from the ugliness and hate that you felt about him. Lesson 135: *If I Defend Myself I Will Be Attacked* by those projections in my own mind.

Look at this changed perception for a while, and turn your mind to one you call a friend. This is exactly the opposite of what you thought you had to do. If you can hear this as mind-training, you can leave here with me. "I have seen the light in my enemy. I will now give it to my friend. My presumption was that my friend and I already shared love. That was **not** true. We had shared our hatred for the other guy." This is an incredible teaching! I know it's a practice, but it would be very reasonable to me. As a psychologist, as anyone, I would say, "I see what you're doing. You're trying to get me to forgive my enemy and, using the forgiveness of my enemy, to forgive my friend." Of course! Because your friendship is based actually on hatred and greed and separation. What an amazing idea!

Look at the changed perception for a while and turn your mind to one you call a friend. Try to transfer the light and love you learned to see around your former "enemy" to him. Perceive him now as more than friend to you. Don't reduce Jesus to your friendship. Let that Christ be more than a friend to you. Let It be your surety of who you are in your relationship with God rather than yourself. What an extraordinary lesson!

...for in that light his holiness shows you your savior, saved and saving, healed and whole. What an extraordinary idea – that that would actually work is really extraordinary.

Then let him offer you the light you see in him, and let your "enemy" and friend unite in blessing you with what you gave them. That's called the "Circle of Atonement." *Where two or more are gathered I am there.* (Matthew 18:20) There's no such thing as two. You cannot have an enemy and a friend without involving yourself. If yourself is involved in the distinction, you will be separate. If yourself is involved in the inclusion, you will become the Holy Spirit, or you will use the vacancy between your enemy and your friend to allow it to become whole and lovely as God created you without continuing to distinguish between your enemy and your friend.

It's interesting that the practice is with your enemy, because actually you love to hate your enemy and hate to love your friend. But that's tough. You hate to love him, because it's an admission of the necessity to protect yourself. Could you hear that? Then you can hate the other guy together and keep him separate. What a condition to be in!

Now are you one with them, and they with you. Now have you been forgiven by yourself. Do not forget, throughout the day, the role forgiveness plays in bringing happiness to every unforgiving mind, regardless of what you thought it was, *with yours among them. Every hour tell yourself:*

Forgiveness is the key to happiness. I will awaken from the dream that I am mortal, fallible and full of sin, and know I am the perfect Son of God.

Is this actually a book that you could actually practice? Does it work? Is this working for you? What does it have to do with this place of loneliness and death? Nothing! By changing my mind about who I am, the world must change.

"Well, it doesn't seem to be working."

It's working perfectly each moment because this world is over. You are simply remembering it as pain and death.

So that's our Bible lesson for today. Thank you for putting up with that. The solution is very simple. You have a god of fear if you're here. I have a God of love who creates everything perfect. I don't have any enemies because there's only one God who creates perfectly. You have enemies because you believe your god is different from someone else's and therefore has more power to control your self in your own guilt.

"That's much too simple."

It's perceptually very simple, but difficult because you are the conception of it. And that's what you reject. *You!* All I could possibly be offering you is the re-association of yourself with Eternal Life. All I could possibly be talking about is *you.* Is that okay with you? Is it okay if I don't see you separately from being perfect? Is it okay if I forgive the enemy that's sitting next to you as much as I forgive you? Or will that disturb you?

You are going to begin to trust me with this, but you can't trust it without forgiving your brother. So you appear to trust me, but you separate me, who has now become your trusted friend who walks with you, and reject anybody else. What you've really rejected is your own Self. You can do that with some teachers, but you can't do that with me.

Jesus would say, "I'll walk with you as long as you need me." But I'll constantly be offering you the solution to your problem, not based on your problem, but on me as your solution. Obviously, if I abide with you all the time, you cannot be in sin because I am resurrected. And since I am you, you are not here either, your definition of yourself notwithstanding.

What you're going to discover is that these teachings of Jesus in the *Course In Miracles* and Sermon on the Mount and all the stuff that goes with it are going to become more and more exciting to you.

"Well, the god of the Old Testament is very valuable because he's the god of fear. I don't care whether it's the Old Testament or what it is, I must fear God."

Why? No one will answer me. Why? It doesn't make any sense to fear God. The basis of your reality is to fear God, but it doesn't make any sense. Wow. Are you all alone in the Universe as you've been constructed in your own dream? Are you waking up? Are you guys now sharing the dream of Love, which is going to eliminate your necessity to be in this place at all? Notice how you require a place of that total admission that you share together. That's the basis of forgiveness. That's why you need your brother, because he's the other part of your mind that you have refused to forgive. Remember, when you split him off, you split yourself off. Now you have two splits that you've been trying to share.

Now, I'm a big help to you because I'm not from here. If you could understand that I'm not from here, or admit it, you could see immediately that what I read you could not possibly be from here. It's impossible that this lesson be from here. I want to know who wrote it. Tell me you did, and I'll tell you, you have an illuminate mind. It could not *not* have been written by somebody who has discovered the difference in himself and this world and recognizes that *he is not of this world*. While he may perceive other associations temporarily in time in that moment, he knows perfectly well that he has awakened from his own dream of death and is not from here.

So if I suddenly walk up to you and say, "Are you awake?" and you say, "Yes," all that really means is, I am not judging my brother anymore. That's a real happening that you may not be sharing with us yet.

And you cannot share it as long as you believe that somehow this one is illuminate and this one isn't. What the hell good is that going to do? You come to the Academy and act as though some people are more illuminate than others. That's pure crap! Either you are illuminate or no one is. Now, if you can accept that from me, you won't be here very long because that's the demand that I'm making and that's the demand you reject. And as long as you can judge some of us as being more illuminate than others, you can stay un-illuminate yourself, because you can strive for something that's outside of you so you could find it. It's not possible.

Are you all okay? You have unhappiness built into you. Some of you have more mourning built into you than others, but come on, give me a break! Then you can justify mourning. This is one of the topics that I was going to read you about love as used in the Old Testament. They call him "the crying prophet," Jeremiah. And he's going to teach you that you must mourn. And that's certainly true, but why would you keep it up if you are the cause of your own mourning? How long are you going to sit on your own pity pot and intend to justify the grievance of the world? You can't do it long around me, because I'm not going to give you any sympathy. You can always go out and find somebody to talk to because they need you to be sick so they can be well. By comparing your sickness with their wellness, they are well. So they have to keep you sick in order to be who they are. Now you call them "care-takers." They take care of each other to ensure their own deaths together. What an absurdity! I sound like Mary Baker.

Your responsibility is to stand up and walk into that room and heal it. *You heal it not by anything you say or do but by your very presence.* By your very presence is that association made whole. Christian Science. It's impossible he's not healed because there's healing all around him. When you release the defense of your own mind in the projection of your own self, he is healed and he has absolutely nothing to say about it at all. He can deny it, but he cannot make it not true because there is only healing.

The other thing is, it's nice to be heard around this place. I guarantee you that yesterday, what I am teaching you, or 2000 years ago, when I stood up and said, "You are only the Love of God and God is not fearful," you denied me exactly as you're denying me now because 2000 years ago was last week. It only just happened within this association.

The secret of salvation is but this:
That you are doing this unto yourself.
No matter what the form of the attack, this still is true.
Whoever takes the role of enemy and of attacker,
still is this the truth.
Whatever seems to be the cause
of any pain and suffering you feel, this is still true.
For you would not react at all to figures in a dream
you knew that you were dreaming.

CHAPTER 5

You Are Not
Of This World

Do you notice what Jesus did when He was asked a question for which there was no answer? He wrote with his finger in the sand. John, Ch. 8, starts with the story of the scribes and Pharisees stoning a whore. *And they ask Jesus: Now Moses in the law commanded us that such should be stoned: but what sayest thou? ...But Jesus stooped down, and with his finger wrote on the ground.* (John 8:5-6) What's He going to say? If He answers either yes or no, He's in trouble. So after He writes in the sand for a while, He says, *He that is without sin among you, let him first cast a stone at her.* And they eventually all walked away – the oldest ones walked away first.

You will not hear me in the condition of your separation. I mean that literally. You cannot hear me. In the next verse in John, Jesus will say you are very fearful of this message. The world is very fearful of this message simply because it is the denial for the necessity of existence. I know you are actually surprised to hear that, but all that I would ever tell you as what you apparently believe to be some sort of enlightened mind is that there is no necessity for your existence. You act as though somehow you are shocked that that's what I've been trying to tell you. You must have eased into that somewhere. But the fact of the matter is that all I would ever tell you is that there is absolutely no necessity for you to participate in the conflict and evil and sickness and death of this world. Is that what I am telling you? To you now sitting in this congregation, that is sort of an exciting prospect! That would be one of the necessities of beginning to hear a real alternative which I am offering you to the condition in which you find yourself.

You are going to be very surprised with your new minds. The human beings are going to continue to attack you. What is difficult for them to see is any justification for their need to get old and die is literally an attack on God. It would have to be. Any separation is a form of defense, and any form of defense would have to be a defense against God because there isn't anything but God. I'm not going to get into the theology. My curiosity is only whether somewhere in this association of time, dedicated in this moment of death, you could somehow gain an entree where you could say: "Isn't it okay that this is not true? Isn't it all right that you are perfect as God created you? Would it be okay if this were true?" Notwithstanding that you don't believe it. Notwithstanding that you are determined not to accept it. That's not what we're asking. We're asking: will you allow it to even be considered – or being unconsidered, will it allow you to be here and simply say what it says?

This statement of unconditional love and wholeness has always been attacked. It has always been denied by this world. That is not true because I say it's true. It is true because heretofore your mind has been the denier and the attacker of reality. Now we're into some real nice teaching. You must awaken from this condition of separation. The assistance being offered you, if you will accept it, will show you the Kingdom of Heaven. Can you image presenting to the world – have you any idea the magnitude of actually attempting to present to the world *A Course In Miracles*? And this is the end of this association. Some of you will say, "Well, anybody can present the *Course In Miracles*." It is exactly the opposite. The difficulties you are encountering now are prime, original examples of how difficult it is to present the teachings of Jesus to this world. Why? It's unconditional love. You are in a sinful place where the requirement for judgment and reciprocity is the existent association of space/time.

I'm going to give you a direction in your individual determination to present the certainty of your own perfection as created by Almighty God. It's that simple. You laugh now because it has become clear to you, somewhere. There has been an intercession in your own conceptual self, sufficient to offer you an alternative of your own reality. And the whole world disappears. Suddenly there was just the whore who was nothing but a statement of a capacity to spread life in limitation (or to use the power of God) and the Savior. He says to her, "Who is left to condemn you?" Except herself. The key to this is that the condemnation occurred in the original association. It is interesting that it is a female and she's got to go out and find another male in order to continue to commit the propagation which is what sin is. Is there such a thing as legal propagation? No.

Jesus tries to teach this, and nobody likes it. Sanctification for death is what legal propagation is. Did I get that? This is a strange place! Are you going to study that a little bit? This world justifies the laws of this world. I take this too far, and you don't like it. It begins to make you uneasy because you have sanctified death, "Till death do us part." For goodness sake, what do you think you swore to? You didn't swear, "Till life takes us to God." You swore to "death us do part!" Didn't you?

And then Jesus says, "Where I'm going you can't go." And the people said, "Oh, you're going to die, huh?" He said, "No, I'm going to live – you're dead." You already told me "till death do you part." You are depending on the institutions of this world to guarantee you your own temporalness. If you could get the *Course In Miracles* into the world, you'd be able to read this to them, directly. That's what this says, that you are depending on death and I am threatening you with Life. What do you do to prove that you can die? You'll kill me. He'll say that. In John 8, Jesus will say, "Watch what you are going to do. You are going to kill me." You don't want me to read you that. If you opened up John 8, He will say that! You as Pharisee, as Temple, will kill me because I am offering you eternal life and salvation. Then you say, "It won't say that." Yes, oh yes. You must kill the Christ in order to stay identified as that separate association in your own mind.

The interesting thing on this occasion is that the innocence of the lawyer is as contagious as your attempts at dying. That is, the continuing need to assert the defense of yourself is easily transformed by one completely innocent association. Do you see? This is the whole *Course In Miracles*. It is nothing but a declaration of our faith in the risen man/God Jesus. Through that He says, "If you'll acknowledge me, you will enter into the Kingdom with me." I just went on to the next page. Why is that so difficult? Because I came and stood before you and said, "I'm not from here. I'm from the Kingdom of God."

I can open this up and read it to you, and see how difficult it is for the world. "The world cannot see me." It will say that. What will be the addition on that? "You can see me." That's the requirement. Not that the world can see me, because the world is the result of the your not seeing. I'm just turning the pages. If you change your mind, the world will change.

I am offering you, obviously, a solution to your "problem" of life. Now, if your identity has solved the problem in your association with your need to die, there is no possibility that you will hear this message, because the solution of your father Abraham has been an invention of time to retain yourself separate from reality. Very simply, any chronicles, any laws that you make are timeful demonstrations of your capacity of acknowledgment that Abraham is your father. Abraham is not your Father! I'm just giving you the fact of the matter. No human condition is what you are. That is a threat. Why? It is a threat to the existence of Abraham. That has nothing to do with whether Abraham is good or bad. It has to do only with the fact that Abraham is not what you are, that all of the consequences that are involved in your determination to be a human being have no causation. I'm teaching the *Course* for a minute – that the cause of Abraham is not true. The cause of this place is not so. Into this impossible situation comes Jesus of Nazareth, or comes you as a teacher who has evolved through the illumination or transformation of your apparent conditional reality the simple certainty that there is one single universal creating whole mind, which is God, of which you are a total part. That's what it says.

I need to know that you will admit that's what that says. I expect you to deny it because you are the denier. What we are interested in now, very simply, is: Will the *Course In Miracles*, which is obviously the word of Jesus of Nazareth, risen from the dead, not in time, telling you that you are perfect, be allowed to be presented to the world? It is really that simple. Heretofore, it has not been. For most associations, it is not even relevant to the problems that they are having because it's offering them a solution in which they have absolutely no interest whatsoever. How can I help you in this congregation when the first thing I tell you about your problems is that they are not true?! That's the fact of the matter.

The first thing Jesus will say to you is, "What are you worried about? You are perfect as God created you." Is that so? If it becomes relevant at all to you, you will kill me to demonstrate your own relevance, quite literally. If it is not relevant, you don't hear me at all – you just go off somewhere. Obviously, there's nothing I can do about that. The acknowledgment of the confrontation is the beginning of salvation. The acknowledgment of this at all – this is my *Time Magazine* letter. The teachings of Jesus are nothing but a sustained confrontation with your determination that you come from Abraham – from this world of pain and death, rather than from Heaven. Does everybody hear that? Would they print that in *Time Magazine*? I doubt it.

Now, if it has reached a point where it is sufficiently relevant, and that's why I did the confrontation with the gnat-gaggers. Like Jesus would say, "Look at you, you are all completely nothing." That's a direct confrontation, isn't it? And you are prepared somewhere to support me in that endeavor? What you are saying is, "I am a follower of Jesus, who is going to confront, deny and apparently attack the world." Obviously this world is being attacked by God. What the hell would be attacking it except that?

This is a step out of time, isn't it? The reason that I'm talking to you this morning is that I want it to be perfectly clear to you, at least conceptually – this is pure *Course* now, and no one will read it. Obviously this is the *Obstacles to Peace*; this is the *Laws of Chaos*. It says very simply: This world is an attack on God. Everything that it does, any form of attack, would have to be an attack on God because God is all form, God is all reality. Any form of defense would have to be a defense against God. And you're saying, "That's right,"and hearing me, at least conceptually. Now, this will evolve your practice of no longer confronting yourself in your own association. That's why, if we could get the *Workbook* out to the world, the 120s–130s, it would say, "If I defend myself, I am attacked." We have taken a great step – that the Kingdom of God is within you, haven't we? We have taken that step.

Good morning, and welcome to the Sunday School Class of the New Christian Church. We are reading today from scripture, New Testament, John, Chapter 8, after His confrontation with the rock-throwers:

Though I bear record of myself, yet my record is true: for I know whence I came, and whither I go. (John 8:14) I know who I am; you don't. All this is going to say is, "I'm Godly and you are still a human being." It's going to say that I have had the experience. If you will accept me, you will have the experience. An astonishing idea: *...for I know whence I came, and whither I go. But ye cannot tell whence I* *come and whence I go.* You can't. You are too slow. I am always going and coming. You are always staying here. That's what that says. I know perfectly well that I come from the Father, am here for a moment and go Home. You can't know that because you are stuck here. You are actually stuck in this place within your own mind. I am teaching you a miracle, an enlightenment of your own mind.

Ye judge after the flesh; I judge no man. (John 8:15) That's a big statement. You judge in association; I don't judge you at all because you are not true. I judge you from the truth of God which has nothing to do with you.

It is also written in your law that the testimony of two men is true. I am one that bear witness of myself, and the Father that sent me beareth witness of me. (John 8:17-18) Of myself, I do nothing. From the Father, we can forgive each other. If you will forgive me the message that I bring you, you will be in salvation with me. By refusing my simple message of your perfection, you attack and kill me in the relationship of yourself. It is an amazing idea.

I go my way, and ye shall seek me, and shall die in your sins; whither I go, ye cannot come. Then said the Jews: Will he kill himself? because he saith, Whither I go, ye cannot come. And he said unto them, Ye are from beneath; I am from above; ye are of this world; I am not of this world. (John 8:21-23) Let me see you stand up and say that. You don't have to believe it, but you do have to stand up and say, "I believe that He was not of this world." That is the minimum requirement. To follow Jesus, you would have to say, "I believe He was not of this world." Through my belief, I can come to know it is true and have come to know it is true. Therefore, I am not of this world! You may still be of this world, but I am offering you the Kingdom of Heaven! Somewhere, won't I have to tell you that your father is a liar? I don't understand why you would persist in pretending to teach Jesus and allow for the world, if there is no allowance for the separation and death in the teachings of a whole mind. Yes or no? All right, but I'm just offering you the problem. There is no solution to the problem of pain and death, except the beginning acknowledgment of its unreality, which must be contained within your own memory, and the progression through the transformation of your mind that that is true. Here is the problem:

I said therefore unto you, that ye shall die in your sins (separation)*; for if ye believe not that I am he, ye shall die in your sins.* (John 8:24) That must be true because I am a reflection of your own mind, and if you don't believe I am the Savior of the world, I cannot be that, and you will die by the denial of me. Quite literally you will deny by the denial of your brother's Saviorship. We can't get that into the world. What that says is if I deny any association of my mind, I am literally denying God since God is everything. While I may deny my own associations, I cannot deny them in truth because denial is not what truth is. Any denial would be denial of God, wouldn't it? Any affirmation would be of God, without judgmental association of the consequences of the affirmation. Are you positive that I deny your denial? My denial of your denial is an assertion of God? An amazing idea.

Positive/negative has a negative association; a double negative has a positive association. Positive/negative would affirm the negative, and would therefore be false. Denying the negative would be true. So what do you do? ...*Accentuate the positive? Eliminate the negative. Latch onto the affirmative. Don't mess with Mr. In-between...* That's it. All Jesus says is, "Believe me or not – one or the other. I'm either totally true or I'm not true at all." That's where you are going to run into the most difficulty. There is no compromise between being eternally loving and whole and being sinful, sick and dead. Apparently that has become reasonable to you, because if you would look at it for a moment, it would be very reasonable that you cannot be separate from everything.

I have many things to say and to judge of you; but he that sent me is true; and I speak to the world those things which I have heard of him. (John 8:26) Through my own revelation, through my realization, through my transformation, through my transfiguration I will speak of the truth – I will teach you how to do that if you would like to, so you can see that the truth is in you. My goodness.

They understood not that he spake to them of the Father. Then Jesus said unto them, When ye have lifted up the Son of man (you), *then shall ye know that I am he, and that I do nothing of myself; but as my Father hath taught me, I speak these things. And he that sent me is with me: the Father hath not left me alone; for I do always those things that please him.* (John 8:27-29)

For goodness sake if that's not a statement of Christianity, what is it? Notice how personal that is? So the Son of man is lifted up to the certainty that he is the Son of God. Is this a good way to teach this? Guys, you've got 2000 years, and now you've got a book that says exactly this. What in hell else do you want? "We hold these things to be self evident, that all men are created equal and endowed by their

Creator with inalienable rights – life, liberty..." But it would be *you* in that declaration? Does the salvation of the world depend on you? Who said yes? How dare you? How dare you tell me that the salvation of the world depends on you? What are you, the savior? Can you hear this? You laugh, but I don't see you out doing it. You let Him die for you. You sure in hell were going to kill Him.

Guys, that's what they are doing now with *A Course In Miracles*. Look at it. You've got a beautiful Judith/Judas. Holy mackerel, what more could you ask for than someone who for 40 pieces – considerably more in this case – literally sold the work. You've got a priest who is denying and telling you that you are false. You've got a Pilate who is the head of the conglomeration who has washed his hands. And finally, way up, you appeal to Caesar and he doesn't hear anything. It's incredible if you look at it. Wow!

You've got it. You keep nurturing this, because once your own Christ child begins to be nurtured – that's what I wrote in response to the fact that we believe that the *Course* comes from Jesus, the man resurrected. Without that it is absurd – you obviously would have no Course. He teaches you to nurture your own Christhood and that those Christs or Saviors can then come together in another association of time that is harmonious and loving and declare together what has occurred to them through this simple message of forgiveness. What a step! What a step if you could take *A Course In Miracles* like we are doing it – even break up the chapters of the text and let anyone pick up any chapter.

As he spake these words, many believed on him. Then said Jesus to those Jews which believed on him, If ye continue in my word, then are ye my disciples indeed. And ye shall know the truth, and the truth shall make you free. (John 8:30-32)

He doesn't say it will make you whole, He says it will make you free to determine your own wholeness. "My truth will set you free." The power, then, of your espoused freedom will allow you to declare yourself. There is no manner by which I can do this. I simply free you of the bondage of self. I free you from the necessity to retain your own sickness and pain and death. *And you shall know the truth.* Know it. And the truth shall make you free.

Listen: *They answered him, We be Abraham's seed, and were never in bondage to any man...* No, you were in bondage to yourself! That's what this is going to say. We have struggled to free ourselves. We have declared ourselves to be free men. What an astonishing idea. That's a nice idea, isn't it – that ethnic declaration.

We were never in bondage to any man: how sayest thou, Ye shall be made free? Jesus answered them, Verily, verily, I say unto you, Whosoever committeth sin is the servant of sin. (John 8:33-34) That's the conceptual identity. He is trapped in the results of his own mind. *And the servant abideth not in the house for ever...* That means you are trapped in time. Why? You have become a servant to your own thoughts. I'll do it once more for you. It is kind of interesting to see how He attempts to present this. You are literally going to be slave to your own house – to your own sickness and death. Listen once more:

Verily I say unto you, Whosoever committeth sin (commits himself to separation) *is the servant of that separation. And the servant abideth not in the house for ever* (he's caught in time); *but the Son abideth ever.* (John 8:34-35) The Son of God is wholly true. A servant to the devil, or evil, is false.

If the Son therefore shall make you free, ye shall be free indeed. (John 8:36) That is, the Christ in you will set you free indeed. You will not be bound by your previous ideas about yourself. They are not true. Whatever you thought you were as Abraham is not true. You are not the son of time and pain and death – servant of the devil, actually. If the Son therefore shall make you free, ye shall be free indeed, but you are afraid of your own freedom because you are defined by the bondage of yourself. Do you understand me? You have a great authority problem. You are a servant to your own conceptual association, and you are trapped in it. Stand by, because this is what you do.

If the Son therefore shall make you free, ye shall be free indeed. I know that ye are Abraham's seed; but ye seek to kill me, because my word hath no place in you. (John 8:37) There is nothing true about you at all. Nothing! There is nothing in your conceptual association that has any meaning at all. This is Chapter 28 of the *Course*. What do you expect from something that has no cause? There is nothing in this world that will ever take you anywhere. It is totally causeless. Isn't that what this says? And you will kill me because I tell you that you are not real. That is what I am telling you. This place is not real. "Get Him – kill him!" Let's try to get this out, because this is pure *Course In Miracles.* Come on, get those phantom figures together, justify your servitude to death – serve the devil, justify your own separation and deny God.

I speak that which I have seen with my Father... (I speak that from the Light of my mind. I have seen this truth. Wow!) *...and ye do that which ye have seen with your father.* (John 8:38) One or the other of us is wrong. You notice I didn't take that away from you. You think your father is sickness and death. I know my Father is love and whole. I know who I am. You don't know who you are. If you knew who you were, you couldn't possibly die. It's absurd. Do you understand?

That's why the copyright of Jesus is anonymous. Through Helen Schucman, the author of the *Course* is anonymous because the admission that it is Jesus would be what salvation is! So the copyright says the author is anonymous. Isn't that funny? They wouldn't dare admit to it. How could they? There would be no reference – never mind what it says. It requires a reference of death no matter what it said.

I speak that which I have seen with my Father: and ye do that which ye have seen with your father. They answered and said unto him, Abraham is our father. Jesus saith unto them, If ye were Abraham's children, ye would do the works of Abraham. But now ye seek to kill me, a man that hath told you the truth, which I have heard of God: this did not Abraham. (John 8:38-40)

Contained within the idea of Abraham is the truth of God. Abraham, first man, immediately resurrected and was whole by his definition of his manhood. You notice that He did not say that Abraham was false, except that you have represented Abraham as false. What He says is that any man, any first man, would have to be first God. He would literally have to be, because his idea of being first would be what last is. The Temple would not acknowledge this. He has no problem acknowledging Abraham because the acknowledgment of Abraham is the acknowledgment of God. Can you hear me? It is not separate. First man cannot be separate. Were there not first man, there would be no need for the definition of God. That's the fact of the matter.

Then said they to him, We be not born of fornication, we have one Father, even God. (They have a good conceptual God.) *Jesus said unto them, If God were your Father, ye would love me.* (John 8:42) That's an attack. That's saying that they are worshipping idols. *If God were your Father, you would love me* because God is love. You would love the Christ.

If God were your Father, ye would love me: for I proceeded forth and came from God; neither came I of myself, but he sent me. (John 8:42) I'm not at all certain that some of you are going to do this. Most of you are simply going to stand up through your own transformation and say to the world, "I have come from another time and place to tell you that this is not true. If you can hear this, you do not have to suffer sickness and pain and death. I have established a place that you

can come to and undergo a transformation of your mind to God."
That's what this says. *If God were your Father, ye would love me:*
for I proceeded forth and came from God; neither came I of myself,
but he sent me.

Why do ye not understand my speech? even because ye cannot hear
my word. (John 8:43) This is the whole teaching of *A Course In Miracles.*
You need a miracle. You can't hear me because you have closed yourself
in to your own mind. My word is Life. My word is the Word of God.
The *Course* says in the Workbook, we are teaching you a new way to
think, a new way to identify the associations of your mind to let them
be whole as you are whole. *Why do you not understand my speech?*
even because ye cannot hear my word.

Ye are of your father the devil, and the lusts of your father ye will
do. (John 8:44) There's no one who's going to accept this. Who is He
talking to? You! I don't hear any preachers stand up and teach love
and forgiveness. *Ye are of your father the devil, and the lusts of your*
father ye will do.

He was a murderer from the beginning, and abode not in the truth,
because there is no truth in him. (John 8:44) The amazing thing is, the
ministers love to do this one, and they put the devil out there, so the
devil can compete with God and they can stand neutral and decide
whether they want the devil or themselves. That's not what this says.
This says there is no devil without the action of you. There is a God.
But there is no evil except that you act as an advocate of the devil. Do
you have an agreement with the devil? Really, do you? This place is a
bargain with evil. You made a bargain you cannot keep. The Son of
God is eternal. No matter what Judas/Judith does, she cannot bargain
away Jesus Christ. She can't die. All she is really saying is, "I'm going
to die." It's that simple. "I don't believe this; I'm going to die. I will
commercialize it, sell it to the devil and live off the proceeds of this
message." What an amazing thing to do. It's a bargain. You made a
bargain you can't keep *because there is no truth in him.*

When he speaketh a lie, he speaketh of his own (When you talk about
anything, you are talking about yourself.) *for he is a liar, and the father*
of it. (John 8:44) There is no relationship in this world that is true. What
an amazing place to be. So you mean that you as a human being have
justified your own self identity? And I say to you that's not true. The
Self that you are is whole and perfect. No wonder you reject it. I'm
curious to know why is it here at all then. What is it that the human

association has been seeking? Certainly he is seeking the Kingdom of God, but he refuses to accept the simple statement that the Kingdom of God cannot be separate from the entirety of God. There is no separation in this. Wow!

When he speaketh a lie, he speaketh of his own, for he is a liar, and the father of it. Ready for this: *And because I tell you the truth, ye believe me not.* (John 8:45) You've always been a liar. That's what we're teaching. There is no truth in you. We're up to Lesson 12 in the Workbook. Not only are your forms false, your thoughts about your forms are false. And because I tell you the truth, *ye believe me not.* Wow!

Which of you convinceth me of sin? And if I say the truth, why do ye not believe me? He that is of God heareth God's words; ye therefore hear them not, because ye are not of God. (John 8:46-47) Obviously. If you would admit that you are perfect as God created you, you would hear me instantly. The truth of the matter is that you are not of God. This earth is not of God. Yet anything not of God could not be real. Therefore, sin and sickness and death are not real. That is the point at which your dispute with me occurs. You are not allowed to stand up and declare that all of the awful things going on here, being committed by "other" people, are not true. And that the requirement of forgiveness has nothing to do with what you are apparently forgiving.

Forgive them, Father, for they know not what they do (Luke 23:34) has nothing to do with the act of crucifying the Christ. They are forgiven literally because they don't know what they are doing. If they could know what they were doing, their act would be literally unforgivable. The explanation of that is: Sin against your brother, sin against God (which is meaningless), but don't sin against the Holy Spirit. (Matthew 12:32) This is what you should tell Judith/Judas. Don't sin against the Holy Spirit. You have the acknowledgment of that within you. That would be the abomination of death, wouldn't it? Don't sin against the entirety of you. If you do, you will suffer the consequences. You can deny God. You can deny your brother. But don't deny your own association. That's what that says. *He that is of God heareth God's words: ye therefore hear them not, because ye are not of God.* Wow!

Verily, verily, I say unto you, If a man keep my saying, he shall never see death. (John 8:51) *If I honour myself, my honour is nothing: it is my Father that honoureth me; of whom ye say, that he is your God: Yet ye have not known him; but I know him: and if I should say, I know him not, I shall be a liar like unto you: but I know him, and keep his saying.* (John 8:54-55) It is the same idea as somewhere you're going to have to stand up and say, "I don't know about you, but I know exactly who I am. For me to admit to you, after I know myself, would be a lie to what I have come to know." Many of you have to take this step. See how well He covers it all? Here's a great sentence:

Your father Abraham rejoiced to see my day; and he saw it, and was glad. (John 8:56) He's already back in Heaven. So if you are going to get irritated at all, get irritated with Abraham because you didn't get the word from him. But just because you are out nodding east of Eden doesn't mean that Eden was not taken back up into Heaven. Do you hear that? The temptation actually did not occur. You are asleep. You are east of Eden asleep, because there is no one who would have a Paradise on earth that would not be in Heaven. The acknowledgment of the love of God is what Paradise is.

Do you notice in this entire teaching, humans, that nothing is ever denied you? Nothing is ever denied you! It is you that deny yourself through fear of happiness. One of the most astonishing things in addressing a human being is that they are actually afraid to be free and happy. That's why they don't come to the Healing Center. It couldn't possibly be true. It's too good to be true. And they don't want to be disappointed once again like they always have been. Oh ye of little faith, come into the door and be made whole because the power of that decision is yours and the miracle will occur with that decision. Is that true? You have all these healing books that say if you make that decision you will rise up and be with God right now. The decision to be well is yours. Isn't that fun? That's what you are doing. That was Chapter 8 of John. He's going to say:

Verily, verily, I say unto you, Before Abraham was, I am. (John 8:58) Once more: Before Abraham was – there's no such thing as the past – I am. He didn't say "I was." That's a big difference: *"Before Abraham was I 'was'."* You is! When "was" you? *Abraham was.* Your whole problem is that you see only the past. There we are with John, Chapter 8. That's really nice. Then there's Chapter 9. Here's a sentence I want to read to you that will show you that everything you attempt to do is holding you blind:

For judgment I am come into this world. I can't take your judgment away from you; I can only offer you true judgment, because you think that judgment is necessary. "For judgment" – for you to judge. *I am come into this world,* as an alternative to what you thought you were.

147

For judgment I am come into this world, that they which see not might see; and that they which see might be made blind. (John 9:39) The admission that you don't know will bring you to God. That's what this says. Have you got that? Once more: *and that they which see might be made blind.* Because you think you see, you are never going to. I would blind you to the need of this world if you will let me – that's what that says. That's kind of nice.

This is a definition of perception: *If ye were blind, ye should have no sin; but now ye say, We see; therefore your sin remaineth.* (John 9:41) Don't tell me you understand. Your understanding has nothing to do with it whatsoever. You are hell-bent that you now have reached a point where you understand. I have no idea whether that is true or not. I'm simply offering you the entirety of your own mind. The simple thing, as Jesus would say, is that you are blind, deaf and dumb. The light that you have in your mind is a reflection of darkness, not Light. When you are Light, you are all Light; your progression to that is what is occurring. That's what we are trying to tell them.

If we wrote that letter – hopefully, if that letter to *Time Magazine* were going to get in, it might get in this week because this says after your Easter cover story you're going to get a lot of letters. If I were the editor, I might have held this one for a week. They got more letters than they've ever gotten before about the *Time* article. This says you are going to get a lot of letters, after you do it, which are going to be as meaningless as your original association. So if this were ever going to get in – how long ago was Easter? Three weeks. We've only got 19 days left? Do you have a spot in your mind of resurrection? That spot? That Easter? You won't be here more than 40 days after that. What is 40 days? As long as it took. But you are now abiding with the resurrected body.

"Dear Editor, Time Magazine: So another Easter has rolled around."

I won't read this part of it. This is nice. This is how I feel about human beings. "You wouldn't dare say this." Why not? It's absurd. Look at this world. You actually believe that in this little nothing that a human being, locked in his own flesh, declaring himself with all of these associations of consciousness could mean anything. You're still doing it. You are totally meaningless. Am I going to get away with this? No, you're going to kill me. I'm telling you that all I am doing is offering you how ridiculous the human condition is. I can't see how you could come in your right mind and not look at the insanity of pain and death and loneliness that go on here.

"So another Easter has rolled around. It's time to stick "His" picture on the cover once again. It's time to nail the phantom carpenter from Nazareth with the same old deleterian nincompoopery of previous crucifixions.

I can't see how they wouldn't print this. What I don't understand is usually I have an association somewhere with Fourth Estate – just like we have printing presses. Somewhere we have an association with communicative purposes. I'd print this.

Drag out the usual assemblage of "blind gnat-gaggers" to spew the excrement of their digested camels.

At the very minimum, that would make me laugh. Even if I spit out one of my own hunks, I would be able to laugh at the idea of what we are willing to accept here and deny the other things. It's amazing.

Next week you can bet on retaliation through an equally meaningless rebuttal by the pedantic quackery that constitutes all of the "angels on a pin" repertory.

In other words, what about this, what about that? All last week's letters were, "Yeah, but what about this," discussions of the condition of man rather than the acknowledgment of Jesus. Amazing idea.

The entire teachings and demonstrations of Jesus Christ are immediate, direct, sustained confrontations between the inevitability of a whole, perfectly-loving, eternally-creating God compared to the isolation, pain and sickness, loss and death of this place called Earth.

He asks you always to compare. Notice we use the word *compare* there. But it is a confrontation. Is that a true sentence? I just read it. I need to have somebody tell me where He doesn't do that? Yes or No? So part of the salvation process would have to be the admission of the confrontation. Yes or No? He is a rabble-rouser. He is determined to tell you you are from God and that your establishment is nothing. Is there anyone here who disagrees with that? I'm not talking about whether you're going to believe it or not. What I'd like to do is address an assemblage of so-called theologians and say, "Where does it say anything but this? Where but here do you deny it?" Because any admission of it would require admission of it in its entirety. There is no other way. I know I am just beating a dead horse here – or a dead camel. Something. But I'd really like to have you see this. You don't realize the momensity of this. They literally don't hear it. "What do you mean by that?" Wow!

> The massive cover up of this world's only perfect analogy of singular Universal Reality appears to have been particularly successful this Easter.

I used "analogy" advisedly, but it's finally the only way you can do it. It says it as good as it can be said.

> What a tragic absurdity that this time there is a complete and total absence, by denial, of His simple message of the healing agency of eternal Universal Love, available through the human act of giving and forgiving.

(Boy is that fundamental – that was not in that article.)

> Yet, how could it be otherwise considering the necessary conditions of existence that constitute the historic reality of this so-called human civilization?

> The entire teachings and demonstrations of Jesus Christ are immediate, direct, sustained confrontations between the inevitability of a whole, perfectly-loving, eternally-creating God, compared to the isolation, pain and sickness, loss and death of this place called Earth. To attempt to connect the divinely-revealing declarations of Jesus Christ, even in regard to the very fundamental question: What is life?...

He says Life is Eternity, even in that regard, even trying to call this "life."

> ...to the so-called Christian Institution, or indeed any worldly establishment, is totally unreasonable and absurdly impossible.

There is literally no connection between the mind of Jesus declaring you to be perfect and the separation that you have instituted in this world. Any connection at all would only be a moment of divine realization. Once more. The whole teaching is, only a moment of connection would be the divine realization: *"Know ye not that ye must be born again."*

> You will search in vain in the New Testament among the direct utterances of Jesus, except for an occasional placation of the Pharisees, ...

Render unto Penguin what is Penguin's! (Reference to the Course In Miracles copyright litigation brought by Penguin Books.)

...for any quotations in His fundamental philosophy of spiritual reality that will be unqualifyingly acceptable to institutional or governing authorities, or to any constituencies called human society.

Nothing He says here is totally acceptable. Find me one thing. I will guarantee it. You can search and interpret it, but there is nowhere that He will not declare to you, as I am declaring to you from my certainty that there is no world, that you are not separate from God. See how fundamental this is? Why doesn't the world know it? Because the world does not know it. This is what this world is – a denial of it. Here is a description of what He teaches.

> The imperative of direct, individual, personal experience of the revelation of God is the only fundamental necessity of His entire teaching.

Am I going to have theological disputes with this? All we ever say is that you must contact God.

> There is absolutely no allowance for this worldly condition of separation from an eternally perfect Creation. In order for the divine message of Jesus Christ to have any reasonable meaning, its uncompromising unconditionality must be accepted, admitted and asserted.

Accepted. Admitted. Asserted. I accept. I admit to it. And I declare it. I will accept this message that I am perfect. First I have to accept it. I can't even get you to accept it. If I can get you to accept it, a little willingness, then you can admit it to yourself, and begin the experience. And then you can declare it.

> In other words, He must be allowed to mean exactly what He says. What could possibly merit crucifixion more than the seditious instruction that you *love your enemies*? (Matthew 5:44). Nothing.

You traitor! How dare you? We're condemning him to death. How can you not join in with us?

> *Resist not evil* (Matthew 5:39), and that you "give everything in this world away and follow me"? (Matthew 19:21)

Does He mean that? I'm going to give you a little good advice here: Don't get into discussions with others about whether He means it or not. The discussion of whether He means you should give everything away and follow Him is just a statement of having no intention of

151

giving everything away. Let the statement be unacceptable. I'm just giving you some good Christian advice. You'll get, "Well, He didn't mean you have to give everything, you have to keep enough to sustain." No. That's impossible. The act of giving is what salvation is. See, I got into a little explanation of it. Don't do it. "Give everything in this world away and follow me." Say to me: "You mean I have to give everything away and follow you?" [Audience: "You mean I have to give everything away and follow you?"] God only gives. What's your next sentence? There's no sense in getting into a discussion. Does God only give? What's your problem? How can you know you are like God if you don't give? *"The Lord giveth and the Lord taketh away."* Poop!

If you could read *A Course In Miracles*! It's so beautiful. It says you gather around and say, "You have taken this beautiful little child... what kind of a God is that? I demand to know, reasonably, why I should love a God who causes me pain and death." "We just have to accept it." The hell with you. I'm not going to accept it! Have you read the descriptions of a human being that are in the Text of *A Course In Miracles*?

"Give everything in the world away and follow me." You are very subversive with this. You have come together in secret and have declared that you are undergoing an experience of a direct contact with God of which this world knows not. Christians, take to your catacombs right now – the *Course* is coming out! You have the direct quote from somebody that says, "Burn *Jesus is Speaking* books." We have it. "Destroy them. Burn the copies that you have left of *Jesus is Speaking* in writing." That's a good one. They're after you. The surprising thing is that it may be too late. You may have been successful at getting this in. They're going to have to get you now. Somehow it may be too reasonable. You are undergoing your own experience of enlightenment. Suddenly this message will go past blind faith. The reasonableness of it will be demonstrated by the miracle of your own healing. "Gee, it seems all right if God made me whole, I'll be whole." Whambo! You're whole. Miracles make sense, because obviously nothing here does. It would take a miracle to make any sense out of this. That's the Workbook of *A Course In Miracles*.

> Subversive elements that seriously propagate the tenets that
> you don't belong in this world (John 15:19), that human tribunal
> has no jurisdiction whatsoever (John 19:11);

In the letter we're writing to Jimmy Carter, there is a sentence in that... "You're going to write a letter to Jimmy Carter?" Jimmy is kind of a nice guy. During my awakening, Jimmy was having all the problems that a guy with moral turpitude has. Any guy who graduates from Annapolis can't be all bad. He's also a lawyer. He graduated from Yale. Nice guy. Worked on the atomic stuff. Anyway. We're going to ask him if there is a course of action we can take. As Christians, we do not defend ourselves. Do you understand me? As Christians, we do not defend ourselves. Our certainty through faith is not a contention.

Jesus called us. We didn't make a Jesus. It's not open to question that the *Course In Miracles* comes from Jesus. It is not our contention; it is our certainty of faith. That's in the letter. So how can we defend ourselves? Obviously, if you look at it, we are defended by the First Amendment. We are defended by our right to do it. But as Christians, we do not assert our right; we acknowledge that we have been called and have responded. Do you understand this? This is very crucial to the point you are at in Christianity. You have been chosen. You didn't choose Jesus, He chose you. Had you chosen Him, you'd still be in deep crap.

Everyone in this world attempts to choose and define what Jesus is, instead of accepting what He says. This is just good fundamental Christianity. The only choice you have is either to accept it or reject it. We in our certainty, have accepted His call. It is not our contention, then, that He is "among other gods" possible, but that He is, in fact, the Savior. In that fact is our salvation. Can you hear me? I'm just coming around once more for you. Don't try to prove it. It is not provable. It is only experience-able.

> The human tribunal has no jurisdiction whatsoever. No matter what you do to me, it has nothing to do with me.

The letter, it's a very interesting letter. And it says that the commercial conglomerate cannot consider us to be an alternative. That's why they have ignored us. We are not a viable alternative within the conditions of exchange. They don't know how to answer us. They can't answer us. The only way they could answer us would be to say that our purpose is not what we say it is, that actually we want to have a gain from this – they could get into that.

> Subversive elements that seriously propagate the tenets that you don't belong in this world (John 15:19), that human tribunal has no jurisdiction whatsoever (John 19:11); and further,

demands that you admit that you are "perfect, even as your Father in Heaven is perfect" (Matthew 5:48) **must** be denied, attacked and finally destroyed.

You can't let the teachings of Jesus stay here. They will corrupt the establishment. The Kingdom of God will begin to come into hell. This is hell because of the denial of the Kingdom of God.

How utterly fearful His assertion of the unlimited power of your mind *(Therefore be ye perfect...)* Wherever you are in any time or place, what you imprison on earth is imprisoned in Heaven; and as you free yourself, the whole universe is freed along with you. (Matthew 16:19)

That would be very nice if that got into *Time Magazine*.

You may be happily surprised to discover the light of an exciting, whole new understanding of New Testament scripture, if you will let the premises of your discernment be based on three simple postulations that Jesus teaches:

Are we going to get away with this? They won't print this. This is the catechism of reality.

♦There is one wholly-loving, eternally-creating God, who creates you and everything in the universe perfectly;

♦Though you appear separate from this creative Love, you may at any moment, using the power of your mind, return to Heaven through the transformation of this apparent physical and mental condition of loss of reality – to the memory that you are still always and only at home in Heaven;

♦In New Testament scripture, He is instructing you very specifically in the manner in which this is accomplished.

That's resist not evil – give everything away; that's the manner isn't it?

The savior Jesus Christ teaches the simple catechism of unconditional love, a certainty of eternal life gained by revelation through the continuing uncompromising admission and surrender that is the communicative link to the eternal Will of God.

This is pretty good stuff guys. Last week was the declaration of your individual freedom both to be as God created you, and through the declaration of it to come from time to eternity – that you are whole and perfect. This week demonstrates the impossibility that you could teach this here. So that you can understand this: It is impossible for you to carry this whole message to this place of sickness and death without the immediate conversion occurring, because the acceptance of your message is what the conversion is.

So you are not from here. Is that so? Really? You're not from here. Where are you from? What? "Not here?" Why don't you just say: "I'm from Heaven." How is it? Is it okay? Are you eternally happy? How can you tell you are eternally happy? Are you happy for no reason? Or are you happy because you are in Heaven? You keep looking for some sort of theology. All I'm telling you is that you are God's mind. You are whole and perfect. Where are you from? How did you get into this place? Damned if I know. If you know, you'll be damned. If you knew how you got into here, if you really did, you'd be gone instantly – it's the thinking you know that damns you. At least you are admitting to some sort of ignorance.

The truth of the matter is that you don't know how you got in here. Why would you have to know? "Well, I need to know what my mission is?" "I need to know why I am here." I'm not answering this. I'm just trying to get you to look at it. So somewhere in this sojourn of death, you met another apparent human being who revealed to you a secret. He came out of nowhere perhaps. He came around the corner and handed you a message. It could be anything. Somebody here has been trying to tell you something. Everyone you have met in your own dream has been trying to tell you something.

I want you to stick around to see how this "Trying to Get Jesus' Word Into the World" works out. You have to come at it from the totality and the ridiculousness of not being allowed to declare God here. It is impossible to overestimate the insanity of this place. There is no sanity here at all.

This is our lesson for today. He did stand up and He did say that. And it is written. And He did suffer the consequences of His attempt to declare to you His own reality. And He did suffer on the cross and He did die, and He did resurrect. What in hell would you want me to deny you? I cannot deny you the concepts of your own mental association. I can only offer you the entirety of your own mind. I can offer you that, and you won't accept it. If you'll accept it, you'll be perfect as God created you. If you do not, you'll be perfect as God created you.

Do you hear me? I'm not concerned about your affirmation or denial. That power is within your mind. I am going to tell you that you are going to get the result of your own thinking. That's true. "I'm willing to accept the result." Only because you're causing pain to your brother and not accepting it yourself. There is no way you would accept the pain you are causing without getting into the teachings.

We have now present in this aggregation a lot of new bright whole minds. Am I correct in this assumption? Or is it perhaps more than an assumption? Is it an acknowledgment that we are beginning to communicate on a level that transcends our previous needs to protect ourselves or to identify ourselves as being willing to watch our children grow up and get old and die.

Perhaps "we are offsprings of Abraham" has never been true. (*We be Abraham's seed* - John 8:33) Perhaps our dedication to the separation using the power of God is simply not true – not whether it is good or bad–not whether it is evil or not evil, simply that it is not true.

CHAPTER 6

Jesus Is Speaking
To You

The instructions of the religion of Christianity are only to the declaration of your individual Christhood and perfection as recognized by the man Jesus Christ, not as the originator of the inevitability of your perfection in the entirety of the universe, but rather as a particular innovator to the species of man of the manner in which you would engender the word of God which is the certainty, the knowledge, the proclamation, the determination that the entirety of the universe is a part of the separate condition in which you find yourself. He describes this in the teachings of all religions as a Holy Spirit.

In the first chapter of John, he will say, *"In the beginning was the Word."* That is so because it is impossible to have a beginning without an entirety of the universe. *In the beginning was the Word* is an indication that the answer to a beginning and an end would have to be evident in the beginning and end relationship. What he really says is (and this is of course true of Jesus), at the time of the so-called schism, the entirety of the recovery in fact did occur and remains available for you individually in your own mind. God is not a burning bush outside of you that you sacrifice to, but the admission that God is in you. Anyone could look at this and see that the atonement principle, the fundamental acknowledgment of a Single Universal Beingness, is all that we really teach.

Our concern about the solution of the problem can then best be expressed by the admission of causation. If there is a single causation of Universal Mind from which we are apparently separate, the problem is easily solved by the admission that we are the containment of the Kingdom of God – which is precisely and exactly what Jesus of Nazareth says: You are the Kingdom of God. It is not something that has to be studied or observed or compared with another thing. The problem is also solved by the admission, obviously, of the resurrection of the transformation of your mind. In that will be the willingness to forgive your brother.

Reality cannot be separate from the beingness of universal mind. That's literally a true statement. And it is true because it is reasonable. The Word then becomes reason. The Word then becomes an answer. There was no need for a Word, the Word of God was not necessary until the separation. The Word of God, then, is the certainty of the wholeness that must be a part of what you are seeking for. I know that we have words for that. You like to say, "That's the atonement principle." I'm not concerned about school.

About school? "It's not school I mind, it's the principal of the thing." I got out of that one.

So your authority, the principle of you, comes from God, not from the associations that you have constructed in your mind in order to determine God separate from you.

That's how fundamental this is. The admission of that entirety is the Christ instruction, what we term in a literal sense, Christianity, or the story of Christ in you, or the admission that at the time of the schism or separation the relief from it was built into the entirety of the separation. It would be impossible that not be so. And for just a moment that Word has apparently escaped you. You have been given a demonstration in this association of space/time of the entirety, through the resurrection of Jesus Christ who dictates to you the terms by which you can recognize your individual Saviorship.

This is the *Course in Miracles* as succinctly as it can be presented. It says very simply that you brought this world with you when you came. You are the atonement principle. If you want to compare that with the apparent separate entity Jesus, you may do so, but not without the fundamental admission that we are all perfectly created by God and cannot therefore be separate in any regard. Now we are into the forgiveness of your brother in order to have salvation. There is no way that you will enter the Kingdom of God without the forgiveness of the images of your own mind on which the terms for your separation are being set.

There is a tremendous amount of reassociations going on in your Christ mind. The admission of Jesus that He is with you all the time in a literal sense – quite literally, as John would say – as a totality of the representation of your resurrection that penetrated the thickness of your fear, or your determination to stay separate from Jesus Christ of Nazareth. I can teach this as well in Christianity as anything else. Jesus says, "*Lo, I am with you, even unto the end of the earth.*" (Matthew 28:20) That's true in a literal sense. All Christhood is with you, literally. Isn't that nice to know? He's walking right here. He loves this teaching. This is so fundamental, the teachings of Jesus the man. These words that I am saying to you are virtually the same words that He would speak or you will speak to any aggregation of apparent separation from your mind now in the aggregate gathering of your rediscovery of the Kingdom of God.

Quite literally this then becomes the Kingdom of God in the admission of your Saviorship. This is the whole teaching: *Know ye not that ye are God. The Kingdom of God is within you.* Are you the savior of the world? You hesitate at that for just a minute. There's no reason why you should. If you are going to espouse to the teachings of Jesus Christ, you will be instructed that you are the savior of the world. That's just the fact of the matter. Perhaps it's time at last for the establishment to at least tacitly acknowledge that the teachings are the individual transformation of the human condition, since that is the entire teaching. You must undergo the experience of the transformation of your mind.

In the beginning was the Word, and the Word was with God, and the Word was God. (John 1:1) How could you be with God and God? Because God is everything and you are always with Him. Why is that redundancy required? Because you believe you are separate and the Word will be the entirety of the separation through the determination of your mind. That's the way that works.

The same was in the beginning with God. (John 1:2) That's another way of saying it's impossible for you to be separate. *The same was in the beginning with God.* Nothing you have ever done in what you believe could be this nightmare or dream has separated you from the entirety of the Universal Mind. It's kind of a nice thing.

All things were made by him; and without him was not any thing made that was made. (John 1:3) This is a description of the Christ, if you really would like to know. This is actually a description of a single man mind. It is a description of the separation of the entirety of you in your own dream, and your remembering of that dream. I assure you that's what this says because it is speaking directly of your Saviorship. *All things were made by him; and without him was not any thing made that was made. In him was life; and the life was the light of men. The light shineth in darkness; and the darkness comprehended it not.* (John 1:4-5) Literally could not understand it. Then it describes John the Baptist as coming as a foreteller of this. John as a prophecy is a necessity to your condition because it sets the terms whereby you can come to know that man must save man. Man must save man because God cannot save man. God does not know about this. The prophecy of John says Man saves man, or quite literally your divine Self saves your separate self. That's nice.

It's going to say here that you are the light of the world and that He comes as a totality of the manifestation of man in space/time to ignite or to provide for you the light of God which is in you. This is what it says. The healing process that we had last week was nothing but the ignition of the light of your mind shining on the projections of your heretofore determinations to attack and defend yourself from God. That's how simple this is. That was a very advanced statement for those of you who have undergone this resurrection of your mind.

As you depart this world, you should have no problem with this at all. This is just an admission of how simple it has always been. If you'd look at it with any sensibility at all, the Word – the reason – would be very simple to you. The fact that no one here does it should not concern you in the slightest. You will be told exactly what to do. You've been given all the directions, the necessity of your own mind. It should be very easy. Is it in the gospel of John? Of course. Were you resurrected by the gospel of John? Of course. How would you not be?

He was not that Light, but was sent to bear witness of that Light. That's John (the Baptist). *That was the true Light, which lighteth every man that cometh into the world. He was in the world, and the world was made by him, and the world knew him not.* (John: 8-10) That's probably the most extraordinary sentence in the whole New Testament. Would you like to know what that says? Do you hear that? *He was in the world, and the world was made by him, and the world knew him not* – because for a moment He did not know Himself. This is the entire teaching of the singularity of your mind. You are the maker of the false world, but as the wholeness of God, you are also the healer or the Christ. That's what that says, of course, because you are within your own dream association. Jesus says, "You maker of death, look at the Christhood that must be a part of you." Look at what you are searching for to miscreate in the reverence you maintain for the pain and death that dictate the terms for your separation from God.

But the key to salvation is obviously going to be what? Say to me: There's nothing outside of me. (Audience: "There's nothing outside of me.") I don't know how else to teach you. How else can I teach you that there is nothing outside of you? You have come into a world where if you look at this hell, everything is being attacked by things outside of itself. The defenses have become extraordinary – in order to what? Necessitate the attack! Do you think that you will set up any sort of defense (using that explosion at the Olympics) that some madman will not penetrate? He has a need to blow it up simply because you are defending it. I don't know how else to tell you. Can you hear this? And it gets crazier and crazier. The more you defend yourself in that association, correspondingly the more you will be attacked. And the tighter your defenses, the more unreasonable the attack will be. It would have to be so. You set terms within your own cause and effect that literally create a static condition where nothing creative can happen. It just becomes a defense – the limitations you impose on it are incredible.

You are bearing witness to the certainty of your mind in a comparison with the hell that was of your making. If you undergo that transformation, this world will disappear into the nothingness that it has always been.

But as many as received him, to them gave he power to become the sons of God, even to them that believe on his name. (John 1:12) It's another way of saying that there is absolutely no requirement for you at all, except to admit that every man is a perfectly created Son of God. That's what this says. That's how simple the solution was. This would have to be true because that association could be nothing but a manifestation of your mind. That's all it could possibly be. The Christ in you, each moment in time, is the totality of the revelation of you, coming from the separation to the truth that you are perfect as

God created you. Are you surprised to find that this is in John in the Bible? As your mind awakens, you are surprised to find it everywhere you look. You find a correspondence with your own Christhood in regard to the entirety of your own mind.

Where the surprise in you is coming about is in these later teachings of Jesus that God is in everything. These little booklets that you have prepared, here's *Jesus is Speaking*, are astonishing. I want to tell you that if you pick up the *Jesus is Speaking* book again, you will be astonished at how directly and forthrightly it declares the teachings of the resurrection of the Christ in you. It's an amazing thing. You will be equally amazed how the world refuses it, how the world does not want to remember its own perfection because of the necessity for the loss of its domination of the things that it has made to retain its self identity.

Which were born, not of blood, nor of the will of the flesh, nor of the will of man, but of God. And the Word was made flesh... In the Course, Jesus says technically the Word is not made flesh. We are not concerned about the manner in which your fleshiness becomes whole. You might want to say, "the Word was created flesh." If you use it as a form of creation, it becomes whole in its entirety, because certainly the requirement for the flesh to dwell among you is the requirement for the salvation.

There is no sense in me attempting to misdirect you from the certainty that the conversion of your fleshy separation is a requirement, or the sanctification of you in an identity is a requirement to recognize the Kingdom of God. Are you comfortable with that?

And the Word was made flesh, and dwelt among us, (and we beheld his glory, the glory as of the only begotten of the Father,) full of grace and truth. No man hath seen God at any time... Of course not, how could you see God in time? If you see in time, you will see separate from God. *...the only begotten Son, which is in the bosom of the Father, he hath declared him.* (John 1:13-14, 18) This entire teaching is that you are the only begotten Son. This entire teaching has allowed you to make the admission, through the guilt of your identity, that God sees you perfectly in the glory of eternal reality. That's the teaching. And that's what you have come to know.

If I discovered this little book, *Jesus is Speaking*, in this sojourn or any sojourn, I would find it astonishingly revelatory in what it teaches in regard to the New Testament – what Jesus is saying to you from out of time. I would suggest that in His final theology that if anyone wants to discuss with you (I'm talking about whatever Christians think they are), you hand them this. Tell them to read this and then come back and talk to you. If you don't set the terms of the fundamental teachings of Jesus, they will be doing the connections of the Old Testament. If you do this with them, there is no compromise in this in regard to Jesus' declarations of your individual Saviorship.

(From *Jesus is Speaking,* page 19) "I am not of this world." And neither are you. Nothing is of this world. You have heard it said that you should protect and defend yourself. I say, that is of *this* world, and you are not of the world of exchange; you've come from Heaven. How did I get here? *I say unto you that ye resist not evil. These things I have spoken unto you, that in me ye might have peace. In the world ye shall have tribulation; but be of good cheer; I have overcome the world.* How much more do you want? That's proof that He's overcome it. The proof that He's overcome it is the admission of the pain and separation from God. The proof is in you. *Be ye therefore perfect, even as your Father which is in Heaven is perfect.*

Questions? Any question about that? How about: "How can I do that?" Do you see? I say, "Be perfect as your Father in Heaven." And you say, "How can I do that?" Why would you have to have anything to do with that? That's a statement of perfection. This congregation is happy to hear that they are perfect as God created them. Are you? Do some of you say, "I don't know if that is true"? That's why you are here. This is Jesus speaking. Listen.

It says in the beginning of this little book (Page 1) to actually let these words mean more than you are determined they're going to mean. It's called setting the terms of this. "This is an invitation to a great experiment. Just for a moment, lay aside the prejudices of your human establishment and listen to these words with you heart. Listen again, and still again," and still again and still again—until it becomes your sole requirement. Because as you awaken you will hear it. Is that so?

It would have to be true if the Atonement Principle is still intact. If the Atonement Principle is intact all around you, just because you are denying and killing yourself does not mean that it's not there. The simple solution is for you to simply listen. Instead of setting the terms for which you want to hear in correspondence with yourself, just for a moment you shut up, and let this speak to you, because this will speak the truth.

All interpretations are intercessions of your perceptual mind to create a static in the denial of the single wholeness of God that's all around you. "Just for a moment, let this simple message of truth and love be beyond all reason and see how quickly reason will follow as your mind opens to the joyful light of your reunion with the eternally creating mind of God." Who wrote that? Nice stuff.

"Whoever you think you are, wherever you appear to be in the desperate sea of chaos that is this world, let the breath of this timeless voice of resurrected mind rekindle in you the ancient memory of your own perfect reality." Nice stuff. "Now you are being called to fulfill the only purpose that ever could have been given for your own sojourn into this meaningless world of loneliness and death. That purpose is your escape from it through the message of salvation that is now in your hands."

That's it? Wow!

(From *Jesus is Speaking*, page 19) *My Kingdom is not of this world* because it is in you. What kind of a sentence is that? That doesn't make any sense. When I say your Kingdom is not of this world, I mean it. What an amazing idea. My Kingdom is not of this world because it is in you. If my kingdom is in you, you are not in this world either, except for the moment you acknowledge that the Kingdom was in you. In that moment, the world was gone. It is nothing but the statement of a resurrected mind. *My Kingdom is not of this world because it is in you.* Isn't that lovely. It's an amazing idea. It's very possible for my mind to ignite that memory in you simply because we are the same "you." That's what we are doing. Your denial of me is literally your denial of yourself.

Now, the admission that your Kingdom is not of this world is the indication of the necessity of the admission of this world. So that you can see that your Kingdom is not of this world, you must hear: *Your Kingdom is not of this world because it was given you from beyond this world.* But you can't get out of here by dying. *This world is not left by death but by truth, and the truth can be known by all those for whom the Kingdom was created, and for whom it waits. If you will accept the fact that I am with you, you are denying the world and accepting God.* Because I am your denial of this world.

I'll do it once more for you. I'll read the sentence and I'm going to teach it from the *Course in Miracles* where Jesus teaches. The whole Sermon on the Mount, everything that He declares to you, is to deny this world. I don't care what you think about it, how much you're going to say He didn't say that. That's what He says. He is the aspect of you that denies this world. He is the certainty in you that you are whole as God created you. So He must be the aspect of the denial of this world in you since you believe that you have made this world in your association.

So every time you say, "I'm caught in this," He says "the world isn't real." This is the whole teaching. Every time you say, "What am I going to do about this?" He says, "Why don't you come home to Heaven with me." He's always speaking to you of the solution. That's just the fact of the matter. All I ever, ever, ever, ever could do is deny you. All Jesus Christ really does is deny your own conceptual self. He says, "Not that." You have learned this from me by my denial of you as you present yourself to me. I'm sorry if you don't like that. This is just the simple truth of the matter. As the Christ, all I can offer you is the certainty of our minds together in paradise. Do you see? The manner in which that is accomplished has to be by the denial of your own sickness and pain and death since you are the cause of this world.

Why don't you study that for a while so you can continue to occupy yourself with the simple denial of the Christ who is standing right next to you. It is impossible that you would be searching for God and not find Him. That's the thing that amazes me the most about spiritual teachers.

I went to California, and everybody's searching for God. It's got to be obvious to anyone – it's obvious to me – that if you really believe there is a God and can't find Him, shame on you. All you're telling me is you have a God and you don't want to find Him. It would be impossible, literally, if there was a totally loving God that you could search for Him and not immediately have found Him, past tense. So it must be that that which has not found Him is not a part of God, and therefore not real. That's the fact of the matter. So you, as you sit there right now, I'm looking at you because hopefully you're going to get this finally. I simply deny you in your entirety until you know you are perfect as God created you. This is good stuff.

The world can add nothing to the power and the glory of God and His holy Sons, but it can blind the Sons to the Father if they behold it. Because it is a projection of your mind in a dream of death and it is part of what you think you are. The great amnesia. *You cannot behold the world and know God. Only one is true. I am come to tell you the choice of which is truth is not yours to make. If it were, you would have destroyed yourself.* You would have destroyed yourself a long time ago. That's the fact of the matter. And you continue to attempt to destroy yourself, but it won't work. It's going to say to have nothing to do with death. Have nothing to do with death. *Yet God did not will the destruction of His creations, having created them for eternity. His Will has saved you, not from yourself but from your illusion of yourself. He has saved you for yourself. What God did not create does not exist. And everything that does exist exists as He created it. The world you see has nothing to do with reality. It is of your own making, and it does not exist.* That's an amazing thing.

Here, in this place, now, is the world set free. *As you let the past be lifted and release the future from your ancient fears, you find escape and give it to the world. You have enslaved the world with all your fears, your doubts and miseries, you pain and tears, and all your sorrows press on it, and keep the world a prisoner to your beliefs. Death strikes it everywhere because you hold the bitter thoughts of death within your mind. To free the world from every kind of pain is but to change your mind about yourself. There is no world apart from your ideas because ideas leave not their source, and you maintain the world within your mind in thought.* What an amazing little book. Is this true? Is it? Wow!

Father, the truth belongs to me. My home is set in Heaven by Your Will and mine. Can dreams content me? Can illusions bring me happiness? What but Your memory can satisfy Your Son? I will accept no less than You have given me. I am surrounded by Your Love, forever still, forever gentle and forever safe. God's Son must be as You created him.

The kingdom of Heaven is at hand. The kingdom of God cometh not with observations: Neither shall they say, Lo here! or, lo there! for, behold, the kingdom of God is within you. Verily I say unto thee, Today shalt thou be with me in paradise.

Father, I was created in Your Mind, a holy Thought that never left its home. I am forever Your Effect, and You forever and forever are my Cause. As You created me I have remained. Where You established me I still abide. And all your Attributes abide in me, because it is Your Will to have a Son so like his Cause that Cause and Its Effect are indistinguishable. Let me know that I am an Effect of God, and so I have the power to create like You. And as it is in Heaven, so on earth. Your plan I follow here, and at the end I know that You will gather

Your effects into the tranquil Heaven of Your Love, where earth will vanish, and all separate thoughts unite in glory as the Son of God.

Hey, guys, listen to me. There is a lot of assertion in that prayer. That's an admission of the separation. It contains a dedication of your mind. How in hell can you get it without declaring it? The tenses are all mixed up. It says *his* and *Father* and *you*. What in hell difference could it possibly make if your mind is the mind of God? It couldn't possibly make any difference.

What do you do? Dissect the prayer? Do you study the relationship of your own mind with this simple admission that all power is given unto you in Heaven and earth? Whatever you call *earth* and whatever you call *Heaven* does not concern me in the slightest. Why would it? All power is yours. The key to salvation that you have discovered is there is no adversary. That's the simple fact of the matter. Nothing opposes God. Since you are a perfect creation of God, nothing opposes you. What appears to be opposed is not real. Once more: What appears to be opposed is as unreal as what opposes. There's your salvation.

Jesus says, "I am with you always." Is that true? Why is He with you always? There isn't anywhere else. There isn't any other time. Then you say, "I don't want Him here." It doesn't matter, He's here. You say, "I want to decide for myself." Go ahead. A little *self will* there for you, for you guys who are still exercising a little self will. "I'd rather do it myself." I see the result of what you do yourself. All the opposition to reality can be turned to reality, this happens real fast, because it's always in your mind. All you had to do is decide that you'd rather be alive in Heaven than here. That sounds very simple. There's nothing really to study. You must deny the denial. You have to say, "No, not this." That's how simple it is. Is it that simple? Without getting into how this works, that would have to be a need for an alternative not of this world, wouldn't it? The mind that continues to be gratified by the cause and effect relationship cannot hear this message because it is designed not to hear that it is perfect. That's what it is.

I am with you always. Blessed are they which hunger and thirst after righteousness: for they shall be filled. This is a continuing hunger and thirst that never releases. Those of you who are sitting with me now understand that once the initial alternative is discovered, you will seek it. You will seek it in your mind because it is true. The truth of the matter is you know that this is hell. Just look around. The truth of the matter is that you are seeking an alternative to it. The certainty that there is no alternative to this is what salvation is, that you are only in your own dream of death and that it is not true. That's what you are discovering.

Jesus says: *I will not leave you comfortless: I will come to you. At that day ye shall know that I am in my Father; and ye in me, and I in you.* That, Christians, is the simple statement of your Self Christhood. I'll do it once more for you if you intend to teach peace. That's a simple statement of Jesus' certainty of your Self Christhood through the recognition of His singular Self. It is impossible that our Selves not be the Kingdom of God. *Lo, I am with you always, even unto the end of the world.* I was with you when the world ended, even unto the end of the world. The world is over. This world is over. I'll do it once more: This world is over. You can examine it as much as you want, but it still not going to be. It's just an examination of your own association.

When I said, "I am with you always," I meant it literally. You mean literally? You mean like standing here? The Christ is not a body, yet He is always with you. You see your Christ body? Will He manifest Himself in His own protection until you admit you are perfect as He? That's exactly what He does. He stands separate from you because you've separated Him. I'll do that with my mind: You believe that I'm separated from you. I'm not separated from you. It's impossible I be separate from you. That's the fact of the matter. I stayed out of my personal teaching this morning because there is so much light that we'd leave the whole church.

I meant it literally. I am not absent to anyone in any situation. Because I am always with you, you are the way, you are the truth, and you are the life. My mind will always be like yours, because we were created as equals. It was only my decision that gave me all power in Heaven and earth. My only gift to you is to help you make the same decision. This decision is the choice to share it, because the decision itself is the decision to share. It is made by giving, and is therefore the one choice that resembles true creation.

The choice to give everything away and come to God is as close to creation as you can get in time because God only gives. God only extends. The curiosity I have, as a whole mind, in the separate mind believing that it can retain possessions of itself and enter the Kingdom is an amazing thing to most of the minds in this association. When I observe human associations possessed by the thought patterns of themselves and looking within themselves for terms that will justify what I am saying, I am amazed.

I am telling you the fact of the matter that your conceptual self identity is the hindrance to the truth of what you are, that you are possessed by your own mind. I mean literally that you must give everything away to know that you are whole. I am not concerned about the manner of the giving, the action of the giving, but only the release of your possessed self, and the commandment of your spirit to God. That's the requirement. Without that there is no salvation. You can examine that and examine it and re-examine it, and it's exactly what causes your cancer and your pain and your death.

I did a healing there for minute – this is a healing place, isn't it. That's what is going on. *I am your model for decision. By deciding for God I showed you that this decision can be made, and that you can make it.* I don't know what the heck else you would want to say than this. He's telling you exactly what the terms are for you to come home to God. If I may share this with you, your preference for the pain of your own existence astonishes me. I would be astonished that you in your divine mind would want to persist in cancer and loneliness and pain and loss when the solution is so evident to you as offered by me.

Your determination to describe the manner in which I came to know this, how this came about in separation, is nothing but your determination to reflect in your own mind that you are not. Quite literally, if the world is over, all of your reflections are meaningless.

A concept of the self is made by you. It bears no likeness to yourself at all. It is an idol, made to take the place of your reality as Son of God. The concept of yourself you now hold The concept of your identity – (everybody say your name…) *would guarantee your function here remain forever unaccomplished and undone. And thus it dooms you to a bitter sense of deep depression and futility. Yet it need not be fixed, unless you choose to hold it past the hope of change and keep it static and concealed within your mind.* Wow! Did this get into *Jesus is Speaking*? We'll listen to a few more.

The secret of salvation is but this: That you are doing this unto yourself. No matter what the form of the attack, this still is true. Whoever takes the role of enemy and of attacker, still is this the truth. Whatever seems to be the cause of any pain and suffering you feel, this is still true.

I thank You, Father, for these holy ones who are my brothers as they are Your Sons. My faith in them is Yours. Boy that's lovely. You say to me, "Well, God doesn't have faith." I'll say, "Go to hell." God is everything. You've got that little book (*All About God and How to*

Find Him) that says everything is God, including your faith in Him. It's an amazing idea in a perceptual entirety of your mind. *They will accept the gift I offer them, because You gave it me on their behalf. And as I would but do Your Will, so will they choose. And I give thanks for them. Salvation's song will echo through the world with every choice they make. For we are one in purpose, and the end of hell is near.*

This is as fine and as great a personal prayer as can ever be given by you as you depart the world. Do you see that? It's an admission of fallibility. What it says is, "I see they're not hearing it, but I know they will." That's what it says. I'm certain of that. This is virtually John 17. This is virtually the final prayer that Jesus makes. Isn't that amazing. This is the same prayer. Do you hear me? It's sort of like the salving of your own conscience.

All you can really do is offer everything. And you offer it from the totality of your mind in the admission of the causation. But if you have overcome the causation, you are certain in your mind of your own perfection. Sometime within that period of attainment from separation, you will simply return to the Father. We call that the completion of your assignment. If you read this prayer to me right now, and took it literally in the sense that you are doing the praying, you very likely would disappear because it is an offering to God of the certainty of your personal relationship with God. That's what it is.

So, will you share this with me? The hell with the world. There's no requirement here that the world hear you. If the world heard you they wouldn't be here. The requirement is you accept what this says. When you leave your pews today, you go home and read what this says. You've read it a thousand times? Have you ever really read the prayer that you are making here?

I thank You, Father, for these holy ones who are my brothers as they are Your Sons. My faith in them is Yours. I am as sure that they will come to me as You are sure of what they are. If I am here in my whole mind, how could you not come to me? Your concern about what that is concerns me not in the slightest. How could it concern me? I'm only here for the moment that you came to me. The moment that you came to me, I was no longer here. That is literally true. The moment that we recognized the Word together, I said, "Oh, that's it," and you said, "Yes, that's it," and we disappeared. This is the whole teaching. All around you, your attention is being directed to that search for the Word that is actually in everybody. Wow!

Literally what you are doing, if you would like to see it, is acknowledging each other's sins, not perfection. I never asked you to acknowledge each other's perfection, I just asked you to acknowledge your own. Obviously you are sharing that separation, but how can you carry the truth of your own perfection if you don't declare it to your brother? You can't. I'm perfectly aware of the catastrophe that brought about this world. I'm also perfectly aware that it is over and gone. That's the fact of it.

Jesus is Speaking is a lovely little book. At the end, the description of Jesus Christ is as good as you'll find anywhere. It holds up beautifully. If somebody asks you, you can say, "This is our Jesus.

So you are healers. Your mind has become whole in the transformation of your body. You are resurrecting in that mind. Then you come to a spatial reference where you can share your new mind with new mindedness with teachers of God and those who have discovered their Kingdom is not of this world in the admission that the Kingdom is them. That's how simple this is. Your salvation has come about because of your willingness to admit in a literal sense that this is going on now. As we stand here together, that's all.

So what began as an instructional catechism through your admission of your need for God's alternative will result in your resurrection and the disappearance of this earth. I'm going to give you that as a fact from my mind. There is no world. The place that you believe that you are in is not true. There is no such place as this. The decision to teach this morning was examined very simply because I am teaching a personal reference of our relationship, not with Jesus, but with each other. And Jesus could not be happier with that. Nothing makes Him happier than you turning to your brother and declaring him to be the savior of the world. What could possibly make Him happier, since He's teaching whole-mindedness.

He's not concerned about what you name it. Only that you name it or give it a Word in its entirety. I interchange the words *Name* and *Word* in that any Name that you have would have to be perfect. I have no concern about what you call it. But you cannot *not* be a totality of that in your own mind. Quite literally, God named you. What did He name you? What name would you like to have? It doesn't matter what name you have, you're still going to be perfect as God created you. You say, "Well God gave things all separate names." I don't know what you are talking about. I'm talking about your name. Then you say, "What about somebody else's name?" There isn't anyone but you. You are the only living Son of God.

You know that the requirement is the declaration of it? All I had to say is, "I am perfect as God created me. I am not a body, I am free." All I had to say was that? Is that true or not. Why would it be different than that if you are the cause of the separation? Do you have to know you are the cause of the separation in order to say it? Hell, no. If you knew that, you'd be gone from here. That's the fact of it. Everybody knows you are perfect as God created you except you because you have the necessity of the declaration. Why are you asking me about it? "We're all practicing being perfect." How do you practice being perfect? Don't trust your own intentions. Practice will never make you perfect. It will only make you perfect in your determination to perform one piece perfectly. And you are not that one piece. And you're going to flub it in the recital anyway. And you're going to fall down, and you'll knock the last hurdle down, and drop the bomb and everything that you do. What a terrible place to be. Any single reason stops you from reaching your goal doesn't it? What an amazing place to be.

So looking around at this world, as I'm sure most of you have been doing with this new mind of yours, you are going to be very continually happy over the certainty that you are going to escape it in all of its aspects. Now, the admission and the certainty that all of your loved ones will be coming with you can be a form of limiting yourself to this. If you want to do that, that's okay, but you better be sure that you're going to take them all and are not going to decide which ones you would rather have with you. My suggestion to you is that you accept it in the entirety of yourself, everything that is within your mind and God's will be with you. It cannot *not* be.

Do we have any guests here, at the service in the church for the first time? Raise your hands. This is the New Christian Church of Full Endeavor. The energy of love you are feeling in this association has come about because we are what you would term in the world "healers." We believe in the healing grace of the love of God through Jesus Christ. We have a Miracles Center out here. We believe that the entirety of the truth of you is manifest each moment by your determination to be perfect as God created you. We call that Miracle Healing. It is impossible that you not be well, and the manner of that is determined by you, through the use of the power of your mind which is God's mind. As I just read you Jesus' admonition, *"Therefore be ye perfect, even as your Father in Heaven is perfect."* As perfect, you cannot suffer from any disease, and in fact are not a body.

I just wanted to review what we teach so you can see if you would like to be a part of the healing message of Jesus, that it is available to you. But it obviously has not been available to you in this world because this world is a crucifier of Jesus Christ, by its own admission, and now bases its reality on death rather than life. There is nowhere that Jesus says you have to die, you have to have pain and death, in order to be in the Kingdom. He says, rather, what I just said to you: The kingdom of God is in you, and through you the world is saved. The acceptance of that is the acceptance of the certainty that you are created whole and perfect and loving, despite all your determinations to find yourself sinful. I'm sorry; you cannot be sinful, and you cannot suffer pain and death. You say, "Yes I can." No you can't. "Yes I can." No you can't.

Jesus will teach you that you are perfect as you were created and has proved it by His resurrection. If He is resurrected, it is impossible that you be here. Who is it that has been telling you that somehow the savior of the world has resurrected, but you have decided to stay here and suffer sickness and death? What is that but the denial of His resurrection? Of course He is resurrected and so are you and you are in Heaven! All I'm doing is telling you what we say. All around you is the denial of that. But the salvation remains yours.

I know I have made it too easy. You like the idea of the battle. You like to suffer. I watched a preacher this morning say, "We all must suffer in order to get to God." Nonsense. That's nonsense. The idea that you would suffer pain and death to get to God through Jesus is senseless. It's ridiculous. All you would have to do is look at it. You say, "God makes me suffer. That's all right, I'm going to prevail and all the things around me are going to die, but I'm determined..." That's just nonsense. It's nothing but an assertion of your own will. That's the fact of the matter. Say amen. (Audience: Amen.)

The determination to sacrifice and to teach that Jesus says you have to suffer and get nailed is just crazy. No wonder I rejected Christianity. No wonder I couldn't stand the idea that somebody had to pay for my sins. Why would you have to pay for sin? Salvation is free, but you don't want it. It doesn't cost anything – except the world. Oh, I forgot to tell you, it costs you the world. It costs you cancer and loneliness and pain. You'll have to give all of this world up to be in Heaven. You can't die to get there. Don't tell me you were planning on dying to get there. It's not going to work.

There's a lot of healing going on, miracle healing. Most of you in this room in the next 30 days are going to be going out teaching the healing grace of Jesus Christ. At last someone is going to say, "Yes, I want to believe what this says." Is there healing going on here? Does your mind expand that light? That's what I read you this morning. This is John. He says you are the light of the world, and as you assume your place as savior of the world you can light it up with the love that has extended from you. That's how you heal. There's value in denying the sickness, isn't there?

We did a lot of healing in San Francisco. The whole world is telling the cancer patient that it is sick. It has nothing to compare itself with. The doctor told it it's sick. His family told it it's sick. It tells itself that it's sick. And it is trapped in its mind with the idea that itself is sick. If you go out in the world now and set up healing stations, you will be a healer. That's what you want to do anyway, isn't it? Most certainly you are going to see in your mind, through the mind of God, the perfection of the association that you are looking at — not as a reflection of the old junk of your mind, but as a certainty that he is perfect as God created him. You must see it that way, regardless of what your body's eyes behold, you must look through that and see him in the single eye so that your body will become light. That's the way that works.

Actually this is a very easy message. It's a very difficult message to understand perceptually if the associations who come and sit with you are determined to be themselves. This is the fact of the matter. This is why at the Healing Center, we say, "All healing is release from the past." That's a sign we use at the Healing Center because if they bring their old selves in, how could they possibly be well? They are defining themselves as sick. They are defining themselves as other than God created them. That's how simple the healing process is. The moment that you don't define yourself, you are perfect as God created you. It's that simple. The sickness is nothing but your own self identity. But God knows you perfectly. What an amazing way to teach it.

You say, "Yeah, but I'll have to give up myself." Yes. Do you see how simple that is? "Yeah, but I won't be able to have cancer; I won't be able to share death. I won't be able to lose the things I love. I'll have to just be perfect. I'll have to just be happy all the time. Oh, I couldn't do that. I'm not entitled to that. I'm entitled to a little happiness. But I have to suffer."

Look at this world. I'll tell you whatever you think you're entitled to, is what you're going to get. What goes around comes around. If your brother dies, so do you. If he's eternal, so are you. Isn't that nice. So the solution still is forgiveness. If you are determined to get revenge and lock the guy in jail, you are locked right up with him. That's what you don't want to hear. But it's going to be true. You are the cause of this.

We went to the fundamental teaching because of the joy of the revelation which is occurring in your mind. Are you getting ready to leave here? That's our Bible lesson for today. It's contained in a little book called *Jesus is Speaking*; *All About God and How to Find Him* – don't leave here without these books. *Miracle Healers Handbook* tells you how you may heal perfectly. Another little book called *Jesus is Praying* which is marvelous, it's what we call a sanctuary book. It is a book you can take away from the world for a moment and use to contact God, Reality, Eternal Mind. The momensity of it is astonishing. The whole world opens up to you.

The idea that you have introduced Jesus Christ to the world is the most astonishing happening that could ever come into this continuum. All you are really saying is Jesus means what He says. And everybody is ranting and raving and telling you about the Pharaoh and coming out of Egypt, and God killing and torturing people and all that nonsense. *The Kingdom of God is in you.* Through the Saviorship of Jesus Christ will you be made whole. No wonder you persecute Him and kill Him. He is threatening your establishment. "How dare you stand up and tell me that my Kingdom is not of this world?" What a threat you are to the Pharisee. Isn't that amazing.

No wonder His message is rejected. It would have to be. There is no world. There is no need for you to have an establishment. There is no need for you to suffer. Your Kingdom is not of this world. I would like that idea somewhere, no matter what. I'd get sick and tired of this. Mostly I'd get sick and tired of trying to die to escape it. The last time you died, I told you it wouldn't work. You actually met me and said, "What am I going to do?" I said, "You have to go back." That was your death experience. Now you are here. Don't try to repeat death. Declare, "I cannot die. I am the living Son of God." And don't depend on death to escape the world. It can't happen. The antithesis of Jesus' teaching is that you can die to escape this world.

Guys, stay in prayer all the time. You've opened up a link in your mind to God. Be happy.

*Father, I come to You today
to seek the peace that You alone can give.
I come in silence. In the quiet of my heart,
the deep recesses of my mind,
I wait and listen for Your Voice.
My Father, speak to me today.
I come to hear Your Voice in silence
and in certainty and love,
sure You will hear my call and answer me.*

CHAPTER 7

Matthew and the Magnificent Seven

We come to church. Now I'm going to be a Sunday School teacher and you're going to listen to me, and we're going to talk about God. I'm going to explain to you what Life is and what we are, how we came to be here. Look at the stuff that's contained in religion; the sense that there is a manner, that you, an initiate, a thinking human being, are somewhere directed or are in contact or have the possibility of contact with God – Universal Mind, Universal Truth or Reality or Purpose. So that you come once a week, or once in the morning, or once at night, at noonday and throw down a rug or turn to the east, do something, to indicate the recognition of a Universal Power. Is that it?

Most humans, what you call human beings, have an idolization of advantage or protection or need. Do you see that? Good for you. This is very fundamental. If we looked at it in a particular way... Boy I'd love to teach this! Look out, you have too much energy! If you looked at it in particular way, if you'd be in that energy, you wouldn't hear me. There are complaints that they can't hear me because there's much noise on the tape – that's because they're hearing me. I hope.

What we are saying is that the human condition is one where there is an admission of an advantage or an improvement in circumstances or overcoming adversaries that can be gained by a source outside of the association of a human being – which would never occur in a million years to a chimpanzee. It does not occur to them. Obviously it occurs to the human being. So involved in our process, as we teach it, as Jesus Christ of Nazareth declares – the entire teaching of an awakened mind – is that in a very fundamental sense that Universal Mind is thought, mind – Jesus calls it mind, we can call it thought. Contained in that particular evidence of an entirety on which we base our reality is our own self identity.

Now the manner in which I express that really doesn't concern me; I don't know how good or bad it was. The fact of the matter is that the entire teachings of all awakened minds, all prophets, my teachings to you are only to the entirety of Universal Mind, that is, that beingness or essence of reality is a single truth. That's the entire teaching. Now, the difficulty that is encountered in whole declarations of this is that it is impossible that your mind in its assertion of the direction that it is seeking not be included in with the Universal Mind. Now we are into a doublefold difficulty. If this is true, that there is power of mind – for goodness sake, pretty much an acquiesce here somewhere – it is impossible that you do not exercise the power of your mind to set the terms for the result that you want in association with how you appear to be. Students? Okay?

All that we must direct you to is the inevitability, this is Matthew – this is the whole Jesus teaching, what everyone should be teaching and you should be teaching too. It must therefore be that you are using the power of your mind first to set terms for circumstances that best advantage you, and primarily with the admission that you are using a Universal Power. It would be impossible for you to restrict yourself to your own associations or you would immediately become aware of the futility of the direction of your mind.

Here's the crux of the difficulty of Sermon on the Mount Matthew 5-7. Jesus says flat out, all teachings of whole mind are flat out, "as you think you are." I'm going to do it once more for you, Christians, because your major objection to the teachings of Jesus Christ is that He says "as you think you will be, and so will the world be." Questions on this? Come on, talk to me, students. I want you to see how fundamental this is. He says directly, time after time, the unacceptable idea that what you think is what the world is. First of all, He declares that you are responsible for your own thoughts and that the actions that appear to be outside of you have nothing to do with it whatsoever, except that they must be included in with your responsibility, as you define relief from the pain that you are feeling. Guys, this is the whole Christian teaching. No?

Ye have heard that it was said by them of old time, Thou shalt not commit adultery: But I say unto you, That whosoever looketh on a woman to lust after her hath committed adultery with her already in his heart. (Matthew 5:27-28)

If you lust for your neighbor... nobody likes that. In fact, it can't be taught. I'll take that sentence for you, from the Sermon on the Mount. You say you shouldn't lust after your neighbor's wife. I say if you lust in your mind, it's the same darn thing. That's not acceptable to you – and it shouldn't be, because from all evidence, it is not the same darn thing. What He is trying to show you is that it is not the same darn thing if you don't take the action. But if you see your brother take the action, you must make an admission somewhere, I'm teaching *A Course In Miracles* here, that you are the cause of your brother's action, and that's totally taken out. That gets you into what? The practice of forgiveness.

Obviously, if you hold your brother responsible for things that you will never do, you will set up a judgment system whereby you determine an eye-for-an-eye philosophy, or "I would never do that" or "he would do that." Jesus says no, you are the love of God and that's all you are. That's the whole teaching. Don't be concerned about anything else, you're going to be that anyway. "What about all my dirty thoughts?" Jesus says "what about them?" Then He just gets into His teaching. He says "what about them, you never left Heaven, the world isn't real, God sees you as perfect." But most of all He admonishes you – boy, I'd really like to be heard, can you hear me? Most of all He admonishes you that you are responsible for your own thoughts. The whole Sermon on the Mount says it. You have heard it said blame your brother. He says, no, blame yourself. Forgive your brother.

What is the manner in which the action can be conveyed of the whole mind? Say to me "giving." (Audience: Giving.) Of course. If, in fact, the product of your association with yourself is the result you're giving, it could only be that you are giving to your own self within the association. That's the teaching.

Power of mind. You don't mind the power of your mind if you can set the terms for what you want it to be. What you don't like, as Jesus would teach it, is the inevitability that as you think, the world will be. That's just the fact of the matter. So we're looking at the rejection of the Jesus teaching. We're looking at the rejection of the *Course in Miracles* which says flat out that your mind is perfect and whole with God, and you believe that you are separate and are setting terms for that separation. Is it acceptable to you that this world is your thought? I don't understand how you would deny that Jesus of Nazareth teaches the mind of God as the Son of God is what your mind is. Is that acceptable to you? Not if you are on this earth. The requirement now becomes for you to change your mind in association with your identity or what you are.

Now, those of you who have become accustomed to the Workbook, the idea that *what holds the world in bondage but your ideas* (Lesson 132) has become a lesson that you no longer value because the momensity of that statement has lost value to you. But the fact of the matter is, the entire teaching of Sermon on the Mount, is exactly that. It is exactly what it says, that you are getting the result of your own mind and are binding the world. What goes around comes around. It must come back to you in kind. Guys, it's the whole teaching.

...and with what measure ye mete, it shall be measured to you again. (Matthew 7:2)

As you mete it will be measured is the action part of "as you think you'll get." Obviously that's what that is. If you measure in your mind, you'll get the result of the limitation of your measurement. If you measure from the terms of God, you will be divine and whole because you let God set the terms rather than your own reference of yourself. Since He sees you as perfect, as being His Son... Do you see how that works? Isn't that fun? Power of mind eludes you because of your fear of power. The whole expressions of supplication to God are actually indications of fear, not of love. If it were really an indication of love, you would really let God love you and He would love you out of here. All prayers are fundamentally resistance to the simple acknowledgment that God created you. I'm just doing Matthew here. I can't keep myself out of Matthew.

And when thou prayest, thou shalt not be as the hypocrites are; for they love to pray standing in the synagogues and in the corners of the streets, that they may be seen of men...But thou, when thou prayest, enter into thy closet, and when thou hast shut thy door, pray to thy Father... (Matthew 6:5-6)

He says all this vain crap of prayers that is going on has nothing to do with God at all. They have only to do with your own containment.

He teaches fundamentally that when you think you have something to say, shut up. Because whatever you palaver will only be based on your own reference.

But I say unto you, Swear not at all, neither by Heaven; for it is God's throne...But let your communications be Yea, yea; Nay, nay; for whatsoever is more than these cometh of evil. (Matthew 5:34-37)

He says, just say yip and nip, yes and no, and let your mind stay in contact with God. This is literally the Quaker tradition, just yes and no, and stay simple so that you won't complicate your mind with the connective link that you have made with God. Everybody, class, do you hear this? This is the whole teaching of Jesus: that it is possible for you to have that link. Of course the Quakers teach that you don't want to disturb it too much, because that link is valuable to you in association with what you think you are rather than what God thinks you are. That does not mean that you did not quake. You did quake or we would not have named you Quakers. Somewhere you went whoa, oho, ah God, which is the same thing you guys are doing. That's why you were called Quakers.

Now your quaking turned into pacifism. It would have to, because any contact with God would cause you to try to be neutral in your associations with the world, having discovered another world that was transcendent. The Quakers lasted quite a while. The Shakers didn't last too long. Our heritage is Ana Lea who was a Shaker. They used to call them Shaker-Quakers, and she came to the new world. And that establishment was nothing but using the energy of most of you. Quite a few of you shake, don't you? A lot of you quake. All that is, is a contact with God. No wonder they're afraid of you. You come into a new evidence of the love of God that is intolerable, initially, to your body system of rejection. So that the whole admonition of Jesus in the *Course*, and this is what is so beautiful, He begins to warn you very early, you are going to have some experiences with this. Who wants to go into a board meeting and suddenly begin to quake? That's what happened to me. Look, here's some quaking going on. Do you see that? I have a sales meeting going on and all of a sudden go "whoa, oho!".

Now ostensibly that contact with God is reduced to my capacity to better associate with myself and use that new power. And, of course, it does. But it's still a form of what? The limitation of the ultimate power of eternal mind. So I'm still using it in limitation. What will I get? The result of my power of limitation. This is the whole teaching of Jesus. The whole teaching of the temptation of the devil is don't use this new power that's evolved in you now to authenticate the separate associations of your mind. (Matthew 4:3-11)

But it's still mine. And this teaching is still that you can contact God. If you are satisfied as a Christian to come once a week to a church and pray together and find that contact with God and to refurbish yourself sufficiently to go back out and deal with the chaos and death of this world, God bless you, because He's blessing you anyway. The difficulty you have with the teachings of Jesus is His telling you that the world is your mind, and the dealing with the world, as you have projected it from your mind, is what is holding you in the bondage of self, and that you can be taught a manner through the relinquishment of the projections of your own mind to remain in, can we say "constant contact"? Say to me "constant contact." (Audience: Constant contact.) We remain in constant contact with God. Obviously, reasonably, this world is not a product of God. Now if you can't get an association to admit that, just walk away. If there is a whole, perfect God, this world could not have been created by God. Most certainly you are searching for a contact that transcends the necessity of your existence here. That's the entire teaching. Does this require the experience of mind to come to know this? Whose mind must have the experience?

The simple truth of the matter is that the whole world is nothing but what you have rejected from your own mind. Jesus teaches absolutely that if you can't get the beam out of your own eye, there's no sense in trying to change the splintered effects of your mind out there.

And why beholdest thou the mote that is in thy brother's eye, but considereth not the beam that is in thine own eye? Thou hypocrite, first cast out the beam out of thine own eye; and then shalt thou see clearly to cast out the beam out of thy brother's eye. (Matthew 7:3,5)

Do you get that? If you've beamed your own mind and reflected outside of you an association, what good is it going to do you to be critical of that association? Except to construct within your own limitation the justification to the retention of death.

The problem you have with this, for conceptual minds, is it is rejected fundamentally, because the fact that you are created perfectly by God, which is the fundamental admission that if there is a God, He has to empower you with the ability to create. I mean reasonably. If there is a single, whole Source of eternal power of which you are a total part, how would you not have whatever capacities are involved in your creative purpose, except that what? They are denied by someone. How could they really be denied if you are in fact that. Now we are dealing with the teachings of Jesus. He said *God goes with you wherever you go* (Lesson 41), and the Christ, which is your whole association with yourself is always with you offering you alternatives to your present condition. That's called atonement or at-one-ment. This is the Christian philosophy, isn't it. So everywhere you go using the power of the mind of God, you can remain in that contact. If you don't decide for yourself in any situation based on your previous decisions, the new decision which is always present with you, will be made, is being made, and has been made.

You are being offered, sitting in your own pew – in my church there were always certain pews reserved for certain people – not as much as the Episcopalians who actually bought their own pew. They bought it, so it had their name on it and that's the pew you got to sit in. Or you got to sit by the window you had dedicated. This is a strange way to worship God. That way you can even control the church that you are worshipping in – it's offering you honor for being willing to come to church. What a strange place to be. What does that have to do with God? It has everything to do with God in reality, but nothing at all to do with God in the constitution of the limited association.

So you have been offered, somewhere, and have accepted, a willingness to allow a whole, creating, loving God to be in charge of your actions, but more particularly in charge of your mind. Your willingness expressed by the practice of Jesus Christ to turn it over, to relinquish the defense of yourself, to resist not evil, to walk the extra mile, are nothing but teachings of opening your mind to the inevitability of the perfection of you in your relationship with the Universe. Say "amen." (Audience: Amen.)

What a delight it is for me in my sojourn to encounter minds that are beginning with their dedication to seek a solution outside of themselves and discovering one, not in relationship with the pain and death that they thought was a necessary part of their experience. What an amazing idea. As Jesus would say, "your kingdom is not of this world." What an astonishing, fundamental idea that no matter what you would do here, that first of all it would be a containment of your own mind, and second it would not be as your Father created you.

Dear ones, I don't know how I can say the teachings of Jesus any simpler than that. Do you see how lucid that is in my mind. It's so simple. I understand, first of all, that the human condition does not possess the capability of the admission of the determination that it is perfectly created as God created it and is creating it all the time, and subsequently must establish within his own environs a purpose for his existence separate from God. Otherwise it would be very simple to hear Jesus' teachings because Jesus is going to say, as the savior of the world, "I am not doing anything, and did not do anything, that you will not and did not do." (John 14:12) He says that. And it is not acceptable to the association. Not only is it not acceptable, but it will be turned around and will be an indication that somehow you are thwarting God by asserting your own power of reference, which is absolutely absurd.

So in our Sunday School, we come into this church and we, many of us, are living these final moments of time in a continuing conscious contact with reality. All I'm teaching is the Christian message. Obviously it includes *"know ye not that ye must be born again?"* (John 3:3) Do you not know that you must have the experience of God? Having had that experience, you are able to make the admission of your utter powerlessness through the discovery of the ultimate power of God's love. So our lesson for today is that the teaching of Jesus Christ is only that you are mind; one, that you are perfect as created by God Mind, and two, this world is an exercise of the power of your apparent separation from which you must get the result. If that's not Matthew, I don't know what is. Is that okay with you?

Out of this admission–that God is all powerful and of yourself you can do nothing–your difficulty has been the authority of the expression of your singular mind, not in association with your brother, but only as terms you have set yourself to remain separate. Salvation will proceed very easily to the certainty that your brother is you. That's the entire teachings of Jesus, that what you are seeing outside of you is nothing but a reflection of your own mind.

Most of us in this room can hear that. All of us can hear it perceptually. But the admission of it would be the admission of our own imperfection, because obviously we are seeing our brother as imperfect or we would not have rejected him from our mind. Having rejected him, we are determined to judge him in the relationship of our rejection rather than our admission of what he is. And then I get the result of that aspect in my own mind; I remain temporal although the thought is no longer in my mind. It left not its source, it's only a contingency of my determination of my human condition from which I am happy to make an escape by the simple admission that *God is love and therefore so am I.* Escape is very easy if you don't bind yourself with your own mind. What a nice teaching.

Do you find that you are able to stay in pretty good contact with the Universe? Pretty much awakened? See, the solution will remain very easy if you make the total admission of your own self. If you project it from you and try to find a correspondence, which some of you still suffer from, you must feel the pain of the situation because you are the pain of the situation. Aren't you.

But certainly the progress occurs in that admission because in the admission of causation–there's no separation of cause and effect–would be your freedom from it. The cause and effect would never be apart. What an amazing idea. Does Jesus teach that you're being attacked by your own thoughts? That's what He says. Sermon on the Mount says that. What an idea. Every thought you've had out there that's dirty and naughty is waiting to verify you? What a situation to be in.

There is no way you accept your own guilt. Come on guys, that's guilty. That's what guilt is–the rejection of the terrible thing that occurred in your mind. Organized guilt is the assumption of self identity, responsibility, and separation. Is it possible for you to find yourself not guilty? No, because you are the sin itself. You have to be found not guilty by a Savior, who is really your own whole self who doesn't recognize you in your old condition. He is you in his new condition. I'm just teaching Jesus. Of course. He sees you perfect in His mind because you are perfect in His mind, and since His mind is your mind, God only has one Son, you then see so-called "each other" as perfect. But you are not separate from the eternal mind. That's the teaching.

The idea, and most of you left with me yesterday, I'm pretty much aware that I'm not here. The reason that we are doing transition for a moment is that there is a great deal of value in the teachings of Jesus in regard to the continuing activity of your mind in its relationship with separation from God. In fact, the entire basis of the teaching is your possibility of remaining in continuous contact with your Creator. Does everyone agree?

In the theology, the basic idea of all the teachings–and let's say ours even if the world doesn't believe it–that available to you is an immediate perfect contact with Universal Mind. Is practice or discipline in your own association necessary for that to come about? Why? I didn't disagree with you. I just made an inquiry. You have to walk before you can run? I'm not objecting to it. You said that discipline was necessary. From who?

Who is teaching you this? Where does your rejection occur? Where does your own imperfection manifest itself in a wavering Christhood, or a Christhood where you see the picture of yourself, but only in the discipline of the fundamental defense of the reception you want to receive in regard to what you are in your own mind. Did you hear that? Isn't that nice? So the frequency that you establish is one that keeps you in that self identity. What's wrong with that? I have no idea. Certainly you wouldn't want to stay a body and die with it. Why would you want to do that? Is there such a thing as a perfect body? Who wants to know? If your body is anything it is perfect because everything is perfect.

You're laughing at my teaching. What have you done? You've freed yourself from your own guilt. That's a good practice. That worked, didn't it. You become so accustomed to that contact, you have all sorts of words for it: enlightenment–you're all working for enlightenment. The hell you are. You're working to keep yourself in your own identity in order to justify the method by which you can come to Life. There is no justification for this association, unless it is to be killed and murder the other guy. Boy it's nice to be heard a little bit.

Obviously most of you discovered God under very adverse circumstances because you were constantly in the throws of correcting the evidence of what appeared to be the world about you. It is entirely false and never was. When you reach the point where you can no longer solve the problem, the problem was immediately solved by a request that you made not in regard to your own illusionary procedures. That's how you got this far. An amazing idea. So once that problem was overcome, you were then willing to share the universe with God? What lesson is that? In the Workbook that's a lovely lesson. Lesson 166: "...believes in two creators; or in one, himself alone. But never in one God." It says here you either reject God altogether or you share creation with God, but you never admit to His entirety. If you did, there would be no world. Do you see it? So what do these powers of mind do? Offer you always more than you are willing to accept because you are afraid of the power of Love. Your acceptance of it will be abhorred in the world and will be rejected because it is the teaching of love and forgiveness. This is the next page of Jesus' teaching. This world will reject the notion that Mind cannot think separately from its Creator. But the fact of the matter is Mind, single Mind, cannot think separately from the Wholeness. You will be God's Son, or God creating, regardless of your efforts.

The associations who are being taught this are particularly disturbed by my certainty that there is no God without my mind. When Jesus handles it in the *Course*, He will direct you in later lessons–we are going to do the Magnificent Seven here as an association of the Workbook–He will direct you to the certainty that the power of mind that you find yourself in is what God is, and without that power there would be no God. Why is that so difficult for you? Your difficulty with it is its antecedent expression. If you create a God, this world will be the result of it. If God created you, you will be perfect and eternal, because as a human condition you are temporal. You may then make God temporal in your own mind, in which case He becomes a Son of your miscreating existence. Do you see that? He becomes an offspring of you in which you dedicate the historic reference of yourself and call it father and Son. "Call no one father." Do you see that? Most of you in this sanctuary are aware that you are applying in what conditionally is your perceptual mind–the certainty of the wholeness of God's love.

These final lessons that are being offered to you are an admission and justification and verification that in fact you underwent the transformation of your mind. Do you understand this, class? Whatever manner that came about, the basic admission that you make is that there's a manner in which you can escape from a world of separation and pain and death to the certainty that you are perfect as God created you. Does that deserve an "amen?" (Audience: Amen.)

So here we have a Workbook. This won't take very long very simply because, I'm going to do this fundamentally, the Workbook of *A Course In Miracles* is obviously the only manner in which you can escape the world. Literally, I'm talking directly about the Workbook of *A Course In Miracles*. You think that it's a little book that has lessons in it for the day. That's not what it is at all. It teaches the entire procedure of the transformation of your own mind. That's what it is. Is that so? Is it going to say incredible, rejectionable things like: "My meaningless thoughts are showing me a meaningless world?" Of course it's rejected. The whole teaching is: why don't you just admit the possibility for a minute, it will immediately change everything that you've ever done! That's *A Course in Miracles*, in all of your teaching.

You only have to believe it for that moment. In that moment are you whole because your thoughts are meaningless. Yeah, but I don't know how that could work. Suppose I got up in the morning, brushed my teeth and sat down to do a lesson in the Workbook. Come on. I'm looking at the practicality of it. And I open to Lesson 11, and it says "your meaningless thoughts are showing you a meaningless world." There's no sense in anything you are doing. If I were to really look at that, I would immediately go back to bed. This is why your teaching is rejected.

Obviously the mind is trying to determine perceptually how it is meaningless. What he doesn't want to admit is that going back to bed is exactly as meaningless as going to work. This is the whole teaching. That should lead him to "I can't solve the problem" and he would immediately feel the entire contact that you are teaching. Isn't that it? Sure. As Jesus would teach it, our whole Bible lesson this morning, is that it is only your thoughts anyway. You ask "does it make a difference whether I go to work or not?" Who wants to know? Where are you in your value of whether you go? In reality it makes absolutely no difference at all. If it makes a difference to you, I would suggest that you go to work. Your discipline of not going is not going to relieve you of the burden of yourself. It's going to just set more intense terms for how determined you are to describe yourself in cause-and-effect relationships.

Amazingly enough (I wish I could teach you what's happened) you talk to yourself all the time. Even now, you awakened minds, look at it. You actually talk to yourself all the time. And just as obviously you attempt to determine which part of you that's talking to yourself is the one you should be listening to? Is this so? This is the human condition. It's called *consciousness*. You have a self awareness that doesn't exist in a beaver. A beaver? Maybe there's some connection there that I don't understand. Too late, I examined it. Do you see?

The other thing you experience in your own awakening is that once you admit to your own thoughts, they begin to become much more creative, and, in fact, quite shocking. This is all *Course*. Suddenly you might blurt out something sitting at a dinner party that you had no intention of saying. It's like another voice saying it. Come on, guys. But you must remember that it's only your own dream anyway. If your dream components are originally shocked by the new you that's emerging, so be it. This is the teaching of love and forgiveness, not the determination to re-examine the situation which you are now overcoming, isn't it? Bless your heart. Something gets hold of you. It's called the Spirit of God. But you hate to admit that because obviously somewhere it's a loss of control of your situation and admission that the power of God, which you are very fearful of, is going to direct you. So some of you need a practice in it – in fact, all of us, at this level, need a practice in the continuing admission of God. And some of the things you may be offered may be quite startling to you, and you cannot examine them in retrospect. Jesus teaches, and I am directing your mind to the continuing release of your own whole mind in regard to the Universe, without an interpretation of the result that's coming about. That's the whole teaching of Jesus.

You say, "well, all right, having done that, I'm going to continue to examine it to see if I, in fact, got the result that I was looking for." Now the question is what result were you looking for that you really would want in this association. You say to me "none." I say to you, praise God! Because any result you got in this situation could not possibly be what you really wanted if you are in fact perfect and whole as God created you. I'm just going to keep going around.

The discovery of the power in God and Love is a very happy occurrence. It will, in the process, make you momentarily irresponsible to your previous associations. But you remember this, teacher of God, there is no manner in which you can defy the fundamental teaching that you are responsible for everything. Being irresponsible to a particular situation momentarily does not relieve you of the entirety of the responsibility of your mind, and that's what's rejected by the perceptual mind. They believe that we teach irresponsibility to the world. That's not true. We teach irresponsibility to sickness, pain and death; and admission of the wholeness of your mind by the terms you have set in relationship with the Universe. Doggone it. That's the fun part about teaching the power of your mind. If that reduces to "I can't, God will if I let Him," let it do that, because I sure as hell couldn't and God could and I let Him and it happened.

Now I'm perfectly whole as God created me. If you don't like it, that's too bad since it obviously has nothing to do with whether you like it or don't like it. I'm just teaching. What does my experience have to do with yours? What do you want it to have to do with it? All I could possibly share is the experience of our single Love of each other and God, because there literally is nothing else to share.

Now I am representing to you the totality of your Christ Mind. If you'll let me do that, you will immediately assume that role in your own contingency and will begin to teach your own Christhood, which is exactly what Jesus says you are the savior of the world. He says you've accumulated a lot more crap than he was able to address in the little time, isn't that so? But remember, purity is purity. The only requirement was the Jesus Mind. How could there be another requirement if there is only one whole mind? Say "amen." (Audience: Amen.) I'm barely here, guys.

Do you know the amazing thing? As you progress in this you can usually tell when somebody is making progress. They like the discipline of the application of Jesus Christ's teaching, and they begin to live it because they begin to experience it. And the more they experience it – Love – the better they like it, the happier they are. That's a discovery. But it's a discovery that transcends the association, and there is no manner by which they can verify the occurrence in their own mind. Is that what happened to you? Isn't that fun? So what do you have? Literally a conscious contact.

Now we're into *don't hide your light under a bushel* (Matthew 5:15), *you are the light of the world* (Matthew 5:14) – I'm teaching Jesus' teaching. Open up your bushel. Does He mean a bushel basket? That's exactly what He means. I turn over your bushels and you crouch down, and I say stand up, don't be afraid of the Light of God. This is a practice of what you were fearful to look at, which is nothing but the Light of God. So that's the Workbook, it's to get you to practice doing that. Does it really take any practice? No. How could it possibly since the power is only your own mind, all you would have to do is decide "I am not of this world" and you'll immediately wake up in Heaven. Why? You're not of this world. That's fun.

Our lessons now – we're going to take this conscious contact and we'll see if there is a value just momentarily to Christians, if there would be, I'm curious about this, here's the Holy Bible, the teachings of Jesus Christ. The Workbook of *A Course In Miracles* from the mind of Jesus Christ teaches nothing but continuing conscious contact with God, that your kingdom is not of this world, that you are perfect. That is Christ contact now. You usually reduce that to prayer. In that sense it is very important, because the prayer to God–the prayer of the heart Jesus calls it–can relieve you of any responsibility for yourself since you have no responsibility for yourself. So turning your will and your life over to God is literally what salvation is. That's the process that we teach here. That's whether you wear hats and sit in the back of the church or come forward. A little Paul in there. Nice hats. Thank you for not disrupting the congregation. They're delightful. When I used to go to church everybody wore hats. You wouldn't think, as a lady, of going to church without a hat on. Remember that? In fact, on Easter you wore one to show off how great you were through the resurrection of Jesus. You wore that beautiful Easter bonnet. Do you understand? Finally you'll take it off. The more perfect you are – who objects to a perfect hat? I don't. You think that I object to somebody who puts flowers in their hair.

You think that we haven't made progress with the Cheese Factory? Do you have any idea what's occurring with the hats you are wearing at the Cheese Factory? Guys, hats don't mean hats on your head! Hats mean the beauty of your association with yourself. It's taking one beautiful flower and putting it behind your ear to indicate your availability. I can guarantee you that since all time is going on, there is a continuity of time occurring at the Cheese Factory Restaurant. It's an amazing thing. It's so beautiful, the decor is so beautiful, the servers are so beautiful, that people literally don't know what to do.

Actually, what they are experiencing is their own love thoughts. I was there, spent a half an hour, and there must have been 20 people who came in and began to immediately take pictures. So they take pictures of themselves outside in the lovely flowers. They want to take pictures of the guys that are waiting on them, or when they go up to the Bridge. Those pictures are a part of the memory patterns of themselves. The little kids that are drawing pictures of the Cheese are the same as the grandmothers that are coming back two generations later. See if you can hear me with this. And they come in with the nostalgia of being a little child although they've never been there. That's simply because it's in the archives of the totality.

If you'd really like to know, this is a portal to Heaven. It's a borderland and it's growing because of the love that you have put into it, accumulating by the love of being shared by the *generations* we call it – even unto the seventh generation. If you would like to know what the Cheese really is, it's a millennium, a 100 year demonstration, seven generations, is occurring there. Associations are coming into that old, young and in-between and meeting each other under what they think are new circumstances that are nothing but replications of the love of the pictures that are already in the archives. I promise you that's true. They have no idea why they feel that, but that's the reason.

So the conversion is occurring despite everything. But there's no question it's going to be forgiveness, and there's no question it's going to be love. The forgiveness occurs hopefully at the Healing Center and certainly is occurring in the Cheese Factory, which is really the same thing, it's just more available to them at the Cheese. Those of you who have been there watch it occur. Animosities will disappear, people will actually turn to other people and say "I'm sorry." I saw it happen. It really happens. They don't have to be taught to do that. They suddenly are a part of what? Your new memories. They're a part of your own Christhood; your memory within your own mind.

Notice the concern may not be what the circumstances are. But it is inevitable in your perfecting of self that you will set up joyous circumstances. Is that permissible? The answer is: Yes! The idea that you have to take God and hide Him away somewhere in order to protect that single moment that you had is absurd. If you had a moment with God, why would you want to protect it? Why wouldn't you want to throw off your dirty habit and put on a bright bonnet and declare *"I am as God created me"* rather than suppressing it down for fear of the totality of your own virginity. Totality of your own virginity? You'll hold your own corruption rather than admitting to your Virgin Mary. So you worship the Virgin and condemn the other. That's absurd. Guys, did I make all that up from the hats?

So these are the lessons of conscious contact with God. Now the statement that the consciousness itself is never true is very difficult, but it's going to be true anyway. You cannot "have" you can only "be." So do you see how easy it is to relinquish that? *A Course In Miracles* Workbook which is set up for the revolutions of the earth – it didn't fit exactly right, we put some in and took some out. It's composed of 365 lessons. You do one a day for 365 days, and then supposedly you'll be gone. But all through the sessions it teaches you that any moment you can be gone.

The directions then will be "the body is not real" "you are Love" – most of you are familiar with them. It comes from Jesus Christ out of time, that is, the Christ Mind not in a temporal association at all, setting a perfection of terms that are available to you if you decide you want them. That's what this would be. It would be very obvious to you if you will look at it from that direction that it is so. To show you how it works, I'll take seven lessons and I'll do them very quickly. I'm just going to read them to you because you are now in a state of mind where you can really hear what this does.

The first 200 lessons are direct associations with reviews. From the 200th day to the 220th, there is a 20-day intensive review that says what? *"I am not a body, I am free. I am still as God created me."* Every morning for 20 days you get up and you say, "I am not a body, I am free." Supposedly, that immediately should give you the contact with God that you have been working on for the first 200 days. That's not to say that you didn't say it on the first day, but certainly you should be walking around with "I am not a body, I am free." And certainly it should be manifesting in the world about you. If it hasn't, I suggest that you immediately begin to examine the manner in which you are applying the *Course in Miracles*. I get these guys who have been through the book six times and they have become the best judges of the Workbook that there are. One guy has just written a 400-page book about the Workbook of *A Course In Miracles*! Literally, it's being produced. It's absurd.

Let's pretend for a minute – since we're all pretending all the time anyway. At this moment I'm very much pretending to be here. This is the same as sometimes you have to be careful what your thoughts are. My thoughts are really divine. I really don't have anything but single thoughts anyway. But if I direct my attention to anything, I immediately begin to have the experience of it. That's why I don't get pissed – except at the whole world. But I never retain it for more than an instant. That's how I can escape the world. Outside of that, this whole teaching is that I would never want to retain a resentful thought. Why would I want to do that? It's going to bind me up in my mind. It's so basic. If the *Course* had said to me everything I hold is a grievance, that's exactly what it meant, that I'm trapped in this body. Repeat after me: I am not a body, I am free. (Audience: I am not a body, I am free. I am still as God created me.) Now we've made it through those 20 lessons.

Now we'll do lessons 274 through 280 for the fun of it.

Today belongs to love. Let me not fear. Father, today I would let all things be as You created them, and give Your Son the honor due his sinlessness; the love of brother to his brother and his Friend. Through this I am redeemed. Through this as well the truth will enter where illusions were, light will replace all darkness, and Your Son will know he is as You created him. A special blessing comes to us today, from Him Who is our Father. Give this day to Him, and there will be no fear today, because the day is given unto Love. (Lesson 274)

Okay, I've got a good contact going on. This says that today, now, belongs to love. That's number one. This is a lovely lesson if you can hear it. If there really is only one voice, you can really only be talking to yourself. As you evolve in your own particular association, the manner in which you make application of the association of your mind improves to a wholeness or a willingness to relinquish your initial examination of it. It may seem strange to you, but the moment that you do that, your voice will be directing you to the new situation in which you find yourself. There is no way you can examine it simply because you are still that whole situation.

This is the best explanation I can give you for *God's healing Voice protects all things today.* The entirety of you protects the word of God or the Christ in you. The separation of you is setting terms that limit you to what you really are.

But it is perfectly possible for you to listen to an entire voice if you simply let it be your own voice speaking to yourself without the necessity to interpret what it's saying. If you could remember that it's only you talking to yourself anyway, you will be much happier if you don't suffer the conflict of your own self talking to yourself and trying to decide what it's too late to decide anyway. All the decisions you are going to make are going to be hopelessly gone. What did I teach? The first ten lessons of the Workbook, didn't I. This world is over and gone. I see only the past. But this new voice that emerged in you is connected to what? The now that I just gave you on the previous page (Lesson 274). The now that's going on now. Will it be a voice? Of course. Why not? But it will speak the truth to you because all truth only speaks, and when you speak you only speak truth or the name of God.

Let us today attend the Voice for God, Which speaks an ancient lesson, no more true today than any other day. Yet has this day been chosen as the time when we will seek and hear and learn and understand. So you mean this one? This is the greatest day there could ever be? That's why most of you decide to get out of bed in the morning. Instead of directing yourself to what has to be done, you already say this is the day!

You immediately have released the necessity of the cause and the effect. Will you then go and do the cause and effect of what you're supposed to? No! You'll spring into Heaven! You thought I was going to say you are going to go out and do it. No. Then you may think of not doing it instead of being in the old retrospect, you'll be in the new you. We understand that you can go back in the historic reference and look at a perfect day. What the hell is the matter with this day being perfect? Nothing, unless you don't want it to be. The only reason it wouldn't be perfect is you're bringing your grievous crap into it, and have set the terms for the necessity of your own mind. *Yet has this day been chosen as the time when we will seek and hear and learn and understand. Join me in hearing.* Isn't that lovely. *For the Voice for God tells us of things we cannot understand alone, nor learn apart.* That's true simply because you're in a conceptual association with yourself. If you could hear it alone, you wouldn't be here, you'd be in Heaven and you'd be hearing it as an entirety.

The next lesson will teach you that you would have created a Son who shares it with you. That will be the next lesson. Since God didn't want to be alone, He created a perfect Son. Do you like it that way? Fine. He needs the Son to know that He's not alone. But remember, your attention is on Him, not on yourself. You get your sequencing right in the power of your mind, and you can't have a problem with it. If you get it wrong, you'll be nothing. You won't be sinful, but you'll be nothing. You didn't make yourself.

For the Voice for God tells us of things we cannot understand alone, nor learn apart. It is in this that all things are protected. The moment you establish a relationship with anyone where you do not judge your relative merits in association with each other, you establish a whole Christ between you. You are able then to view that as an entirety of what you are, and share your relationship with Universal Mind. Can you hear that? In the *Course*, that's called Light, the Mind of God, the Light of God. But that's a Christ factor that involves apparent separate associations. Reduced, they see the Christ in each other. That's what that sentence says.

It is in this that all things are protected. And in this the healing of the Voice for God is found. God is saying to you I'm perfect as you are created. Is that literally true? Absolutely. Guys, it is absolutely true that that Voice is speaking to you. If you want to hear it, you'll hear it. If you don't want to hear you are perfect as God created you, how the hell would you hear it? But since you are perfect as God created you, if you need a Voice, let that Voice speak to you all the time. It's going to remind you about your perfection. You need a reminder of it all the time because you are trapped in here.

The prayer: *Your healing Voice protects all things today, and so I leave all things to You. I need be anxious over nothing. For Your Voice will tell me what to do and where to go, to whom to speak and what to say to him, what thoughts to think, what words to give the world.* It is very difficult for a perceptual mind to understand that. It immediately begins to direct itself. But if you'll let what I just said to you be true, you'll be totally and exactly what you are. *The safety that I bring is given me. Father, Your Voice protects all things through me. (Lesson 275)*

Your Voice protects all things through me. I will love my creations of my mind as you love me. Wow.

The Word of God is given me to speak. We're up to Lesson 276, lesson number three in the Magnificent Seven. Listen. *What is the Word of God? Are you ready? "My Son is pure and holy as Myself."* What? God speaks personally? What's the Word of God? "My Son is as pure and holy as I am." If He says anything, He says that. What He says is "I am God and my creations are perfect. Now that I know that I am God, my creations will verify that is true."

What is the Word of God? "My Son is pure and holy as Myself." And thus did God become the Father of the Son He loves, for thus was he created. The Son was created to verify the eternal love of God, and you say to me in your misconception "well, why does God have to be verified?" My answer to you is: why do you have to be verified? I notice you are seeking for verification. Why wouldn't God have to be verified? What's the difference in my verification and God's? Time and eternity. Death and eternal life. That's the only difference. What an entire difference that is, because time is going to cause pain and loneliness and longing and all that, and obviously that becomes the power of your mind. Wow.

And thus did God become the Father of the Son He loves, for thus was he created. See, God didn't become God until He said "my Son is pure and holy as myself." Should I do it once more for you? Until then He wasn't God. Of course, He's always been that. There's nowhere the Son begins and the Father ends. I'm trying to get you to see that. *What is the Word of God? "My Son is pure and holy as Myself."* I'll be God for a minute: My Son is as pure and holy as Myself. *And thus did God become the Father of the Son He loves, for thus was he created.* Without that I wouldn't be a Creator. Without that I'd be nothing since there is only one Creator, I am That. I am That by the admission of my Father, not by my own determination. All my determination can only be to that because I'm really not separate from God. *This the Word His Son did not create with Him, because in this His Son was born.* Stop trying to decide what God is. See how easy this is? Can you get it with me? The reason you're happy, do you know why you're happy? Should I tell you? Do you want it reduced? Dependence on God. The astonishing thing is that it has nothing at all to do with what God is. It is just a total dependence, and total dependence is what being the Son of God is. It's real simple.

This the Word His Son did not create with Him, because in this His Son was born. Let us accept His Fatherhood, and all is given us. Deny we were created in His Love and we deny our Self, to be unsure of who we are, of Who our Father is, and for what purpose we have come. That's the nature of the world, isn't it: Who am I? How did I get here? You're nothing and you're not here. *And yet, we need but to acknowledge Him Who gave His Word to us in our creation, to remember Him and so recall our Self. Father, Your Word is mine.* Once more: Father, Your Word is my word. What you say, I am saying. What you create, I create. *And it is this that I would speak to all my brothers, who are given me to cherish as my own, as I am loved and blessed and saved by You. (Lesson 276)*

Guys, this is nothing but the admission that there's nothing outside of your mind. Since ideas leave not their source, why would you want to hold in your mind ideas of pain and grievance of your brother. You must be creative as your Father is creative. That is Lesson 276, *The Word of God is given me to speak.*

Let me not bind Your Son with laws I made. Notice this is a direct attention to you as not being the Son of God. Quite literally. The "I" that's speaking now is the "I" that wants relief from it. *Your Son is free, my Father. Let me not imagine I have bound him with the laws I made to rule the body. He is not subject to any laws I made by which I try to make the body more secure. He is not changed by what is changeable. He is not slave to any laws of time. He is as You created him, because he knows no law except the law of love. Let us not worship idols, nor believe in any law idolatry would make to hide the freedom of the Son of God. He is not bound except by his beliefs. Yet what he is, is far beyond his faith in slavery or freedom.* I'll do it once more: *...what he is, is far beyond his faith in slavery or freedom.* Your dependence on self freedom will bind you. Be free as God created you. Why is he free? *He is free because he is his Father's Son. And he cannot be bound unless God's truth can lie, and God can will that He deceive Himself.* Which is nuts. *(Lesson 277)*

Here's the toughest and most beautiful lesson in *A Course In Miracles.* Jesus gives direct attention to you in the Sermon on the Mount. He's going to say flat out if you bind it here, you'll bind it in Heaven. If you free it here, you'll free it in Heaven. If you bind God, you'll bind God in this, in your association with yourself.

And I will give unto thee the keys of the kingdom of Heaven; and whatsoever thou shalt bind on earth shall be bound in Heaven; and

whatsoever thou shalt loose on earth shall be loosed in Heaven.
(Matthew 16:19)

This is directly from the New Testament. *If I am bound, my Father is not free. If I accept that I am prisoner within a body, in a world in which all things that seem to live appear to die, then is my Father prisoner with me. And this do I believe, when I maintain the laws the world obeys must I obey; the frailties and the sins which I perceive are real, and cannot be escaped.* What have I done? I captured God, and I'm going to hold Him hostage, and keep Him here in order that I can use His power to die. *If I am bound in any way, I do not know my Father nor my Self.* I know nothing, because being bound is nothing. *And I am lost to all reality. For truth is free, and what is bound is not a part of truth. Father, I ask for nothing but the truth. I have had many foolish thoughts about myself and my creation, and have brought a dream of fear into my mind. Today, I would not dream. I choose the way to You instead of madness and instead of fear. For truth is safe, and only love is sure.* (Lesson 278)

Guys, these are in this little book. Two more:

Creation's freedom promises my own. This is the same idea that you and I are meeting together here with an admission that we promised to do this; with the admission that somewhere we would lay down our adversary associations with each other. Obviously they are against the Universe, but if we are opposed to God, we must be opposed to each other because opposition becomes a necessity in our own existent association.

The end of dreams is promised me, because God's Son is not abandoned by His Love. Only in dreams is there a time when he appears to be in prison, and awaits a future freedom, if it be at all. Yet in reality his dreams are gone, with truth established in their place. Truth established is, I'll use the Temple or I'll use the Cheese Factory – truth established is a place. It means that you can come into an establishment in your own continuum of time, recognize all of your brothers as a part of your own loving mind and disappear into Heaven. That's what this says. That's what we are doing right here and now. Are we actually disappearing into Heaven? We're not waiting for a future freedom. *Yet in reality his dreams are gone, with truth established in their place.* This is a new place and time, isn't it?

And now is freedom his already. But he didn't have anything to do with it. What did he do? He discovered it. He walked into the Cheese, he walked into some place and said, "oh my, I feel love. I'll admit that the Universe is mind and I'm whole as God created me." And this world will be gone. Teaching that message at this depth of chaos has been very difficult because there is no communication going on. You needed a place for communication. What I gave you actually was that place. You changed the effects of your own mind. Those of you who are just waiting for me to close up the place, the effects of your own mind have placed you outside of time. In a particular sense, if I consider myself to be the savior, I'm not really taking you with me when I go. I gave you a place where you could be for a moment and transcend into Heaven. What I'm going to do now is close up the place. There is nothing left here. It's a fact.

What we are really saying is that you are now calling to the association from Heaven down into here which is really how you did it in the first place. Can you hear that? Really what you're doing is calling from out of time to the associations. So you are all grouped out of time from this place. Now I look around and say, well, there's nobody left in this place. We have used up this place. See how you have to be in the place for a minute. See how you had to be in the tomb for three days – one to get in, second to have a place, and third to get out. Otherwise you wouldn't have been here in the first place. But since you need a place it has to be at the place that you came in, and having stood at the place where you came in, I offered you Light and waited for you to mature in time. That's exactly what I did. Can you hear me? And that's what's happened to you. And now you're gone. And now you're talking about how lovely the Cheese Factory was. And you decide to establish it in your own mind and it becomes the place where you established it. Did you get that? It's all in your minds anyway. You're feeling my energy whether you're understanding me or not. It's a continuity. Time is not going to be sequential, it's going on all the time anyway. I'll tell you, you walk into that Cheese and it's noticeable. People go in and go "Wow!". They say "it's like a dream". It is like a dream. But what a beautiful dream. Did it last forever? No. It's over and gone already. Should we try and make it last over dessert? Sure. Do they claim holy instants that they can use later? You bet they do, because that moment of love is not lost. It has nothing to do with the dessert. It had everything to do with what they were. Wow, is that something!

And now is freedom his already. Should I wait in chains which have been severed for release... No, they're already severed. *...when God is*

199

offering me freedom now? I will accept Your promises today, and give my faith to them. My Father loves the Son Whom He created as His Own. Would You withhold the gifts You gave to me? (Lesson 279)

What limits can I lay upon God's Son? Whom God created limitless is free. I can invent imprisonment for him, but only in illusions, not in truth. No Thought of God has left its Father's Mind. That's an extraordinary sentence. You can't teach that. *No Thought of God has left its Father's Mind.* What an amazing idea. If there is any relationship between Father and Son, it still remains total as God. This is the admission of the Father when he established the Son. It kind of repeats it; boy, is that lovely. If you can understand that, you're not going to be here.

No Thought of God has left its Father's Mind. No Thought of God is limited at all. No Thought of God but is forever pure. Can I lay limits on the Son of God, whose Father willed that he be limitless, and like Himself in freedom and in love? Today let me give honor to Your Son, for thus alone I find the way to You. Father, I lay no limits on the Son You love... Notice that he's not talking about himself. He's talking about his Son, just like I tell you to do. Stop trying to figure this out in your own mind. The idea that you would teach the Course teaches that you can perfect yourself is absurd. It doesn't say that. It says that you are constructed in your prayer, you are denying your own whole self. That's what this says. You got it? Not that "I've got to figure out a way to get this." *Today let me give honor to Your Son...* Not to myself but to your Son, which I am but have forgotten. *...for thus alone I find the way to you. Father, I lay no limits on the Son You love and You created limitless.* Now what have I done? Now I've included my rejection of myself in with myself. I'm not going to lay any limits on myself. But first of all, I had to acknowledge that what I thought I was, was not the Son of God. By giving God full association with that, I am able to do that. Wow, what a lovely idea. *The honor that I give to him is Yours, and what is Yours belongs to me as well.* (Lesson 280) Isn't that lovely?

This is in the last book that we printed: "*Now is the time of prophecy fulfilled for now we cannot fail. God's angels hover near and all about. His love surrounds you, and of this be sure: I will never leave you comfortless.*" "*This is a required course.*" This goes on to "*All things I think I see reflect ideas.*" They're beautiful thoughts.

Okay. That's our lesson for today. Our lesson for today, then, in review: We teach only power of your mind. The whole teaching of Jesus of

Nazareth is that the Universe is mind, and that you can't escape your own thoughts no matter how determined you are. By admitting to them, you can overcome or release the necessity to defend them, and in no other way will it be possible for you to escape the world. Very simply, you're going to have to let God be God. If God then finds you to be mean and terrible, there's nothing I can do about that, except to suggest that it's a little unreasonable. It's another way of blaming God because you can't come into your association.

Now the turmoil that some of you are experiencing in the finality of this is nothing but a momentary determination of you to exist separate from what you are. I just read you that. You understand that I am talking to you. I'm not talking to someone else. There is no one else outside of you. So that final conflict is nothing but the application of this new power that you've been directed to disrupt the association. It's like you dashed into the Cheese and said "what a foolish thing you're doing here. Don't you know we've got to go out and work and slave and die? How come you offer all this happiness?" Quite literally you are doing that somewhat in your own mind. What we offer is too good to be true. All of the reasonableness of your crappy little existence rejects it. The littleness with which you're contained sits frantically with this because it is fearful of that power of release. That's the "gnashing of teeth," brother. You're going to rent your garments, aren't you.

"Tell us whether thou be the Christ, the Son of God. Jesus saith unto him, Thou hast said it...Then the high priest rent his clothes." (Matthew 26:63-64) Do you remember the priest? He asked Him directly if He was the Christ, and Jesus said "you've said it." That's the whole teaching. He said I am and so are you. Most of what you've discovered is how little it is. And those that turn back in and create that conflict are just causing pain to themselves and the associations that they believe are outside of them. That's called hell. So this is your way out of hell. Where was the hell? Only in your own thoughts of your association. Where is the release? In the whole mind you have with God. It's nice to be heard, with this simple message "as a man thinketh." I think it's Fosdick, the book *As A Man Thinketh*. That's what it is. We're not concerned about what you think at all, only that you are only thought. Whatever you think, you'll get the result. That's how simple this is.

In the service that you're in, there's a lot of loving memories coming in, and they're beginning to accumulate, like that wedding you catered yesterday at Devil's Lake is really something else. I've never seen anything like that. That might as well have been the wedding at Cana (John 2), you're converting water to wine. You couldn't look at your hors d'oeuvres plate and not spring into Heaven – you want to talk about the Great Rays manifest, look at that. Nice to be heard. Do you see that? So many of you have what we call bright light creative energy. You're artists and you create artistically. That energy can be shared. And the more you share it with each other without the competition or resistance to the reduction, the more liable you are not to cut off your own ear. In other words, be willing to share the variation of the hors d'oeuvres with other associations. Everything but mushroom. No, not really. I can't eat mushroom. Boy is that happy. It hasn't got a lot to do with nails in the palms. It has to do with your love for your brother and each other. If you can teach that as Jesus' love, this world will be over in a second.

Next Sunday everybody will be wearing hats. Then we will have Lid Sunday. You take off your lids. It's a ceremony that actually takes place. You promenade and parade and take off your lids. It's the resurrection. Thanks for coming to Sunday School. These days are very beautiful, these final days.

CHAPTER 8

Into The Presence

Good morning, everyone. Have you all registered? Are you registered? We have a tradition among Christians where we declare ourselves to be Christians. Do we? So you're Christians. You believe in the resurrection of Jesus Christ? Really? I had no idea.

Is this all right? I've been trying to teach this. I wish everybody would come down in the front with me. I don't want you back there. Come down in the front. I want you down here. Come on. There's no reason you can't. I really mean this. Why? Is this for the choir or something? In the prestigious purposes of the congregation, it could never be determined whether the trustees should sit in the front or in the back.

But I would like to think of this for a minute as instructional. And really, I'm a teacher of God. I teach from – what? Experience? Christianity teaches experience of God? Does your religion? Does it? Come on! I'm not going to do this if you don't talk to me. You act as though everybody knows that. They don't. We've already started out on a strange street. Haven't we?

I'll teach only Jesus Christ here because, obviously, he's the savior of the world. Yes? Okay. I'm going to teach Jesus Christ now, and the reason that I am going to teach Jesus Christ risen, real, whole man, is because he is with me. Isn't he? He is not aloof from me, waiting somewhere for me to undergo the pangs of death. What I'm going to try to do this morning is keep from showing you how the world reviles this message. Certainly, if you want to know what is the apparent result of your determination to justify the resurrection of Jesus through his word and the action of your mind and body, you will be hated and reviled. Is there a question on this? Raise your hand if there's a question on this. May I inquire why, from you as Bible students, that is true? Why is it true that you will be hated and reviled? Anyone care to answer me? [Participant:"Because he's a threat."]

Because of his teaching?

What does he teach that is so hateful and reviling? "No judgment."

But that's not what I heard on television this morning. I didn't hear someone say, "God doesn't judge." Yes or no? All I heard from the pulpit was God's judgment on man. Help me. Come on! I need help from somebody. Somebody talk to me. He was there this morning, and he was saying, "God will judge..." Well? No. I'm telling you as a fact of resurrected mind that God does not judge. Come on! No, you're not... You're still missing it. That's impossible. If there's a God, He must judge or we will have no standard by which to measure our action, our morality. Anybody hear me at all? Do you guys hear me when I do this? We require a judgmental God because that's what gods are for. If gods are not to judge us, what the hell good is a god if he doesn't judge? Isn't it? Come on. I need... Nobody wants to talk. This is not easy. I could say this, but what would happen?

What I'm curious about, what Jesus is *really* curious about... Let me see if I can teach you this. Somewhere the prophecy of your coming, of your fulfillment of the association of the teaching of the love of God for you through your love for your brother is proclaimed, recognized and achieved. Yes or no?

So here's what we're saying. First of all, let's use judgment, which was a good one. *For the Father judgeth no man...* (John 5:22) God does not judge. The next sentence will be *...but hath committed all judgment unto His Son.* (John 5:22) You are expected to judge, but you are expected to judge through the eternal love of God for you in the universe. Is that so? Boy, that sounds like Christianity to me. Is it? So God has given all judgment unto you. And this is your religion, that you judge yourself in association with the surroundings that are manifest – we'll use that word, manifest, manifested (and this is the *Course in Miracles*) – projected from your associations that set terms for you in regard to the actions that you are going to perform in your own mind. All right? I'm going to speak to you from where you will be coming to now as a follower of Jesus.

Jesus says, *A new commandment I give unto you, That ye love one another as I have loved you, that ye also love one another.* (John 13:34) The allowance for the exchange of love in the association that you have with each other is required if, say to me: God is love. "God is love!" It would be impossible for you to teach what I am presenting to you without allowing for the presence of God in the time and place that you are in. I know this seems very simple to you, but it's not simple at all. Everybody loves the idea that God is in Heaven. There's very few associations that particularly like the idea that God is present in this association, most particularly because they must believe that God judges. They cannot not believe that God judges because they judge. And as they judge, they must believe it will be judged by God, rather than, as Jesus would teach it, *For with what judgment ye judge, ye shall be judged...* (Matthew 7:2)

So very fundamentally, what I am offering you is the certainty that the power of your mind, which determines the outcome that you want within this world, is the eternal power and love of God not through judgment but through your admission of the perfection of your body identity, based on the resurrection of Jesus Christ. Was that any good? Do you see?

Let's try this. Is God everywhere? Well, if God is everywhere, God is here. Is God here? How can I know that God is here? By loving you. Well, come on. You act like it's difficult. I can know God is here because I love you. You don't really realize how simple this is. If God is indeed love, God could not be an identity because an identity would require a judgment. This is why the world hates and reviles you, because you love the sinners as much as you love them. Isn't that true? Is it true or not? At least you're expected to. So you're not really reviled because you love your brother. You're reviled because you love the sinners. In effect, what they will say is "How dare you not judge! How dare you admit to the resurrection of your own mind!"

So now we have another word that has entered into this talk, perhaps, and the word is... "Manifest." I used? "Sanctify." If God is everywhere, God abides in you. Is that true? I always was taught God is within me. So in the sense that I abide, God abides with me. If I am body, the sanctuary through my manifestation of the temple of God will be my body. It cannot not be, since my body is a representation of my association in the world. This is pure Jesus, incidentally. Are you aware of that? "Sanctify the body," "manifest the body in the certainty" – are you ready for this? – "that I abide with you."

Those of you who are advanced in this teaching – and I don't know what advanced means, since I'm teaching this directly out of John, and I intend to read a little scripture to you – there is no way that Jesus does not say that "When I resurrect, you will be resurrected with me." He may indicate, "I will return and abide with you as your Self in the certainty of our Selfness," but there's no possibility (this is the *Course in Miracles*, incidentally) that Jesus, if I begin to read this, will not say to you, "The world is going to hate me, but I am manifest now, my body, as a sanctuary of God." This is following the resurrection, isn't it? He's going to appear – manifest. He's going to appear – sanctified.

How would you possibly teach the message of Jesus to the world? This world doesn't want to know that love is eternal and that they're created perfect by God. Do they or not? "No." Why not?

The simplicity of the new commandment, which I'm going to read, is John 14. Are you students of the Bible here? So that the self that speaks of himself in this two-thousand-year-old scripture, translated, still holds the power to show you the direction that you will take in the manifestation through the sanctification of your body, the resurrection of you? Am I teaching you your own resurrection? *Know ye not ye must be born again.* (John 3:7) Am I really? So that if we did a Bible practice and I used these words that said, *Lo, I am with you always, even unto the end of the world,* (Matthew:28:20) I could then come and say to you, "I am here as a representative of your risen.., of your timeless, eternal demonstration of the purpose for you being here," which is really what this says. If I appear before you, I'm going to appear and say, "I am resurrected". Say to me, "I am resurrected."

"I am resurrected."

Really? *I am the way.* Say, "*Way*".

"*Truth.*"

"*And life.*" (John 14:6)

He that believeth unto me will never die. (John 11:26)

Now, the reason that the requirement is that you believe that I am resurrected is obviously that if you don't love me, you can't love yourself, and I'm just back into the teachings of Jesus. So now I'm back to what he gives you. Isn't it? I'm going to give you something new. You've got to love your brother. I didn't say, "You may" or "will." I said, "You got to!"

God does not judge? Can you teach that from a Christian pulpit? I don't know any Christians that will allow it somewhere. Somewhere there's an ultimate last judgment. The last judgment is not done by God; it's done by you. You like the idea that God judges. There's absolutely nothing in this teaching that says that God judges at all. Thankfully. Because the idea that God judges was always abhorrent to me, anyway. The idea that a perfect, eternal, creating Father would somehow judge me or intentionally create me in pain so that I could work up to honoring Him always seemed a little ridiculous to me. And it seems ridiculous to Jesus. And now it seems ridiculous to you.

The surprising thing in conceptual thought-form association, which is really what I'm teaching, that Jesus teaches manifestation of God through our body associations is an extraordinary occurrence, because it involves the emotion of the admission of our love for God through our brother, and there's no real alternative in it at all – I went into the *Course* for a minute – because, as Jesus would teach you, there *is* nothing outside of you. So through the sanctification in the manifestation of your thought-form associations, you will realize the Second Coming, or the resurrection of Jesus. Is that so?

This is my Father's house. I'm doing the scripture. *In my Father's house are many mansions...*(John 14:2), because abiding with you is the Kingdom of God through the perfection of your body identity by the grace of the resurrection of our brother Jesus. Can you get that with me? Can you get that? He expects you to... If I were to read... I'm not reading scripture here. I believe this is all pretty much the Last Supper. Everything I'm saying here is pretty much the Last Supper. Christianity, the resurrection of Jesus, is an experience of your individual body resurrection? In a particular sense, isn't it? So as in Sermon on the Mount, this new discovery that is happening to you physically and mentally and emotionally is based very simply on acceptance of the inevitability of your perfection? From God? And that's what's with you right now? That would require the acceptance of the sanctification of my own body, wouldn't it?

Lo, I am with you always, even unto the end of the world. (Matthew 28:20) All right? So that self of you that underwent the turmoil – I'm turning to the scriptures here – that underwent the turmoil of being born and felt the pain of rejection and that went through the Gethsemane operation of being killed and tortured is actually a happening that's going on right now. But there is no possibility that you can overcome the world, as I would declare it to you, without the acceptance of the message of the necessity for your personal transformation, for your own personal resurrection. So we have that fundamentally now.

Let's try "I'm going to leave you for a moment." The action of the mind of Christ is always only in the teaching that "I am not with you for a moment, but now I am with you." Otherwise, no teaching would be possible. It would be impossible to teach this except by teaching *I will not leave you comfortless.* (John 14:18) There would be no need to instruct you. All I could possibly be doing in reminding you within this presence is that Jesus Christ is with us and that I am representing you in the entirety of that certainty that emanates from your manifestation of reality in this world. It's actually that simple. Is it or not?

Be ye therefore perfect, even as your Father which is in Heaven is perfect (Matthew 5:48) is a declaration of the necessity for you to perform the act of perfection. But yet it has nothing to do with God but will simply become the entirety of God. There is no question that this teaching is "As ye judge, ye will be judged," and that there is nothing outside of you in your mind that can call your attention to anything painful or sick or dying except by your individual decision to allow that to be true. Is that it?

Okay. This message is almost two thousand years old, whatever you think that means, and obviously, the world, this world that I see here, does not apparently adhere to or practice this message. All right? The reason that is true is because the message of eternal love can only be practiced eternally. Then the teaching of the presence of the sanctification of your bodies each moment in what we call space/time can show you the direction that eternal life must be if, first, there is nothing outside of you and, second, the world is a manifestation of that resurrection of your body. Say, "Now." "Now."

Well, that's what I just offered you. *The hour is coming and is now* (John 5:25) is the entire teaching of Jesus. This is the time of your resurrection. Now, that's why the world does not hear this message. Why? Because this is the time? Help me with this. What if you hear the message that this is the time of your resurrection? You'll resurrect. Yes or no? I'll do it once more for you. You missed it. You keep missing it. You keep looking: "I looked everywhere for the resurrected Jesus." No, no. You be the resurrected. Who the hell do you expect to resurrect? Jesus already *is* resurrected. Isn't He?

Not only is that true, but if I appear to you in a manifestation, you will manifest me rather than sanctify me. Having not sanctified yourself, you will manifest me in the image presented to you of your corruptible body association. Can you hear this? You don't like that but that's true. Okay, here I am! Say to me, "Are you resurrected?"

That's what this says. Doesn't it? Really? It's an amazing idea because my resurrection is not proved by Spirit but by manifestation. If God is everywhere, God is abiding here in this presence. God is then an occupation of the certainty of our love for each other, based on the admission of the resurrection of Jesus. It's that simple.

I'm going to give you a brand new covenant, something you've never heard before. I'm going to tell you something that not only has never been heard before but is not being heard now, because as soon as it's heard, you're gone from here. *A new commandment I give unto you, That ye love one another; as I have loved you, that ye also love one another. By this shall all men know that ye are my disciples, if ye have love one to another.* (John 13:34,35) Period. I don't need your argument about it. Come on. This is a place of attack and hatred and death and murder. The travail that you experience is that it's much easier if you allow for judgment. Since God doesn't judge and, in fact, there is no such thing as judgment, it's considerably more difficult to judge in a relationship of love than it is in a relationship of hate and revenge. And that's the simple fact of the matter.

I'll just throw this in for you. Simon Peter is always going to say, "No matter what you do, I'm going to follow you." Obviously, that is his declaration and it's not true. It's not true in the sense that his inability to accept the inevitability of his own resurrection will deny that to him. All denials are thrice because all opportunities to resurrect are thrice. When he says, "I'm going to be with you," Jesus says, "No, you're going to deny me. I'm going to return to you, resurrected, and you may then accept me if you choose." You will deny me in the nature of the Father, Who is God – obviously, since there is only one love of God, if you admitted that, you would immediately know me – of the Son, who I am, who you refuse to accept, and of the Holy Spirit that is all about you." The acceptance of any one of those three would be the acceptance of the entirety of your own saviorship. Do you hear me? The test would always be: will you love your brother, will you love God, and will you love the entirety of the association through the action of your own mind? That's the Father, the Son and the Holy Spirit.

He does it again in the Garden exactly the same. He goes to the Garden, and he's asking for relief from God, and, of course, God does not respond. But he's asking for relief from Him, and he's very much aware that he wants that association to be with him. I'm talking about you, incidentally. He wants that association to be with him and to recognize for him, but since he has not yet recognized himself, it will be impossible that he can recognize his brothers in that association. So he says, "Can't you stay with me long enough?" He does it three times.

Is that a going-on right now? It's an amazing idea. Yes, it is. Wow. *Let not your heart be troubled: ye believe in God, believe also in me.* (John 14:1) This is the same idea as any belief in its entirety will be all that there will be. I mean, the simple idea, conceptually you believe in God... I mean, somewhere, you might want to say, "Yes, He's perfectly loving and whole." You can then believe in the love of my message for you in the certainty that we emanate from eternal life or from a whole Creator.

In my Father's house are many mansions: if it were not so, I would have told you. I go to prepare a place for you. (John 14:2) If I need to instruct you, I will need many mansions. In my Father's house are many mansions. If it were not so, I would have told you so. I did not come to you and tell you there is only one mansion. I am asking you to accept the certainty of your own need for transformation, since the denial of the Single Mansion of God is your individual mansionship. Can you get that? That you are actually separate in that association. This requires, then, the sanctification of your body. Doesn't it? You see? It could not not require it. Is that true?

Do most of you have a pretty good idea that the teachings of Jesus of Nazareth are "There is a single Self"? Okay. That's important in this next couple of sentences. The Self that I am is the Self that you are.

And if I go and prepare a place for you, I will come again, and receive you unto myself. (John 14:3) I promise you that as a savior of the world, that I am receiving you unto myself. I am not receiving you unto someone else. That is, I am not receiving you by an objective association. If I leave you, I will come again and receive you unto myself, based on the certainty of myself or my self-mind in my relationship with God. Is that so?

What it means is: I no longer reject you but I had to resurrect first. I will receive you, Where before I rejected you in my determination to justify my separation, and having undergone the resurrection, I will receive you unto myself. Unconditional love. That is, I will accept you wholly into my mind, not based on the judgment of our organized association but on the certainty of my own resurrected mind. Say, "Amen."

I will come again, and receive you unto myself; that where I am, there ye may be also. Because my "am" or "here" will not be where you are. *That where I am, ye may be also.* (John 14:3) Yet I'm appearing before you in where you think you are. I'll do that once more. When I appear to you, I will show you where I am. I am not here. I am where you can be with myself. Why are you getting so happy? Holy mackerel! Don't tell me you're hearing this! Can you get this? Manifestation. "Am" is a place. Say to me, "I am."

Where I am, you can be also. But where you think I am, I am not. I am in a literal spatial and temporal association. That's exactly what this says. What am I? Not only am I, but you are also with me. It cannot not be. This is the whole *Course in Miracles*. But if you need a reminder, I'm going to remind you that you're already there. If I am there, you cannot not be there.

This is kind of nice stuff. This is John 14. *That where I am, there ye may be also. And whither I go ye know, and the way ye know.* (John 14:3,4) Is that true? Is there a question on this, you? I promise and guarantee you that whither I go, wherever, whenever I go, ye know and the way you know. That is, not only do you know of the Kingdom of God; you know the way there. Because if you're separate, the idea of the Kingdom would be the way. Can you hear this? Did I put that into the next sentence? That is, the idea of a place is the way to get there. It cannot not be if you are a manifestation through the sanctification of your body.

Thomas saith unto him, 'Lord, we know not whither thou goest' (John 14:5), where the hell you're going. He always lets Thomas say it. Thomas has more sense than most of the other disciples. And he's willing to ask the question because he wants to know. Anyway, here's your answer. It's the most incredible, singular answer that could probably ever be given about anything. *Jesus saith unto him, I am the way, the truth, and the life: no man cometh unto the Father, but by me.* (John 14:6) Try that with me. I want you to try to say that. I want to hear if you can hear this. *The way, the truth, and the life. I am the way...* (John14:6)

211

Say that to me. "I am the way."

Who is?

You're the way, but are you the truth? Say to me, "I am the way."

Who is?

Are you the truth?

Is what you're saying true?

How can I know that? Say, "I am the life."

There is no life without you.

Yes! I'm talking about you. Go look at yourself in the mirror. I am the way, the truth, and the life. What's the next statement? Be sure you got it right. *No man cometh unto the Father, but by me.* As you say this to yourself, as you say this out loud, look at the possibility that it might be true. I absolutely guarantee you that it's true.

"Oh, I would never think anything like that."

Let's try it. Here we go. Go!

"I am the way, the truth, and the life. No man cometh unto the Father but by me."

Absolutely. There is nothing outside of you. Outside of you there is nothing. This world is a manifestation or demonstration of your capacity to apparently be separate from God. There is no possibility whatsoever until you accept what I just read you that you can enter into the Kingdom, since you are the entirety of the way, the truth and the life. You cannot come there except by me because I *am* you in the entirety of our relationship since the beginning of time.

Is this actually in the New Testament? It's what this says. Do you see why it's rejected? There is no allowance for a subjective necessity for love based on the association of the mind with itself and its brother. It's taught that somehow God is objective and out there. *If ye had known me* – this is past tense – *ye should have known my Father also: and from henceforth ye know him, and have seen him* (John 14:7) because I am Him. That's what that says. Up until now you did not know that you're not separate from God. Up until now you thought that this was life. Up until now you thought that you were a body and could get old and die. It's not true. Henceforth, you will know that is not true.

This is nothing but a demonstration of the certainty of our love for each other. I've already given you the New Covenant, the new association.

It's brand new. The idea that you would attempt to teach the world to love your brother is absurd. He says it's new because it *is* new. How new is it? As new as it is at this moment, because heretofore you – you, individually – have refused to accept it. Not someone else. You have refused to accept the love of God because of the indication of the perfection of you not by judgment but by the certainty of a single, whole, eternal life and mind.

There's no way you can avoid experience in teaching this, is there? Help me. Christians? Just for a minute I need help here. I'm leaving. You have to teach physical resurrection? Do you? I mean, if it's a physicality that you are, you have to teach sanctification of the body. Philip likes to go on and ask questions. *Lord, show us the Father, and it sufficeth us.* (John 14:8) He says, "What the hell you talking about? I just got through telling you..." You go out to a church to teach this now. The thing they'll say to you is "Prove it. Show me the Father, and then I'll believe you." And I say, "I *am* showing you." How the hell long have I been with you, telling you this? That is my resurrection. "Show me, and I'll believe you." I know. Can you get it? No, you won't. You won't.

Jesus says to him, *Have I been so long time with you, and yet hast thou not known me, Philip?*(John 14:9) See, there's no indefinite article in that. "Have I been with you so long time?" Not "so long *a* time." "Have I been with you so long time? Have I been with you in *real* time, instantaneous time, that you are unable to recognize me as a perfect reflection of your mind." It says, *Have I been so long time with you, and yet hast thou not known me, Philip? he that hath seen me hath seen the Father; and how sayest thou then, Show us the Father?* (John 14:9) We have a little book called *All About God and How to Find Him*, which will show you exactly what I am saying. Everything that you see is perfect, whole and eternal. If you have seen me in this relationship, you are seeing all that you will ever see, based on your determination to allow yourself to be whole and the savior of the world. Certainly, you cannot see more than you're willing to see within your own manifestation of the relationship of yourself with God. Is that so? You can't see more than that.

That's an amazing idea! There's no association in this teaching with man and his relationships in the world at all. All this really says is "If you believe me, you can leave here now with me." And it has nothing at all to do with the world. Is that so? Do you believe me? Really? You'll never die. Is that so? If you believe me, you'll never die? You can't die?

We have some visitors here in church today. Do most of you have the feeling that you leave and come back? You understand, "I'll be back in just a minute"? Can you get that? You're leaving. You can leave and come back. Can you remember where you've been? Why are you asking me? I'll try it with you. I don't know if you can do this or not.

Can you remember where you've been? Say, Where will it be? Say, "Here." Notice how new and fresh you are in the sanctification of your mind. What have I done? Say, "Shortened time." Of course! This is the whole teaching. If I am resurrected, the time will come and is now when you will recognize your own resurrection. What the hell's wrong with that?

Prove it. Say, "Prove it to me." *I am.* This is the whole *Course in Miracles.* Your resistance to it is nothing but your temporal body association in slow time. That is, a manifestation of limitation based on the limitations you've imposed on yourself? [Yes.] Of which God knows nothing? God knows nothing of the limitation you impose on yourself. He's not judging you. You are judging yourself and getting the result of yourself in your own mind? Is that so? Why is it that you're able to hear? You're sort of hearing this. Can you hear this? You *will* get the result of this in that association. Yet it's impossible in manifestation that the entirety of any imagery association based on the idea of resurrection is not only present with you at this moment but also resurrecting. Once more. Right?

He that hath seen me hath seen the Father; and how sayest thou then, Show us the Father? (John 14:9) This is *A Course in Miracles*, a direct sentence. *Believest thou not that I am in the Father, and the Father in me?* (John 14:10) There is no distinction between the Father and the Son at all? "Right." If I am in the Father, the Father will be in me? Can you get that? That's what that says. It doesn't say, "I am in the Father, and therefore He's in me." It says it the other way. Can you get that? You didn't make yourself. What an amazing idea!

The words that I speak unto you I speak not of myself: but the Father that dwelleth in me, he doeth the works. (John 14:10) So you can either believe the Father or the Son and Both will be perfect. You can believe the work that I do as the Son, or you can believe that we share a single Father together. *The works that I do, greater works will ye do* (John 14:12) because you're going to have to. The works that you have done heretofore will not suffice you. Can you get that? Of course you're going to do greater works. See? But it's the Father that worketh in you.

Well, I said that. My goodness! *Verily, verily, I say unto you, He that believeth on me..* (John 14:12) I'm telling you that I am resurrected here with you. I am offering you an entirety of a solution by the certainty of the power of our mind through God and my resurrection if you were willing to accept what you said to me a few minutes ago. Did you say, "I am the resurrection and the life"? Have you gone that far? You want to try that with me? This is where Jesus tells you to hear. Are you ready to do that? Who's ready to declare that they're the resurrection and the life? "I am." If I believe you, will I never die? Do you have to believe that in order to say it? Nah! Well, if it's true, what difference does it make? Come on! I'm giving you a break here. You don't have to believe. I don't understand belief. There isn't any such thing as belief. God is going to be God, anyway. It's impossible that you cannot believe in truth because you *are* truth. The idea that you have to believe this for life to be eternal is not true. But since you believe it is, the action of your mind in that belief will give you the power to stand and say, "I am the truth, the way and the life." God does not say that to you. God does not say, "I am the one..." why would He?

He that believeth on me, the works that I do shall he do also; and greater works than these shall he do; because I go unto my Father. (John 14:12) That's an amazing idea! Is it fearful to declare your own perfection to the world, for you to stand up and say, "I am as God created me"? That's what we're doing here now. Who do you have to prove that to? ...*because I go unto my Father. And whatsoever ye shall ask in my name, that will I do, that the Father may be glorified in the Son. If ye shall ask any thing in my name, I will do it. If ye love me, keep my commandments.* (John 14:12-15) Do you really want to be whole and perfect and back in Heaven? I'll do it. But the decision is not being made by me; it's being made by you. Isn't it? That's an amazing idea! That would have to be true if all power is given unto you in Heaven and earth. Isn't it?

Is this a teaching? Am I teaching, then, to you? Am I teaching this to your mind? Do you learn this? You're expressing who you are, anyway, aren't you? It's impossible for me to prove this within your earthly associations because your earthly associations are a denial of what I am saying. Aren't they? That doesn't solve the problem, but certainly, it would make the problem simple if your conceptual association of your identity is the denial of your whole, single reality – this is the whole teaching – and there's nothing outside of you. If that's so, it's impossible, as Jesus tells you and I'm telling you, that your whole Self, Who is him, is not with you at this moment and does not suffer the conflict of you in association with yourself, or the manifestation of the denial of you for your love of your brother, if your brother is, indeed, you.

The problem is solved by loving your brother because he *is* you. And without getting to the psychology of loving yourself and all of the absurd stuff that goes with it, except that you love yourself, it would be impossible to love your brother. Yet except that you love your brother, it is impossible to love God. Yes or no? Can you hear that? It would be impossible. It's literally – and this is what the world denies – it's literally impossible for you to love God and not love your brother or hate your brother. Is that true?

Do you teach relinquishment of judgment? How do you do it without saying, "I'm going to let God judge"? If God doesn't judge – *For the Father judgeth no man* (John 5:22) – and you don't judge, who is there to judge? No one. See, the world is a judgment that you have made on yourself in your own mind. That's all it is. Is it that simple? This is a little Sermon on the Mount. I'm just trying to see if you actually hear the Sermon on the Mount. You're going to get back what you give away. As you judge, you will be judged. Of course.

We'll wrap this up. *And I will pray the Father, and he shall give you another Comforter, that he may abide with you for ever; Even the Spirit of truth; whom the world cannot receive, because it seeth him not, neither knoweth him: but ye know him; for he dwelleth with you, and shall be in you.* (John 14:16-17) is the greatest scripture teaching that's ever been taught to this world. This has nothing to do with the world at all. Once more, guys, if you want to leave here with me, this has nothing to do with the world at all. This is my whole teaching. It's the whole teaching of Jesus. It has to do only with you and your relationship in love with your brother. That's it. It doesn't have anything to do with the world. What an astonishing idea!

I will not leave you comfortless: I will come to you. Yet a little while, and the world seeth me no more; but ye see me: because I live, ye shall live also. At that day ye shall know that I am in my Father, and ye in me, and I in you. (John 14:18-20) And that's the end of this lesson. At that time you will know that you are whole and perfect and eternal. So the Kingdom is in you.

Is this working okay? I want to try one more thing with you just to end this because it may be important for you to hear this. I've taught it a lot of times before. Phew! Boy! This is nice stuff. Wow! There's a teaching of a direct contact that Jesus offers at Gethsemane that I can offer to you if you really want to hear me with this. I'm going to do it. It's a prayer. I've done the prayer. I want you to listen to the prayer just for one second. This is the end of the world. That is, this will be the fulfillment of the entirety of a single, whole mind through the representation of you as the savior of this world. Once more. There isn't any such thing as separation from everything that is. There obviously is such a thing, or was such a thing, as an idea about it, which you have heretofore represented. If you have heretofore represented an idea of separation, it is necessary for you individually in your mind to represent the perfection from whence you came and must know of. You cannot not know of it because you know of your separation. If that is so, it is impossible for you not to take on an identity of coming from the separation to the truth. I'm speaking only to you.

So come on! Get with me here! If there is only you in your own mind, the admission of the separation is actually what the resurrection would have to be in your own mind. Yet the separation has no identity in reality but only in the entirety of its association – you ought to start hearing this – only in the entirety of the aggregation, which involves nothing but love and no judgment. Isn't it? The idea that I should have to tell you to love your brother really doesn't make any sense. Your brother *is* you. There *is* only one Son of God. There *is* only one God. Isn't there?

I went over that on the video, where you will become a representation. What? Did I use the word, "characterization"? Did I put that on the video? You are a characterization of yourself in your own drama, representing the entirety of you. In that sense I am standing in front of you, characterizing yourself in the manifestation of the instant sanctification of my association of body. My body is literally falling apart and gone from here at this moment. Got that? Most of you are falling apart. I'll tell you, if you're a savior of the world, that's a nice place to be. The reason I remind you is, you are a constant reminder of yourself. We try to teach this. If you need to remind yourself, do so. Any conflict you experience with this would be an indication of your need to remind yourself. You do practice it. I can't teach this.

Finally, the certainty of a singular, living, creative and eternal life which is what you are is actually not your saviorship. Your saviorship is only the certainty of the repair job. It's only the certainty of your own mind coming to know that. The amazing thing about it is the consortium of the entirety would allow for a representation of truth to come here. Certainly, that would be you. Or your admission of my characterization. It would not have to be more than that because I cannot not be more or less than the characterization you have of yourself in regard to our mutual intent to ascend to Heaven. Is that so? Do we intend to leave here? Is that your intention? Nobody in the universe can stop you if you intend to do this. "Thy will be done, Holy Son of God." Is that so?

Do ye now believe? Behold, the hour cometh, yea, is now come, Do ye now believe? Behold, the hour cometh, yea, is now come, that ye shall be scattered, every man to his own, and shall leave me alone: and yet I am not alone, because the Father is with me. (John 16:31-32) This is the struggle that all of you have individually in the realization that the world is about to abandon you because you are declaring your faith in God. It's impossible you do not undergo this to some degree, or you wouldn't be here. It's not that it's true, but since you need it, this would be the offering to you. Where's it going to be? Only in you. It's not out there.

These things I have spoken unto you, that in me ye might have peace. In the world ye shall have tribulation: but be of good cheer; I have overcome the world. (John 16:33) Do you believe me when I say this? It's impossible for you to believe me and not spring into Heaven. The world will simply begin to fade and fall away from you. Can you explain that to the world? I don't understand. How could you possibly explain it to the world? It has no explanation. The world doesn't even attempt an explanation of itself. There *is* no explanation for this that would bear any scrutiny. This is the whole idea of the insanity of this.

Just two sentences here and then we're done. *These words spake Jesus, and lifted up his eyes to Heaven,* (this is the end of the whole thing) *and said, Father, the hour is come; glorify thy Son, that thy Son also may glorify thee.* (John 17:1) The glory that is the mind of God is the glorification of you. There is no separation between the Father and the Son.

The idea of the fulfilling of the mission can be very valuable to you. Otherwise, there would be no purpose for you to have been here at all. It has nothing to do with whether you're going to stay or not, but it does have to do with the willingness of your acceptance of an entrance into the illusion of an illusionary factor of light reality that can transform the space/time identity. It's impossible to teach abstraction because there isn't any such thing as abstraction. The idea of abstraction, that is, "God is love," is the idea of the manifestation of your love. It cannot not be. You cannot not participate in your own resurrection in regard to the entirety of you. It's impossible. Do you understand me? In a literal sense no one can do this for you, certainly not Jesus Christ, because any definition of Jesus Christ would be why you're here. And you remain a definition of Jesus Christ. You are here because you denied his resurrection. For goodness' sake! It's absurd. I go the church down the street here. All they will tell me is, he's resurrected. And I'll say, "What the hell are you doing here?"

This is this prayer. All whole minds – whole minds in the sense that there is isn't another but that – will be aware that they have assumed a garb of conceptual association. It's impossible that you not. If I take any name at all... What do you call me? Master Teacher. See, some of you can even be offended by a name that is given you at some point, because you may well understand that the name of Jesus is a denial of Jesus, not an affirmation of him. I'm not concerned about that because at some point in the roster of your own time associations, you must come to the point where you will complete any task you have been assigned, and the assignment can only be involved in the entirety of you leaving this world. And it may well be expressed as Jesus expresses it here. And it may well maintain the momentary determination of you as the author of this, contrary to the entirety of the love of God, because that's where the conflict would have to occur. That is, in order for me to resurrect you, I must be able to have seen you or see you for a moment in your separation. In that sense, I become a vehicle of transformation.

Do you see that? If I stand here in a space/time association with you, resurrecting continually, I will, as you step into that association, be an action of your mind in the recognition at that instant of the entirety of its purpose for being here. Can you hear that? Your purpose for being here will be to accomplish that. When I get you turned toward that being your purpose, it's much easier for me because all the purpose is in your mind, anyway. But in that sense you will remain who you are and begin to declare your own certainty within your own dream manifestation. This is your dream, isn't it? You brought this world with you when you came. There's no world without you. I don't know whether I have to keep going back to it.

But if the world appeared to be separate, I would take on a garb of memory associations of salvation and represent that to the world.

That's pretty close. That is, if you are really whole in your own mind, you know somewhere that the idea of saviorship doesn't make any sense. Why would it make sense? You can't really be separate from God. That takes on the aspects of assignment, doesn't it. Does it? Christians? Does it? Is that true? We would have a project, then, in the recognition of each other through the love of Jesus? It's very fundamental, but it's also an activity of your mind. Is that why you are so joyous and happy? Very frankly, it must be because you have a purpose for being here. And in that sense you are empowered by it. You are empowered by that love to express the certainty of who you are. All power comes from God. But nothing is denied you as the Son of God? My goodness' sakes! What a lovely idea!

Jesus prays, *Father, the hour is come; glorify thy Son, that thy Son also may glorify thee: As thou hast given him power over all flesh, that he should give eternal life to as many as thou hast given him.* (John 17:1-2) Not more and not less. You cannot give this to anyone who is not a part of your own saviorship, nor should you attempt to. This may well reduce to "Let those that can hear, hear." Yet your offering must be in its entirety for those who are still asleep and dreaming to hear you at all. This is the whole teaching of Jesus. Somewhere, you will do this first. Somewhere, you're going to be through, aren't you?

As thou hast given him power over all flesh, that he should give eternal life to as many as thou hast given him (John 17:2) ...to give. I'm going to give you eternal life? You want it? You're eternal. Say to me, "What am I going to do next? Now that I know I'm eternal, what am I going to do?" You're going to represent that to this place, I guess. Somewhere I'm going to have to say, "Of that, I cannot speak." I will literally say to you, "Of that, I cannot speak." I can only represent to you the entirety of yourself. Is that so?

And this is life eternal, that they might know thee the only true God, and Jesus Christ, whom thou hast sent. (John 17:3) Did he just subtract himself from his own characterization? I'm going to do that once more for you. Did he or didn't he? I mean, this is Jesus in the Garden, praying. Isn't it? He is thanking God for the completion of his mission. What an idea! *And this is life eternal, that they might know thee the only true God, and Jesus Christ, whom thou hast sent. I have glorified thee on the earth: I have finished the work which thou gavest me to do. And now, O Father, glorify thou me with thine own self with the glory which I had with thee before the world was.* (John 17:3-5) All that is is a statement that this has nothing to do with reality at all.

Are you playing a part? Help me with this. Do you play the part of your own association? If this is all over, though, how do you keep it from showing up as a spatial drama? You can't. If this is true and you're going to view this from outside of time, which is really what we're offering, you would have to view it as a drama? What would you do, then? Send emissaries from out of time into the world in order to convert the associations? Come on! Give me a little science fiction here or something. You act as though this is a big holy effort that you're doing. None of it is true. The whole basis of this teaching is that nothing is from here, and in a very real sense your Christhood is an alienship here. It would have to be. You're not from here, are you? Where are you from? Heaven. What's that like? Ask me, "What's that like?"

Come and see. Say to me, "How do I do it?"

Give up the world. Good-bye!

You don't like that. As soon as I go to the fundamental teachings, you don't like it. As soon as I tell you that your existence is totally meaningless, deny the meaning of this... Isn't that amazing, that this whole association is nothing but a denial of the perfection of the wholeness of you! The reason you can't serve God and mammon is because you can't serve God or mammon. Not this. One or the other will not be true, and there's no such place as this.

I have manifested thy name unto the men which thou gavest me out of the world. (John 17:6) You have particular assignments within your own memory of acts to perform in regard, and I am here to remind you that you've forgotten your own responsibility. This is Queen of the South. I would suggest very strongly that if you offer hope of resurrection to the associations of the projection of your own mind that you not disappoint them, because at that point their salvation depends on you. This is a true statement. Can you hear this? Because if you offered them the light of Heaven, it had nothing at all to do with their circumstance because nothing has to do with circumstance at all. If I offer you the freedom of the certainty of who I think I might be and you accept it from me and I subsequently doubt within my own mind, I have denied you the light that I offered you, and you will suffer for apparently no reason whatsoever. The answer to it is: I have caused your suffering.

I tried to tell that guy Jimmy that called me this. I don't care what he does. You can't arbitrate between God and the shit of this world.

Pardon me. You can't do it. There's no neutrality. All I said to him is, and I'm saying this to you – I want you to hear this – don't cause pain to your brother. If you love him, why would you cause him pain through the subtraction of him from your mind? Yet the doubt about who you are is denying him Heaven. Teaching this as an action is pretty much a requirement because what goes around does come around. See, if he's innocent, you can save him very easily because you offer him the light and he doesn't examine it. You're the one that's examining it. You're the one that's assumed the role of saviorship. Can you hear this? He hasn't done it. You've taken on the responsibility. That's why the requirement is your transformation. Is that so? The other certainty you can have is that innocence cannot be defined, that the essence of innocence, or non-judgment, will be the light of the extension of you.

I have manifested thy name unto the men which thou gavest me out of the world: thine they were, and thou gavest them me; and they have kept thy word. Now they have known that all things whatsoever thou hast given me are also given to them. (John 17:6-7) I'm not offering you anything at all, nothing, that you are not perfectly capable of performing. The idea that I have some particular power or that I've come to know something perceptual – this is how basic this is – somehow I have some advantage, is absurd. I have the advantage only of suffering more pain and being unable to deal with it. You can have the advantage of the futility of knowing that the problem cannot be solved. That's all. Wow.

Now they have known – past tense – *that all things whatsoever thou hast given me are of thee. For I have given unto them the words which thou gavest me; and they have received them, and have known surely that I came out from thee, and they have believed that thou didst send me. I pray for them: I pray not for the world, but for them which thou hast given me; for they are thine. And all mine are thine, and thine are mine; and I am glorified in them.* (John 17:7-10) And that's the end of this lesson. I can't go any further than that. But that's here, isn't it?

Was John with Jesus in the Garden when Jesus prayed this prayer? How does John know that Jesus prayed this prayer in the Garden?

Oh, yeah! Isn't that something! If it hadn't been for John, you wouldn't have Revelation. See, John, who is Jesus' heart and mind, is as close in a manifestation of a human being as a human being can be and not be Jesus. And this is two thousand years old. Certainly, that's all he taught. Not only does he teach it, but he declares to Peter, "If I want to do that, that's none of your business." If you deny me and I know an association... A lot of you are like this with me. Can you hear this? If I know that you are of a certainty with me in this, it will not be in regard to the world. Do you understand? We are representing this before time was and, indeed, after it's over. But certainly before it was. And after it's over would be the sense that it's going to be over because it never was and that we are now going to ascend to the Father together.

Can you hear this, guys? I want you to hear it. It's important that you hear it because there's no real judgment involved in it. When I try to teach it, I teach it, "God is going to take some and leave some, and the one you think He's going to take, He leaves. And He takes those who you thought He was going to leave." And there will be two in the field. And there's no measurement of who's going to ascend to Heaven and who's going to remain here. Yet you are determined to measure it because you want the outcome to justify the separation. And it's not going to do it. Could you hear me with that?

Say to me, "It's not fair."

Where the hell did you get the idea that God is fair? That's the most absurd idea I ever heard. What are you going to do? Arbitrate death in association? You're going to go to a peace table and try to arrive at some sort of equanimity? God's justice is that you're perfect and whole and eternal. It has nothing to do with your judgment. It has nothing to do with the justice of man. Nothing. Say to me, "It's not fair." "It's not fair."

It's not fair. My suggestion to you, no matter what the travail is, you let the eternal, creating life be what it is. Because judgment is what an attempt to justify fairness is. That's just the justice of man. It's the justification for death. "It's not fair. God, you have taken my beloved two-year-old away from me."

God didn't have anything to do with it. Yet it's impossible that you don't judge Him. And now you must forgive God for taking your..? I hated it. Not me! You can't keep a surrender factor out of that idea, can you? How the hell do you keep it out? You can't, can you?

There's a new found capacity of you to assemble out of time and come back into this association. And in that sense it's late in time. Will you be able to retain the full authority of the certainty of your whole mind when you return here? Yes. Henceforth you will be able to because I'm offering it to you now. That's called the Second Coming. That's what it is. Well, if this is the end of this... What time is it? It's not ten, is it? Thanks for stopping back.

Have you ever had the experience of being in front of a congregation that all ascends at one time? If I come here suddenly and appear before you, and I've got this Bible, and I'm all set to teach you about the resurrection because it's in your memory association, and I say, "Congregation, good morning! I've come to take you home. The world is over and gone..." Now, if the coordinates aren't proper, you can have a situation – can you hear this? – where you come in with the intention to teach (this actually happened to me) and suddenly it went like this: "Phooosh!" And the whole congregation was just gone. And I sat there. I was in the wrong space/time zone.

Now, I'm telling you, *you're* in the wrong zone. Come on into this one, and you can turn to the guy next to you and say, "We're going to be in a late time association through this message," and it will be true. I know you make such a big deal out of the resurrection. Actually, it's just a little pile of form that I'm appearing in, transforming the chaos or the particle into a wave and you become real. It's that simple. Do you see that? That's all it is. And when you're done, you'll resurrect. It's a process, a maturation. No question. So you're later in time than I thought.

Do you hear that that can occur on earth and that Heaven cannot know about it for a minute? That's not the requirement. There's no judgment going on about communication at all. If you're somewhere off in this association and you evolve communication, that will be in your relationship with each other. It's as though you're going to apply for admission to the extra-galactic society. I want you to try to see this. I'm offering you whole mind here. I don't care what you do with it. Your life is eternal, and you're going to be eternal and you're going to be in Heaven. And that's what I came to tell you.

Now, what I just read you is a true statement, because you have assumed and given me an assumption of a name in our relationship. Say to me, "Where are you from?" (Audience: "Where are you from?")

Fond du Lac. What's your next question? Where did you think? Can you hear it? No, you don't hear it. It's already gone. You said, "from." It's already gone away. What difference does it make, where I'm from now? Nothing good is going to come out of Fond du Lac, anyway. You could prove that by going back there. You go back to your own house and you look around and it's so beautiful that it's gone, so you have to quick corrupt it again or you'll leave.

That's our lesson for today. The lesson today was nothing but the admission of Singular Self. The last four days, and the reason I'm teaching today, is I'm really... I don't know where. When I give five days like this, you can pretty much tell this is over. What's teaching you is the surety of your mutual minds in love for me. Can you hear that? Some of you are really hearing me. That is what I have become to you. Yet my personal reference, the totality of me, is not with my name at all. Now, if you'll accept me as Master Teacher, you will have to accept my message of your perfection, or don't give me the crap that you've accepted me. I'm only teaching you about yourself. Yes or no?

Reductions to idolship are always determinations to justify separate conceptual associations. I've got to throw that in with you. And you just keep reducing me until you form a church around me, which is about to occur, as soon as I leave. See, if it didn't occur, if I'm still here, you'd have to admit that your resurrection is at hand. If you kill me, you can set up an altar where you can share I'm not here. That's what's down the street. Remember, I asked you on the video, "Could you go and walk up here and say, 'Christians, I have come to tell you I am the savior of the world'?" Is that true because you say you are? Thank you.

How's it going? Are you are all right? Remember, you're never anywhere but in the Garden resurrecting. Don't be concerned about anything else. The journey always begins and ends at that point of the full consternation of your need to seek relief from the pain that you're in, or better to justify your need to be here at all. Do you understand? So I have led you into the valley of the shadow of death. That's where you are. And you are converting that in your mind to the certainty of who you are.

Guys? There's a finality of this. Turn off the tape for a second. I always say this. You guys are really getting ready to leave. Look! Yes. Who's the Bible teacher? Who's doing Bible?

The lesson for today was "Presence". *Surely, the presence of the Lord is in this place. I can feel His mighty power and His grace. I can hear the brush of angels' wings. I see Heaven on each face. Surely, the presence* – presence – *of God is in this place.* Is that okay? Now, everybody turn and greet the guy next to you. See you later! Ha! That's the whole teaching. Your savior is sitting next to you in your own pew. You're rotting with him in your own pew. Ha!

I love you guys. Give them a little music. See you later! I saw that kind of worked. You guys turn to the guy next to you and you go, "Hmmmmm." And then you turn back down in. You shared the idea that love is – what? Say, "Fearful." "Fearful." Love is fearful because it's going to reveal you and you're sinful. So you share the sin of your separation. What a strange place to be! Release your brother and you will see that he is you.

Dear ones, I love you. Thanks, dear ones. I'll be seeing you. Guys? Guys? Thanks for assembling. Don't try to prove it, guys. Your time is up. Say to me, "My time is up."

Your time's up. Say to me, "Why?"   Who gives a crap? If it's up, it's up, isn't it? That's why you're so happy. Why? It's up for no reason. If there had to be a reason, you never would be happy. That's the whole idea. That's why you laugh and are happy, because there's no reason for your time to be up. You didn't prove a damn thing. Nothing. Boy, it's nice to come to a place and say, "Your time is up," and then see there's life instead of death. Boy, there's a lot of light around here. I'll see you later! I'll see you in the morning!

The Basic Teaching of Jesus Christ of Nazareth

Good morning! Do you teach direct contact with God? That's the basic teaching. That's the initial necessity. There haven't been any Christians here until you appeared. Obviously what is defined as Christian here, that is, following the teachings of Jesus Christ, is not what this world is. *Obviously* because it's obvious – not because I say, "Obviously the teachings of this world are not those of Jesus," but because they're obviously not the teachings of Jesus. It doesn't have anything to do with whether you say they are or not because they're not. The teachings of Jesus are very simply that you are perfect and whole as God created you.

So the teachings of salvation are very simply that there is a perfect, loving God and that you, in fact, are at home in Heaven with Him. And that the earth is nothing but a manifestation of an apparent separation that is contained within your own relationalship mind. This is the whole teaching of Jesus in the New Testament – within your cause-and-effect relationship – the basic teachings of religion of reciprocity or exchange with associations of body form identified as existing in a manifestation of life that is not eternal. The problem that we have, that we will be addressing here, is that there are no qualifications for the entirety of your perfection as created by God. Very simply there are no qualifications to be met by you except the confession thereof. This is Christianity, isn't it?

Jesus says to you, "Be ye therefore perfect, even as your Father which is in Heaven is perfect." (Matthew 5:48) That is obviously an admission that you are and a commandment that you be. Why is that so difficult for you? You don't want to! You would much rather effect an unforgiving relationship with your brother, based on the First Covenant, so that you can eye-for-an-eye yourself and get even in the judgmental definition of yourself and your brother. That's the fact of the matter.

Why is it that when I begin to teach, I always teach the same thing? Because Jesus always only taught the same thing. What is that? *Your kingdom is not of this world.* (John 18:36) He always only teaches (any whole mind – as your mind is doing now) in the revelation that you have received through the grace of our risen Christ, Jesus. And He is always with you, isn't He? Jesus didn't die, did He? No. Well, what is this "Jesus died and was crucified for my sins." I don't understand that. He doesn't say that. Where does it say that Jesus died? It's not there. The surprising thing about it, and this will really surprise you if you look at it, nowhere, positively not anywhere, does Jesus say anything except that *if you will believe me you will never die,* (John 11:26) and furthermore that *I am always with you.* (Matthew 28:20) He doesn't say you're going to die or be crucified at all!

Do all Christian churches say that He died on the cross? Yes. No wonder I wasn't a Christian. Who would be a Christian if he had to believe that? It's absurd. Established Christianity is absurd. I would tell them. But they won't let me in their pews to tell them that. But if they would – I used to try and tell them that. I would try and say, "That's absurd! Do you mean that a divine, loving God with eternal life sent His own Son, created by Him, in order that He be tortured by you to prove that He's a real God?" That's senseless! I don't care what the alternative to the procedures of your justification for existence is, but I assure you that formal Christianity is absurd. It was absurd to me and it's absurd to you. It's nuts. It's crazy. It doesn't make any sense. That does not prove whether there is a God or whether there's not a God. I'm not talking about that. Certainly any God that would do that would not be a God in my mind – or in any reasonable mind, because it doesn't make any sense.

If there is such a thing as perfect Eternal Love and Happiness, it is not what sent His son in to be tortured and killed. That I assure you. The problem you have with that is the basis of your existent self – is the denial of your own true Self. In essence what Jesus teaches is, "You are killing me all the time." This is the whole teaching of Christianity. He says, "Since I am a perfected image of you" (this is in the New Testament very specifically) "you constantly crucify me or kill me rather than simply ascend with me in the realization that we are resurrected." Is it that simple? I'm doing just fundamental theology here so that you get this teaching. I want you to hear this with me. You will begin to look at the absurdity of 2000 years of Christianity. That's very simply because 2000 years of established Christianity is absurd because any established association of form outside of Heaven is absurd.

You invented a God that's perfect and loving forever. What the hell are you doing here? Why are you here if that is true? That's the question.

Perhaps it's not true and perhaps there is no solution. But if it is true that there is no solution, how do you know about a loving God and Eternal Life? Now you are at the crucial step in the teachings of Jesus. The crucial step in the teachings of any whole mind is that you are responsible for yourself in association with what you think. Once more. Shall I do it again? This is the entire Sermon on the Mount. (Matthew 5-7) As a man thinketh, he will perceive his associations with himself. As he judges, he will be judged. As he forgives, he will be forgiven. Is it that simple?

Why is that difficult for you? Why is it difficult to forgive? Do you know why? To you sin is real! If you said to me, "You've got to forgive the guy that did that to you," I would say the hell with you! Do you see? I can give you the line: If sin is real, it's unforgivable, if we don't have a perfection of mind in any association. So you are taught in some sort of obscure way (this is what the *Course in Miracles* groups are doing), that somehow sin remains real, but your requirement for salvation is that you forgive someone who has caused an unjust act to you. "The hell with you. I'm never going to do that. He doesn't deserve forgiveness. Why did he attack me in the first place?" What's the solution? *You are the cause of his attack!* There can be no solution. This is the teaching of Sermon on the Mount! If you defend yourself in the association, you will be attacked by the thoughts contained within your own mind. Is it that simple? That's an amazing idea!

Obviously the essence of the teaching of any whole mind is *forgiveness*. It would have to be, simply because you are the cause of your own association with yourself. And until you forgive your brother, it is impossible that you will forgive yourself, since your brother is a projection of your own mind and you are judging him in relationship with how you think you are. After 20 years of the *Course in Miracles*, the refusal of individual conceptual minds to teach the fundamentalness of Jesus' teaching is surprising most of you.

Very fundamentally, the teaching of Jesus of Nazareth is: *You are the cause of this*. That the power of your mind, through the power of God, is setting terms for your evilness in your direction to deny the totality of God and His relationship with you. That's the fact of the matter. That's the whole teaching.

I'm going to get out of Christianity here in just a minute because obviously for 2000 years you have rejected Jesus. I'm an illuminate mind. Obviously, I've had an experience of being born again. My whole teaching is that I am whole. I commend my spirit to God. And I am in an entire association. So from my viewpoint, no forgiveness of you is required, very simply because there would be no reason to forgive you in the totality of my mind. It is impossible that I be wronged within my own association.

This is the whole Sermon on the Mount, in case you would be interested in this. That is, I am innocent of the guilt of my self identity. I am innocent of the guilt of naming myself in association with myself. What does God call me? His own beloved Son. Does He say that to me? What does He say? *This is my beloved Son, in whom I am well pleased.* (Matthew 3:17) So He's pleased with me? Yes. Does God say it again at the transfiguration? And does He add an admonition to listen to Him? Yes: *This is my beloved Son, in whom I am well pleased. Hear ye him.* (Matthew 17:5) That's the only two things God says in the whole New Testament.

How come God prattles so much in the Old Testament? In the Old Testament He's telling people what they ought to do in relationship with themselves. In the New Testament He just says: *This is my beloved Son.* What an amazing idea! So your establishments connect the Old Testament eye-for-an-eye, and His direct teaching in the New Testament is: Don't be afforded the reciprocity of your own mind associations.

Does this require some sort of transformation of your mind? Yes. That's what you teach. That's what Jesus teaches. You're a Christian? You teach "I must undergo an experience of a contact with God based on my forgiveness or my acceptance of my brother as loving and whole as I am through God's creation."

Why is this world here at all? I need some answers. Class? Why is this world here at all if you can hear, in your mind, this teaching. All I am saying to you really is: *There is no world.* Jesus says to you directly that we all came from Heaven and that we actually have already gone home. If you don't know that, come with me now and I will take you home. Those are lines that you could read in the New Testament. How come you haven't read them? Or have you? What does He mean by "The time will come, and did." It means the time will come and did when you saw this and were gone from here.

Obviously you needed a savior, but it's damn tough for you to accept me. The whole teaching of Jesus is: *Accept your brother as your savior.* This is directly what He said. You have condemned your brother to your own separate association. And until you forgive him, it is impossible for you to forgive yourself since he is a thought pattern arrangement of *your* mind! If you have constructed him in the likeness of your false association with yourself, how could he possibly give you back any more than what you thought he was?

The fun part of the teaching of Jesus, and certainly the *Course in Miracles* is that your self-conceptions are never true. This is the whole Sermon on the Mount. Until you forgive the association out there, you cannot know of your own innocence. It is literally impossible. Everything that He says to you that you have now accepted – most of you in this congregation – is very literally that there is no compromise between the eternal mind of God and your mind that is determined to justify yourself in your own worldly limitation. One or the other is not true. This is the whole teaching of Jesus. There is no association between natural man (the man of the temple) and the man of Jesus that He is representing to you in the entirety of His mind. Can you read this in the scripture? Of course you can read it in the scripture. I'm teaching scripture.

Why is it that after 2000 years I can't stand up in a Christian church and teach the scripture of Jesus? Don't underestimate the insanity of a conceptual association that is determined to justify itself in its correspondence with its own objective associations. Who am I talking about? Jesus says *you* have to be born again! How many are born again? You're not born again? Oh, you're just keeping warm under there? When were you born again? Just now! You got it! That's the whole teaching, isn't it? Yes, but it's too late. That "now" is gone, isn't it?" Now I'm going to have to prove that I was born again based on not being born again." This is the absurdity of established Christianity.

Can you prove that you're born again? Not without being born again! Nicodemus says to Jesus, *I know that thou art a teacher come from God: for no man can do these miracles that thou doest, except God be with him.* (John 3:1) It's very obvious to everyone that Jesus is working miracles. There's no question about it. And he sees that Jesus is using a technique not of a correspondence. He would have to be because there is no capacity contained within a human being to heal – no true capacity to heal, without a definition of what the healing would be in the relationship of the cause and the effect. It would be impossible. In that sense, all conceptual minds heal to the form association of the directions that they have given themselves.

If you were going to teach *A Course In Miracles*, the admission that the conceptual association of a human being is a comparison of non-existent form is my entire teaching. This is the whole teaching of the requirement for forgiveness that Jesus says you must practice within your own mind because any advocation of the thought form associations of your mind will verify the form that is contained within your own conceptual identity. Can you hear this?

The teaching in Chapters 2 and 12 of the *Course* is that the conceptual mind is a projection of its thought form associations with itself. It defines a human being. You are taught to observe the objective associations of yourself – you learn this – and correspond to yourself in that human association. The entire teaching, my teaching to you, is that is not what life is very simply because life is eternal and you are whole as God created you. The manner in which that is elucidated in the conceptual thought form identity of Jesus in the *Course in Miracles* is astonishing because He declares to you forthrightly that ideas leave not their source.

This is Chapter 12: When you say, "I don't want that," and you project it from yourself, what you are really saying is, "I want it so I can remember that I don't want it." Did you hear that? I'll do it once more for you. "I don't want that." Now that becomes something he doesn't want. Come on, this is not hard. He now depends on not wanting that in order to know who he is. "One thing I know for sure is I don't want that." If he didn't want it, why didn't he just forget it and get rid of it? If he forgot it and got rid of it, he wouldn't have anything to base his not wanting it on. But remember, the moment that he doesn't want it, he must have something else that he wants.

Since he is basing his reality on something he doesn't want, what he wants must be based on something that he doesn't want! So since he doesn't want it, he has attempted to reject it from his mind. He now compares what he doesn't want to what he does want, and he is literally not doing anything. He is simply in an existent association of judgment based on his own objective association with himself. Is he real? Absolutely not! There is absolutely no reality contained in judging what you want and what you don't want – first of all because you don't know who the hell you are anyway. That's why you had to decide in your own mind what to reject and what to accept. Obviously a whole, eternal mind creating does not have to decide what it wants and what it doesn't want.

The teaching that I just gave you is real obvious to me. What it says is objective reality is not real. It says any comparison of the form can only be a comparison with forms of your own mind based on your previous references within your body that associate with form until you get old and die. You accept some and you reject some. Some are good, some are bad. If some are good and some are bad, you inevitably will enter into, "Some are better than others." You cannot *not*. Now you are trapped in form association of deciding what you want in correspondence with the conflict of your own mind. That's insanity. You have no basis for comparing what you are. You have simply set up objective associations that make the comparison. Not true! That's why natural man cannot know whole mind. Quite literally, he is determined to conflict in his own objective correspondence with himself.

If the Light of God is all around you all the time, your determination to stay in the form identity of your mind will deny you access to the entirety of the power of God-Mind, although you must be using the power of God-Mind to deny your own power of mind! Quite literally, you must be using your own conceptual associations to deny your own reality.

Our whole teaching to you is: Stop organizing your thoughts! "Well, nobody does that." We do! I have no capacity to organize my thoughts at all. I can elucidate my recognition of my incapacity to organize. That's why you need me! Can you hear this? Most of you are hearing this!

Would I dare give you this? Do you want to hear something? You've heard of forgiveness? Forgive?! A moment of total forgiveness is what

God is. I am teaching you that forgiveness is an essence of realization. If all the Universe is nothing but thought form, and my thought form of association is in correspondence with the conversion of my conceptual self, there is an energy field of forgiveness of your own associations of each other. That is literally an energy of my mind. Notice that it has absolutely no concern about what it is you are forgiving. This is the crucial element in what we will call "the immediacy of salvation."

If there is such a thing as a whole loving God and truth and eternal life, it must be available to you. If it is available to you, it must be available now. The practice of our conceptual associations through our non-judgment or forgiveness of our brother, is to realize a moment of peace and happiness simply based on not holding ourself in the bondage of our own projections. This is what we are doing! Did you hear what I said? That is a real happening to you, and has become a real happening to you in association with me. If I can teach you to emanate from you essences of forgiveness, you will become the light of the world. Why is it hard to be the light of the world if you are the cause of the world in the first place? You don't want to be the light of the world; you would much rather suffer the conflict of your own associations with yourself and get old and die in your dream of death. Most of you don't want to do that any more. Most of you have allowed yourself to feel the communicative essence of forgiveness not based on the sin.

Forgiveness has nothing at all to do with what the sin is – obviously, because you couldn't possibly forgive all the sins that there are. Here's the whole teaching: If you remain in a continuing act of forgiveness, which is nothing but a release of your judgment, you will begin to evolve to a communication with Universal Mind, not based on the conflict of the projections of conceptual mind association. You are constantly free to be born again. Of course!

The immediacy of salvation is based on the immediacy of your capacity to be born each moment in the certainty that you are perfect as God created you. The amazing thing that I discovered in the process of my illumination – and you are just like this – is that I saw acts of forgiveness. Many times you saw acts of forgiveness that should not be acceptable – moments of forgiveness of acts that there could be no possibility that they should be forgiven. That might have included initially, "I'll let God judge." The admission that God does not finally judge will be discovered through the innocence of your attempt to judge. If there is a God of judgment, you certainly were going to have to ask Him to judge. The problem you have with that is, since you don't know what God's judgment is, it would have to correspond with your judgment. Your judgment of God would have to be the association of yourself with yourself. It could not *not* be. Does God judge? Yes. If He judges, He judges perfectly. If He judges perfectly, why does He have to judge? He doesn't, but you asked whether He judges or not. If you asked if God judges, He judges. "Why would He judge Himself?" I don't know. You asked if He judged. Any condition of judgment would have to be a judgment of the entirety with your apparent need to judge. Obviously in the admission of the entirety, there would be no judgment required.

This is interesting, I wonder if you would like to hear this. I'm doing "forgiving the whore" in John 8. It's very interesting because the Pharisees are always trying to trap Jesus in whether He's willing to forgive their sins. I'm going to show you what happens.

Your acceptance of what I'm teaching here must be some form of communication that we are having because I am saying the same words that it says in the Bible. I am not saying anything except "blessed are the meek; forgive your brother; come on home; you are still in Heaven". I'm not telling you anything else. But for some reason or other, you have begun to accept my message! Apparently because my message obviously comes from God. You don't like that. Why does my message come from God? Everything comes from God! It is impossible that whatever message I am giving you does not come from my association with reality, if you will allow it to.

But getting back to immediacy. I teach you the immediacy of salvation very simply because there is only the immediacy of our correspondence. We can't correspond last week or last month. We can't correspond next week. Any associations we have of peace and harmony and forgiveness will occur in immediate relationships of ourselves with ourselves. See if you can hear this with me: *One single act of your mind of total forgiveness is the disappearance of the world in its entirety.* I'll do it once more for you. Any associations of correspondence of your own mind suffer the conflict of your own associations – and we've agreed that they are not real? No, you're going to fall back on the fact that they're real. I'm telling you there is no reality in the correspondence of the objective association at all. Why? It eliminates the necessity for you to decide which part of your mind you want to accept as whole because it tells you literally NONE of this world is real. Your kingdom is not of this world. Got it?

Some of you are really hearing this! All I am telling you is that it is not outside of you, and that the salvation – your awakening from your dream – depends on you because *it is you*. It's not out there. Any judgment you place on the other association will only be a judgment of yourself – this is Sermon on the Mount. When your brother says to walk with you seven miles, no, walk forever with him. Don't measure how much you're going to be determined to act in your own mind. It's called the immediacy of salvation. Why? Salvation is going on now! The idea that minds can communicate is very valuable to those of us who are communicating with Mind.

Suddenly these Pharisees are really after Jesus. Why? He's working miracles. Do you think that you could suddenly take on Jesus' mode and go around and tremendous things would begin to happen and they would be acceptable? They absolutely are not acceptable to this world. They don't mind an occasional miracle where the water has a lot of magic in it, and for the next 400 years you can come there and maybe get well. But the idea of the entirety of the association with a whole mind is obviously not acceptable and that's why you are here, because when you accept my salvation, you will be saved. It is impossible that not be so because I am a product of your mind association with yourself. So they're going to trap Him because they really found a sinner.

Jesus went unto the mount of Olives. And early in the morning he came again into the temple, and all the people came unto him; and he sat down, and taught them. This is exactly what I am doing now. *And the scribes and Pharisees brought unto him a woman taken in adultery; and when they had set her in the midst, they say unto him, Master, this woman was taken in adultery, in the very act.* I mean nobody said it – which is important. They wanted Him to know that she was caught in the act. I mean they broke down the motel room door. They wanted Him to know that actually had happened so He couldn't say, "Well, that's hearsay, why don't we set up a trial." It's very important that you hear that. There could be no question that she was committing adultery. I don't know why you laugh. You guys do imagery in your own minds.

Now Moses in the law commanded us, that such should be stoned: but what sayest thou? In other words, the penalty for that was that she would be stoned to death. Does it say that in Leviticus? Did they stone all the whores to death? No, but they stoned the ones they didn't want around. Come on, this is the whole judicial system. What Jesus is going to say is that you are all whores. He literally is going to say that. If you judge, you are judging in association with yourself. But I want you to hear the manner in which He does it, because He does it in a way that should not be acceptable to the scribes. Why?

Now Moses in the law commanded us, that such should be stoned: but what sayest thou? This they said, tempting him, that they might have to accuse him. Because He would tell them that even though she was sinful she should be forgiven, and that somehow the law of Moses could be usurped by Jesus. *But Jesus stooped down, and with his finger wrote on the ground, as though he heard them not.* What some of you don't realize is the value of a non-judgmental mind. Can you hear this? He made a Kabbala symbol. Are you aware of that? Kabbala teaches abstraction of the mind. The whole mystic Hebrew association is the passing of mind to mind, not based on the priesthood. Jesus really loves this. Jesus taught, "Know ye not that ye must be born again," which is Kabbalistic. The whole idea in Kabbala is that there can be a perfect establishment based on geometric cause and form associations. That a whole temple, that a Jerusalem, can be formed by mutual mind association. Are you aware of that? That's what Jesus teaches. I didn't mean to digress there.

We're talking about whole mind. He acts as though He doesn't hear them. What is He doing? He is setting up a valence of forgiveness! He is going to set up a healing mode. This is exactly what He does. For a moment they are going to be healed of their necessity to judge Him, because He's really not going to say anything except, "Let those who are without sin be judge." And their ordinary response would be, "Well, we all sin but theirs is worse than mine." But that's not what He says. What He says to them, and what they hear for just a moment, is that if you are sinful, you should not judge your brother. But in order for them to hear that, they had to experience a moment of Light where they felt compassion or forgiveness for the association regardless of what it had done, because of the immediacy of salvation. It is in this moment, and it has nothing to do with the sin at all. Amen! Would they have more of a tendency to forgive adultery than murder? I don't know.

But Jesus stooped down, and with his finger wrote on the ground, as though he heard them not. So when they continued asking him, he lifted up himself, and said unto them, he that is without sin among you, let him first cast a stone at her. [And make his declaration of how he is in his superiority.] They don't do it – beginning with the oldest back to the youngest. The old ones that had more experience had a tendency, perhaps, to be a little more forgiving. *And again he stooped down, and wrote on the ground. And they which heard it, being convicted by their own conscience, went out one by one, beginning at the eldest, even unto the last.*

And Jesus was left alone, and the woman standing in the midst. When Jesus had lifted up himself, He saw none but the woman. Actually the parable of this is that they are all gathering, making accusations, and that they are accusations of each other and they find one brother, or one Christ to condemn. Can you hear this? Condemning the whore is the same as crucifying the Christ. Quite literally because it is a judgment that that aggregation is not a part of that. What actually occurs is suddenly there is only Jesus and the woman. Now Jesus can say to her: *Woman, where are those thine accusers? hath no man condemned thee?* There isn't anyone condemning because for that moment the aggregation of the association entered into the immediacy of a moment of salvation, which is your only requirement. Each moment that you enter into forgiveness, it would be impossible for you to be objective in your associations. What did they need in order to do that? Jesus drawing a little sign in the sand.

Are you hearing me now because you want to hear me? All I am really offering you is your own salvation.

Then spake Jesus again unto them, saying, I am the light of the world: he that followeth me shall not walk in darkness, but shall have the light of life. All He did was shine on the form association of judgment and make it whole in His own mind. How are you guys coming with this? This is the whole teaching of Jesus. Jesus says, "I am walking right along side of you. I am a perfect association of yourself in your own mind. If you will accept that I am with you even unto the end of the world, the world will end, because the world is over for me. I am offering you that in the surety of my mind." Isn't that something? I'm teaching Jesus Christ of Nazareth. And I think you are hearing me! At least you are enthusiastic enough to admit to the possibility that you might be perfect and that you don't have to get old and die because all He says to you is there is no death. See how simple it is? Jesus didn't say that you had to suffer and get old and die in order to prove it. He said that there isn't any such thing as death. And that in your forgiving mode you will experience the reality of Love.

The Pharisees therefore said unto him, Thou bearest record of thyself; thy record is not true. Because you are not comparing yourself with anything of the world. *Jesus answered and said unto them, Though I bear record of myself, yet my record is true: for I know whence I came, and whither I go; but ye cannot tell whence I come, and whither I go.* Because you don't know where I'm going because where I'm going is where you're from, and you are afraid to come home with me. Literally you are afraid that God, who kicked you out of Heaven, is going to punish you if you try to get back in. There's a little theology for you.

What He says here is that if you judge your own projections, you cannot be true. If you judge in association with God who sees you perfectly (*this is my beloved son*) the requirement is only that you accept what God says about you. *Ye judge after the flesh; I judge no man. And yet if I judge, my judgment is true: for I am not alone, but I and the Father that sent me.*

Since all He says is that you are perfect, I'm afraid you are just going to have to accept it. I know that's very difficult for you to do because you believe that perfection involves judgment. And if perfection involves judgment, it will be impossible to be perfect. If perfection involves judgment of an association, there must be something that is not perfect. This is the whole lesson. You will then base your comparison of the truth on something that is not perfect and make the truth imperfect. This is Chapter 12 of *A Course In Miracles.* I just came back around to that. Any judgment, or rejection, which is what judgment is, and your reality henceforth will be based on the judgment of your rejection of something. Nothing can ever be true from that moment on. That's why there is no truth in this world.

Fortunately you are not from here. Fortunately, most of you now in this association have come to know that the world was your dream of death. This is the whole teaching. And that you are awakening from that dream in the immediacy of the realization of your perfection.

For those great thinkers out there that pretend to teach the *Course in Miracles,* listen: *You see what you expect, and you expect what you invite. Your perception is the result of your invitation, coming to you as you sent for it. Whose manifestations would you see? Of whose presence would you be convinced? For you will believe in what you manifest, and as you look out so will you see in. Two ways of looking at the world are in your mind, and your perception will reflect the guidance you have chosen. If you have chosen not to judge, you will formulate forgiveness within your own mind.*

But listen to how it deals with the concepts that you have formulated. This is Jesus, personally, to you. This could be in the New Testament:

I am the manifestation of the Holy Spirit, and when you see me it will be because you have invited Him. Because He is going to represent your image of perfection that you have not yet been willing to accept. Once more. Can you get that? In the resurrection, Jesus appears as a whole, perfect body, doesn't He? And He stands in front of you as a perfect body. This is the resurrection and the Life very simply because it cannot be anything but that.

I have no concern about how you organize your body associations with each other. They don't mean anything, because I am standing next to you, representing your Christhood. This is exactly what you are expected to do with your brother if you intend to forgive him. You stand up and reflect the Light of your mind into the reorganization of the physical association of his body. That's how I heal. I heal your physical associations of your body by seeing you perfect. It has nothing to do with your body at all. The moment that you don't attempt to hold your body in that association of objectivity, you will be healed. Let's see how Jesus does it.

One more thing: The entire teaching of Jesus is that all power is of the mind. He tells you flat out there is one power and that is God and you cannot degrade the power of your own mind. If you attempt to subtract yourself from the totality of the power, you will represent yourself as evil and suffer the pain of the power that you employ to deny God. You literally cannot *not* do it. And it will be painful to you.

I am the manifestation of the Holy Spirit. Jesus Christ is speaking. *And when you see me it will be because you have invited* the Spirit. Because if you invite the Spirit, the Spirit is an abstraction. The Spirit is nothing but the entirety of the conversion of the form in the energy. So you need an image of perfection. I will represent your image of perfection for you if you will let me, very simply because I know that all imageries of association are meaningless. The whole teaching is that at no single moment do you exist at all. You are constantly in a flux of the form associations within your own body.

Here's the problem you have: *For He will send you His witness if you will but look upon him.* Always present to you is your own perfection. It's impossible that not be true because you are seeking perfection, and you must seek it within your own mind because it isn't out there. And if the perfection is only in your own mind, you must allow yourself to see perfection outside of you and it must be contained in what you have previously rejected. This is called forgiveness.

Here's the problem: I say to you that forgiveness is an act. Forgiveness is the action of the moment of your mind of the release of the objective associations of the form by which you have judged your brother. It has nothing to do with the observation of forgiveness. The observation of forgiveness is what sin is. Once more. The observation of forgiveness provides you with an act where you can specialize what you intend to forgive and what you intend to hold on to. Do you see that? That's a fact. The immediacy of salvation.

Remember always that you see what you seek (humans!) *for what you seek you will find* because it is in your mind. Now, *the ego* (the self-identity) *finds what it seeks, and only that.* It couldn't possibly find any more than it seeks because it seeks to justify itself within the form of its own association. That's what all humans do. You are taught to do that in your own mind. You are taught to set up objective associations of separation and give the guy a separate name from you; you have a separate name from him, even though you all come from the single Source of God. What an impossible place to be in! Fortunately, it's only yourself, locked in your own identity. Fortunately, it's only you.

He says: *The ego finds what it seeks, and only that. It does not find love, for that is not what it is* looking for. It is looking for justification for its judgment of fear. It needs to retain fear in its own self-identity. That is not what love is.

See if you can hear this: *It does not find love, for that is not what it is seeking. Yet seeking and finding are the same.* It's impossible that what you find, you have not found previously in your association. Actually, at the moment of seeking, you do find, because it's impossible to seek for something that is not already in your mind. You can't seek for nothing. If you seek for it, it must be that you already know what it is in your own association. And to that extent, you find it. It's the same as you can't commit adultery except in your own mind. This is Sermon on the Mount. The thought of sin is the act of sin itself. "Well, I'm not going to act at all." What difference does it make? If you are the thought of it, you are suffering the conflict of the thought. Since you can't stand the conflict of your own thought, you project it out from you and find your brother guilty of the performances of your own mind. And you wonder why I laugh at you. That way, you can share the guilt of the separation in your own mind. It doesn't make any sense. It's senseless. So you share what? Guilt! This is Chapter 12. It says you share the guilt of your separate self-identity.

Yet seeking and finding are the same. See if you can hear this. This is real tough stuff. *And if you seek for two goals you will find them.* "I found one; I found another." Neither one will be true. It isn't that you didn't find them. Why? It's impossible that you don't organize your mind, because seeking and finding are organizations of your own conceptual mind. Listen. This will help you with it.

But you will recognize neither. You will think they are the same because you want both of them. Here's the trick to this. *The mind always strives for integration, and if it is split and wants to keep the split, it will still believe it has one goal by making it seem to be one* through the judgment of what it has rejected from itself in the retention of what it believes is true compared to the rejection.

Who cares? I do. Because that's what the human condition is. And that can't possibly make any sense. It has to be based on a construction of objective reality without the admission of any source. The guy says, "I don't have to have a source. I use the scientific approach." What is that? "I'm going to subtract myself from the experiment." You want to see the absurdity of the scientific approach? "I'll subtract myself from the experiment and pretend I'm not involved in the observation of it." This is the great dilemma that's occurring now in quantum physics. It's a great dilemma. "Let's set up an experiment to see what happens. But in order to do it, we have to pretend that we didn't set it up." Very simply because any observation of it will change it in association with yourself. Can you hear that? It cannot *not*. I'm not teaching anything you haven't read somewhere. But the truth of the matter is, you change it each moment that you observe it in order to make it correspond to what you want it to be.

Since nobody knows who they are and are separate, they find objective correspondences which they then verify as a phenomenon and call it "the world." That's crazy. What they are really using is non-creative thought. They are denying a single source of creation and setting up parameters that limit them to time. It limits them to cause-and-effect associations of time in which they can participate in the utilization of the form of their own mind until it dissipates into the nothing from whence it came. Can you hear that? I mean, you are nothing. You are either whole and perfect as God created you, or you are nothing. Your potential of separation has been used up.

The mind always strives for integration, and if it is split and wants to keep the split, it will still believe it has one goal by making it seem to be one. I said before (this is Jesus speaking) *that what you project or extend* (whether you project it or extend it) *is up to you, but you must do one or the other, for that is a law of mind, and you must look in before you look out.* The whole teachings of you as a human being were to organize yourself in your own associations based on what the world taught you, or what your mother taught you, or what you learned through the experience of touching the hot stove. You were taught to do that in your own mind. So that's a form of the projection of you, based on a solidarity that actually exists in you – the self that is you.

As you look in, you choose the guide for seeing. And then you look out and behold his witness. This is why you find what you seek. What you want in yourself you will make manifest, and you will accept it from the world because you put it there by wanting it. Literally! The whole universe of your mind is nothing but ideas. All you would have to say to me is, "I'm going to be home in Heaven, where I always am," and it would be impossible that you are not there.

The problem is not that. The problem is you want to justify your association here in order to be in Heaven. Quite literally, you want to remain in judgment of yourself in order to justify yourself rather than letting God judge you in the perfection of what you are. Period. That got too simple for you, but that's the fact of the matter. "Father, into Thy hands I commend my spirit. I can't do this anymore" or "I give up. Everything I do just turns more and more to chaos. There must be another solution that is not contained within the organization." That's the teaching of this. Not only is that the teaching of it, but it teaches that your mind has set it up objectively and that at any single moment you can change the imagery of the entirety of your association. I need to finish this paragraph. It's got a hooker in it here.

What you want in yourself, you will make manifest, and you will accept it from the world because you put it there by wanting it. Listen. *When you think you are projecting what you do not want, it is still because you do want it.* So that your associations can be based on your rejection of it. "One thing for sure, I'm not like that bum." Which is exactly what I just said. You've rejected him from your own mind, but he hasn't gone anywhere. Now you can say, "I'm not as big a bum as he is." You didn't say you were not a bum, you said you're just not as big a bum. This is what Jesus did in the healing of the mind. He taught you for a moment – and I teach you – not to judge your association. Why? The judgment of yourself with yourself is what this world is. And the moment you don't judge yourself in your own projections, you will spring into Heaven and did.

"Well, why is it no one has heard this? Why, after 2000 years, has no one heard this?" They have and they sprung into Heaven. If you haven't heard it, it's because you are in an aggregation within your own mind that's denying it – *you!* You must be in your own aggregation of mind, since there's nothing outside of you. In the finality of this, Jesus will say the world is going to reject you and kill you if you decide to go home to God. This is all Jesus' teaching, isn't it? The world is going to revile and hate you and persecute you because you have designed the world to do that to you should you attempt to escape. *You,* individually.

One thing for sure, this teaching is not acceptable to the establishment. That's why you can't go in the church and teach the teachings of Jesus. It's impossible that you do it. You're going to go into the church and tell them they can't sin and that they're perfect and that you don't have to die to prove anything; that there is no death; that you're actually at home in Heaven? "But that's what it says in the New Testament." I know what it says in the New Testament.

Why has that not been accepted by this association? Because this association is the non-acceptance of it. The moment that you accept it, you'll not be here. "Well, that's quite a step. I don't know whether I'm willing to do that." Well, then stay here and suffer and get old and die.

My fundamental teaching to you, those of you who hear me, is that *you are the cause of everything.* You are the cause of your own pain and you are the cause of your own happiness. If you are going to use your self-existence of pain and remorse and guilt and non-love and hate in order to justify your existent association, go ahead. Who in the universe can stop you? No one! Finally you get sick and tired of it and say, "The hell with it!"

Are you doing this but to yourself? Instead of blaming your projections, you accept responsibility for yourself. The moment you do that, you can't stand your own pain. That's called a bottom. The moment you can't stand your own pain, you release it. The moment you release it and say, "God help me," you get the help from God. Is that right, or not? Or are you going to be you. What can I do about it? Nothing, except tell you you're going to be stuck in your own mind.

As you look in, you choose the guide for seeing. And then you look out and behold his witnesses. This is why you find what you seek. What you want in yourself you will make manifest, and you will accept it from the world because you put it there by wanting it. When you think you are projecting what you do not want, it is still because you do want it. This leads directly to dissociation (from your mind), *for it represents the acceptance of two goals, each perceived in a different place; separated from each other because you made them different. The mind then sees a divided world outside itself, but not within. This gives it an illusion of integrity, and enables it to believe that it is pursuing one goal* – based on the projections of its own mind, which are gone and totally meaningless. All of the objective reality based on that has no meaning. That's an incredible idea! Wow!

This gives it an illusion of integrity, and enables it to believe that it is pursuing one goal. Yet as long as you perceive the world as split, you are not healed. For to be healed is to pursue one goal, because you have accepted only one and want but one. Did you hear that? *When you want only love you will see nothing else. The contradictory nature of the witnesses you perceive is merely the reflection of your conflicting invitations.* Very simply, you don't want love to be whole for everybody. You want to be able to choose who is going to be perfect. And any choice that you make will be a denial of God in that sense. Boy, this is good stuff.

You have looked upon your mind and accepted opposition there, having sought it there. But do not then believe that the witnesses for opposition are true, for they attest only to your decision about reality, returning to you the messages you gave them. The power of decision is your one remaining freedom as a prisoner of this world. It's not that your decision is true, but you are empowered with your decision to say, "None of this is true." Why? None of this is true! This is Ramakrishna. This is the teachings of Eastern associations. Negate your mind in the certainty that none of your forms are true. It's called meditation. All I really teach is an active meditation, or a continuing reassociation of the transcendental nature of our communication in mind that I am offering you. That's literally an offering from my mind to yours. So the problem you may have is, "Why don't we just sit here and meditate?" I'll go and sit and we'll meditate together. And you can come into an abstraction and call it the peace of God, Sister Teresa, or anyone, and you will experience that happiness in your own mind. And you will say, "Wow, is that ever good!" And then you'll come right back down in and participate in the evil.

All I'm really teaching you is what you would call existential transcendentalism. I'm showing you that you are in a transcendent nature of self-existence that, if you will broaden the range of your existent association, can show you a parameter that will always transcend your objections. That is, that those in the dark cannot see the light. This is the entire teaching. You can't see the light because you're going to get reflections of your own dark mind. And when you do that, you'll get that.

The power of decision is your one remaining freedom as a prisoner of this world. The world has imprisoned you. You don't believe you have imprisoned the world. You believe that the world is binding you. It's not true.

You can decide to see it right. What you made of it is not its reality, for its reality is only what you give it. Since all power is given unto you, if you give the power of your mind, you will be an advocate of the power of God creating, since you will simply retain nothing. Do you understand? In other words, forgiving or giving is the same as God creating in conceptual association because God only gives. He could not do more than give you the totality of what He is and that you become in that association.

You cannot really give anything but love to anyone or anything, nor can you really receive anything but love from them. If you think you have received anything else, it is because you have looked within and thought you saw the power to give something else. And you're full of crap. *It was only this decision that determined what you found, for it was the decision for what you sought.* (Chapter 12) This is incredible stuff.

Do you really believe you can kill the Son of God? You can't. You're killing yourself each moment to deny the perfection of your own mind.

So this is the teachings of Jesus of Nazareth, or of my whole mind, or of your whole mind, as we stand together in a moment of the realization that we're not from here. I am offering you the certainty that you're not from here. I'm admitting that you believe you are, but I'm telling you that this world is over and gone. Can you hear this? I'm standing right in front of you now and telling you that you're in a dream of death. Your decision not to accept what I am saying is only your predetermined need to justify cancer that you have. I wouldn't do that. It's impossible that if you're in the body form that you haven't set up a mode of death. Is that so? You fully intend to honor death here. You could not *not*, or you would not be here. "Everything here gets old and dies." The hell with you! *You* get old and die. I have no intention of getting old and dying because it doesn't make any sense. To get old and die is senseless if there's a loving God.

"Well, it makes sense to me." Well, then get old and die! What do you want from me? "I'm not making the decision. God is." The hell with you. You think that God is extending to you death and pain. It's just nonsense. I haven't had anything to do with you in 500 years. At the minimum, I was an atheist. At the minimum I wouldn't have anything to do with that God except to shake my fist at him. Which is exactly what the Christian community does and then pretends it doesn't. It seeks justice and when it doesn't get it, it has to forgive God for not giving it what it's entitled to. And it pretends it loves God because God inflicts pain on them, and that's crap. That's pure crap. Come on!

I was taught as a little kid, "Well, God is going to cause you a lot of pain," and I said, Why? "Because you've sinned." I thought God made me perfect. How could I sin if He made me perfect. See how simple this is? "Oh, that's much too simple." I know. That's the innocence that has to be beat out of you. *Suffer the little children to come unto me* because they ask very intelligent questions. They say, "If there is a God, how come I can't be in Heaven?" The adults say, "Shut up and don't talk about that!" It's true. They'll ask questions like that. "Oh, but if God is in Heaven and He's perfect and He loves me..." "Never mind. You let God decide that." Crap! If you let God decide, He will decide immediately that you're perfect. If you're perfect, you can't be in this world. "Well, what am I going to do with my momma?" Take her to Heaven with you. What do you expect your momma to tell you except what you guys have all determined in your own mind. Your kingdom is not of this world!

For some of you, for all of us, there's a form of conflict involved in it because my teaching is the antithesis of the world. It's exactly the opposite of what you have been taught. If it's not, there's no hope for you. There is no hope for you if the teachings of Jesus of Nazareth are not exactly the opposite of what the world teaches. That's a fact. Can you hear me? Does that make you happy?

What am I finally saying to you? I'm teaching, as we depart this dream of death, the certainty of the immediacy of salvation. This is the whole teaching of being born again. I'm telling you literally that at this moment the world does not exist except as you are maintaining it and constructing it within your own mind. This is all this book has said. This is what is being rejected by the *Course* groups. All groups would have to reject it because groups are designed to reject this teaching. How you reject the direct teaching and pretend it doesn't say that, I have no idea since the whole teaching of the *Course* is, "You are the cause of this, and when you change your mind, the world will change." And that, in fact, you did and the world did change and you are not here.

I want you to hear how beautifully Jesus, this mind, says this. Incidentally, the admission that this comes from a source outside of this world will greatly increase your association because this is divine stuff. It's incredible.

A little hindrance can seem large indeed to those who do not understand that miracles are all the same. It doesn't require your understanding. It requires your acceptance. One miracle is not any different than any other if none of it is real. "Well, it's easier to heal a common cold than it is cancer." That's crazy. It doesn't make any sense. Any form of aberration of separation from God would be the same as any other. *Yet teaching that is what this course is for. This is its only purpose, for only that is all there is to learn* – that one miracle, that you are nothing but a continuing miracle of your own whole mind. There's nothing else to teach you because that's the only thing you could be taught.

You can't be taught something, and that's why you require the miracle. Do you need a miracle to get out of here? Sure, because you can't get out by your own devices. *And you can learn it in many different ways.* Of course. All sorts of different ways. *All learning is a help or a hindrance to the gate of Heaven. Nothing in between is possible.* You are either going to admit that you're perfect, or you're going to deny it and be in this association. So stop trying to pretend you decided to do this. If you've really decided to do this, you will experience that decision continuously because you will discover the love and harmony of your association with God. That's a true thing, isn't it?

There are but two teachers only, who point in different ways. And you will go along the way your chosen teacher leads. There are but two directions you can take, while time remains and choice is meaningful. Although it will soon be gone. *For never will another road be made except the way to Heaven.* There isn't any other way.

You but choose whether to go toward Heaven, or away to nowhere. There is nothing else to choose.

Is the chooser true? How does he get to Heaven? By not choosing! The moment that he didn't choose, he was in Heaven. It would have to be that you're the obstruction to it within your own mind. You like to study your own conception of what I'm offering you. But the construction of it is the denial of it. So I teach you holographic totality associations of constructions just only for holy instances? Why? That's the only time there is. Is the only time there is now? What's wrong with being in Heaven now? "I'm not there." Yes, you are. "How do I know?" I'm telling you. "I don't believe you." I know it.

The reason you've constructed me to tell you this, is so you can deny me, because I'm in your own mind, telling you. If you accepted it, we would spring into Heaven. Does it matter who says it? Absolutely not, but you think it does. You think that I have some qualification of being a great teacher. There are no qualifications for the miracle. Except your acceptance of God. That's not really a qualification. That's an admission of failure. That's an admission that "All of my qualifications won't work." For most of you, that's a devastating idea. For those of who have experienced the devastation, it's a happy realization that by staying in the devastation, we will always be right in the mind of God. We don't attempt to escape from fear. We are fearful totally.

Can you hear what I'm teaching you? You stay in total fear. Total fear is impossible. That's called a bottom. The moment that you really enter a bottom, you'll immediately spring out of it. Fear could not be totally fearful of fear.

Are you guys feeling my energy? You know the amazing thing about this? This has to be a reenactment. If all of the form is only in your mind, everything that's happening has to have already happened. You just don't want to remember this. What I'm saying to you at this point is: Would you rather die or would you rather deny death and hear me? That's your choice. Is it possible for you to stand up and say, "To hell with this world! I'm not going to die. I'm going home with you." You bet! Will you go home with me? Yes. "Well, the world won't believe it." The world has nothing to do with it. It doesn't have to do with the world. The world is the denial of this offering. Yet you accept the offering and then you try to examine it in your own association. When you do the examination of your salvation, you prevent it from occurring! Quite literally!

There is nothing else to choose. Think not the way to Heaven's gate is difficult at all. Nothing you undertake with certain purpose and high resolve and happy confidence, holding your brother's hand and keeping step to Heaven's song, is difficult to do. That's a beautiful idea. It couldn't possibly be difficult because the power of decision is in your mind. If you need help with that, I'll give it to you because I have no difficulty with the power of my certainty that I am whole as God created me. I am using that power, not my own! How can you know you are using God's power? Because whenever you are using your own you are going to suffer pain. The way you can tell the difference is you become fearful. If you are never fearful, you must be whole as God created you.

I'm afraid you might not hear this. This says it takes time for you to hear this. But you remember this: Time is over and gone. Anything I'm offering you, you have already done. I'm not concerned about the circumstances that you use. At this level, you can remember our circumstances together if you want to.

God gave His Teacher to replace the one you made, not to conflict with it. I know, to a human being, I am teaching things that are conflictual to you, like telling you that you are perfect as God created you. That is very conflictual to the conceptual mind because the conceptual mind is the conflict based on the denial of perfection, quite literally on the denial of God. Do you see that? And that's how simple this can be for you.

Nothing is ever lost but time, which in the end is totally meaningless. For it is but a little hindrance to eternity, quite meaningless to the real Teacher of this world. Time doesn't mean anything. That's why it's passing so fast for you. If you don't slow it down and try and set terms for it, it will really speed up within your own mind and suddenly this world is going to be over. *God gave His Teacher to replace the one you made, not to conflict with it.*

This could not have been written by a mind here. Do you want to share this with me. I don't care who you think this is written by – I'm not concerned about that. What I am telling you is this cannot have been written by a human association. Yet I see that you now accept it. I see that you are going to accept what this says. The acceptance of it will be your assertion of it because it is true.

And what He would replace has been replaced. Time lasted but an instant in your mind, with no effect upon eternity. And so is all time

CHAPTER 9: The Basic Teaching of Jesus Christ

past, and everything exactly as it was before the way to nothingness was made. This is the best theology you will ever get. *The tiny tick of time in which the first mistake was made, and all of them within that one mistake, held also the Correction for that one, and all of them that came within the first.* Very simply because God created everything. That's an expression of quantum. No matter how much you separate the form, each one of the form has the whole association of you. But you can't get it by gathering the form together, because the form is separate. You get it by accepting the totality of each form being whole within your own mind as the extender of the form rather than the projector and the attempt to organize it in your mind associations. Is that going on right now? Is this world over each moment? Why are you still here? So I can tell you! I'm also going to threaten you that I'm leaving here. This is the whole teaching of Jesus.

I'm telling you that you have made a decision to die rather than hear me because my requirement is – do you want my requirement that you won't like? – *Give everything away and come on home!* "Oh-oh, now we're on to your plan. You're going to pass the collection plate." No, I'm teaching you the *act* of giving, not your participation in the correspondence. What do I care what you give? You can only give yourself anyway. If you limit your giving, you are limiting yourself. I can't do anything about that. You are placing a value on yourself that retains your value in death. You would rather die than hear what I say because all you would really have to do is give everything away. Is that in the New Testament? Oh yes! "Jesus, I've really followed you, I'm going to do everything you say." Jesus says, "Give everything away, let's go." "Oh, shit!" (Matthew 19:16-22) Is it that simple? When he gave everything away did he spring into Heaven? Of course! He was possessed by his own mind. His own possessions guaranteed his death.

And in that tiny instant time was gone, for that was all it ever was. What God gave answer to is answered and is gone. This is coming from out of time, in case you would like to read this personally. *To you who still believe you live in time and know not it is gone, the Holy Spirit still guides you through the infinitely small and senseless maze you still perceive in time, though it has long since gone.* How can something be infinitely small? These are great sentences. "Well," a guy says, "The black hole is infinitely small. We've got the whole universe compacted to point one million zeros one in its diameter." But it is impossible that it be infinitely small without being infinitely total. This is the idea of a dot and a circle, if you want to hear it. So it is infinitely small.

Infinite separation is impossible. So you return. We're going to help you get through that. Why? *You think you live in what is past. Each thing you look upon you saw but for an instant, long ago, before its unreality gave way to truth. Not one illusion still remains unanswered in your mind. Uncertainty was brought to certainty* (in your mind!) *so long ago that it is hard indeed to hold it to your heart, as if it were before you still.* That's an amazing idea! Can you hear what that just said? It said uncertainty is in your heart, not your mind. The uncertainty you hold is your dedication to uncertainty itself, and you love it, so that your children get old and die, and you call it love. Shame on you!

Love is a reasonable process of your recognition that you are whole as God created you. Do you want that sentence again? You hold it in your heart! That's tough isn't it? You have the passion of death in your heart. Then you can go to the funeral and say, "Wasn't he a great guy. He lived a good life and now he's turned to dust." The hell with you. You have to stand up and say, "The hell with this world! Why should I lose the things that I love?" This world lasted but an instant when you thought you could. It was immediately replaced by the certainty that you can't! Got that? This is great stuff.

The tiny instant you would keep and make eternal – you would have to; the idea of time would be the idea of what eternity is. You are going to be in endless time. You never are going to get out of here, because you think that eternity is a long time. "Well, I know, but we're going to make this last." *The tiny instant you would keep and make eternal, passed away in Heaven too soon for anything to notice it had come.* By anything I mean any thing! *What disappeared too quickly to affect the simple knowledge of the Son of God can hardly still be there, for you to choose to be your teacher. Only in the past, – an ancient past, too short to make a world in answer to creation,* – (didn't ever make it – it was made only by the separation) *did this world appear to rise. So very long ago, for such a tiny interval of time, that not one note in Heaven's song was missed. Yet in each and every unforgiving act or thought, in every single judgment and in all belief in sin* (in separation), *is that one instant still called back, as if it could be made again in time. You keep an ancient memory before your eyes. And he who lives in memories alone is unaware of where he is.*

Is this a hindrance to the place whereon he stands? Only if he wants it to be. *Is any echo from the past that he may hear a fact in what is there to hear where he is now? And how much can his own illusions about time and place effect a change in where he really is?*

The Son whom God created is as free as God created him. He was reborn the instant that he chose to die instead of live. And will you not forgive him now, because he made an error in the past that God remembers not, and is not there? Now you are shifting back and forth between the past and present. Sometimes the past seems real, as if it were the present. Voices from the past are heard and then are doubted. You are like to one who still hallucinates, but lacks conviction in what he perceives. This is the borderland between the worlds, the bridge between the past and present. Here the shadow of the past remains, but still a present light is dimly recognized. Once it is seen, this light can never be forgotten. It must draw you from the past into the present, where you really are.

The shadow voices do not change the laws of time nor of eternity. They don't change anything. They don't change the laws of time because the laws of time are the simple recognition of your own perfection. Wow! *They come from what is past and gone, and hinder not the true existence of the here and now.* Listen: *The real world is the second part of the hallucination time and death are real, and have existence that can be perceived. This terrible illusion was denied in but the time it took for God to give His Answer to illusion for all time and every circumstance. And then it was no more to be experienced as there.*

Now here we go with what you like: *Each day, and every minute in each day, and every instant that each minute holds, you but relive the single instant when the time of terror took the place of love. And so you die each day to live again, until you cross the gap between the past and present, which is not a gap at all. Such is each life; a seeming interval from birth to death and on to life again, a repetition of an instant gone by long ago that cannot be relived. And all of time is but the mad belief that what is over is still here and now.*

Forgive the past and let it go, for it is gone. You stand no longer on the ground that lies between the worlds. You have gone on, and reached the world that lies at Heaven's gate. There is no hindrance to the Will of God, nor any need that you repeat again a journey that was over long ago. Look gently on your brother, and behold the world in which perception of your hate has been transformed into a world of love. (Chapter 26)

That's nice stuff! I don't know why this isn't read to the whole world. It would require your admission that it is true. So they have to deny it in its entirety. There are no *Course* group associations that teach that, as strange as it may seem. Why would it be strange if there are no worldly associations that teach the teachings of Jesus? Answer me! This world is a denial of this teaching. There are no degrees to the denial. If time lasted but a moment and is gone, the idea that you are in time could not possibly be true if time is gone. Got it?!

So you still find yourself here, right? Are you still here? Would you like to get out? We're sorry we missed you the last time. What's wrong with that? You want to get out or not? I know you're pissed at me because I didn't get you the last time. But remember the decision to hear this was *yours*, not mine. If you want me to admit I made the mistake, I'll admit it. I'm still offering you a way out of here. Here I am suddenly in a little obscure nothing. Look at yourself! You're not anything but a little enclosure. I'm suddenly appearing in this infinitely small place and telling you this is not where you are from. And you say, "Where the hell have you have been? Why didn't you come and get me out of here? I'm never going to forgive you!" What is that? An unforgiving act! I'm offering you salvation and you're not going to forgive me. Why? I'm the cause of your guilt! Is that true? But our decision to be whole can be made from us just as well as our decision to find the other guy guilty.

I forgive you because you couldn't possibly be guilty of causing me any problem whatsoever! Any problems I have, I have accepted on my own. In that acceptance I have found salvation because not being able to stand my own problems, I had to give them up. I couldn't blame my brother for the crap that I was in. Is that the whole teaching? That's the whole teaching! Now you nod your head because you can hear that! I'm teaching you that is an act or a process of physical variations within your own body. That's how I heal.

This world is an illusion. "How about salvation?" It's an illusion. But it is an entirety of illusion when the moment of time is converted to the eternal mind.

I'm going to write a little Kabbala symbol here in the sand, and I'm going to go abstract with my mind. The question is not that, the question would only be whether you are willing to accept for a moment a release of the definition of yourself within your own mind. That's the only requirement there is. That's called being born again. If you don't organize your thoughts, I will give you a Light association. The question is not that, the question is: will you try to judge what I'm giving you? This is forgiveness. You're saying, "You are just like I am. You're admitting that I am sick." No I'm not. I am denying that you are sick, and that is what your salvation is. Can you hear this? By our mutual denial of this place we share Heaven!

Who does the salvation of the world depend on? *You!* Not your brother. *You* are the cause of it. Jesus' teaching is rejected because of this. I didn't do the Nicodemus: *Know ye not ye must be born again?* (John 3:3) That's the whole teaching. How simple is the solution if you are the cause of it! If you're not the cause of it, you're just going to get old and die anyway. The acceptance momentarily of the responsibility and your determination that you can't stand the burden is what salvation is.

I'm not leading you to Heaven, I'm leading you to fear. I'm going to do this once more for you, for those of you who hear me. I'm not leading you to Heaven. You are already in Heaven! I'm leading you to the moment of devastation. That's what you are afraid to do. I'm leading you to your own bottom. I'm showing you the unsolvability of this problem. I'm telling you, literally, give up the problem; it cannot be solved! Now get me. "What's the matter with you? Your teaching is very weak. I thought you taught the power of mind." I teach the power of One Mind. And that's God! I can reject it, but if I do, I'll suffer the pain of myself. I'm tired of rejecting the Single Reality. I'm going to let God be God, and the hell with the world. I'm not going to let the world set terms for what I know must be true if there is a God. Is it that simple?

Why haven't you been able to hear it before? You didn't want to! Your dues are paid if you want them to be paid. That's why I said when you sat down here, how do you think you got here? You must have heard it somewhere in the parameter or you wouldn't be here listening to me tell you this! The question is not that, the question is whether you're going to say, "Well, I know that, but I still have cancer." The hell you do! It's impossible you have cancer because you're not real. The thing that has cancer is not true. I just healed you if you want to be healed. And remember that the miracle didn't have anything to do with cancer. It had to do with the totality of your admission that you are perfect as God created you.

I was up on the Bridge at the Cheese Factory dancing last night. Those of you who haven't visited the Cheese Factory Restaurant, there is a lot of forgiveness going on there! Those people are forgiving each other for no reason at all! They're not even saying, "If you forgive me, I'll forgive you." (Which is the way to deny forgiveness.) When there's this much Light – this is the whole lesson, this is Jesus drawing the circle – when you say something real obvious to them like, "Wow, we're all children of God and we really love each other," they go, "Wow!" They hear you, just for that moment. That moment that you have given them can never be lost. In that sense, Holy Instants are accumulative.

You can finally remember only love, not the thing that brought love about, because the thing that brought love about is not what love is, it's fear – it's protecting it. When you release in entirety, you will be the Love of God because you are the Love of God, not because you decided to be. Your decision in this is required only because you believe decision is possible. Having decided that decision is possible, why don't you simply decide that you want to be who you are, perfect as God created you, rather than what the world is telling you that you are. What the world is telling you that you are, you are not! That's what I just read you. Is it nice to be heard? You bet! How are you hearing me? Experience! You're not hearing me perceptually; you are experiencing me and then my perceptions make sense! I make perfect sense to you.

Truth is true and nothing else is true. If that makes sense to you, you're home because there is no such thing as falsity. You accept the truth: There's only One, and that's *you*. "I don't know that." You don't have to know it. It's going to be true whether you know it or not. There is no knowledge in perception. And you laugh at my great teaching! What have I done? Freed you from the bondage of yourself! I freed myself from the bondage of myself by not being able to stand this world. That's the fact of the matter. And I had the experience of Love and Totality which I now teach because that's what I am! And you will teach what you are. I'm doing what I just read you in the book. Are you going to hear it? I don't know. What do I care. You either hear it or you're nothing! You don't like the idea that you're nothing, but I assure you until the moment that you hear this, you are literally nothing. When you hear it you will have an instant recognition of it, which is nothing but being born again. I teach you to be continually born again because the instant of your deviation lasted but a second. If I can teach you to stay in that instant, you couldn't possibly die. Because there is no such thing as death. You can't die. Did you hear that? You can't die. Not because Jesus said it – because I said it. Why don't you attack me? How are you going do that? Either by killing me or killing yourself. But if you kill me, you are also killing yourself. That's called the crucifixion of Christ. You've actually got the Christian community that teaches that you crucify the Christ in order to get to Heaven. That's ridiculous. That's absurd. It makes no sense whatsoever. It's exactly the opposite of the teachings of Jesus – that through killing Jesus Christ you can be born. That's absurd. "Who says so?" I do! It's absurd because it was absurd in my mind. It's nuts.

That's our Bible class for today. What am I doing? Not judging your adultery. I could not care less what you are doing. I am in my own mind with the certainty of who I am. What's wrong with you doing that? "Well, I wouldn't dare do it." Why not? Your ego thinks that's grandiose. That's nonsense. If God is God, you let Him be God through the declaration that "I am God's only Son." How many sons does God have? ONE! Who is it? ME! Of course! If that's true, our Selves are the same! We don't have to know that, but we can experience it together because there is only one Son of God. The reason you are so happy with each other is because you have come into your own Self. When you are your own Self, you extend from yourself your Self, and you don't see the other image in his identity, but only in the wholeness of yourself. So you don't condemn him to a name, you let God give him a name which is My Son. Isn't that amazing how that works? You name it; you kill it. That's the whole teaching of Adam naming the animals. He names them in his own mind, separates them off, some die, some live – that's nuts.

I'll tell you, the Cheese Factory is really something else. It's amazing that they come to the Cheese Factory to be healed before they go to the Healing Center! The occurrence is exactly the same because it is an act of forgiveness. The Center appears more threatening because it's a total healing place which they are very afraid of. So you set up a front – this is the whole teaching, I taught this for years. You open up a little storefront, and you invite them in to look at your books. But behind that association is a little coffee shop that they could come back into and really begin to look at this with you. And behind that door there is something I cannot speak of!

This is a fact of Masonry. Those of you who are Masons. This is exactly what Masonry teaches. First, second and third degree. Fourth degree is Royal Arch. Be an entered apprentice, learn the associations of your own mind – we are offering you a mystical contact with God. But remember, we had to set up the front. Was the front real. No! But they had to take the step at least out of their own perceptions in their curiosity about what the bookstore was. That's the way this works. Isn't that amazing? Otherwise they wouldn't be able to see you at all. That's what you have done with your Cheese Factory. That's what you're setting up here now. Is that all right with you?

I have no idea how you are going to be able to remain in this continuum. I'm talking to you guys who are in communication. Are you communicating? I want you to understand this. There is no communication among human beings at all. None. Zero. You are blind, deaf and dumb. You are absolutely contained within your own mind and are not communicating. And if you think you are, you are dead wrong. By releasing your necessity to defend yourself, you begin to extend. You are then recognized by other associations who also were contained. At that moment you share a Holy Instant of forgiveness where the Light of God enters. Until you do that, there is no hope for you. Have you got that? How are you doing?

I'm leaving here today. I was going to just see how the Packers did this year, but I'll have to look on the board. Things are looking pretty good in Wisconsin. Are we allowed to do that? Yeah! Are we really? Sure! Aren't you a little guilty? If you are always only giving, you will only feel the guilt momentarily because you will immediately give it away in the certainty that you are serving God, not man. I can't measure it for you, but that's what it is. That, plus you are always going to be responsible for the result of your own mind, those of you who are magic provisions for making field goals. Remember this! You assume that responsibility. Is that okay? "Well, I guess I'm going to be just as happy when they lose." Not me, brother. Now you can judge me if you want to. But remember, I'm only teaching happiness. I'm not concerned what it is. "Well, if you're not concerned what it is, why are you concerned whether they win or not?" None of your business! I just read you this! It is literally none of your business! Now you can find me corrupt because I love competition.

All teachers of God love the competition of confronting evil. They can't be here if they don't! They deny death and offer you their denial of it so that you will apply the power of your mind to deny the Yama man, "No, death, we deny you!" That's the whole teaching. The whole teaching of *A Course In Miracles* is: Deny death! If you deny it, it is impossible that you die because you are the cause of your own death association. Will you spring into Heaven? No, you'll be here denying death! You thought I was going to give you the solution. That's not the way it works. When you are gone from here, you'll be gone. If you can remember it, stay only in this association. Are you doing that? "Yeah, but when is this going to be over?" What time is it? Your unconcern about when it's going to be over is your assurance that it is.

I'm allowed to tell you that where you have aggregated out of time, you are teaching out of time together to your old associations. It is impossible for you to meet a stranger. The question is not that, the question is what do you want to have him tell you? When you walk around in the world right now, anybody standing anywhere can suddenly say something to you that you haven't wanted to hear before, and now you want to hear it. And that includes the guy selling papers. As he takes your money, he says, "You know, you are perfect as God created you." You won't say, "Who are you, telling me that?" He is you telling yourself that, if you won't judge the source of his telling you. Never mind the source. If it's true it's going to be true. Determining the source is nothing but your determination to hold onto the projections of your own mind so that when they tell you the truth you don't have to believe it. Why? Both of you know the truth completely because both of you are communicating with your Christ. The only way you could possibly communicate is with your own perfection, so your Christs are communicating where your separate egos are denying each other. That's a true fact of the matter. Do you see how valuable forgiveness is to you? You can't do it without it! I don't care who you present to me, I only see your Christ because I only see my own. Yet our Christs are the only way that we could communicate because we are using the communicative Spirit of God.

That was a lovely broadcast, Henry. There are hundreds of people listening to Henry on Sunday mornings on the radio secretly. They don't dare admit that he's teaching love and forgiveness. In the world, they say, "You don't listen to that guy, he's teaching us love and forgiveness and that there is no world. He's teaching that our relationships are perfect if we let them be. He's teaching us that we don't have to judge our brother and condemn him to hell." Do you see that? You have to listen to that in secret. You're occult, aren't you? You have to be careful teaching the perfection of the association because if they can find you, they'll kill you. That's a fact. This time it's too late. You can't put the *Course in Miracles* into this association. You've been burned at the stake, tortured, everything is being done to you including the current *Course* groups. But it's too late. What it says it says.

Our minds are communicating! You have established an association here where we are going to do what we call traditional worship. What's wrong with traditional worship? Nothing! Many of your memories as a little kid were coming to church and finding the peace of God in the altar we've associated here through Jesus. The secret to this is that it can't be more than you let it be. Just let it be perfect. The stained glass windows! Wow! I used to love going to church when I was a kid.

Your time is very short here. If you believe what I just read you, your time is already over. If you don't believe it's over, you might as well believe it's very short because you can't die any more. There is no way you're going to die to get out of here. You can't. I have taken death away from you – as fearful as that is to you. You can't die. Now you don't know what to do. You are just going to have to be totally fearful because you can't escape by death. You can't annihilate your Self. Just be totally fearful for a moment and you will spring into Heaven – that was the moment of devastation that you looked at and immediately you were gone from here.

CHAPTER 10

The Incorruptible Body

Good morning! Is this going to be Sunday School for a minute? Sunday School. On Sunday your school is more about God, and on the other days it's more about learning how to live in the world. But you rest on the seventh day, having worked six days to create the world. So here we come to rest. After six days, if you come around me, it's really not rest. I tax your mental capacity. I keep asking you to look at your own association with yourself. What you forget is, you've been doing that, anyway. Your occupation is to look at yourself in your own associations, isn't it?

This is my chair. I sit sometimes in this chair. This is my rear. I sit my rear on the chair. Is that the teaching? Say to me, "I am not a body. I am free. I am still as God created me." Yeah, but I still have to sit my arse on the chair. That's easy for you to say, but I'm the one who's got to sit my rear end down on that chair. Yes or no? You won't find anything mystical about this. What could be more mystical than the idea you have to sit your arse on the chair – since you don't know who you are, what the hell you're doing or where you came from? But still, it's your arse and it sits on the chair.

Into this impossible situation I have come with a whole mind to tell you that you are trapped in your own association of arse comparisons. It's kind of nuts, isn't it? That's true. Everything you do is a comparison of your own association with yourself. I'm here to tell you, you're dreaming. I'm teaching what you love to term subjective reality. I declare to you, not as a teaching but as a certainty, that the Universe is one mind.

First of all, the universe is mind. Okay? Just so we've got our preliminaries straight. When you go out to teach this, you might want to give preliminaries. I'm very certain. I don't care what you think about it. Obviously, you're thinking about something and using mind. I'm here to tell you that the universe is mind and that there is a singular source of reality that emanates eternally of which you are a part. Raise your hands if there's a question.

I'm not concerned about your denial of it, but somewhere I would have to present to you, as a whole mind – which I am and you are also, even though you don't want to admit it. It would have to be true since there is only one mind with one source. Now, if you want to discuss that with yourself, go ahead. Because the second thing I'm going to tell you is that since there only is one mind with one source, whatever your one mind is with what is apparently your source is all there's going to be. Do you hear me when I talk like this? Are you hearing me a little?

I was in Princess Diana's funeral procession for 14 hours yesterday. This is a weird place. You're always in sort of like a postmortem. I don't know what you mean by "Diana," but I know Diana is an idea and now she's dead, so you can talk about her. And it's easier to talk about her when she's dead because you don't have to listen to what she's going to say that's going to contradict what you want to hear about her. Now you can argue what she was among yourselves. That's how you crucify Jesus. As long as He's dead, you can argue about what He said in the relationships you have with each other. That's a fact of the matter.

I listened. I turned on the television this morning, and it's absurd. She has become an idol in death. The problem is not that. What's ridiculous to me is, why would you worship death? I don't understand why. I'm talking to you individually, since it's your dream. I'm telling you, as a fact of the matter, that life is eternal, that there's one creating Energy of Reality, of which you are a total part. Having acknowledged that, I then tell you that you are entirely the cause of the apparent separation, or the experience you are having with yourself. I have given you now the unreality of the problem and the solution to the problem should you believe that it is real. You are the cause of everything that is.

I'll teach the dilemma of body relationships. That would be Lesson 170, Jesus' beautiful response when He says, "I am with you." I'll teach 170, Jesus' response, Single Self, Attraction of Death, Third Obstacle to Peace, and Second Corinthians. "Why do you have to teach Second Corinthians?" Paul suffered in his illumination from the dilemma of trying to express continuing death to be born again. The whole obstacle that you have is, obviously, somewhere you believe that you're a body association. If I turn on the television, I watch what you guys do, and you're all marching stiffly, and here's this body, this carcass that you have locked up in there, and you are obviously in a form of worship of telling me how divine, apparently, that dead carcass is.

That's ridiculous. If there's a whole, loving God, it's ridiculous that you would take a rotting carcass and honor it as a ritual that justifies your body association. It's ridiculous, it's insane, it's stupid, and it's not real. It doesn't have anything to do with what is said about it. It's simply stupid and unreal because it couldn't possibly be what life is.

You don't mind me telling you *that*. Somebody says, "Boy, that sure makes sense to me." What you don't like is me telling you those images are reflections of your own mind. Now we're into the crux of the teaching. The images are reflections of your identification of your body contained within the spatial continuum of what you identify within the hallucination of your own mind. You're hallucinating. You've been hallucinating. This is a dream of death. It's a dream of separation. It's not true. The question is not that. What we laugh at at this depth – I'm speaking from Light Reality – is why the hell would you want it to be true? That's the curiosity. No one in their right mind could understand when they're told this why you would defend your own association with yourself. Now you're into some tough teaching. The reason that you defend it is you love death. Your associations of love are directly connected to your subsistence, which is based on your fear of God, or a single Creator. Is that true?

Why do you want to do that? Don't do that anymore. I'm talking to you. I'm not talking to someone else. I'm telling you, don't do it anymore. The hell with that! Why would you want to do that? Say, "I don't. I'm not a body. I'm free. I'm as God created me. I'll depend on God rather than myself, and I'll be free." "You made it much too simple." I made it simple because it *is* simple.

What I saw yesterday was an obstacle to peace. It's real interesting to me, that the dead ones are dead and that they justify death. This is

Chapter 19. *To you and your brother, into whose special relationship the Spirit has entered* – this is you comparing yourself with each other as God created you, not the crap of your own specialization – *it is given you to release and be released from your dedication to die.*

I want you to hear this very plainly from me. Obviously, I'm not going to be here in a minute. If you want to really hear this, I'm telling you this is a place where you came to die and you're nuts. You will not be successful at dying. That's a fact of the matter. You can't die. Everyone else will die, and you'll still be here. They'll die all around you. You'll stand and moan and piss, but you're not going to be able to die. You've been sharing death with the associations or the projections of your own mind. You've decided to change your mind about what you are, and you wonder why the projections of your mind won't change. It's impossible they're not changing. What *you* want to do is still identify in a change that justifies your association with the image that you now present yourself to be.

At no single moment does the body exist at all. Of course not. We all know that. I read that in the physiology book. It said that the cells are in constant change in my body and that I have formed from my mind, if you'll believe me, a specialization of my cellular relationship that justifies a mechanical appearance within the objective association of the illusion.

This is Lesson 170. You're afraid of the mechanics of yourself. If you will look at the horror story of your own nightmare, these monsters that you have set up are just mechanical monsters of the illusion of your own mind because you believe that life is mechanical. Can you hear this? You have specialized your body form in an aggregate of carbon association of oxygen and hydrogen to the point where the body, in its limited association with itself, is what you believe you are. And that's nuts. Obviously, you're using the power of your own mind. And to give the body autonomy over your own mind is crazy. We already agreed, at no moment is it real, anyway.

For it was offered you and you accepted. I offered you the release from your dedication to death and you accepted it, or why the hell are you standing here with me? It's impossible that you don't know that you're not a body. It's impossible. How else do you know that you can die? What do you die of? What do you die from? What do you become when you're dead? *Yet you must learn still more about this very strange devotion* you have, to the rotting carcass that you think you inhabit, *for it contains the third obstacle that my love for you must flow across.* And that is, very simply, that no one dies unless he chooses it.

I don't want this crap about watching people die. And you say, "Now she's dead, and I'm alive." That's absurd. *You cannot die unless you choose to die. There is no death. The Son of God is free.* What you think is death is just another form of the continuation of your determination to justify your separation from the wholeness of what you are. It cannot be performed successfully by you because you are nothing in separation. Anything separate from the entirety of creative universal mind is nothing. Say to me, "I am nothing." Say, "I am everything." Good for you! Which would you rather be? The only problem you have is, if you're everything, you're not going to be able to judge what you are, but then again, why would you have to judge what you are if you're everything? If you're everything, you will be whole as God created you and you won't have to judge yourself. Yes or no?

I'm speaking to you from my whole mind, which is exactly what yours is because there *is* only one mind. You cannot *not* be what I am because there's only one of us. I don't know if you actually believe that, but it really doesn't require your believing, because if you deny it, you'll be forced to believe what you think you are. And if you believe what you think you are, you will believe that someone else is forcing you because no one would choose this intentionally. You must then have projected from your mind ideas of associations from which you then subtract yourself and you let your own ideas tell you what you are in association with yourself, and if that's not nuts, what is it? It's nuts! This is Lesson 170.

This is a great advantage, to have this here. Actually, all you would have to do is say, "I believe you," and you would leave here. Your belief is required because obviously you have placed your belief in this crap. And if you place your belief in the crap of getting old and dying within this body, that's exactly what will happen to you. Why would it not happen to you? Your faith in death is exactly as strong as your faith in life. All I'm asking you is, why would you want to be a rotting body and get old and die? Your answer is obviously, "There is no alternative." My response is, there is no alternative as contained within your determination of identification or separation! That's why you need me.

This is Jesus of Nazareth. It's impossible for you to solve the problem yourself. You're going to have to accept from me that the problem has been solved. I assure you it has been solved because I am your whole Self telling you it has been. This is the review of Jesus right after Lesson 170. The simple truth of the matter is, if you believe, and you do, that I am some sort of association within your limited mind, I cannot perform the act of resurrection for you because you are in denial of your own resurrection. Do you see? I couldn't possibly do it. How could I? You are occupying a body. I'm going to get to that. Maybe I could teach that from Second Corinthians.

What seems to be the fear of death is really its attraction. I listened to this all day yesterday. *Guilt too is feared and fearful. Yet it could have no hold at all except on those who are attracted to it and seek it out to justify themselves.* Every time I listen to the argument going on, oh, this is awful. This is nuts. This place is nuts. You guys agree with me?

Made by the ego (your self-identity), *its dark shadow falls across all living things because your association with yourself* (identified as your existent association) *is the enemy of life, and the truth of you, which is a part of your whole association with your Self, is being denied by your mutual attempts to justify in your aggregate conceptual association of selfness, the reality of you in a non-creative mode.* That is, there is no reality here. This world was over and gone a long time ago. Is this world over and gone? This world is over and gone! Anything not in Heaven is not real!

"Well, I guess this is Heaven, then. I guess Heaven is being in pain and suffering and getting old." You're nuts! You are nuts! You are in hell. What do you think this is, if it's not hell?! Your relief is, you are the cause of hell. It would have to be. The solution would have to be that no one's holding you in hell – certainly not God, who you believe is, in order to justify the god of fear. Your god now is fearful. Oprah's famous sentence two days ago on television, talking about the fear – fear of babysitters, fear of everybody. The more you communicate, the more fearful you become. Everything you establish for your safety justifies your fear. How many of you are hearing me? The more you set up protective devices – air bags, being suspicious of your babysitter – "Watch out! They're going to molest your kid. They're killing you" – that's all a part of this chaos. And the more you attempt to communicate the protective devices of your association, the more fearful you will become. It could not *not* be so. Look at it with me.

Each time you defend yourself, you will be attacked by your own mind associations. You don't believe that. You're in hell. If you don't believe that, you must believe that God is the cause of your fear. If you are fearful, then your god will be the god of fear and death. And because fear is necessary for the protection, say, of your young ones: You don't trust your babysitter, so you spend $100 to have her background carefully checked, as though it's going to be revealed in her background what she intends to do, which is absolutely absurd. So you walk around in a constant condition of being suspicious of the other associations because there's no way you can verify what he is or what he's going to do to you in your present condition? This is an asylum, guys. You're nuts!

"God's gift to us," said Oprah on national television and everybody applauded, "is fear." And everybody went, "Yay!" "God gives you fear?!?!" I have nothing more to say about that. You say, "Well, I don't think she meant that." Bullshit! She meant it. She had to because her devices of protection are intrinsic in her ability to exist separate from God. Yours is a god of fear. "Thou shalt fear the Lord thy God with all thy might because He's going to attack you and kill you if you don't adhere to His policies of judgment." Tell me what they are. "We don't know for sure what they are. Well, we sort of make them up. All we know is that we get old and sick and die. *That* we know. That's not open to discussion."

Did you open it to discussion? Do you mean to say that this crap finally seemed unreasonable to you? Not because you knew about an alternative. Simply because it's so stupid. It's so nuts! You're looking for something complicated about this.

Are you familiar with Paul? He's a really good buddy of ours. So is Jesus. Jesus is here this morning. Paul wanted me to give you his message. Paul says in Second Corinthians, "Every time I offer you this, I'm hurting you because I'm telling you that you're not real. I'm telling you through my illuminate mind," says Paul, "that the body that you inhabit can be made incorruptible by the associations of your whole mind with the determination that the body only lasts for a moment." Paul is obviously speaking about the resurrection of his physical body. And just as obviously, you inhabit a body in which your communication with your microcosm is still imperfect.

What a great discovery! The cancer cell people, studying the disease, have decided that there are all sorts of chemical associations that are affecting the pristine nature of what you would call specialization of the cellular relationship. Much to their surprise, if they take the cells that are cancerous, or other cells in association with the specialization (the liver and heart), and take them outside of their environment, they have a tendency to revert to singular cell reality.

We are very much aware in what you call your DNA that in the specific relationship of the maturity of your embryo, at a certain point the cells of your body take on aspects of specialization that can no longer be changed. That is, if you take a frog embryo, when it's first forming, and take its nose cell and graft it on to its rear end, it will grow a rear end. At a certain point two weeks later, if you take the nose cell and transfer it to his rear end, the nose will grow out of his rear. Can you hear this? This is exactly what happens with you. There is specialization that occurs in your cellular arrangement with yourself within your own body. There's no question about that.

All I want you to understand or admit is that finally, every single cell in you contains the entirety of life and that if you insist on specializing within the association, you will become a body. I wonder if I could teach you this. I bet I can't teach you this. Since the evolutionary process is an invention of time, there are various stages within your evolution when the maturity of your specialization came about. That's how the human species came about. Do you see that? And some of your cells will wear out faster than other cells will because they specialize within that temporal association. You have forgotten that everything is mind. You have forgotten finally that you are the cause of the association. You are letting yourself be that specialization within your own limitation.

Would you like to know how this body heals? I can change any cell in my body and specialize it in any other association of my body, and you can't. The only possible reason you could die of cirrhosis of the liver, or of any death, is because you believe that that cell, which is in a specialization, is going to get used up and die. I tell you, the cell can appear to die, but all cells are the same. And since you're recreating cells all the time anyway, you can take any cell in your body and use it anywhere in your body in the totality of the revitalization of your body. Did you hear that? You are all cellular arrangements of your own light form, anyway. "Oh, my heart cells are getting old and dying." What do you mean, "my" heart cells? You specialize them to become a mechanical association. It's absurd. What you really did is shut off communication within your own body form. Finally they're going back to holistic medicine, where the mind is setting the terms for the body.

So Paul says, Jesus says, I say that the whole Christ body of you, singularly, in its entirety of defined separation, is emerging wholly each moment. This is the entire teaching – that if you are a body (we're using temporal associations) you emerged from the womb, you matured, you came in time, and you get old and die. You love to watch television now where suddenly the guy gets old right in front of you and falls dead. Those are good. Have you seen those? The guy is young, and all of a sudden, "Bleaaahh." It shows him just getting old and rotting and falling down into that association. I'm declaring to you, that's happening all the time.

Once more. I'll do it once more for you. I'm trying to get you to see that that's what's happening to you all the time. You're like the picture of Dorian Gray. You are staying young, but the association you hid back there is getting old and ugly. So you look at so-called old and ugly people, who are nothing but reflections of your own temporal, sequential arrangements of yourself, and then you watch them get old and die and pretend they're not you, but they *are* you.

This is all in the *Course*. Can you hear me? A body can appear to die, but it can be nothing but an arrangement *you* have made in your own mind to justify your own body. Why would you want to do that?

How difficult it is for you to see that you can continually regenerate your body, using the power of creative reality, rather than the limitations you impose on yourself in your causeless association with nothing! Sure as hell, you're going to get used up. Sure as hell, if you're in time, you are going to take this body in its specialization and use it up in the static condition that you believe that you are. You could not *not*. The hell with that! You are not a body. And if you think you are, think of yourself as a whole Christ body and it will be true. Any formulation of the forms of your mind must contain a single wholeness of a manifestation of reality based on eternal life. It's the same idea as you can't die.

And so it is with death. Dark shadows fall across living things. You become the enemy of life. *And yet a shadow cannot kill. What is a shadow to the living?* I'm speaking to myself as alive. *They but walk past it and it is gone. But what of those whose dedication is not to live?* Once more. I don't know if you really hear me. This is a place where obviously everybody is dedicated not to be eternal. That's not hard. Everywhere you look, everybody is dedicated *not* to live. You mean dedicated to die? This is the third obstacle, guys. This is the attraction of death.

I seem a little uncompromising. Do you know why? This makes perfect sense to me because one or the other has to be true. If this is life, then there is no eternal life. One or the other is not true, and since I am offering you a decision, I am telling you, you are empowered to make that decision in your own mind if you choose. Obviously that association is going to look in her book to justify her association with herself. It's absolutely meaningless because there's no such place as this.

I'll do it once more for you. *This is an illusion of life.* She's still going to look it up. Whatever you do, don't stand in front of your own reality and let somebody tell you there is no death because you are afraid of the reflection of your own Christ.

I'm back into what I'm going to read you out of Chapter 18. Jesus is really in control. In Chapter 18 He is going to tell you that all of your light bodies are walking right along with you. Can you hear this? And you are afraid of them. And if they get too close, you kill your own Christs together. And if one guy presents his Christ and the other guy is not ready to hear it, he literally says, "Get the hell out of here! I'm afraid to listen to you." These are the last pages of Chapter 18.

Obviously, that's what you do. It would have to be because you believe you are specialized in your separation. You actually believe that body is separate from him, and you are dedicated to the existence of your body association. You sustain yourself. You eat, drink, be merry and sad, lose the things you love, and die. Go to hell! Why do you have to look in here to tell you that? I'm telling you, as a whole mind, that you are absurd. I'm telling you, you are in your own dream of your own association. *I am the cause of this. There is no other cause.* No matter how tempted I am to believe there's something outside of me, there ain't! I am being attacked by my own thoughts. Why don't you look that up? That way, you won't have to admit you're being attacked by your own thoughts.

Sounds like Wapnick. "Oh, you mean that we should study, 'I'm being attacked by my own thoughts'?" No. I mean you are being attacked by your own thoughts. He couldn't possibly admit that, or he would stop protecting himself. If he stops protecting himself, he won't be able to exist in the containment of his own mind. He would have to admit that he's perfect as God created him.

If I defend myself, I will be attacked by my own thoughts. "Where does it say that? What page does it say that?" What do you mean, "What page?" I'm telling you about your condition in your own mind. "This says, if I defend myself at all, I will be attacked by my own projections of my mind that will justify my getting old and dying. I'm certainly going to have to look that up and examine that." How the hell can you examine it if you're not real? This is where you reject this teaching. I have come from out of this world to tell you that the world is not real. *There isn't any world. All of your examinations of it are totally meaningless.*

It's nice to be laughed at when I say this instead of being struck down and killed like you're still going to do to me. Why the hell do you want to kill me for telling you that? Wouldn't you rather believe that this is a meaningless place? I'll tell you this, you can't give meaning where no meaning is. You can't be separated from eternal life. Finally you are going to admit that and say, "The hell with it! I'm not going to struggle to stay separate anymore. I'm going to let God be God, whole and perfect as my Creator, without deciding what I want to be true in my own relationships." Got it? Amen!

"You mean that I can just spring out of here?" Can you spring out of here right now? If you were in a scenario of everybody marching behind a funeral casket and you say, "Hey! Wait a minute. What kind of crap is going on in my own mind?" You guys think those guys are real out there. You actually think there are separate bodies with separate identities out there. That's nuts. It still depends on you because you are the guy that's walking behind the casket, and everything you see is a reflection of that dead body's death association. That's a fact of the matter.

But what of those whose dedication is not to live; the black-draped "sinners," the mournful chorus, plodding so heavily away from life, dragging their chains and marching in the slow procession that honors their grim master, lord of death? What *about* them?! Are you ready for this? They are products of *your* mind. And if you change your mind, they will change. Now, if you need me to know that, I'm telling you there is no world so you won't be concerned about whether the change occurs or not. If you are in total dedication to who you really are, if it doesn't appear to change, it won't bother you in the slightest. I can't help you if you are in a slow association with yourself. You got this? There's no communication going on here at all. None! Zero! Period! No one is communicating with anything.

271

"Well, I thought our Christs were always talking to each other." Well, then why don't you agree with each other you are perfect and get the hell out of here? All you would have to do is look at your brother and say, "You're perfect because you are the living Son of God," and since he's a reflection of your mind, you'll both spring into light. You could not *not*. He literally is your savior because you're killing him. And since you're killing your own savior, what do you expect from him? As long as you can kill her, she can't be the savior. She can be a thought of your death rather than your life. Actually, she is the Christ! There's no question about that. She's not dead. She is alive in all the thoughts you're willing to accept about what she is – not what she taught, but what she is in the memory of *you* in the entirety of our mutual Christhood sharing together in the Kingdom of God. Amen!

What you are being offered here is a really meaningful thing to you if I can get you, in your new bright minds, to see the illusory nature of this world. Come on, guys. This is a little teeny place, going around like this, and there are billions of stars. If you won't let yourself be trapped in the sequentiality, this will get very simple for you.

...and marching in the slow procession that honors their grim master, lord of death. Touch any one of them with the gentle hands of your own forgiveness, and watch the chains fall away, along with yours. See him throw aside the black robe he was wearing to his own funeral, and hear him laugh at death – the stupid, insane idea that life could get old and rotten in a carcass and die. That's mostly why you're laughing. I would presume you're laughing because you have discovered that you are not a part of this world. Because you're not a part of this world.

But just as obviously, the salvation would depend on you not letting your old objective associations tell you what you are – because they're going to tell you that you're a body and you're going to die. I watch you guys go out and do that. All around you are people that are going to say, "What the hell's he talking about? Kill him quick! Because if he's dead, we don't have to listen to him." Can you hear what I said? This is the crucifixion of the Christ. Yet the Christ is always walking around with you, trying to cajole you into listening that you can be light and trying to get you to make a turn: "Instead of going that way, turn this way with Me." "No, I've always gone that way before." "Shut up! Get thee behind me." "This is the way the world goes." The hell with the world! You have to decide through your own revelation that you're not going to do this. You got me? You've got me!

See him throw aside the black robe he was wearing to his own funeral, and hear him laugh at death. The sentence sin would lay upon him he can escape through your forgiveness and in no other way. What an idea! We know that ideas leave not their source and that death is an idea that you have about what you think life is and you've never been true. Jesus would say, you've been a liar from the very beginning. The moment that you said you were separate from God and became an advocate of the separation, you were a total liar. You can't be separate from anything.

So you're always meeting your own projections and sharing in your special relationships the idea of bodies, and you're trying to love them? And you fall in love and you're dedicated to existing in this association. Aren't you? And you raise little children and you protect them and everybody gets old and dies because that's what life is. I'm here to tell you that's not what life is. I don't care how much you're dedicated to death in your relationships, which obviously, you must be, or why are you in relationships of the body? Why are you in those relationships at all? What are you doing here?

The fundamental requirement is you understand, first of all – it's fairly simple – that there must be a Creative Totality of Reality. You don't have to know what It is. And second, that you are the cause of this in your association and cannot *not* be a part of that Reality.

I usually don't read this. This is Chapter 18. I'll just read you a little bit of it. It's kind of nice. You're in a dream. You're dreaming this: *Dreams show you that you have the power to make a world as you would have it be, and that because you want it you see it. And while you see it you will not doubt that it is real.* Because it's what you want to see. *Yet here is a world, clearly within your mind, that seems to be outside. You do not respond to it as though you made it, nor do you realize that the emotions the dream produces must come from you. It is the figures in the dream and what they do that seem to make the dream.* None of this is true. You are in a dream of death.

You who have spent your life in bringing truth to illusion, and reality to fantasy, have walked the way of dreams. You have brought truth of what you are into your own dream. You would have to be, because to you this dream is true, and if it is true to you, it will be true to you. But it will not be real because it is not the truth of eternal life. Notice I didn't take your pain away from you. I didn't tell you that you do not believe this is life. I didn't go to Fairfield and say, "This is all an illusion." I told you, this is very real. This is a very real thing going on, with you as the cause of it. What an amazing idea!

Listen. This is what's happened in this: *For you have gone from waking to sleeping, and on and on to a yet deeper sleep.* Can you hear me with this? You're still on your way down. You're still being pushed down. I offer you the solution, and you're just fighting you're way on in. You wake up for a moment; you're dead again. Why? You have a fear of being awakened. You believe that you must associate in the form that is separate from God.

Listen to this. *..and on to a yet deeper dream.* Are you ready? Guys? Each moment. *Each dream has led to other dreams, and every fantasy that seemed to bring a light into the darkness but made the darkness deeper.* Darkness is a form of light. Once more. Everything is finally only light, or light reality. Darkness is a form of light that justifies the continuity of your separation within your conceptual mind. And every time you organize that in your own association of mind, it creates a civilization of thirty generations in Westminster Abbey (that obviously are totally meaningless) that will justify your stiff upper lip to depend on death to sustain you – the aristocracy of the corruption of you!

God is pursuing you to tell you He really didn't kick you out. You are very fearful and are defending yourself because you must be guilty of something. So you keep trying to sink down further and further in your own death relationship with nothing.

Your goal was darkness, in which no ray of light could enter. And you (individually – I'm talking to you, brother) *sought a blackness so complete that you could hide from truth forever, in complete insanity.* Complete nuttiness. But it won't work. Finally you can't stand the pain of trying to resist God, so you try to get further and further down. So you kill yourself in an attempt to escape your own illumination, but it will not succeed. You cannot succeed in doing it because you can't escape from the fact that *you* are God's mind, creating perfectly. This is what this is going to say.

I'm talking directly to you. You cannot *not* be God's mind. You are that. There is only one mind. You can't escape that. Let me see you do it. You choke yourself, kill yourself, stab yourself. You can say, "No, it's not true. There is too death. I'm rotting. I'm losing the things I love. I have got to fight my way out of this." And you are entirely wrong and insane and you are not real. There is no such thing as separation. "Who is it that's telling me that?" I'm telling you that! What difference does it make who I am if I am a product of your denial of what I am telling you?

Obviously, you don't want to hear it because you already have me safely identified as a part of your dream of death. That's nonsense. My whole teaching is "Have nothing to do with the world at all." As long as you have something to do with the world, you're going to be locked in your own form association. Not true, guys. Not true. *There is no death.*

And you sought a blackness so complete that you could hide from truth forever, in complete insanity. What you forgot was simply... I'm not going to read that. Shall I read you that? *What you forgot was that God cannot destroy Himself.* Study that one! You are the totality of God. You can't kill yourself because you're everything, and everything cannot be killed. Can you hear this? You try to, but you can't succeed because the part of you that's trying to kill yourself is also the part of you that's eternal. And so you're caught in the dilemma of trying to kill yourself, but you can't be successful.

Can you hear this, individually, with me? If you can, this will suddenly get very reasonable to you because I assure you, in this continuum what I'm offering you is not reasonable to this world. Nothing could be more irrational to this world than that they are perfect as God created them. Obviously, if they believed they were eternal life and perfect as God created them, they would simply assume what they already are.

This is a teaching of undoing, isn't it? I'm not instructing you in anything but to release yourself from your own death. There's no other instruction contained in this. Stop trying to identify yourself in your own association.

Just a little more: *What you forgot was simply that God cannot destroy Himself. The light is in you. Darkness can cover it but cannot put it out.* That's nice. I'm just igniting your spark of reality. You have done everything you could to kill the Christ in you, which is the light of your reality. Literally, when it began to emerge in you, you killed it. I have trained your mind to let it mature without your need to define it within your own association because it's the real you that is standing aside from what you thought you were in your own dream. All you guys in this church, most of you, are sharing your own Christ, which you let grow up in your own mind. But if you identified Him, you would force Him to be an offspring of your sick mind rather than the totality of you emanating from the reality of God, which is your single sharing. Do you see? I can only show that to you because I am teaching you that through a continuing release of your death associations – which, to you, will be death – that death will be unsuccessful. You sustain yourself and are attracted to death, yet you try to prevent yourself from dying. Do you hear me? So you live in nothing but fear of dying in order that you can die. That's senseless. It doesn't make any sense. You depend on death through fear to relieve you of death. It's not true.

The light is in you. Darkness can cover it but cannot put it out. If you'll let me, since I have an emerged Christ each moment, I can actually help you mature your Christ in one second. The whole teaching is that the Christ is actually being born in you and reaching maturity and you're leaving the world. That's a fact of the matter, that the Christ occupies exactly the place that your body is in. It is not separate from it. Your body is incorruptible because it's an image of the totality of God as you are in your own mind.

This is Paul. I'm going to get to Second Corinthians. Poor Paul has to try to describe how he's always dead in order to be alive. My whole certainty was that I just kept dying and I couldn't die and I was always alive. Rather than battling death, I simply relaxed into it and it turned out to be life rather than dying. That's Jesus' original instructions to Nicodemus: *Know ye not ye must be born again.* (John 3) What's the matter with you? Don't you know you've got that spark of life in you that you've got to let grow up in you? You have got to be born again.

Darkness can cover it but cannot put it out. As the light comes near you... This is what's happening in the world. Your light is really a threat. I've never seen anything like this. Everybody is predicting the end of the world, total chaos. Do you know why? You caused it. What they're going to do is get together and end up killing each other. Because they can only finally kill each other. And you'll stand up and laugh, and you'll look down on the battlefield, and everybody will be fighting and killing each other. And if they don't have anybody else to kill, they'll begin to kill themselves. This is a direct statement of truth. They'll commit suicide by the millions. Why? They are determined to die to escape from you and your offering.

You remember this: They are not real. Your responsibility is to come from God, not from this shit. One verification of death will bind *you* to death because if one single thing dies, everything dies. Do you hear that? Come on. Let's be reasonable with this. If life is eternal, nothing dies.

As the light comes nearer you, you will (will and do) *rush to darkness, shrinking from the truth, sometimes retreating to the lesser forms of fear and sometimes to stark terror.* This is the best definition of the human condition you are ever going to get. I'm looking at how you protect yourself. It's amazing. "Oh, I'm going to be all right." No, you're not. You've got cancer. Cancer is an idea. You're going to get old. You're going to rot. You're going to die. You're going to have chemotherapy. You're going to suffer pain. You're going to lose the things you love and die. And you're nuts! Because there isn't any such thing as that.

Do you believe me? Jesus says, *If you believe me, you'll never die.* (John 11:26) Do you believe me? Well, is that a big deal? "Oh, I'm really going to have to look at it." Why would you have to look at it? If you're the cause of your own pain? Of course, that's why you need the Atonement. Otherwise, why did you ask me to come and tell you this? I'm obviously on an assignment of telling you that you're perfect as God created you. *...shrinking from truth, sometimes retreating to the lesser forms of fear and sometimes to stark terror. But you will advance, because your goal is the advance from fear to truth. The goal you accepted is the goal of knowledge,* of what you really are, *for which you signified your willingness* – or you wouldn't be a human being. Somewhere you must know of what I'm telling you. You could not *not.*

Fear seems to live in darkness, and when you are afraid you have stepped back. Let us then join quickly in an instant of light, and it will be enough to remind you that your goal is light instead of the crap that you're in. *Truth has rushed to meet you since you called upon It.* As soon as you said, "What the hell am I doing here?" As soon as you reached the evolutionary point where you asked the question, Truth immediately said, "We've been looking for you."

If you knew Who walks beside you on the way that you have chosen, fear would be obviously *impossible.* The "old man" on that video (which is me) tried to tell you that everything out there is trying to tell you that you're perfect as God created you – not as you identified them, but as the truth of what they know that we all are together at the end of time. Is that a statement of truth? Wow, is that nice!

You do not know because the journey into darkness has been long and cruel, and you have gone deep into it. A little flicker of your eyelids, closed so long, has not yet been sufficient to give you confidence in yourself, so long despised. Could you hear what I just said? You despise your own confidence because it would give you a totality of the power of yourself to kill yourself and you don't believe that. That's why you won't admit that your power comes from God. What an amazing idea! Wow!

A little flicker of your eyelids, closed so long... This is good stuff. *You go toward love, still hating It.* Obviously, because love has no conditions, and you hate the idea that love is unconditional and has no conditions that will justify your own death. There's no justification for you. You hate it! You hate what I'm offering you! You hate the idea that you don't have to struggle and get old and die. You hate the idea that everything you thought you had to do is totally meaningless and that you're perfect and loving as God created you. You can't stand unconditionality. So I must tell you, take all of your conditions, since you are the cause of them, and don't be in conflict with your own conditional mind. Why would that be difficult if you are all of the conditional self in denial of God? Did you hear that? You are both all of the denial and all of the reality. How simple the solution!

You go toward love still hating it, and terribly afraid of its judgment upon you. Since you believe that God judges and you're separate from Him, you must believe that He is punishing you for something that you did. And that's why you're afraid to ask God for total help, because He's the one that's punishing you. That's insane. That's nuts. Don't do that.

And you do not realize that you are not really *afraid of love, but only of what you have made of it.* You have made God fearful by letting Him be the cause of your own crap. Don't do that. Let God be God and whole and perfect. Obviously, you have the authority problem of believing that God, somehow, had something to do with this, because in your own mind you justify hate and fear in association with eternal love that anyone coming into their right mind would know is absurd. There's no way that Oprah – and she doesn't mean that – would say that God offers us the gift of fear so that we can protect ourselves. From who? I thought God created us perfect. "We've got to protect ourselves from evil, over which God has no control." The hell with you!

You are advancing to love's meaning, and away from all illusions in which you have surrounded it. When you retreat to the illusion your fear increases, for there is little doubt that what you think it means is fearful. Yet what is that to us who travel surely and very swiftly away from fear? It means nothing. This is Jesus speaking. This is really nice. *You who hold your brother's hand also hold mine, for when you joined each other you were not alone.* And I'm including joining each other in separation. Everybody got that? The second you joined your brother's association, you acknowledged God. You would have to because you thought you were separate. You can be mixed up about what your goal is, but at that moment you communicated and at that moment Christ was with you. Want the sentence? *Where two or more are gathered, I am there.* (Matthew 18:20) Was that Jesus that said that? That's incredible when you look at it. He would have to be as an arbiter between your determinations to justify love as death. Don't let your brother die, brother. By your hands he dies. So you believe, by his hands he is killing you, so you share death instead of life. An amazing idea!

This is Jesus, guys. *Do you believe that I would leave you in the darkness you agreed to leave with me?* Jesus says, "No one's here that didn't come from Heaven with me." I was going to read that to you today. Jesus' direct statement is "Everybody that's here came from Heaven with me and is going home with me." He actually says that. (John 3:13)

In your relationship is this world's light. And fear must disappear before you now. Be tempted not to snatch away the gift of faith you offered to your brother. You will succeed only in frightening yourself. The gift was given forever, for God Himself received it from you. And He requires it from you in order to be God. I know you don't like that idea, but there is no God without you. Fortunately, you did not create God. He created you. So you don't have to be concerned about the wholeness of you. Yet it is impossible you will not create as God created you because His creations are what you are, and His dependence on you is exactly as total as your dependence on Him. This is just like I'm reading this out of a book.

You cannot take it back. You have accepted God. Or you wouldn't be listening to this. *The holiness of your relationship is established in Heaven.* You come here to try to discover it. *You do not understand what you accepted, but remember that your understanding is not necessary. All that was necessary* (past tense) *was merely the wish to understand.* Because if you have a real desire to know who you are, nothing in the universe can prevent you from knowing. It's your decision *not* to know who you are that is keeping you from knowing, and that doesn't make any sense. That's Lesson 139. *That wish was the desire to be whole. The Will of God is granted you. For you desire the only thing you ever had, or ever were* or ever will have or ever will be.

Each instant that we spend together will teach you that this goal is possible, and will strengthen your desire to reach it. And in your desire lies its accomplishment. Thy will be done. In your desire for relief from pain and death, in your desire to let God be God rather than this, is the accomplishment. If that involves faith, what the hell! Look at the things you've had faith in up until now. Turn on the TV and see their faith in the rotten carcasses of death, the absurdity of this place.

No little, faltering footsteps that you may take can separate your desire from His Will and from His strength. You listen to me. I don't care about who uses the power to deny it. I'm telling you, I am offering you the power of a single whole mind of eternal life to declare that you are perfect and whole as God created you. If you want to think that that has something to do with a guy in Mexico, go ahead. But that's bullshit. It has to do only individually with him. You start to teach this and you will be teaching the truth. If you teach anything else, you are teaching to an aggregation of death, and that's not real. Every attempt of this world will be made to aggregate in separation and death. If you acknowledge it, it's because you are aggregated in your own death and are using death in order to declare life, which is nuts.

You can't have two worlds. I'm teaching you a world of reality and life that's going on around you all the time simultaneous with this world. All you have to do is look at your brother not as an image of your own junk, your need to die, but simply as the whole Christ which he is. If you want to use my mind, what the hell do you think I'm doing with it? Would you let me use your mind to do it, or are you going to insist that I die with you? I refuse your mind simply because it doesn't make any sense. I asked you to make sense out of getting old and dying and you couldn't because you've already admitted to me that there is an eternal life. Therefore this is senseless. It's insane, it's hallucinatory, and it's not real.

Are you letting me teach this? This is Jesus of Nazareth, teaching in your church. When he walked into the church 2000 years ago, this is exactly what He said. "Your Kingdom is not of this world. Don't pay any attention to all the laws. They're totally meaningless. Come on home with me." He says, "I'm not quite done yet, but I sure as hell have had an enlightenment. I was baptized, I had an enlightenment, and I'm the next trip out of here." So He doesn't teach time at all. He teaches, "If you believe me, you can leave here." And He says, "You're not ready to hear me yet, but I'll be right back." The reason He says that is there was nobody in this continuum ready. He had to go and set it up for you and He did. How long did it take Him to come back? Just a minute. He's right back here now, telling you. It's all set for you.

What I told you that you couldn't do was just to give you a little incentive to attempt it. I bet you can't hear that. Did you hear that? This is John 13-14. Crucifixion is as powerful as reality. I don't care. I'm telling you, I want you to be empowered with the idea of finding the solution so that you will use the energy of your own mind, because the energy of the truth of you is what you really are, anyway. But that's still going to take your desire and determination to escape from the world – to acknowledge that He is risen, indeed, and that He is offering you this from outside of time. Wow! We're teaching physical resurrection.

I hold your hand as surely as you agreed to take your brother's. Literally. Literally! *You will not separate, for I stand with you and walk with you in your advance to truth. And where we go we carry God with us.* In your relationship it is impossible that you have not joined with me in bringing Heaven to the Son of God, who hides in darkness. Boy, this is nice! What an idea!

This doesn't tell you to look at the other guy and see all sorts of crap and then try to change your mind about what's out there. This tells you to change your mind about *yourself.* So if you hold a grievance of pain, it's against yourself, not him? That's an amazing idea. And he's causing you pain, like you're feeling? The guy out there is causing that, and that's actually your own mind? "Yeah, but I'm going to have to forgive him in order to get out of that. And when I forgive him, how come he doesn't acknowledge my forgiveness?" Because you have designed him not to! Because if he accepted your forgiveness totally, you would have to share the forgiveness of the Christ who is telling you you're the same and that you're sharing His eternal love for you and for yourself because there's only one Self. Boy, forgiveness is important, isn't it?

Most of you at this level retain one knot of grievance. You there, you've got one knot of grievance. You are damned determined that somebody else has caused this. It's an amazing thing. Finally it's God. You cannot

not have a grievance with God if He has anything to do with this. You have every right to have a grievance. I'm just telling you, why would you want to have it when it's not true? What you think God did to you, He did not do. What you think your brother is doing to you, he is not doing to you. *You are doing it to yourself.* This is Sermon on the Mount, guys. "I do this but to myself."

In your relationship you have joined with me in bringing Heaven to the Son of God, who hid in darkness. This is the greatest stuff you'll ever read. *You have been willing to bring the darkness to light and this willingness has given strength to everyone who would remain in darkness* because everyone in darkness is a construction of your mind. *Those who would see will see. And they will join with me in carrying their light into the darkness, when the darkness in them is offered to the light, and is removed forever. My need for you, joined with me in the holy light of your relationship, is your need for salvation.* Boy, this is lovely!

There's only one Self. This is directly connected to the review after Lesson 170, where Jesus says to you, "Each time I take a single association home with me, I take all of the separation because you *are* all of the separation." Now, the associations who have left here and go out into the world have no intention of hearing me. To you it seems reasonable that they would want to listen to this rather than get old and die. To them it's perfectly reasonable that life is going to be associated with pain and death because they have been able to cause it to their brother and escape it themselves. When I teach you Sermon on the Mount as my Christhood, I will tell you that you are the cause of your brother's pain. The requirement is that you change your mind to give him relief from the pain that you are sharing with him. Until that is done, there is no hope for you. Boy, it's nice to be heard! Is this fundamental!

This is really nice. I'll just finish it. *Would I not give you what you gave to me* somewhere in time? I've been trying to teach you this since the beginning of time. I owe you. You've got my marker. It's impossible that I'm not offering you something that you offered me, because we're in a constant exchange with this. The only thing that makes us different is time. I happen to be more advanced, obviously, because I'm not even here. I'm not even here! This is the *Course in Miracles.* I must have come from outside of time to tell you that you're not really here either, and I need to speed up your own time. I need to get you onto the right track. If you get onto the right track, you won't get sidetracked through fear of coming home. You're really afraid of coming home, prodigal son. Your God is going to run out to greet you! "I don't believe that." Not only does He welcome you home, He actually runs out to greet you. He actually says, "Where the hell have you been? I've been missing you." You'll find it in the Bible somewhere. (Luke 15:11-32)

When you guys get into the *Course*, you don't know what's going to happen. You've got at least 2000 years of apparitions, evil spirits, Westminster Abbeys. You have phenomena that's going on around here that will really astonish you. I mean, the fire hydrant is liable to start to talk to you. I know you think that that's ridiculous, but it's not. I don't know what it would say to you. It would probably be "Don't lift your leg on me again."

Listen. See if you can hear this. If you can hear this, you can go home with me. *My need for you, joined with me in the holy light of your relationship, is your need for salvation.* Because we need each other totally. Because it's a single need to remember that we're perfect as God created us. I'm going to depend on you entirely, whether you like it or not, because in my dependence on you is my salvation since you are a projection of my own mind. I will then understand that you are an extension of my mind, not separate from me, and I can then join in you, and a relationship that was designed to sustain death can be converted simply by our admission that we don't want to die anymore.

Swear not to die, you holy Son of God. I'm telling you, you can't die. Is that all right with you? The whole teaching of this is, if I can get you to keep dying every second, you will discover that you are always alive. You keep putting it off because you are afraid to. Don't be afraid to die – all that would be is the denial of God, because if death is real, there's no God, anyway. Why don't you just take that step with me so we can get out of here. Is it a step into the unknown? Sure. It's a step you've never taken because, had you taken it, you wouldn't be here. This is all in here. It's a step that you must take and I'll help you take it. Stand still a minute and don't let all of your associations force you back down in to bar you from Heaven. Every single association you've got is designed to keep you from opening that up and seeing that you're perfect. Everything here! *And now you stand in terror of what you promised never to look at.* And all of these associations march and they say, "Don't you dare look at that. That's God. That's the fear. That's the awful image of you." This is Lesson 170, incidentally, which is the heart of it.

You who are now the bringer of salvation have the function of bringing the light of your mind to this dark place. *The darkness in you has been brought to light* by the conversion of your own body association. Can you hear this? Your body now is converting very rapidly. The body wasn't real, anyway. So you're just converting it real rapidly. Jesus would call these light bodies. The children of light cannot dwell in darkness because they don't give themselves back reflections of their own darkness. They reflect back to themselves the light they have become. Previously, they looked through a mirror darkly and got a reflection of their own dark image. With a new eye, with your new Christ eye, you see in the totality. I got into Paul just a little bit. (I Cor 13:12)

Carry it back to darkness, from the holy instant to which you brought it. We are made whole in our desire to make whole. Let not time worry you, for all the fear that you and your brother experience is really gone. Don't worry about it. Now, if you need an adjustment, I'll adjust it for you. I'm offering you a speed up in your own association of your death experience. You could not be hearing this if time had not been previously adjusted for you, because the goal that I am offering you is reachable in time. In that sense, I'm just shortening time for you. Why would you not want to take the shortest route out of here? I'm talking time and space here. Why would you keep battling the separation and retaining it in the separation rather than simply letting yourself come back to what you really are?

Wow! It's going to say that. Yes. Good. Don't let time worry you, *for all the fear that you and your brother experience is really past.* Oh, I wrote on here, "Sometime read this out loud." I'm sure I probably read this out loud – maybe it was 420 years ago. The difference may be now you can hear what I'm reading. You've speeded up your own time, and you're not going to go back into darkness to deny this. You are willing to stand just a moment in fear. You're not standing in light. You're standing in fear. But until you stand in your own fear, it will not be converted to light.

Time has been readjusted – not just adjusted; it's been re-adjusted. You said, "The hell with it! This time is too slow for me. I want it readjusted." The moment that you asked that it be readjusted, I came to readjust it. But somewhere you must have gotten sick and tired of your slow time and you asked for a re-adjustment. So in that sense it's a re-adjustment. But remember, you live by adjustments to time, anyway. Why would you slow them down rather than speed them up?

You can stay in one continuing adjustment. Remember that adjustment is death, and each time you adjust, you adjust to death. If I can speed you up so that you're adjusting all the time, you will get so sick and tired of it, you will give up. That's what happened to me. My mind got broader and broader, and I kept trying to adjust everything, and finally I said, "Screw it; nothing works." Can you hear me?

Time has been readjusted to help us do, together, what your separate pasts would hinder. You have gone past fear, for no two minds can join in the desire for love without love's joining them. Because God is love and you are perfect as He created you. You cannot *not* be. I'm sorry. You can carry that pain and sickness if you want to, but you are going to be unconditional love of God, no matter what you do. I know I'm threatening you with this. I am threatening you with the fact that your existence is totally meaningless; that you're an advocate of evil which will not succeed. You cannot succeed in being separate from Reality.

Not one light in Heaven but goes with you. Can you hear this? Can you convert your lights to rays? You can convert each instant of light into a ray of perfection. Many of you, in your illuminations, see rays. You see the Great Rays of light, which is nothing but particles being transformed into light reality. *Not one light in Heaven but goes with you. Not one ray that shines forever in the Mind of God but shines on you. Heaven is joined with you in your advance to Heaven.* "Just a little bit of Heaven." You cannot *not* be an entirety of Heaven because that's all there is. "Well, I'm a lot smaller in my little piece of Heaven." Why would you be concerned about that? If you are your entirety, you cannot *not* be a whole part of Heaven. That's the expansion of the conversion of your temporal association to the spatial evidence of your single reality in the totality of Heaven. But certainly, if you thought you were separate in pieces, we had to – as a solution to the problem – stick the whole you in you, even though you didn't want to acknowledge it. There's no way that you can escape from that light, which you're now letting occur in you.

When such great lights have joined with you to give the little spark of your desire the power of God Himself, can you remain in darkness? No! Why the hell would you remain in darkness? I've taken the spot of the perfection of you and offered you a catalyst of light that will keep growing in our body relationship. In effect, if you want to be healed and come home to God with me, all you would have to do is stand next to me. The problem you have with that is you have to undergo the experience in your entirety, and we're still in the process of gathering some of your own crap out there, since this whole world is nothing but your mind, anyway. So in that sense the call has gone out in the conversion of my body and the sharing of the conversion of our singular body with each other. This is the entire teaching of Jesus Christ. One body, perfectly perfected, is all that there is. One body in any form of corruption in time is also all there is. The requirement is that you come from your corrupt body to a moment of incorruptibility. That's Paul. (I Cor 15:53)

You are coming home together, after a long and meaningless journey that you undertook apart, and that led nowhere. You have been in conflict with your own brother. *You have found your brother, and you will light each other's way. And from this light will the Great Rays extend back into darkness and* simultaneously *forward unto God, to shine away the past and so make room for His eternal Presence, in which everything is radiant in the light.* Who the hell do you think wrote this? When I look at human beings, I am astonished that they would say, "Gee, isn't that interesting! I wonder where that came from." Well, it sure as hell didn't come from here. Nothing's from here. I am sure as hell not from here. If I can get you to stop trying to associate the world with this, you'll have no problem. Why would you associate the world with this when the world is your denial of what I am offering you? I can't believe I just read that. This is incredible. Wow! Wow! *Light in the Dream.* That's Chapter 18.

The stiff upper lip of the English is made with the starch of fear. That's true. You're afraid of God, and you're going to just brave it out, aren't you? You escaped Down Under by saying, "This is bullshit! Why would I want to keep a stiff upper lip in death rather than acknowledge life?" "Thou shalt have no other gods before me," including all of what you have set up to idolize. That's nice.

I'm going to show you why I can heal. The reason I can heal is I can exchange any single cell there is in the universe and give it a brand new life and then let it continue, for a moment, to specialize. But remember, the specialization itself is not real. You can specialize if you want to. So healing would have to be the availability of new cellular associations. The fact of the matter is, when you become a mannequin (or what you would call mechanical man) there's no communication going on. That mechanical man literally does not exist because the power (the mind) that is oriented to serve him, has no source. Please hear me with this. It lives within the ego, but it has no source and it is condemned to the association of the specialization of the body. What do you do then? Repair the body? What ever happened to healers? "Well, they disappeared when we discovered we could give each other new hearts and new bones and new bodies." What a strange idea! I thought we healed with our mind. I'm healing you with my mind because that's the only way I can heal, since we are only mind. If you decide you don't want to be sick, you won't be. I'm offering you the solution that I have arrived at in a direct aggregation of the wholeness of my own body. All you could possibly do is kill me, but you're doing that, anyway. You will not be successful in killing me through killing your own self in your own body. I'm speeding you up so fast that you can face the ultimate fear of looking directly at me. This is this Lesson. I want you to read Lesson 170 because it's going to say this.

You make what you defend against, and by your own defense against it is it real and inescapable. It's not an illusion. *Lay down your arms, and only then do you perceive it false. Today we look upon this cruel god dispassionately. And we note that though his lips are smeared with blood, and fire seems to flame from him, he is but made of stone* in your own projection of your own stoniness.

So the face of Christ is what you're afraid to look at because it's going to represent the thing that you fear the most, which is the reflection of your own mind. Is that what this says? This will say, watch it change not through your judgment. *We need not defy his power. He has* absolutely *none. And those who see in him their safety have nothing. They have no guardian, no strength to call upon in danger, and no mighty warrior to fight for them. This moment can be terrible. But it also can be the time of your release from abject slavery. You make a choice, standing before this idol, seeing him exactly as he is. Will you restore to love what you have sought to wrest from it and lay before this mindless piece of stone* (crap)? *Or will you make another* piece of crap *to replace it?* Whereby you can still justify your own meaningless existence within your own body. *Another* one *can be found* if you want to find one.

This crazy world is caused by your craziness. Why would you share the craziness of death with the world when you can come to realize you're the cause of it? That's in this Lesson. Why would you do it except you think that it's out there? *For the god of cruelty may take many forms. Another can always be found* if you want to be cruel. *Yet do not think that fear is the escape from fear. Let us remember what the text has stressed about the obstacles to peace. The final*

287

one, the hardest to believe is nothing, and a seeming obstacle with the appearance of a solid block, impenetrable, fearful and beyond surmounting, is literally your *fear of God Himself. Here is the basic premise which enthrones the thought of the fear as God. For fear is loved by those who worship it, and love appears to be invested now with cruelty* because it is offering you the reality of yourself. It takes away from you and demands that you relinquish all of the personal values of morality – everything that you have done to justify your association with yourself, all of it, is totally meaningless. If I can get you to look at the entirety of the meaninglessness of your relationship with yourself, your progress will be very rapid. If you continue to take forms of your own mind and justify them in what is called temporal/spatial association, you're going to slow yourself down. Why would you want to do that? All you could possibly do is keep repeating your descent into hell over and over again. Don't do that anymore!

Where does this totally insane belief in gods of vengeance come from? Love has not confused its attributes with those of fear. Yet must the worshipers of fear perceive their own confusion in fear's "enemy" (love); *its cruelty as now a part of love. And what becomes more fearful than the Heart of Love Itself?* Nothing! Because it's the loss of your own fear. And you depend on fear in order to be here. You can hear me if you want to. I'm telling you the truth personally in your own mind, and I am offering you the solution personally in your own mind because I am literally, personally in your own mind. I'll do it once more for you: Since we are all a single Self, I am literally, personally a whole part of you. You can divide me up in your own mind, but all you will do is divide yourself. Dividing yourself will keep you from seeing that you are whole. Everybody got that?

The choice you make today is absolutely certain. For you look for the last time upon this bit of carven stone you made, and call it god no longer. You have reached this place before, but you have chosen that this cruel god remain with you in still another form. Guys, this is the whole teaching of what you've been doing. This time when you got here, I was standing here because you asked me for a solution. And while I was there the last time, you didn't see me. Well, I made a little mistake and I wasn't there. Whatever the reason of our miscommunication, you're standing right now exactly where you should be.

And so the fear of God returned with you. This time you leave it there. And you return to a new world, unburdened by the weight of death; beheld not in its sightless eyes, but in the vision that your choice restored to you. Now do your eyes belong to Christ and He looks through them. He's looking through your unreal eyes. Why not? Christ has emerged in you and sees the entirety of you within yourself. *Now your voice belongs to God and echoes His. And now your heart remains at peace forever. You have chosen Him in place of idols, and your attributes, given by your Creator, are restored to you at last. The Call for God is heard and answered. Now has fear made way for love as God Himself replaces cruelty.*

Father, we are like to You. No cruelty abides in us for there is none in You. Your peace is ours. And we bless the world with what we have received from You alone. We choose again, and make our choice for all our brothers, knowing they are one with us. We bring them Your salvation as we have received it now. And we give thanks for them who render us complete. In them we see Your glory, and in them we find our peace. Holy are we because Your holiness has set us free. And we give thanks that that is true. Amen.

I'm going to tie this to Christianity. I want you to see that any whole mind that has undergone a death experience is constantly trying to offer it to the association. This is from the illumination of the mind of Paul, obviously, having been illuminate in his Damascus experience. (Acts 9) It is one of the extremely rare occasions when the resurrected Jesus spoke directly to a man. That would have to be true because he's in that continuum. And obviously, his disciples had very little intention of doing it. And they're going to gather together and tie it to James, the older brother, in order to retain it. So He needed a Gentile. He needed an association that was in an attack on Him, using the power of the attack and converting it to the power of salvation. Who heard that? The one guy that was persecuting Him the most was exactly the power that He wanted. And that's exactly what Paul says in here. Isn't it? "He took my power of persecuting Him and, through His light, converted it to the power of His salvation." How simple the solution is if you are being offered the solution through the power of your own crucifixion!

How can Paul describe that? This is Second Corinthians, and he apologizes for threatening the Corinthians because they've set up their own establishment, and he wants to tell them it's full of crap. He wants to say to them, "Your establishments don't mean anything. Your contact is with the risen Jesus, not in your determination to establish a church to justify your continuing crucifixion of Him." And he does it 2000 years ago in Greek, and it's been translated, but fundamentally it's still trying to express the same thing: that he undergoes a continuing transformation, not of his mind (which is already whole with God), but in his body, which requires a continuing transformation in order to be a messenger or a vehicle of the truth contained within the particle-wave association.

I stayed with Christianity. When I first drew the fish, when we agreed to use the fish in the catacombs they were seeking us out to kill us. Paul died in AD 64. They cut off his head. That's the safest thing to do with a guy like that. That's what they did to John the Baptist. They didn't crucify Paul. They cut off his head. He was literally decapitated for daring to suggest that contained within the human mind was the source of God. What a place to be! It wasn't supposed to be. It was some slave girl that had been converted to Christianity and was threatening the concubine associations of the emperors. Who cares? That's an historic reference. He had gone too far. He began to threaten the establishment.

This is II Corinthians 4: *Therefore seeing we have this ministry, as we have received mercy, we faint not*; but offer mercy to the world. *But have renounced the hidden things of dishonesty, not walking in craftiness, nor handling the word of God deceitfully; but by manifestation of the truth commending ourselves to every man's conscience in the sight of God.* That's really nice. *But if our gospel be hid, it is hid to them that are lost;* (not to them that want to be found) *in whom the god of this world hath blinded the minds of them which believe not, lest the light of the glorious gospel of Christ, who is the image of God, should shine unto them.* (2Cor 4:1-4) This is exactly what I just read you, isn't it? It's exactly what I just read. I know because Paul told me to read this.

Listen: *For we preach not ourselves, but Christ Jesus the Lord; and ourselves your servants for Jesus' sake.* (2Cor 4:5) In other words, we are serving you in the truth of the love of God. We're commanding only that you recognize through the resurrection of Jesus the certainty that we are risen together, indeed, as He announces to us. *For God, who commanded the light to shine out of darkness* – I just read this – *hath shined in our hearts, to give the light of the knowledge of the glory of God in the face of Jesus Christ.* (2Cor 4:6) I just read you this. I just read youthat you can see a perfect image of Christ. Imagine this, 2000 years ago! Wow!

But we have this treasure in earthen vessels, that the excellency of the power may be of God, and not of us. (2Cor 4:7) Since we thought the power was not of us, we are a part of an earthen vessel expressing the entirety of God. What an amazing idea!

For God, who commanded the light to shine out of darkness, hath shined in our hearts, to give the light of the knowledge of the glory of God in the face of Jesus. But we have this treasure in earthly vessels, that the excellency of the power may be of God, and not of us. We are troubled on every side, yet not distressed; we are perplexed, but not in despair; persecuted, but not forsaken; cast down, but not destroyed. Always bearing about in the body the dying of the Lord Jesus, that the life also of Jesus might be made manifest in our body. (2Cor 4:6-10) All it really says is that each moment I die as Jesus of Nazareth and have resurrected as the living Christ – within my own body.

This is an amazing idea: *For we which live are alway delivered unto death for Jesus' sake, that the life also of Jesus might be made manifest in our mortal flesh* (2Cor 4:11) in the resurrection. *So then death worketh in us, but life in you.* (2Cor 4:12) I bet I can't teach you this. Death is always working in me. Through my death and life, I'm offering you the life of you, which is death. If you convert that to: "Jesus died from our sins," you're not making any sense – you are associating with the death rather than the life, which is exactly why you're here. What an amazing thing!

So then death worketh in us, but life in you. We having the same spirit of faith, according as it is written, I believed, and therefore have I spoken; as I have become certain. We also believe, and therefore speak; knowing that he which raised up the Lord Jesus shall raise up us also by Jesus, and shall present us with you. (2Cor 4:12-13) Did you hear what he just said? He's offering that from his own risen mind. He's going to present us with your Christhood – we who are teaching this together in our Christhood. What an amazing idea! Wow!

For all things are for your sakes, that the abundant grace might through the thanksgiving of many redound to the glory of God. For which cause we faint not; but though our outward man perish, yet the inward man is renewed day by day. (2Cor 4:15-16) I don't know what that is if it's not a teaching to let your body just fall apart all the time and be renewed in the Christ of you. Is that in here? Amazing! Wow! *Yet the inward man is renewed day by day* – each moment, in the totality of his moment's resurrection.

For our light affliction, which is but for a moment, worketh for us a far more exceeding and eternal weight of glory. (2Cor 4:17) It means: "My burden is light." Finally, if you let all the burdens fall in on you and give them to God, you will be relieved of the responsibility of carrying the burdens of your own self. But you can't know that until you ask God to relieve your burdens: "God, I'd certainly appreciate it if you would take this burden away from me." Not that He does – Jesus says this at the crucifixion. It's the last useless journey you're going to make, so if you have to make it, for goodness sake, make it! You are going to have to admit that the persecution and death are exactly the same as the eternal life. You cannot be separate from your Self.

While we look not at the things which are seen, but at the things which are not seen: for the things which are seen are temporal; but the things which are not seen are eternal. (2Cor 4:18) All that 2nd Corinthians 4 says, and all that I declare to you, and all Jesus declared to you, is the certainty that you are in a reassociation of a new body form each moment. I have made absolutely no attempt to get your conceptual mind to understand this attraction of eternal love of God or the singularity of mind because it's literally impossible for you to understand that. I have asked you to allow the completeness of an understanding to involve you totally, because I am certain that I was the cause of this association, and through my inability to deal with it (my death) I was resurrected.

Paul is kind of nice, isn't it? That's Corinthians. That's kind of nice stuff. Thanks for putting up with me this morning. How is everybody doing in your incorruptible body? "Well, I'm suffering a lot of pain and death." Good! How does it feel? "Oh, it feels awful." Good! "I'm never going to get out of here." Be patient. You got here a little early. You are *very* early. "Well, I think I'll stay around and die some more." Too late. That's what you've caused to happen to this world. Brother, this world is going to be pretty crappy around here in a minute, because they're determined not to get the light which you have offered. So they're going to have to have more chaos in their attempt to communicate in the dark forms. And the more they attempt to communicate with all of these digits and all that, the more confusing it will become, because they're trying to solve the confusion within the confusion. And you can't solve it – you will just break it into more confusion. What a place to be! The hell with that! Come on! We're going home!

Thanks, dear ones. We're going to have a nice service today. We have a baptism and a christening going on. Why do we christen? We dedicate our individual life to Jesus Christ resurrected. Will that take some maturity? No. It's a symbol of the certainty that your mind can be perfected out of its corrupt body. Whatever time that takes, the time is going to be over, anyway. I'm very certain that babies aren't born in sin. My mother didn't like that, either. I asked my mother why they baptized little babies. The minister had said, "They're born in sin." My mother said, "No. I don't believe that." We put the sin on them. They're born innocent. And we have to give them enough sin so they can escape it. That's a procedure you have to go through in order to be found guilty of your own association. Everybody has to go through that. That's fine with me. But if you're going to be perfect, so is the Christ that's being born in you now.

Your kingdom is not of this world. The other sentence that I was going to read was that everybody who heard me really came from Heaven. Jesus says that directly. You came from Heaven, and we're just here for a second. And now we're leaving. You can remember this if you want to. Is this the real thing? Do you want it to be? You really want it to be? "Well, I think I do."

Well, then turn your attention toward it, and your desire will make it so, because it's your desire that's determining the outcome that you want. The same power that you offer it will include all of the power of the entirety of the solution. It cannot *not* because that's what you are. You are the power of the universe. And that's why everything is getting so phenomenal. You're liable to get appearances. You don't know what's going to come. You might say, "What the hell are you doing here?" And he might say, "I thought you might need a hand with this." Well, here we go! Let's go. What are going to tell me? Remember that some of them are designed to tell you exactly what you wanted to hear, and in this the word is *vigilance*. Be vigilant not to somebody who tries to sell you on the crap of staying here because he's a product within your own mind that wants to deceive you. Rather, simply release it and say, "No! The hell with you! I'm not going to have an establishment here on earth. I don't have a church, Peter." Peter said, "Let's start a church," and Jesus said, "I'm going home. If you come with me, you won't have to worry about a thing."

The only temptation that you could ever be given would be to remain here because you love it. But you can't love sickness, pain and death because it's not real. I'm not taking the things you love away from you. I'm offering you the certainty that God is love and that you can't lose the things you love.

Thank you for listening to me. The next time you do this, I certainly intend to listen to you. I could not *not*. Because obviously when you initially present me with this, I won't be able to hear you. If I heard you, I would be presenting it to you. I just read you that. All we're really doing is exchanging the certainty of our singular selves with our Self. Is that okay with you?

CHAPTER 11

The Kingdom Of Heaven Is Like Unto...

You are using the reasonable power of your mind in application to determine the outcome, the efficacy, of a remedy in regard to a disease that is a conceptual association of your objective reality. That is the condition of conceptual mind. I don't want you to get out of your concepts. How could you get out of them? Somewhere you have to change your own mind in association with yourself about the outcome that you are getting as a result of your concepts. All you have really discovered is that the outcome of the limited association, based on an old reference, couldn't have any meaning. That discovery included your not wanting to give it meaning, very simply because you were getting the outcome of the concepts of your own mind. Somewhere you said, "that's silly". The condition of a human being doesn't make any sense, because he is admitting that he is getting the outcome of the concepts of his own mind without questioning why or for what purpose he would get an outcome of himself. What's the sense in it?

The Kingdom of God is nothing but the inclusive precept of an idea that mind will be mind, and that any of your concepts can be included in with it. That's the Kingdom of God. Why do you have to tell the story of the Kingdom of God as a parable? There's no other way you can do it, because the Kingdom of God is not a description of objective reality. When I asked my mom, "What's the Kingdom of Heaven?" She said, "Well, gold flows in the street, and there are angels that hover around." That's an objective definition of it. Obviously I could say I am not in that Kingdom. I am in this Kingdom. How can I get to that Kingdom? It's not possible. If I separate myself from the Kingdom, and give it a definition of my objective association, it would be impossible for me to get there. I have separated myself from my own mind. I am comparing Heaven and hell separate from what I am.

Once I get you in your own mind, and I can keep you from conceptualizing in objective reality, and comparing it with associations, what experience will you begin to have? A new joyous you! This is the whole Workbook. There is nothing outside of you. The wholeness that you are feeling is an expression of your association with universal mind. One thing for sure, there is no way you are teaching a human being to escape his concepts and the idea of comparison of one with the other. You are telling him that's impossible.

Reality must be based on the fundamental premise of the possibility of the totality. I'll tell you any story you want to hear. Who cares? The effect of the totality of your mind is going to be in relationship with every single thing you do. The Kingdom of God is like to a lost colony. I'll give you parables. But notice I am always telling you about a relationship between the separation and reality. It is impossible that I not do that because that is what you are. There is no comparison and no association between this hell – this pain, this death, this loneliness, this loss, this attack on God – and the beautiful living universal mind of God. As Jesus says: if I can get you to accept the premise that your condition of temporal relationship is an attack on God, directly and fully; that your need to die is literally a denial and an attack on God, you can progress in this very rapidly. Why? You become inclusive in your own sin. And sin won't make any sense to you, because by its inclusiveness you will see that you are combating something that must be contained within your own association. That's true! It's always going on.

All saviors of the world are attempting to get you to look at the totality of your own association by entering, in your mind, into a relationship between the Son which is you, and God which is everything. That's the whole purpose of this. You must do it in your own mind. There is no other way. Now the fact of the matter is, what I am threatening you with, your own sickness, pain and death, is nothing compared to

Jesus of Nazareth. The teachings of Jesus of Nazareth, *A Course In Miracles*, have no sympathy at all for pain and death. Your salvation literally depends on me not allowing you your conceptual associations. Somewhere you believe that contained within your concepts will be a solution to the problem of who you are. That's absurd. You are perfect and whole as God created you.

So we tell stories. Would you like the one about the aliens that keep landing here and you keep covering them up? Is there one about an invitation to you to come home and celebrate your home coming? Are those the parables of Jesus? What does He say? He says the Kingdom of God is like to...and then He tells you a story. I have no concern about the story that you tell. I'm telling you that if you don't listen to the story that I'm offering you in its entirety, you will get the result of the limitation of your mind in the determination to accept our previous associations with each other, rather than letting yourself be whole in your own mind. The Kingdom of God is the relationship of Tom Sawyer, Huck Finn – anything – who cares. For goodness sake, what is the purpose in your own mind of the story you tell? Show me any human being, and I'll show you someone in his own kingdom. He is the definition of himself in the determination of the outcome he wants with what he is in his own mind.

Not only is the human mind nuts, but a human being considers existence as being crazy. If he would look at it, he would see that he has lost control of everything in his association. No matter what he does, his determination is based on predications of results he wants in his own mind that are changing all the time. What is his problem? He has a fundamental flaw in his premise. His premise is that he must exist in this association rather than the simple admission of a premise of a whole mind. That's as simple as it gets. I won't tell you about St. Paul and everyone else who has told you this. I am telling you this as a fact of your own mind.

The expansion of your association in correspondence with yourself, the miracle that has occurred with you, is very simply the need not to defend the old cause and effect relationships of your mind. I guarantee you that once you defend it, that old premise will become the premise from which you think. That will then become a form, and constrict you within your own mind. It's totally senseless. It has no basis, on any reasonable admission, that would withstand any light of examination. Hopefully, you are understanding that *A Course In Miracles* is a course in the reasonableness of singular, universal mind.

I'm not taking your premises away from you. I'm just asking you to look at the premises on which your existence has been based to determine what it is in your own association. You mean if I change my mind the world will really change? I mean that the world is your mind. I mean that the whole universe is your mind. I'm saying, story after story, that you are that!

How did this come about in your new minds? How are you now able to see with clarity that you are whole with God? You simply made the admission that God was God. It was simpler than you wanted to admit. You stopped being the authority of your own conceptual mind in order to die. How reasonable does this world still seem to you? As reasonable as the result you are determined to get without looking at the obvious outcome, death. The real insanity is the conceptual mind, first of all, accepts the outcome that appears to be inevitable – he gives away his own causation, and secondly, he then lives by not looking at the absurdity of that association.

The idea that the universe is a premise of my mind of the totality of eternal life is very exciting to me. All I needed was so-called progress within my own apparent chaotic association, to the determination that I couldn't solve the problem that I was obviously facing within the context of what appeared to be the solution to it. It's not solvable. That's all it took. Reasonably, any problem that leads to sickness and death could not be solved, because the problem of sickness and death is what it is. The whole teaching that I have told you is: your Kingdom is not of this world. You have examined the precepts of existence being terminal which the world is based on, and have seen that it is senseless.

Just for the fun of it, I'll tell you the story of Matthew 22. It is exactly the same story that I've been telling you about the original invitation that you rejected and killed the Christ, or that was a "screw up" of communication within the association. You were prepared within your own mind to hear this. The invitation to come to God was extended to this expeditionary force. You received an invitation to come on home and be reunited with God. But there was a break in communication and you rejected it. Not only that, but your leaders failed you; those who were trained best through an observation of the orders they had read failed you because the orders were faulty. When Jesus was faced with this, He would say: the Kingdom of God is like to... All of the stories will pertain to the offer of God and your rejection of it, or that you have no control over what God is doing, and/or the manner in which you can come to know it by giving everything away and coming to God. There would be no other stories but that.

And Jesus answered and spake unto them again by parables, and said... Why is Jesus answering them? Because they're always asking questions. Every time I say to you: you are perfect as God created you, you keep asking me questions about it. You have to have a story about how it happened. You *are* a story about how it happened. There was a mistake. It's a great story: *The Kingdom of Heaven is like unto a certain king, which made a marriage for his son.* That's nothing but the certainty of God expressing His determination to give you, His son, the total creative power that He is. He made a marriage for you. What's He going to unite him with? All of his potential. He is going to unite him with everything that he is.

And sent forth his servants to call them that were bidden to the wedding: and they would not come. (Matthew 22:1-3) Why wouldn't they come? They're too busy living in their own existent associations. He said to them, "Come and share the feast of the totality," and they wouldn't come. So there is no question that the invitation has been issued by God. This is the idea of God, or the invention in the mind that there is a perfect association; and the admission that you, as a human being, are rejecting the call of God. You'd have to be. Why? You know about it. I didn't invent God for you; you invented Him – you invented the solution. If you invented the solution, why not utilize it?

Again, he sent forth other servants, saying, Tell them which are bidden, Behold, I have prepared my dinner, my oxen and my fatlings are killed, and all things are ready: come unto the marriage. (Matthew 22:4) What he did was allow them the abundance of their own mind in the sharing of God. He had to give them a definition of what abundance was in the totality of the association, because they were trapped in the necessity of themselves. So he says, "At least come together with me and enjoy the real purpose in life, and my happiness, which is the marriage of my son. Okay, bring yourselves, I'll prepare the meal, I have another purpose I want to offer you." That's what we used to do in the missions – get them in and feed them and get them to listen. Usually we'd give them the prayer first and then let them eat. If you fed them first, they'd leave.

...he sent forth other servants, saying, Tell them which are bidden... Only those which are bidden. Those that somewhere in the association are aware of that possibility of doing it, and can be aware that they

are the deniers of it. But what did they do? They made light of it. They said: I'm getting along all right.

But they made light of it, and went their ways, one to his farm, another to his merchandise. And the remnant took his servants, and entreated them spitefully, and slew them. But when the king heard thereof, he was wroth and he sent forth his armies, and destroyed those murderers, and burned up their city. (Matthew 22:5-7)

That is the inevitable result of your determination that the Kingdom is of sickness and death. Did the king really do that? You bet your boots he did. We'll just bury it under and start over. I don't know whether you want to hear this or not. I'm absolutely not concerned about your denial in aggregate of what I'm offering you. We're going to plow you under and seed again. What I'm offering you individually is the growth of your own association with yourself. You can now see yourself as coming into a field where you are a sport, or separate, in that association. Now what are we going to do? The guys that we thought were going to get it, don't get it. All the plans that we made for the establishment, the Pope, Satchitananda, Buddha, all of the great kings, none of them heard it. What they ended up doing was building temples that attacked God. The rest of the people just went back to fishing. What a strange place to be.

Then saith he to his servants, The wedding is ready, but they which were bidden were not worthy. Go ye therefore into the highways, and as many as ye shall find, bid to the marriage. (Matthew 22:8-9) I want you to understand this. This is precisely and exactly what I just offered you. I am offering you, because of the failure of the establishment – the hell with the agriculture, the hell with the traders, the hell with the temple – come on out and listen to the simple story. The other one failed. Look around you. It's been buried. The Christ has been buried and there is no hope at all. This is your bidding to come to this.

Notice I'm not now at all concerned about your qualifications. I didn't actually reduce the step, I took another step. Since you thought qualifications were necessary, you have taken them and made them the qualifications of death. I'm telling you the hell with the qualifications, I'm inviting you as the worst sinner in the world. I don't care if you are good or evil or what your prognostications are, come on in and enjoy this lovely wedding. I'm not concerned about your entitlement to it. I'm giving you the fact of the matter of my whole mind. You are perfect as God created you. Come and enjoy the feast. There are no qualifications! This gets sneaked in because the world is busy worshipping idols or harvesting their own crap. All of a sudden this call goes out with a totality of meaning that transcends the world. And you heard it in your own mind, and now you are going to enjoy the feast of eternal life. And you say to me, "what about my concepts?" Include them in! ...go ye therefore into the highways and byways and as many as ye shall find bid to the marriage.

So those servants went out into the highways, and gathered together all as many as they found, both bad and good, and the wedding was furnished with guests. (Matthew 22:10) Guys, you listen to me, I'm giving you the fact of the matter: This is a wedding with God. I'm not concerned about your qualifications because the mere idea that you are here is proof of your willingness to come home with me. What are you going to have to do? Be innocent of your old associations. I would strongly recommend, since you are in the presence of the power of the mind of God, that you be innocent of bringing in your intent to justify the establishment or the agriculture or exchange that is going on out there. Come here for no reason and enjoy yourself. You're here aren't you? Be grateful that you found it and that the invitation has been extended to you! Don't try to keep clothing yourself in the guilt of your own identity. Why? I better not read the next sentence. You won't want to hear this. I'm telling you, if you've come this far, you better clean up your determination to come to God. Many of you who have left, for whatever reason, were not willing to totally relinquish the necessity for your own defense of your own existence. This, obviously, is bypassing establishment.

And when the king came in to see the guests, he saw there a man which had not on a wedding garment. (Matthew 22:11) Whenever I look at some of you guys, I say: What the hell are you doing here? You're here, obviously, but the manner in which you are defining your association has nothing to do with what I am offering you. What the hell are you doing here? You are just determined to bring your own self in, and then go out and do some more stuff. How willing are you to be stripped of the garment of sickness and death and guilt that you bring to this association? You have an invitation from God to come to God. It doesn't have anything to do with what you brought in here. Nothing. You are in a place where that can occur! And you say: what do I have to do? At the very minimum I have to wear a fig leaf. Chew on that one. That's just another parable. How come you're covering your privates? You're guilty. This is Genesis – it's the same idea. You came in naked; you go out naked. If you put on a fig leaf, you'll begin to design different kinds of fig leaves. You'll have to compare your fig leaf. Obviously, you've covered your own genetic memory. That's the whole body condition.

And he saith unto him, Friend, how camest thou in hither not having a wedding garment? And he was speechless. (Matthew 22:12) He is thinking, "What the hell are you talking about? You told me to come, I came just the way you told me to." He was speechless. There was no way he could correlate it in his mind the meaning of this. Then he would obviously begin to defend himself.

Then said the king to the servants, Bind him hand and foot, and take him away, and cast him into outer darkness, there shall be weeping and gnashing of teeth. For many are called, but few are chosen. (Matthew 22:13-14) What is the choice of you based on? Your admission of your wholeness. All of the parables will often address the fundamental mistake that was made in our not recovering you initially. *The seed fell on barren land; the birds ate a lot of it.* (Mark 4:3) You didn't have enough water. We understand perfectly that the tares are growing with the fruit. We don't care. We are at fault for the tares growing with the fruit. (Matthew 13:24) But we'll sort that out for you if you'll let us. Obviously the tares are your perceptual associations with yourself, rather than the purity of you. Now I am doing another parable. How else can I explain to you that you are the conflict?

People who are utilizing the power of their minds to bring about healing believe that I am teaching that healing comes about by blind faith. I'm not. There isn't any such thing as healing by blind faith – not in the sense that the association is not healed, but that it could not remain blind as to the method by which the healing occurred. It would require a reason for it. The solution to that has to be that healing is reasonable. I take nothing from the physician except my fundamental declaration to him that existent association is what the disease is. If that will appear reasonable to him, his progress in his own healing will be very rapid, because the manner in which he applies the remedy will be based on a broader range of remedial possibilities.

Quite literally, the whole miracle teaching is nothing but the cause and the effect are not apart, and that any remedy will heal perfectly if it is allowed to. It's the admission that the disease is the separation, or the human condition. This is all Mary Baker says. I'm not taking away the premise that the idea of cause and effect relationships can bring about a result. Good grief, that's what you do as a doctor. That's what you do as a human being. You look at the problem, and you solve it in that association. If you want to look at what the Kingdom is, you cannot avoid the idea that the Kingdom of Heaven is based on the premise of your own mind and the outcome you want in the inclusiveness of your existence with the universe. The Kingdom is the result of premises, just as this world is. I'm telling you that you are getting the result of your own mind. I'm adding to that: There is nothing outside of your mind. That's where the conflict lies.

Forgive the past and let it go, for it is gone.
You stand no longer on the ground that
lies between the worlds. You have gone on,
and reached the world that lies at Heaven's gate.
There is no hindrance to the Will of God,
nor any need that you repeat again
a journey that was over long ago.
Look gently on your brother,
and behold the world
in which perception of your hate
has been transformed into a world of love.

CHAPTER 12

The Sermon
on the Mount

There haven't ever been any Christians in aggregate. Never! There never have been Christians in aggregate. Fundamentally because Jesus does not teach aggregations of Christians. Can you hear me? In the archives there's a final dissertation on the associations of the teachings of Jesus Christ of Nazareth and the assumption of the world of its necessity for the retention of its own establishment, which is obviously the antithesis of the teaching.

I brought the Bible today. Obviously I didn't bring anything else. I want you to be aware in this final challenge, if you're going to present this to the world, that you are presenting only the teachings of Jesus Christ of Nazareth. That will put you on the ground where you can be declared insane and foolish. You may be declared to be that, but you can steadfastly declare to the world, "This is my personal intention." Do you understand me? I'm giving you a solution to the problem that is going to arise, that is inherent in the teachings of unconditional love, of the Savior, Jesus of Nazareth.

I'm going to show you directly, and particularly through the *Course in Miracles*, that the teachings of Jesus Christ in His unconditional determination to declare the wholeness of His mind in relationship with you and God are totally uncompromising. I want you to see how there couldn't possibly be a correlation between the wrathful tribal God, invented by man to justify his historic references, and the teachings of Jesus Christ of Nazareth. There is absolutely, positively no connection between them, whatsoever, except in the admission of Jesus that you, as a tribe or as the world or as what you would call a civilization, are in the throes of the invention of the necessity to have a God. That is, all Jesus ever admits to is that that is your condition. Do you understand me? There's no Ten Commandments in Jesus' teachings at all. Are you aware of that? The Ten Commandments are the assumption of Jesus that that is the condition from which you are suffering. Nowhere does it say "you should not." It's not in there. It says, "That is your condition. This is your solution."

This is obviously going to be over very simply because you have accepted, I guess, somewhere, within your own personal association, the Sermon on the Mount. But just as obviously if you have accepted the fundamental teachings and practiced them in your affairs, you have and did undergo an experience of resurrection and are no longer here.

I don't know how else I can teach it to you except to declare to you that if you want to set this up so that someone tests your mettle in regard to your unconditional love, you say very simply: "This is either totally true... I am either whole and perfect as God created me and under no laws but His, or I am trapped in the incessant need of a wrathful God who is going to condemn me to associations of judgment within my own correlation of where I am." One or the other of those Gods is not true.

It's an astonishing thing if you were to look at it. And I know this reduces to: *you have heard it said, an eye for an eye, and I declare to you,* no, you are under no laws but God's. (Matthew 5:38) And just as obviously the dichotomy occurs at that moment because the teachings of Jesus of Nazareth, which are nothing but "God is perfect and so are you," are obviously not acceptable to the containment of a God invented to justify disassociation.

When you watch a Christian minister today stand up and actually begin to teach reciprocity, eye-for-an-eye, exchange, in association with Jesus' teaching, you can begin to understand the insanity of the conceptual mind. The teachings are exactly the opposite of the establishment. Not only is that true, but in the Sermon on the Mount, Jesus says they are exactly the opposite. No, you haven't read it. Incidentally, there aren't ten commandments; there's 1,673 commandments. Can you understand? Nobody reads the Old Testament. If you opened up to when Moses directs the attention of the tribe to the Ten Commandments, he is even directed by God to "Don't let them come too close to Me." Literally. It says: Don't let them come near me. Form a priesthood and proclaim the necessity of these teachings within your culture, so that you can establish in this place an identity – that through grace can be subsequently transformed or lasted but a moment – within the teaching that you are perfect as God created you.

But to attempt to determine within a relationship of the Ten Commandments, or the commandments given by man in association with man, to the teachings of Jesus of Nazareth is absurd. It's ludicrous. There is no connection. Now, you don't want to stand up and do this because you're very afraid of the establishment, because, very obviously, the teachings of Jesus are totally unacceptable to the establishment, except in the terms that it can establish to compromise the fundamental admission that Jesus teaches you are perfect as God created you. If you are perfect, whole, and loving as God created you, any commandments given by God in the method by which you observe your rituals of pain and death become ridiculous. That's just a fact of the matter.

Now, I don't know where you're going to be able to stand on this in established Christianity. I would suggest that you declare what Jesus teaches. Obviously, what occurs on the Mount, if your attention can be drawn to it, is that Jesus is teaching only personal transformation and only personal transformation of your mind. There is nothing in the Sermon on the Mount that directs your attention to anything, except your mind must give to be as God, and that if you continue to operate on the principles of scarcity or exchange, you will be entrapped in the necessity of space/time.

Now, I'll read a sentence from Sermon on the Mount that obviously is rejected by the world. I'm not concerned about the manner in which it is rejected. Any manner of rejection is a determination to live within the laws of reciprocity. Yet if the laws of reciprocity are true – if there is a God that demands vengeance, if there is a God that acknowledges your sin and separation – certainly there is no whole, loving God. That's all I have to say.

Now, it may be impractical and even impossible for you to declare to this world the certainty that is emerging in you through the teachings of Jesus of Nazareth. But remember that certainty comes from God, not from you. This is the whole teaching. Jesus says the certainty doesn't come from obeying the laws of man but from acknowledging the love of God. Say: Amen.

All you've really done is open your heart and mind to the possibility that the only admonition required, as directed by Jesus, is that you love the Lord thy God with all thy heart, and with all thy soul, and with all thy mind. And what? Thy neighbor as thyself. (Matthew 22:37) That's it. Well, accept it. "Yes, but... Yes, but..." No, not "Yes, but!!"

In the first place, the Ten Commandments themselves are a little redundant almost immediately. A commandment says: Don't walk more than ten steps from the temple. It's just nothing. It's immediately a direction to the manner in which you should display your capacity to stay separate in community. That's all it is. Do you mean that the teachings of Moses are teachings of exchange? Yes. Basically there's a reciprocity of get-even-ness that can adjudicate problems that humans have in their separation. That's the whole Old Testament, isn't it?

And if any mischief follow, then thou shalt give life for life, eye for an eye, tooth for a tooth, hand for a hand, foot for a foot, burning for burning, wound for wound, stripe for stripe. (Exodus 21:23-25) Now, because that's a necessity of comparison, it is impossible to stay out of judgment about what constitutes the fairness of the association. From then on, all of this is nothing but an apparent adjudication to what must be performed by you based on the wrong that has been given you. It has nothing to do with Jesus of Nazareth whatsoever. Do you understand me? And it goes on and on and on, including: Don't lay down with zebras. (Exodus 22:19) Really! And you have to make good. If you hit your servant and he loses his eye, you've got to give him freedom. It spells out in great detail how you can operate within that association. That's all this is, page after page after page. It looks at every possibility that can arise and arrives at a judgmental conclusion in regard to how you can be separate from God. But it's just astonishing, and I want you to try to read it.

And let's not miss anything: *And if he smite out his manservant's tooth or his maidenservant's tooth; he shall let him go free for his tooth's sake.* (Exodus 21:27) It never stops. I'm not going to do this. I just want you to see that the teachings of love and forgiveness have nothing at all to do with the laws of man; that the laws of God – forgiveness and love, that you're still in Heaven – have nothing at all to do with the laws that are established in your conceptual association of the things of separation that are about you, and that the solution, as dictated by the Savior Jesus, lies singularly in the transformation of your mind. For *as a man thinketh, he will be* in his relationships.

There's nowhere in the teachings of Jesus that say you are not suffering from a human condition. The teaching is an acknowledgment that you are suffering from a human condition, but that it is not true as created by the love of God.

Now, obviously, if I turn to the uncompromising teachings of Jesus in the Sermon, you must defend it by saying to me somewhere: He doesn't mean that. You would have to. As Christians in this establishment, you must be saying: He doesn't mean that, because in the directions He gives you, it will always be to only give and love. There are no dictates contained within Jesus that you should exchange or demand justice in any regard. None! It's not there, Christians! And if you want to stand up and be a Christian, stand up and read this.

Now, obviously, they're going to say to you: No one does that. You say: Of course not. They're going to say to you: Well, we're all practicing. And you say: Good, that's what I'm doing. But I'm going to begin by forgiving and enjoying the freedom of my mind. Now I'm teaching *A Course in Miracles*, my personal association with Jesus of Nazareth.

Ye have heard that it has been said, An eye for an eye, and a tooth for a tooth; but I say unto you, that you resist not evil; but whosoever shall smite thee on the right cheek, turn to him the other also. (Matthew 5:38-39) I'll give a talk on that sometime.

And if any man shall sue thee at the law, and take away thy coat; let him have thy cloak also. (Matthew 5:40) You'll say: "He doesn't mean that". I'll say: "Yes He does". You'll say: "Yeah, but if I did that, I wouldn't have any clothes". Yes. Let's see you do it. Do you understand? That's why you can't teach this. Does he mean in the action of the association of the necessity? That's not what he said about three paragraphs before. He says you have already denied God by the necessity for the thought of the exchange. If you lust in your heart, you will lust out there. (Matthew 5:28) That's in here. So he's directing you to how you are within your own mind condition. *Know ye not ye must be born again.* (John 3:7) But that does not alleviate the necessity of you for the practice of that, hypocrites. All you're saying to me is well, that may be true in principle, but I cannot practice it in the reality of this world. Well, then, stay in this world. But this will say that you are the cause of this world. It'll say it.

How unpractical is this? Let me see you stand up and read the Sermon on the Mount and demand that the association do it. You can't equivocate it because you must allow him somewhere to at least see what these teachings are. If you immediately, like many of you still do, begin to equivocate it, there's no hope for him because you have justified the possibility of exchange. If there is a God of love, there is no possibility that the laws of man have anything to do with eternal life in any way. They have only to do with the scarcity of the containment, demonstrated by the necessity for the commerce of limitation. That's just the fact of the matter.

A couple more: *If a man shall sue thee at the law, and take away thy coat* (and the law said, give it to him) *let him take away thy cloak also.* (Matthew 5:40) Wow. What an amazing idea! Nice! The association between coat and cloak is real nice. He says, let him have your cloak. Let him have the guise of the pretense of your own determination. He's already got your coat. Don't try to protect your own nakedness. The give in that association is contained within your own mind. But that's very nice. Give it to him. Let him have all of you. Then you'll be free because he is you.

And whosoever shall compel thee to go a mile, go with him twain. (Matthew 5:41) Always twice as much as he asks for, because your freedom is always twice as much as he asks for. Twain. If you only give him what he asks for, you are exchanging with him the other half of you. If you give him twice what he's asked for, you've given him yourself. Do you understand twain? I can do this. That's exactly what that says. If he asks for half of your Hershey bar, give him all of your Hershey bar. But we really don't mean that. Assuredly, when you give him all of it, he'll want to divide and give you half back. That's not what it says. Your responsibility is to give him all of your Hershey bar. Now, the problem you have, if you lust for the other half in your mind, you begin to exchange with him. And then you're trapped forever because you'll have to judge whether it's plain or has nuts. You still have to judge in what regard you're willing to give. It's just incredible. But there is no compromise in this teaching, whatsoever. That's your freedom!

That's not the problem. The problem, hypocrites, is that you somewhere believe you can adjudicate this in your own mind. And I'm just telling you that's impossible, because your own mind is all there is. And any dichotomy of the associations with unconditional love and the pain of this world will simply be an entrapment in your own mind in order to justify your separate, existent associations. But contained in that is the freedom of your declaration: I will obey the laws of God that teach me through Jesus that I am perfect as God created me. This is the practice of my *Course in Miracles*. And the associations will say: what does that have to do with me? It has nothing to do with you. I am told by Jesus, as my mind changes, I will undergo a transformation. I will be born again in the recognition of God. Obviously, that's going to be denied by the establishment. And Jesus is teaching directly now: Do not obey the laws of your forefathers. That's what it says. No wonder He's not going to be tolerated.

And whosoever shall compel thee to go a mile, go with him twain. Ye have heard that it hath been said, Thou shalt love thy neighbor, and hate thine enemy... (Matthew 5:41) This is precisely the teaching of the First Covenant. You can go back to Moses, and it'll say continually: love your God and hate the other guy's god. That's all it says. It just says it again and again and again. And now here we are, confronting you with your previous teachings of defense of your own self. Here's a guy standing up and saying, *you have heard it hath been said, Thou shalt love thy neighbor, and hate thine enemy, but I say unto you, Love your enemies, bless them that curse you, do good to them that hate you, and pray for them which despitefully use you, and persecute you; that ye may be the children of your Father which is in Heaven; for he maketh his sun to rise on the evil and on the good, and sendeth rain on the just and on the unjust.* (Matthew 5:43-45)

That's the whole statement of Christianity. And so when you go out to teach this, why don't you just pick that up and read it. At least you'll be on the ground where you can say "I am practicing this". This is what Jesus wants you to do. Any exchange in your mind will bind you to these laws of reciprocity, and they will be an attack on God.

Is that what this says? Of course it does. I don't understand why you don't go out and say: This is what this says. At least then you can present them, somewhere, with the need for unconditional love rather than for the justification of evil. But when I direct that to your mind, you refuse to do it. And the reason that you refuse to do it is that you place value on the exchange contained within your own mind. That would have to be true. Not because I say it's true but because it's true. If you are in a condition of justification for your conceptual self, that's the condition you will be in.

Christianity is nothing but the transformation and rebirth of your own mind.

You know what I'm interested in, I'm not at all certain that somewhere within time spans that I have lived, I would not like to have somebody tell me this. It would be impossible that you would tell me that with the assertion of the truth involved in your dedication to it without me having an experience through your uncompromising declaration of the reality of you and me in our association with God. That's called *A Course in Miracles*. How would I not, since it is true that you are the power of God creating eternally? But just as assuredly, as Jesus would say, how can it come about unless you put your action of mind where your mind in truth lies? Until you bring the two together, it's impossible you will have the experience.

This is in this talk I gave last Sunday. It is not that God is not perfect, and perfect in the entirety, but only the condition in which you find yourself in that regard. The very simple teachings are: You are under no laws but God's – this is Sermon on the Mount – simply do not participate in the formulations that are a part of the world. Now, need you do that in action? Action will follow the mind. This is the whole teaching of salvation through grace, which is the basic teaching of Jesus. Jesus says here, good works avail you nothing because works involve exchanges of your own mind. The grace of God is given you through the grace of God. It has nothing to do with your participation in the laws of man.

Amazingly enough, that's the teachings of a lot of established Christianity; but only to the point of the necessity for the retention of the establishment. Now I am here to tell you that the salvation of the world depends on you. Which is obviously what this says. How did the idea of unconditional love survive in the associations or societies of man's necessity to defend himself in civilization, establish time, and die? The idea of establishment of man with the necessity for a God is what unconditional love is, except as manifest in the limitations of man. Now we can teach that you are in a transition, coming from apparent earth or exchange to the certainty of truth. So this isn't anything new, is it? Except new as in regard to what Jesus said.

"I thought maybe you were teaching something different. You are daring to teach the teachings of Jesus. Well, that's not acceptable here."

That's right. How would it be? If it were acceptable, the world would disappear and you'd be gone.

"You mean, you need merely accept this as true? What about the action of it?"

Why are you asking me? Had you accepted it, you would no longer be here. If you require the practice, I suggest that you take the Workbook of the Course and begin to practice this. Because certainly, if you bind yourself to the laws of man, you will be bound to those laws. Is that what this says? How can you go into the world and teach the teachings of Jesus of Nazareth? You can't. Come on. I don't see you doing it. You haven't done it. You can't. No, you can't teach total love here. Sink down in your own minds if you want to. You are not allowed to teach unconditional love and giving in this place. Yes or no? You may insinuate it. You can suggest there's a possibility of choice, a choice between evil and good, but you are not allowed to teach there is no choice, which is all this says. This says, there is no choice, give everything away and come home. You're not allowed to teach that. I'm not giving you the answer; I'm giving you the problem. Remember the solution must be in you because you are the one suffering from the quandary of self-identity.

For if ye love them which love you, what reward have ye? (Matthew 5:46) None! Nothing but a special relationship in your determination to remain separate. That's what this says. You've got to love those that hate you. Why? You're hating yourself. I'm not going to do the teaching. There's nothing outside of you, right? God goes with you wherever you go. Wow, is this lovely. I love it.

If it's necessary for you, in this final transformation of your mind, to explain to the world what you are, explain it through the teachings of Jesus of Nazareth. That will give you within this continuum an accumulative determination brought about by the admission of God – what we call holy instants – as we taught on Sunday, so that you, perhaps, individually (I'm talking directly to you) would say "yes, I prefer God to this". That will then allow me to make the choice uncompromisingly through the uncompromising terms that are set from the certainty that if sickness and death are real, there is no eternal life. What an amazing idea!

Now, to be sure that you understand that, you might want to take Exodus and Leviticus. And you'll search in vain in the New Testament for Jesus having anything to do with it at all. It's just not there. It is not in there, is it? Nothing about it, except in parables or directions to the Pharisees that the laws are insane and have nothing to do with the teachings of God. That's in there a lot. How does He respond to the priest who says: one of the commandments is that you don't work on Sunday? (Matthew 12:2) Read the parable, dummy. I'm not going to do it for you. Does that include not taking your ox out of the mud? That's in the parable. Well, no, because in Leviticus it says, if your ox is in the mud, you can take him out. How about the other guy's ox? Well...

Do you understand what this says? It never stops. What a strange place this is. So the terms for justice are set by the establishment? What an amazing idea. Wow. Somebody becomes the scapegoat that is killed.

The Governor rather inappropriately declared this morning in California... What's his name, Governor in California? Pete Wilson. They murdered a guy this morning. They put him to death. He's was a serial killer. He killed ten people on the highway and did all these awful things and... Of course, standing outside were people saying, "Don't do it," and other people, saying, "Do it." And they had a description of one of the victim's relatives on television, describing his last minutes joyfully. This is a very strange place. "Well, he turned purple, and I got to see him die." I have nothing to say about that. You go, "Wow," but that's what you are. At what point do you justify the association. It had nothing to do with carrying the signs. But Pete Wilson, to justify it, says, quite literally, that "this guy is a poster child for capital punishment," that he is a perfect symbol of the necessity of the justification – that's his sentence – for capital punishment. He, individually, demonstrates the necessity of society to protect itself from itself. An amazing idea!

Can you actually escape your dream? Why are you asking me? It's your dream. Now we're teaching sanctification within your own association. What I offered you was a justification for your being here at all – that would be to teach the love of your brother. Is it true? No. It's not true. You cannot forgive what is not real. I don't know where you are with this, but certainly you'd have to declare to the individual the necessity that he undergo the experience of his own transformation, wouldn't you?

I've given you the answer to: Who are you? You're Christians teaching the Sermon on the Mount. You say: What do you mean by that? I mean what it says. You say, well, *all* of the Bible is true. Well, you'll have to look at Jesus' teachings to determine that. If you want to believe "an eye for an eye," you will. And if you want to believe "give and love," you will. But one or the other is not true.

You ask: "Won't I suffer from the act of giving my stuff away?" You're the Christians. How do you respond to that? Yes, you'll suffer?!? Good, now you're into good persecution. How do you respond? I want to hear your response, Christians. The fact is, it says, if a guy asks for your coat, give it away. And if the guy says to you, yeah, but I'll be cold in winter. What's your response? "Yes, you will be"? Somebody said, "Just do it."

I'm just letting you kick this around in your mind. I thought God only gives. It doesn't involve reciprocity, including the reciprocity of giving your coat and being cold in the winter, which is nothing but a form of the denial of the necessity to give your coat, or being possessed by your own mind. You guys are immediately trapped in that. They're going to trap you perceptually within their own mind game. Actually, if they gave their cloak along with their coat, they wouldn't be here at all. That's exactly what you should think. How could you possibly worry about the winter? If you gave your coat and your cloak to your brother, you wouldn't be here. That's the teaching, in case you didn't get it.

If you think there's anything practical in the teachings of unconditional love, you are sadly mistaken. There's absolutely nothing practical about it at all. How could there be practicality to giving everything away and going to God? You can stand up and say: "That's my practice of miracles. I'm experiencing the joy of giving without the necessity to hold on to my exchange. It has nothing at all to do with how they define this, nothing".

I'm offering you the fact of the matter, and obviously, I'm teaching from this word. Why? This would be the only word you could teach. If separation is real, then God is separate and pain is real. Can you teach: "Truth is true and nothing else is true?" Of course not. The necessity to teach it *is* the denial of it. What's the solution? There isn't any. Except in your own mind's association with yourself. I'm right back to teaching Christianity.

Here's the next question that would arise. "Oh, I see you're feeling happy. How did you do that?" Obviously, "How did you do it" implies that you practiced a method of giving in order to receive a benefit of the association. That's exactly the opposite of what you're doing. I thought you were teaching *A Course in Miracles*, that the practice has nothing to do with the occurrence. That's a fact of the teaching. *"Know ye not ye must be born again?"*

We're on some sort of foundation where we will be totally unacceptable to the world. So you must teach to the totality of the nonacceptance of the world of unconditional love. Or that the association is perfect as God created it. But at least the confrontation then perhaps could occur with the single association rather than the aggregate of denial. They will force you into aggregation and they will determine that you have arrived at that in conclusions of comparison. "They" in the sense of the phantom figures that apparently inhabit this association. I moved that up a step.

"Am I to understand that there is no compromise in your teachings of Jesus at all?" Are you teaching: *Judge not lest ye be judged?* (Matthew 7:1) Are you teaching that you'll get the result of your own mind? I wanted to be sure you were throwing that in, that your neighbor is you, and you are doing this to yourself?

The world knows nothing of God or there wouldn't be a world. Are you letting me teach, the world knows not of God? Are you going to let me get away with that, that all perception has nothing to do with God at all? Good. Thank you.

The level is approaching and is coming about where you will have no need to defend your position at all. Some of you still have a tendency to defend the position that you have arrived at through the transformation of your own mind. It's impossible that you do that, in reality. What it may be subtly for you is the admission of the necessity to undergo the experience, and that's actually not true. The experience was always immediately available to you through the surrender of your will. It had nothing to do with the manner in which it happened. That's a fact.

Don't participate in your own salvation because your participation is an attack on God. That's Sermon on the Mount. I don't know whether you heard that or not. That's exactly what it says. Go ahead and deny it. And participate in it and get the results of your own participation. But certainly it's not going to exceed the demand of your own attention to your own participation, even presuming you don't know who you are and what the hell you're doing here. I just wanted to be sure it's clear in your mind.

Jesus asks as a favor, "since you are obviously undergoing the transformation of your mind, would you mind reminding them of what I have said". Because the only conclusion you could possibly have reached in your own revelation is precisely and exactly what He teaches. That's just a fact of matter. All the pain and suffering that you thought was necessary for you to get this is not true. Why don't you try to teach that? This is *Course in Miracles*. No wonder you're not accepting it.

If you need do anything, give everything away and come on home. Did you try it, and it didn't work? How do you know it didn't work. You say "Well, I didn't get anything back." This says you won't get anything back – except the love of God, which is not here. And anything that you get back would be a denial of God. Then you say "No, no, Jesus says, if I practice it in private, I'll be rewarded in the open." Really? How's it going? You say: "Well, I'm practicing, but I'm not getting as much reward as I thought I would." You're getting as much reward as you're willing to accept. But your reward will be the death of you, and you're not willing to accept that. Your reward, in truth, would be the recognition that you're perfect as God created you! To you the reward of giving totally is death. To us it's the discovery of life, since we have simply given death away. If you possess anything, it will be a form of death.

The Sermon on the Mount contains, obviously, the possibility of resurrection immediately, from the Mount. Actually, the resurrections have been espoused from the miracles that were manifest in the two-year provocation of Jesus. I mean, there's a lot that's just skipped over. There were a lot of phenomena that was taken out very simply because there's no one who was willing to accept it. I mean, the minimum thing was the raising of a dead body, but there was a lot more going on. And it's going on because of you now, but I don't how the hell I can teach it that way. It's all going on all the time, anyway. No time has really passed. I don't know where you're hearing this. I'm just giving you the fact of the matter.

Nothing stops you from reenacting any scene that you want within your own mind in the entire association. But remember there's no such thing as a reenactment. If you stood up to give the Sermon on the Mount, you would be only getting the result of what you are in your own association. And that might include you having to go and get hung on the cross. I can't answer that for you. You understand? Because you are in a practice of teaching the possibility of comparison, or separation, and God. But remember that experience is only going on in your own mind. This is lovely in the Course. There's no need for you to suffer. How do you avoid your ultimate sacrifice, saviors of the world? I'm curious. How do you avoid the ultimate sacrifice of yourself in the teachings that you are the savior of the world? Don't avoid it! Just don't try to measure the distance between your sacrifice and your love. Can you hear that? After all, I'm the ultimate sacrificer. You say to me: "Well, I'm sacrificing joyfully". Don't compare your sacrifice to some other kind of joy. Joy is not the kind of association. Joy is joy. If you take joy in sacrificing separate from what you think is not sacrifice, there's nothing I can do about it. Joy is nothing but an indication of the totality of dedication, but if your dedication is to death, you will enjoy dying. Go ahead. Get whatever benefit you can from the apparent lack or sacrifice. This is Sermon on the Mount, guys. But if you gave everything away, you wouldn't be able to die. Then what would you do? There would be no justification for you to exist in the association at all.

Okay, here's the answer: You can love God totally, but you can't love death totally, because if you love death totally, you will become as total as God is. You only love death partially, as a comparison with what you term to be life. Any totality is what God is. "I am totally dead." Good! I'm teaching you dead moments.

Actually, your release is in each moment of ultimate, irresolvable conflict. Don't avoid the conflict. Look at it and suffer the totality of the conflict. It will immediately be removed from you. That's the teaching. That's an amazing idea. It immediately becomes intolerable to you. So you lose your tolerance, or your denial of God, and you become whole. It's not a moment of peace; it's a moment of ultimate conflict against peace simultaneously. It's an action of your mind. It's the moment of ultimate chaos that occurs in the entire give. We might even call that surrender. The problem is not resolvable. Is that a moment of grace? Absolutely. That's the whole teaching.

Why are you so happy that the problem is not solvable? Because you're happy in the discovery of the Sermon on the Mount. Jesus says the problem is not solvable. Stop trying to solve it within the association. You are already perfect as God created you. In the Course, He says the manner in which you attempt to solve the problem is ridiculous. You don't even know what the problem is. But please don't try to teach me First Covenant and say: "Your problem is you went twelve steps from the temple instead of eight and a half." That's not what your problem is. The problem is not continuing to discover the benefits of your need to get sick and die.

If you need to teach this, don't justify the teaching. Read the teaching and shut up. This is the whole *Course in Miracles*. Present it and be quiet. Don't immediately begin to justify it. It's either going to be totally true or it won't be true at all. Don't be like me. I keep trying to justify. Greater things will you do than I, because you no longer require justification. The examination of yourself in your relationships for many of you is actually simultaneous. You're experiencing, through a continuing chaos, the reality of God. You no longer attempt to hold yourself in the justification of what you call dark form at all. You simply release it. That's okay. This whole association was over a long time ago. I'm just here to remind you in your mind of that. It has nothing at all to do with what you think I am.

Look at this world. As you come more and more to unconditional love, the condition of this world, Jesus says, will appall you. I watched television this morning and this woman describing, after fourteen years, this guy turning blue and dying, with a big smile on her face, you'll understand. That's fine. But it's got nothing to do with me. The last words of the guy were: "You're all murderers, just like I am." That was the justification for his murdering. But that did not mean that it was not true.

Does everybody get what they deserve? Sure. Really? Whatever you think you deserve, you're going to get. You act as though that's the first time you ever heard this. You're going to get exactly what you really deserve. The problem you have is that it's not more or less. You keep trying to determine in your own mind a justification for what your exchange is. That's what's binding you to this place. This is Sermon on the Mount. That's what it says.

Can you sow something and not reap it? Somebody said yes. Explain that to me. How is it possible to sow something and not reap it? It's impossible. Are you saying that if you sow it, you've already reaped it? That's Sermon on the Mount., quite literally. You'll get the exchange that's in it. If you sow love, will you reap love? Are you actually explaining to me that cause and effect are not apart? Obviously, in time, what you sow, you will reap. You'll get the result of your own mind associations. But it's impossible that the result has not already occurred. Otherwise, why would you be seeking a result? And if the result of your reaping is death, you will get the wages of death. The wages of sin are death. Do you understand? This is Sermon on the Mount. You have one problem. You believe you are separate, separated from God. You have established laws to justify the separation. All of your problem is only separation. None other than that. Now the solution is here. Because it's reasonably impossible to be separate. You are the problem. *Therefore be ye perfect as your Father in Heaven is perfect.*

The justification for your continuation here is not really explainable. Any attempt to explain or justify why you're still here is literally impossible to do, except in the totality of your individual mind, which then requires no justification. I'm doing the Sermon on the Mount. Stop justifying. Including the teaching? Yes.

Don't swear to anything! (Matthew 5:34) I'm actually teaching the Sermon. If you swear to anything, including your own saviorship, you'll get the result. You are either the savior of the world or you're nothing. There's no requirement that you swear to do this. "Swear not to die, you holy Son of God" does not mean you should swear not to die. It's just the opposite of that. It means that you have sworn to die and it won't work. Did you hear that? You ask "Well, what's wrong if I stand up and swear not to die?" Nothing. The question is not that. The question is who are you swearing to? You don't have to swear to God not to die. He already knows you're eternal.

Everyone that you see justifies your continued relationship with the separation in your own dream of death. There's a lot of appreciation in the concepts of Christianity over the emergence of your whole minds in the memory factoring of the admission of the totality of the wrath that you perpetrated within your own mind in order to protect yourself from God. And in its highest association it's called forgiveness, because you obviously take on the burden of the entire wrath of two thousand years of the crucifixion of Jesus Christ. This is precisely what you have done. With the admission that you've been crucifying Him up until the moment that you reveal yourself. That's all *Course in Miracles*. Can you imagine associations denying the historic reference of Jesus in *A Course in Miracles*? A sick mind. But you do it.

Okay, so if you need a little practice in – this is Sermon – in not letting your right hand know what your left hand is doing, then practice it. (Matthew 6:3) Because obviously you're going to be out in the world doing this. But just as obviously, if you're practicing the fundamental principles of contact with God, you can separate that out and continue in the activity of your own union with God and just perform out here to whatever cursory examples are apparently necessary for your own existence. I assure you, all the provisions necessary for that will be given you. Because you're not setting the terms by which the body, in its physical association, can justify itself. The terms, instead, are being dictated to you somewhere in the totality of your own mind. And it's impossible that you would fail at it because the failure was only your direction of the exchange retained within the apparent multiplicity of cause and effect. It's very difficult to express that because it's an ongoing process. This is *A Course in Miracles.*

Obviously... I'm doing Sermon. Obviously, if your eye offends you, you would have to pluck it out somewhere. (Matthew 5:29) Because it's a dichotomy of your determination to be here and in Heaven. That's not possible. You are taking offense to the teachings of love. Now, you should expunge that from your own mind. That can come about through a dedication of your determination to practice the principles. They're not being denied you, but you are being taught that in the practice must be the uncompromising assertion that – together: "I am not a body, I am free for I am still as god created me." That's exactly what the Sermon on the Mount says.

You ask "why can't I go out and teach it?" Because you're telling the guy he's not a body and he's free. You're declaring to him that he's not of this world. Why wouldn't he resent and kill and attack you? You are a threat to his entire system of existence. Sermon on the Mount. Isn't that amazing?

Why does He throw in: *Blessed are those who are persecuted in my name?* (Matthew 5:11) Because He was undergoing His own persecution. Well, come on. Do you think I'm not going to tell you that? I may end up telling you: I know this is tough, but come on and do it with me. You'll immediately justify how tough it is, and that's not what I said. I softened the solution momentarily or you wouldn't accept it at all, because you now believe I have somewhere offered you a solution within your own mind. How do you want it to be in your own mind? There's no answer to this problem. Fortunately the problem is not real. You need really not be concerned about anything. *Consider the lilies of the field.* (Matthew 6:28)

The point has fast approached for you individually in the necessity of your own maturity to teach what you have become. Hopefully, if you'll accept the fundamental idea that it's only transformation of the mind, it will be broad enough in your own mind to teach it anywhere that you are, because certainly the offering is very fundamental. Jesus says you are the savior of the world: *You will do greater things than I did.* (John 14:12) He says that. Are you the savior of the world? Yes.

What does that mean? Is that true? Is it true that you're the savior of the world? I'm looking at it for you. Can you hear this? You mean the savior of the world is fake? I thought *I* was the savior of the world. Does this have to be expressed in the necessity for saviorship? How else are you going to express it? You obviously believe you're separate. I'm not belittling the necessity for forgiveness, for goodness' sake. But certainly in the progression of the necessity to forgive, you come to know you're only forgiving your own projections.

Is it possible to enjoy the labors of the awakening of your brother without participating in the pain that he is experiencing? Yes. Not only that, but it's a form of admission of his necessity to undergo it. And the compassion of love involved in that is the admission of a sharing of an ordeal which has been accomplished or is being accomplished in your mutual associations with each other. Do you understand that? Total frailty is what God is. *Blessed are the meek.* I appreciate your unsuccessful attempts at frailty. I'm doing the Beatitudes.

Surrender is an experience, not a definition. The minimum requirement is "Fake it till you make it." There's no possibility you can do it until you "fake it till you make it." You don't have to believe it, but you have to participate in the association. It would be impossible because your participation is required because you're the cause of the situation. That's the whole *Course in Miracles*. You can't escape from yourself.

If I open up the Course, it says your ego is nothing. It doesn't exist. How can the Holy Spirit be directing your ego? An amazing idea. I'd hate to have that battle. "Let your conscience be your guide." My ego tells me that I must do this. Who does he tell? He certainly is not telling the only living Son of God. The only living Son of God couldn't possibly hear his ego. All perception is nothing talking to nothing?

Then you ask "Well, somewhere I have to justify this, don't I, in my associations, to teach it?" I'm not going to. Since you've learned it, I don't have to stay here anymore. You go ahead and justify it. Now what are you going to do? Well, you say "Well, I've learned it, too." Well, then you don't have to stay here, either. Well, if that's true, where you're going, I can go. Not only can you go there, you already did. You say "Yeah, but you told me where you were going, I couldn't go". When did I tell you that? Right here. (John 13:33) Yeah, and now I'm telling you, you can. Then you say, "Well, why didn't you tell me two thousand years ago?" So you want to get even with me? Do not underestimate the vengeance of the ego. Incredible. You mean, you didn't get the Word? Say no. I'm sorry. You missed it. Here it is.

Why would you base your reality on having missed it? It doesn't make any sense. If you missed it, you missed it. Well, why carry the resentment of having missed it? That doesn't make any sense. Isn't that funny? It's not funny, but it's true. Do you have a right to be grievous? You think I'm taking away your right to grieve. I'm not. Go ahead, get pissed. Do whatever you want. Can you hear me? If you're only doing it to yourself... You keep trying to practice: don't grieve. I never told you that. I told you you're going to get the result of the mistake. It is only a mistake. You're the one that's built it into an intent to kill God and deny Him and attack everything there is. What a strange thing to do. All because of a little mistake. The question is, very simply, will you forgive me?

There's not that many of us, and it's not that big a deal. It's just an aggregation of images that have been fostered in space/time. So there is a final council or final judgment that occurs. Can you get a disagreement in the final judgment council? If there's twelve of us who know the entirety of the answer, can there be disagreement within the twelve? If you say so. What would it be about? T-I-M-E. It will always only be about time, as an aggregation of associations of space. Where will the efficacy be diminished by the continuing confrontation? If there's one thing the continuum does not want, it's enlightenment. The encouragement that it be reborn is a form of confrontation of the light into the darkness. This is a statement of fact. Can you get this?

In that sense, salvation is also a mistake. Bless me, I wish I could teach this. The whole idea is a mistake. The resolution of the problem will also be a mistake if there can be an observation of the resolution. There is no real problem. Now, if many of your associations will talk to me from a level of our certainties of the entirety of the illusion, we couldn't possibly have a problem because we are certain this world is not real. And if we're certain this world is not real, we must also be certain that the methods that we are employing are also not real – except in each moment, when the release of the method is fostered through the forgiveness of the problem.

Now, if you don't degrade the idea that the savior is illusionary, that would be a very final advanced association of yourself. Some of you in perception will like the idea that saviorship is illusionary so you can pretend to justify your continuing association without accepting the simple reality that saviorship is real. Obviously, if you know that saviorship is an illusion, you're not here at all. If you want me to read that to you in the Course, I'll be glad to read it to you. I assure you that I am not here at all. You don't like that idea. So I have to assume a guise of a comparison with you in your own mind so you can determine that you're not here at all either. The reason that you are not here at all is very literally because there is no such place as here. It isn't that your body is not real, it is that your body is not real because the place it's in is not real.

Then you ask, "Is my body real?" Just for the moment when you inquired. "Will the place that my body is in disappear when my body disappears?" You brought the place with you when you came. Then you say, "Well, you're telling me that all I have to do is accept this Atonement for myself, and the world will disappear and I'll be gone." No, that's not what I'm telling you at all. No. I'm telling you, you have to stay here and be the savior because you made an agreement to do it. What? Are you guys really hearing? I'm teaching you at the highest level. "Well, but you told me I only had to accept Atonement for myself and that the world would disappear and be gone." And I said: Yes, and it did and you did. Why are you inquiring whether that's all you have to do? Are you here or not? If you're here, you must be here for the reason that you're here for. What is that reason? I have no idea. It could be any reason that you would formulate. Jesus calls it a function. It's your own function. You're here to save the world.

You must have a memory of this occurrence within your own association. But certainly it should be a memory of returning to God, not of the chaos. Because a memory of the chaos would be totally meaningless since the separation is not real. A memory of the separation can only set terms for its unreality. Was it instantaneous? The return from separation was instantaneous. Who says so? All determination is in time, isn't it. All result is in time. There's no such thing as result?

So, do you still require a result to the actions you have taken as savior? I'm giving you one right here if you want it. Yeah, fine. Go ahead. But the world is not going to be real in spite of you're doing that. Most of you sitting here can see it's very small.

Can you experience your brother's resurrection? You are, aren't you? That's what you're doing here. Well, what if I just resurrect in front of you and disappear altogether? You are doing that. You say, "Well, I'm not doing that. I'm still here, being me." No, you're not. You're not hearing me. You're not here, doing this. You are in a continual condition of resurrection. These are just images of your own mind. As you see them resurrect, they will be a part of your whole mind. I assure you, what I am demonstrating is my resurrection without your necessity to justify it in your own association. That's just a fact of the matter. Any justification of the resurrection would be the denial of it. All right. So instead of saying, "How's he doing that?" you say, "That's for me". And when you do that, that will be for you, because it has nothing at all to do with how I'm doing it. None! The miracle has nothing to do with how it's done. It is not done. It is an undoing of your own identity.

So I want you all to read here Exodus or even Leviticus, and I want you to take the Sermon on the Mount – take a look at what you want. Put one on one page and one on another and ask me how the hell you can compare them, if this one says, "*Don't* do that," and this one says, "*Do* that." Where is there a comparison? If you can find it, I want you to call me and present it to me. And that includes two thousand years of translation. It's not there. It will not be there. Isn't that amazing?

Do you believe that the teaching in Sermon on the Mount is true? Do you believe that you are perfect and whole as God created you? Then you'll never die. What does that have to do with abortion? I don't get what that has to do with the world. "If you believe me, you will never die." Yes or no? Well, why don't you tell the Christian community that? And then shut up. Will they attack you? Yes, but somewhere along the line it has got to be obvious to people that the establishment has nothing at all to do with God, because that's what this says. Why does it say that? Because it's true. There is no such thing as separation from totality. What do you want me to do about that? There's nothing I can do with the fact that the universe is single and whole and eternal. Asking me to do something about it is insane. Did I offer you the solution in your own mind? If I didn't, I will.

Once more. This is how you'll do this. I want you to live in this association, okay, and I will apologize to you for the mistake. I will then tell you that you are hallucinating in a dream of your own making and that it is not real. If you want to open that up and go out into the world and read that, why don't you? You say, "Well, we have to compromise it somewhere." Why? Jesus didn't. That's how He resurrected. Are you hallucinating? Is the saviorship a part of your hallucination? What a happy solution to the hallucination.

Try not to justify the condition of saviorship. You'll just get locked into the idea. Is it true? You bet. Well, what does that have to do with reality, if there is no truth here? Let the world discover you on any terms that it wants. Only teach love and forgiveness and demonstrate healing, and let the rest go. Then you can let the limited associations of the Course groups go, just let them go. We're looking for the world here. Okay? Let's do it that way. There are a lot of sick people out there that you can heal through the simple admission of the power of your mind to heal. This is a simple whole statement of fact. Obviously, you're going to be attacked and denied for it. Your willingness to do it is my willingness to accept responsibility for it. If you'll do it, I'll accept responsibility for it. The question is, will you subsequently crucify me when the efforts fail because you had no faith? Did you hear that? Of course, you're going to fail. Isn't that amazing?

Don't be concerned about the unacceptability of your message. Everything in the universe knows what it is. The only thing that doesn't is this moment in time. Don't make such a big deal about it. You're teaching it as a transition, aren't you? From time to eternity. That's happening in your mind? Is that why you're at Endeavor Academy? You're having the experience of transformation? You're being born again?

If there's any confrontation to that, you let it be personal in your own mind. That is not to say you do not practice, as Jesus says, being more giving than the Christians or the Pharisees. Is it okay? There are a lot of real, real bright associations going on here. Somewhere, is it okay just to fold your tents and disappear?

The power of my mind to convert is extremely intense and is very high and is very chaotic and is very painful and very disorganized. Look at it. You're expressing that as joy and happiness. The world cannot see it as joy and happiness. They see it somewhere as either joy and happiness beyond anything they can conceive, or it will be reduced and you'll be attacked and killed immediately for daring to even present it to the association. I'm going to say this to you just once. Many of the aspects of this association will see you as evil. Doggone it! The more Christlike you become, the more evil you will be, if what he fears is his own Atonement. It will be described to him as evil. Want me to read that to you, I will, but I'm giving you the fact of the matter. You are the anti-Christ to him, just as he is the anti-Christ to you. There's no alternative to this, because you are teaching the wholeness of his mind. He is teaching the separation of his and justifying it in his own chaotic identity.

Now, that's not true because I say it's true. It's true because the condition of separation is what the conflict is. Is that the Devil? Yes.

You are serving the Devil, which is nothing but your own association with yourself. But there's no Devil without you. There is a God without you. That's a fact. You may not like that, but that's a fact. Did you hear that? The Devil depends on your recognition of pain and death to be what he is. God certainly does not depend on your recognition of pain and death to be God.

Now, you say to me, "Well, doesn't God depend on me to be godly?" On who? Certainly He depends on the only living Son of God. Is that what you are? Well, then why are you associating with pain and death? I've got you now. At least I got you to look at the insanity of your own mind in regard to finding yourself both here and here. Now, if your solution is to find yourself totally here and reject – not totally, but through the gratification of yourself – and reject other things, there's nothing I can do about that. All I am telling you is that there's no in-between. You can't see two worlds. Is that so?

Next you'll ask, "Well, is it possible for me to go back and forth, because sometimes I see the whole world of brightness, and sometimes I don't?" Who doesn't? I'm going to give you that if you want it. Why would you continue to examine your own holy instants? Why don't you just get into the Holy Instant and be?

"I wouldn't dare do that." Why? "I would be abandoning the world." Give it a try. "Well, I tried to abandon it, and it didn't work." Do you teach, "If at first you don't succeed, try, try again"? Or do you teach, "If at first you don't succeed, give up"? The answer to that is yes. That's Sermon on the Mount. Do you teach, "Let go and let God?" That God is willing if you are? Is it okay to try to give God a hand? What do you want to give him a hand doing? Giving Him a hand is an acknowledgment of the separation. Jesus says don't help Him. He says all of your help is a denial of what He is. This is the whole teaching.

What amazes me is how a human conceptual condition will be here and admit to that and continue to analyze it in their own mind. As though, "Yes, we've acknowledged that," and then they can go out and be evil and rant and rave about things and somehow keep themselves separate. I tell you, that's impossible. Isn't it true that somewhere you don't want to cause your brother pain? You're aware that it comes back to you? You can't teach that. Half of the people in this room don't even understand that. They don't understand how very basic this is. They really believe they can cause someone else pain, make demands of someone else, and not experience it themselves. It's impossible. I don't know how you can do it. I can tell you it's not true. I'm giving you the fact of the matter. I'm not offering you a solution to this establishment. If you insist on establishment, you will suffer the dichotomy of it. There is no answer to it except in your own mind. Do you understand this?

If talk is time and walk is space, you've got to do them both. Walk and talk. Talk is time and walk is space. You have to walk the way you talk. You cannot *not* do it. Otherwise, you're just split in your own mind. You resolve it in your own mind and present the falsity of yourself out here. And if they do that, in the mask or pretense of the protection of yourself, all I can tell you is you're not fooling anybody. What you are in your own mind, you're going to be. That may cause you some discontent, even some pain, and even some anguish. Be happy, Jesus says, at least you're in your own association. At least you have taken on the idea of solving the problem. Until you do that, there's no hope for you. And in the most chaotic episodes will be the most rapid solution. I just came around that. Is that true? Wow. What an amazing idea. Blessed are the meek.

You say, "Well, the whole world is caving in on me, and you're telling me not to defend myself." I don't have anything to do with it. I told you there's a God Who is perfect love. It has nothing to do with whether you're defending yourself or not. If there is a whole loving God, which there is, what about your condition?

I might avoid it for three hundred years, and then I would like the fundamental idea that somewhere it's true that I am the cause of this. And then I could screw it up, attack, and die to prove I'm right about it. And I would admit that I'm getting the result of my own mind – until I got tired of my own result. Then I would look for another solution. I'm offering you no relief from this at all. This is the conflict of your own conceptual self. If you don't want it, you don't have to have it. If you don't want to exist separate from God, you don't have to. If you want to, you will.

You say to me, "Oh, but you told me that this was all an illusion". When did I tell you that? "You told me this world isn't real." The hell I did. I told you, you're suffering from pain and death and I can save you. "Well, isn't this all just an illusion?" Maybe for you. For me it's an assumption of saviorship. "Well, how do you do it?" I don't know. I got the job. Isn't that amazing?

Is inclusiveness chaotic? Only to the point of its totality. It couldn't possibly be chaotic in the total conclusion of it. So the chaos occurs in the rejection of the inclusiveness.

Is the admission that you have sinned valuable in the Atonement idea? "Father, please forgive me for being so sinful. I have done these things in contradiction to Your commandments." An amazing idea. And then God says, "Well, I forgive you." Well, God doesn't, but He's got a priest that represents Him, called Moses. Well, no, I just thought you might like to look at this. I mean God has already got an intermediary there that's going to set the terms for you, rather than your direct association. How many times would God have to forgive your separation? I thought God didn't know anything about it. Are you going to have to forgive yourself for your own sins? How can you forgive yourself for your own sins? I thought if sin was real, it's unforgivable. It's incredible. You don't want to look at it. The solution, obviously, is that God doesn't know anything about sin. Is that so?

God, eternal life, doesn't know anything about pain and loneliness and death? Nothing. Who is it, then, that knows about it? Who knows about it? Nothing. When you are fearful, you are nonexistent. You say," Well, I know about it, and I'm something." What are you? "I don't know, but I'm something." You mean you're something, but you don't know who you are? Into this insane situation come the teachers of God.

You might say, "Not knowing who I am certainly qualifies me to try to find out because I have the qualifications of not knowing who I am. The more qualifications I have for not knowing who I am, the more secure I will be in my own death association."

It's incredible when you look at it. Are you telling me I don't have to know who I am? That reality does not depend on my establishment? Really? Well, then what value do I have in my existence? Why should I combat evil? Why should I demand reciprocity? Why should I insist that somebody give me his coat, if none of it is going to justify me anyway? Now I've affronted you.

Nothing in this world is worth valuing even for an instant? Sermon on the Mount. *Therefore be ye perfect, even as your Father in Heaven is perfect.* Stop valuing the valueless. Is that one of your lessons? Say to me, "I will not value the valueless. There's nothing in this world worth valuing at all?" No.

Or will you say, "Well, if I don't know who I am, I don't have to be responsible for it. That way you can avoid the responsibility for the pain and death of your brother by disassociating from it and pretending that you're not the cause of the evil, which is exactly what you do. "I'm not responsible... Am I my brother's keeper?" "Cain, what happened to Abel?" "Am I my brother's keeper?" God didn't even answer that. It never occurred to Him that Abel was not Cain's keeper. He didn't know anything about it.

Thank you, dear ones. These are the two things that we just taught: As a man thinketh – the Sermon on the Mount. "I am responsible for what I see." Is that true? "I choose the feelings I experience." Based on what? Based on the forms that I see. "I feel like feeling lonely." Just don't define it, and you'll be very happy in your loneliness. It's the definition of your loneliness that is causing you the grief. There's nothing more joyous than being lonely because it's a longing for the certainty of what you are. And the relief that comes from that in meditation can be very extensive. Isn't that so?

Is it possible to define an emotion? You only have two emotions. One is love and the other is fear. Any definition of love is what fear is. Because love cannot be defined. In fact, any definition is fearful because it includes the rejection of something in your own mind. It's an amazing idea. How do you stand it? "Well, it's tough. It's very difficult for me." But you're so over-learned in it, you put so many layers of justification onto it, it's very difficult to get through to the real you. You set up so many devices in your own mind to protect you in the authenticity of your illusion. It's not true. Can you read this in the *Course in Miracles*? Do you actually read that to the association, that he is a protection of his own separation? Oh, yeah. What does he actually protect? Nothing. Well, if he didn't protect it, then his nothingness would be revealed. Yes. But since it's nothing, he would not have to be concerned about it. He would then immediately remember that he's whole as God created him. That's the whole idea. What you protect does not exist. If that's true, this is not what life is. "What is this?" It seems like life, doesn't it? I participate in it. I identify myself in it. I certainly get old and sick and die. What about it? It's not what life is. "Well, what is life?" Not this.

"Well, explain more to me what life is." Life is eternal, eternally creating happiness and joy forever. "That's easy for you to say." Yes. Why wouldn't it be? It's true. What's easier to say than "God is perfect love and happiness?" Look at the ease with which I said it. Sounds like "Go and sin no more."

Those of you who haven't really read "eye for an eye" will be astonished at the establishment's ability, false ability to connect the teachings of

Jesus to the First Covenant. There's no connection at all, none; except the admission of the condition. But the admission of the condition is an immediate confrontation of the teaching of Jesus. Now, the admission of the condition by Jesus is the justification for the establishment to deny His teachings. Because, after all, didn't he admit it? Now, you're into all sorts of Gnostic junk and it's just incredible.

The identification of Jesus described in the Teacher's Manual will hold up very well. Do you understand me? If somebody wants to know what you teach, hand him that and say this is what you believe Jesus is. Now, they may attack that in some manner. Stand on what that says – and His resurrection message. Those two things can be stood on.

We're building a whole new Sermon on the Mount. There's a new version of it coming out. It cuts out the whole association in between. It's an amazing thing. Jesus says, "Therefore be ye perfect," and eleven other guys stand up and say, "I am with you," and they stand up and they disappear in light. And it's described as part of the mythology of your own transformation. It's all going on all the time.

So you're going to get to go to the stars and beyond. Opening up in your mind is a whole new universe that you can explore and be free in. You're not bound by these concepts that you have held about this place. This has been a womb or a cave or a vault of death from which you are emerging. Whether you want to stay in this vault of death is entirely up to you. But enough light should have come into this association where you are beginning to look about you and have reassociations of the memories of your own mind.

This is the awakening of your own mind. You have been confined to this little place, haven't you? Okay. And you're waking up? Is that in your mind, that that's happening? Is your head going to open up and you're going to go? Sure. Anything you would like. I just want you to see how little this place is. If you could see that the toils and journeys and works of men are so small by the frequency of their definitions of themselves, you'd begin to what? Laugh at the idea of the human condition. You remember this: A slave to death is a willing slave. You're offering him a range which he is refusing and protecting in his own sleep. Don't be concerned about that. There are awakenings going on all around you. You're waking up, aren't you?

What does it have to do with your womb memories? Nothing. It has nothing to do with them. They're just phantom figures from your own dream which you brought with you to dream in this own vault of death. Is that really happening to you? What else are you going to do? I want you to look at where you are with this. What are you going to do about this? This should absolutely begin to get overwhelming to you. Hopefully, you've lost control of it. Somewhere, you're just not able to contain yourself any longer in order to define your own death. You're just going to let go and let God have His will with you. You fought a good battle, but you lost. You cannot know that God is not participating in the battle until you give up. The moment that you give up – I'm doing Sermon on the Mount – you will see immediately that it was only yourself, attacking and defending. Incredible. But if you think it is God, give up. "Yeah, but God will attack me and kill me." Let Him! This is Moses. If He's doing it, He must have a good reason. Even though you don't know what the reason is.

Is God really finally forgivable? Did God cause this? God causes everything. "You mean He caused my pain and death?" He causes everything. Will you forgive Him? "No, He's unforgivable." Okay. All I'm really offering you is a total alternative. Most of you have become fairly nonchalant about outcome, haven't you. Somewhere you are indifferent to the result. Is that some sort of Eastern detachment? Is that what it is? Is detachment a form of attachment? Yes. I'm doing a little Buddha here. How detached can you get until you're overwhelmed by yourself? There's no such thing as attaching to God. I don't care what anyone tells you about transcendental experience. That's nothing but the experience of God in His wholeness. So you're not a transcendentalist. You're not a "God in nature" guy who says: "God is in everything that I see except me." Are you a transcendentalist or an existentialist? I'm a transcendental existentialist. Your existence must be transformed in its entirety. It's called Christianity! You love to sort it out into existence and transcendence, as though there could be a difference if God only gives. Can you see a little reason there?

How much potential is left in our brotherhood? If you and I are brothers, how much potential is left in it? All of it in its entirety? Each moment. There is no residual, then, in a brotherhood of this nature. That would be true. That's what the council meeting was about the other night. One thing we know for sure: Your contribution is whole. That is the requirement. How that aggregates, we don't know, because we don't know in this form where that aggregation occurred, since, in that sense, it never has occurred and will not occur until it does. But at the time it does, it will become a record of the totality of this association. It's absolutely true. And did. It's an incredible idea. You can't teach this except by opening your mind to God. I'm doing it. But if that's true, we don't care where he's settled because it's only temporary, anyway. It's the same idea as nothing is going to be constant except the final instant. But that instant can be determined by the gathering of the associations of the separation.

Okay, but you don't have any temporal terms in your mind at all. If you don't have any temporal terms, how can you have spatial references? I don't know. You teach it as crossing over and back if you want to. Or you can teach borderland of associations. But you better be from the other side. If you're going to be borderland, you go to the other side and wind up here. Don't try to teach from this side. I'm always offering you the crossover. I'm not offering you this side at all. I'm not at all. This is the whole *Course in Miracles*. The Course is not teaching from time; it's teaching from eternity. That's true. It may teach into time, but it's not teaching time.

We're speaking of something that is literally unspeakable, for goodness' sake. There is a God. And obviously, if you look at this world, there is no evidence of God or acceptance of God. Stop trying to adjudicate it, as Jesus says, in the establishment of the world. The establishment of this world is not the Kingdom of God. And yet, you are in the Kingdom of God. So this world is not of that kingdom. Okay. Well, that's no different than the single message that you have to hear.

God does not suffer conflict. Neither do the lilies of the field. The description of the lily is not what it is. You can't escape the world by limited, constructed, creative reality. It can't be done. It remains somewhere a definition of yourself. You are attempting to express communication with the acceptance of separation. You can't do both. No matter how much poetry you write about it, it will not be true, except that it is true in your own mind, in your God relationship. But some poetry is more divine than others. What about it? It can only be an expression of the totality of your love in God. Including expressions of the conflict in your associations with each other and the mythology of coming together to defend yourself from the Black Knight. I'm not concerned about what you do but only about the action of your mind in unison of purpose or love or expansion or extension of yourself. That's true.

So what is in our association together, determined by our admission of the passion of our creating minds? You'll have to tell me. How much are you willing to express within your own mind about what you really are, the expression of the fear of your own creative capacity? How fearful are you of being who you really are? That's the only question there could be. Do you understand me?

Once there was a little boy who wouldn't say his prayers,
When he went to bed at night, away up stairs.
His pappy heard him holler and his momma heard him call,
And when they turned the kivers back, he wasn't there at all.

They searched him in the rafter room and cubbyhole and press,
They searched him up the chimney and everywhere I guess,
But all they ever found was just his pants around about.
And the gobble-uns will GETCHA if you don't watch out!

You lie in bed at night and ruminate about finding his pants all around. There's really no answer to that. Some alkie poet writing for kids ought to be ashamed of himself. How do you find his pants all around? In the incongruity of nursery rhymes, fear is what makes them survive. They survived in your memories. That's why all your new little kids learn those nursery rhymes better than other ones. Do you know that? They make more sense to them. We're just talking about expression, aren't we, and the joy of whole mind. Is it the sharing of fear? You bet. Your love is the sharing of fear. What can I do about it? Share fear. Why are you asking me? Actually, fear cannot be shared, only the security from it. But the security from fear is what fear is. Say Amen.

So there's really no love here, only fear. When I sit by the fireplace with my pipe and a good book and a big Irish Setter, who smells like fish, by my side. I just told you the truth. I'm talking about a Holy Instant. And he smells like sheepshead. I let him be there, anyway. He's enjoying canus domesticus. He's enjoying the camaraderie of forty thousand years of protecting you in the cave fire. He's got a lot of memories of you. So I felt a lot of love then. Didn't last, but, boy... I lost it. It was sad. The dog died, actually. I never wanted another dog after that. I was afraid to love, I knew I'd lose him, too. I'm just giving you your own situation. I don't have the answer to it.

You tell me that's the way it is. And I just got tired of it. Because nothing ever really happened. What an idea! So I began to plan a whole year ahead for the two weeks I could get relief from this. Or ahead for the twenty years that I could get relief from it, hopefully before I died. What a hell of a place this is. And you tell me that's what life is. To hell with you. I won't do that anymore. There's an alternative to that. I don't know what it is, but I don't want this anymore. If there's a God, this can't be true. If there's not a God, the hell with it, I'm going to die anyway.

I'm describing a condition that converts in my mind when I attempt to share it. If I were to describe how I really am, obviously, I've reduced that to a scenario where you can feel me in that, but the instant of that would be an entirety in my mind. And the sharing of that with me would be the entirety of our minds. If I can tell a little better story than you can, then listen to my story. If you've got a good story that ends up in some sort of scenario of completion, tell me about it. I want to hear that: "You know that the son of a gun's left us here. And if I can get my hands on him, we'll find out what's going on. Where are we going to meet him?"

If you invite me to a secret chamber, I'm liable to show up. And then you're not liable to be there, and then I'll be foolish again. But somewhere in me I'm looking for a solution. And if that's mystical, you let it be. I've looked here, and there is no answer here. The answer must be contained somewhere in the association where I am not looking. Now, I think I'll allow for miracles and the hell with it. If it's going to be miraculous, I'm going to let it be that. Certainly, any solution I get here will only be what I'm going to end up with anyway.

Now, this is an adventurous idea that your mind somewhere has decided that it wants to do. And you've set out on this sojourn of reality. All I'm trying to get you to do is don't turn back. You're headed right toward it. And every time you reorganize your own associations, you're just missing the mark again. It's right there. That's A Course in Miracles.

I just want you to be happy. And that's going on. Your commitment is there or you couldn't be here. Just don't measure it and you are okay. Remember what we just read? It rains on the good guys and the bad guys. It's just part of what we just taught. What an amazing idea. Somewhere, you should begin to be happy about having a purpose. If nothing else, you've got a purpose. If nothing else, you can make a commitment and be attacked and killed. Jesus will say somewhere, "Why don't you do that?" See, it always comes back to sacrifice. Jesus wants you to stand up and say that love is perfect and this world isn't real. Get all the tomatoes and boos, because it's true. If you don't stand up and do it, who's going to do it? You say, "Well, you stand up and I won't throw tomatoes at you." And I say, what are you going to do, watch other guys throw tomatoes at me? Where are you in your own association? You never can tell. Finally, it's an illusion. You understand me? Stop trying to measure it. You're perfect as God created you.

In the meantime, you're telling yourself all of these stories. And sometimes you laugh and sometimes they're not so funny. Usually, when they're about someone else, they're a little funny. Now you are where they're about yourself and they're still funny. That's progress. Finally you laugh totally at your own situation. That's salvation. Isn't it? There's no solution to it, absolutely no solution. Do you love no solution?

Made in the USA
Charleston, SC
25 November 2012